Louis Brownlow, 1945

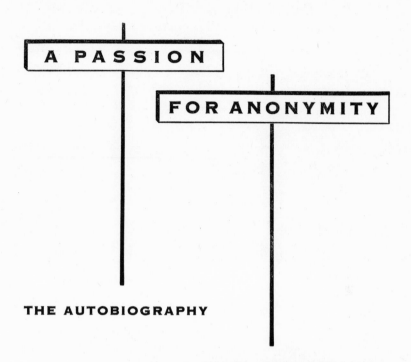

A PASSION

FOR ANONYMITY

THE AUTOBIOGRAPHY

OF LOUIS BROWNLOW

SECOND HALF

THE UNIVERSITY OF CHICAGO PRESS

JA
93
.B7
A3
V.2

Library of Congress Catalog Number: 58-5536

THE UNIVERSITY OF CHICAGO PRESS, CHICAGO 37
Cambridge University Press, London, N.W. 1, England
The University of Toronto Press, Toronto 5, Canada

© *1958 by The University of Chicago. Published 1958*
Composed and printed by THE UNIVERSITY OF CHICAGO PRESS
Chicago, Illinois, U.S.A.

PREFACE

For many years I have been both confounded and comforted by Alexander Pope and that sententious couplet of his:

For forms of government let fools contest;
Whate'er is best administer'd is best.

A fool or not, I have contested for forms of government, always fighting for that form which I deemed the most democratic, but, among the governments that are democratic, I agree, but not foolishly I trust, with that great eighteenth-century poet that whatever is best administered is best. In the first volume of this autobiography I contested the first phase of Pope's apothegm: in this, the second and the last, I come near to agreement with the last phase.

Periods of time have three lives. They are "crucial" to those who are involved in their making; "everyday" to those who are living in them; and "history" to those who, years later, delve back into them. The years covered in this volume of my autobiography—1915-45—are still all three, not only to me but to many of my readers. Some of the years seemed crucial at the time—and do even today. The record of the era is still being written, and, in some important respects, is still being lived by those who witnessed the two world wars and the depression that separated them and are concerned with the lessons and effects of both wars and depressions. The desire to "get on the record" by those who were involved continues; and the desire to understand, shared often by historian and public alike, continues to be fed by those of us who thought we understood at the time, or think we do now, or, having left understanding for others, just want to talk about the era.

My work has been spent largely with associations, in encouraging the gathering in groups of people whose interest in administrative problems was common even if their political beliefs and solutions were not. The American democracy rests on a faith in the ultimate workability of association as a means of solving the common problems of an assembled group, whether it is a town, county, city, state, federal

[v]

government—or political party—as well as on the understanding and leadership of those who have been given the responsibility of dealing with those problems. As a boy in Buffalo, Missouri, the idea of public administration would have meant nothing to me; but politics, democracy, and the needs of a society of human beings meant much. My working life has been largely an effort to discover the relationship among them, to adjust, to preserve, and to enlarge the influence they can have on one another for the improvement of life as a whole. The theories of propinquity, of anonymity, of the effective exchange and development of useful information, all of which were central to the Public Administration Clearing House and the organizations it helped to foster, were evolved from an experience which was as much mine as it was that of the many others who aided, encouraged, and directed my work. Some of my own experiences, as an administrator and as an adviser of administrators, from the Wilson era through the Roosevelt era and later, are recounted in the pages that follow.

For one whose name played so small a part in the public side of the record, the desire to "talk" now may seem a little strange. Anonymity and autobiography are in some ways mutually exclusive. The friends and associates who prodded me to write this tale of mine may be disappointed. Those who expected revelation will certainly be. And since I cannot claim scientific objectivity, I won't pretend to please those who want clear, concise explanations of the what, the how, and the why of the matters of which I write.

What is set down here (as well as the things written in the first volume of my memoirs, *A Passion for Politics*) is admittedly and confessedly subjective and almost completely egocentric. It is my own recollections (no doubt often inaccurate), my own views of what happened, recalled through the mists of many and many a summer and a winter. Its errors and mistakes are my own. I could defend them for what they have meant to me. Their usefulness to others will have to be judged by others.

LOUIS BROWNLOW

ACKNOWLEDGMENTS

For their unfailing support, I acknowledge with gratitude my debt to Herbert Emmerich and my other fellow-trustees of Public Administration Clearing House, an institution rooted in anonymity and nourished by propinquity, which, its mission having been accomplished, was dissolved at the end of 1956. Most particularly among those fellow-trustees I thank my friend the late Marshall Field III for his special encouragement.

I trust that my indebtedness to scores, if not hundreds, of others in the field of public administration will be obvious to any one of them who reads what is set down in the text.

In the making of the book, I have been both assisted and admonished by the wise man, the master of letters, who edited it—Barry Karl. He pruned away many of the more inconsequential things I had set down and hence is entitled to the thanks of any chance reader for shortening it. I owe him more than I can ever hope to repay.

Also, I am deeply indebted to Miss Lucile Keck and Miss Marianne Yates and their associates in the Joint Reference Library of Public Administration Service of Chicago for preparing the index.

The book probably never would have been written and certainly it never would have been finished without the counsel, the drive, and the help of Mrs. Grace Geer Brown. She, my most efficient office manager and secretary, transcribed it, copied it, and copied it again after Mr. Karl had edited it. She has my everlasting thanks.

L. B.

TABLE OF CONTENTS

PART I. WASHINGTON, D.C.

PART II. PETERSBURG, KNOXVILLE, RADBURN, AND CHICAGO

Table of Contents

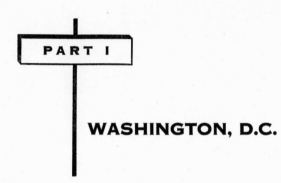

PART I

WASHINGTON, D.C.

CHAPTER I

MR. COMMISSIONER

Tuesday, January 26, 1915, was a balmy day. The omens seemed good indeed as I took the oath of office as a commissioner of the District of Columbia and began my career in public administration.

President Woodrow Wilson had appointed me to a term of three years. I had decided to try my hand for that short period of time at the business of municipal government in order that I might put into practice some of the things I had so painfully ached to do when, as a reporter, I had covered the city halls in Nashville and in Louisville; some of the things I had seen and heard in the cities of Europe and the Orient; and some of the things it had seemed to me ought to be done in Washington. After that, of course, I would go back to work as a newspaperman.

Although at the time I regarded the event simply as an interlude, I was not a little excited by the prospect.

The occasion itself was a formal one. I was doomed to don the morning dress that then distinguished officialdom in Washington from fellow mortals. Armored for the fray *cap-a-pie,* from silk hat to patent leather shoes, I walked in the Florence Court apartment house from my apartment to that of Oliver Peck Newman, then the president of the Board of Commissioners of the District of Columbia.

He was nearly ready, but not so eager, not quite so much in a hurry as was I. Newman and I went down in the elevator and walked to the driveway, where awaited a closed carriage drawn by two dappled gray horses under the command of a Negro coachman who wore a hat just like ours and wielded a whip as an emperor would a scepter. That was the equipage of the president of the Board of Commissioners, and I would have a similar outfit assigned to me that afternoon. The coachman knew, and he knew that we knew, that the knell had rung and that on July 1, the beginning of the new fiscal year, horses would be out; carriages would be out; and motor cars would be in. He knew, too, but he didn't quite realize then, that coachmen also would be out. He touched the brim of his hat with ceremony, flourished his scepter with dignity, and faced with a gleaming smile what the gods might decree, apparently unafraid.

The carriage deposited us at the then practically new white marble District Building at Fourteenth and D streets. I was whisked with Newman up to the fifth floor and we went into his office. In a few moments Major Charles Willauer Kutz, U.S.A., the engineer commissioner, came in.

The Board of Commissioners of the District of Columbia was then, as it is now, composed of three persons—two civilian commissioners appointed by the President of the United States with the advice and consent of the Senate and one engineer commissioner assigned from the Corps of Engineers with the approval of the President. That had been the case since the adoption of the Organic Act of 1878. However, in 1914 under an act of Congress initiated by Senator La Follette of Wisconsin, the commissioners of the District were also members ex officio of the Public Utilities Commission of the District, an arrangement no longer in effect today.

We three decided to continue the current division of departments that reported directly to the board through each of the three commissioners, I taking those that had been reporting to my immediate predecessor, Frederick L. Siddons. We agreed that Mr. Newman would be re-elected president of the Board of Commissioners and that Major Kutz would be chosen chairman of the Public Utilities Commission. With these matters settled, I was ready to take the oath.

The ceremony was set for eleven o'clock in the Board Room. Newman walked ahead and I followed with Kutz. Major Kutz and I had been friends for some months. He had frequently been a guest at our luncheon table, the "Doughnut Cabinet," which assembled daily at the Willard Hotel grillroom. There he had expressed his opinions with candor and vigor, but he had not shared the partisan political approach to affairs toward which so many of us there were inclined. I was astonished when he disclosed to me that he had some misgivings about my attitude, that he was somewhat alarmed that I would violate the integrity of the District service by going too far in my partisan activities.

"Brownlow," he said as we walked toward the Board Room, "one thing you will find here that I am afraid you do not realize, and that is that our subordinates in the District are loyal, able, and efficient. I hope you will recommend no changes in persons except for reasons of improving the service. It is a good group of men and women, and, furthermore, there is very little party politics in this outfit."

There was not time for a response from me. I saw that he had no notion that my political partisanship was based on what I thought were good measures and had little or no connotation with respect to persons. Nevertheless, it was an admonition which, if it somewhat astounded me, still was accepted in the spirit in which it was given. For, as a matter of fact, I held in general the same opinion that he held. But there was no time then to talk.

The Board Room was crowded. All the heads of the departments, all their principal assistants in the District Building, members of the School Board, and the superintendent of education were there. So were a dozen or more of my newspaper friends, many of them accompanied by their wives. Not a few leading businessmen and representatives of citizens' associations were there, along with a goodly number of friends who held high positions in the federal government.

Mrs. Newman, Mrs. Kutz, and my father-in-law, Representative Sims, with two or three fellow members of the Congress were present. Two of my wife's sisters, Edna (Mrs. William L. Beale) and Tom (Mrs. William Joyner), were present.

And above all, of course, there was Bess, my wife. Bess was proud but also wary. She was afraid this sort of thing might go to my head. After all, it was a heady wine and I was only thirty-five years old.

I was to take two oaths. That as commissioner of the District of Columbia was administered by Mr. Justice Siddons, who had been my immediate predecessor. His appointment to the Supreme Court of the District of Columbia had been confirmed by the Senate a few days earlier. It was the first time a retiring District commissioner had sworn in his successor.

Then the other oath, that as a member of the Public Utilities Commission of the District of Columbia, was administered by John Russell Young, Sr., clerk of the Supreme Court of the District of Columbia.

The law setting up the Public Utilities Commission required a special oath in which the commissioner had to swear that he was not the owner of any stock or bonds or other obligations of any public utility operating within the District. It was easy for me to take that oath without any equivocation or mental reservation. Mr. Louis B. Wilson, the paymaster, began introducing me to all the heads of departments (most of whom I already knew) and members of their staffs; and then each of them bade goodbye to Judge Siddons. It took a long time to say all these hails and farewells, but I found that I was quite excited by it all.

Then, accompanied by my wife, I walked down the hall to *my* office. Already the transom over the entrance door, which had borne the legend "Commissioner Siddons," had been changed to read "Commissioner Brownlow." At that door, the entrance of what was to be my own suite of offices, were stationed Amos A. Steele, who had been Mr. Siddons' private secretary, and James Jones, a Negro clerk, who had served as messenger to Mr. Siddons and to several of his predecessors. I had known Steele ever since I had first come to Washington in February, 1904, when he had served in the branch of the Library of Congress in the Capitol that served the House of Representatives. Jones I had met frequently in my visits to the municipal building. It had not once occurred to me that I would not continue them in their employment, and it had not so much as crossed my mind that either of them would be the least bit anxious. But both were obviously apprehensive. It was manifest, but to me almost unbelievable.

Thus under escort and with more than a tinge of the formality of official fuss and feathers, I was ushered into a suite of three large rooms. Entering through a reception room, I came to my own principal office, a great square, high-ceilinged room at the northeast corner of the fifth floor. The walls were paneled in oak. The desk, the sofa, the armchairs, the swivel desk-chair—all were of the prevailing mode of golden oak. The great high windows were closed against the winter air, and the wide expanse of carpet was appropriately red. The huge desk was set diagonally in the middle of the room so that I could command with my eyes the door of the reception room to the left and another door to the right that led into a hall, a bathroom, and a huge private office and consulting room beyond. This was my new world, a world that was destined to capture my imagination and command my greatest and most devoted interest for the rest of my life.

The change manifested itself on the instant. Amos Steele, who for better than ten years had called me "Louis," addressed me formally as "Mr. Commissioner." And then at once there came a stream of callers: heads of the departments of the District government who would report directly to me; persons of lower rank in the municipal hierarchy whom I had known; personal friends, some old, some new; colleagues from the newspaper world, some interested in local affairs, some not. There were others not known to me at all; but all offered heartiest congratulations and predicted success for me in my new position. All gave me the formal title "Mr. Commissioner." Possibly it was a little startling. Possibly it was faintly pleasurable. Possibly I felt a little elation and at the same time a little squeamishness about it all. But what sticks in my memory is that the reporters who came in from the pressroom down the hall—John Martin of the *Evening Star,* who was accustomed to write with anonymous authority, and Graham Nichols of the *Times,* the one-legged demon poker-player of the Press Club—addressed me as "Mr. Commissioner" instead of as the familiar "Louie" to which they both had been accustomed.

Their formality reminded me that no longer was I to look in at the city hall, ready to write with cheerful nonchalance all the news I could get. It reminded me that here and now, in talking to my old newspaper friends, I should have to begin to guard against even the chance slip of information about unfinished business. It brought in upon me with great force my new awareness of the gulf fixed between the irresponsibility of even the most conscientious and careful reporter and the grave responsibility of a governmental official charged with a high obligation—a great difference between casual comment so easily forgiven and forgotten and the impetuous or petulant expression that might be taken to be an official pronouncement.

Yet it was not at all a surprise to me to find myself at that big desk; it was not at all something which had been uncontemplated or for which I felt myself unready. Not only had my interest in municipal government been growing over the years of my newspaper work, but I had known for seven months that I was to be named District commissioner and I had been freely and fully consulted by my colleagues-to-be, Newman and Kutz, as well as by my predecessor, Siddons, about matters in current consideration.

The Newmans and the Brownlows had lived in the same apartment house for several years. We were the closest friends. For nearly two years when I had happened to be in town, I had frequently driven down in the morning with Newman in his carriage. Very often we stopped at the foot of the hill where Phelps Place turns into S Street to pick up Charles F. Nesbitt, an old friend of ours who had been appointed by Newman and Siddons to be superintendent of insurance of the District of Columbia. Not infrequently we stopped farther down on S Street to pick up Robert Wickliffe Woolley, another old friend who then was auditor of the War Department. If the weather was good, we might dispense with the carriage and walk together the mile and three-quarters downtown.

Late in 1909 I had married Elizabeth Virginia Sims, the daughter of a member of the House of Representatives from Tennessee, the Honorable Thetus W. Sims. Judge Sims had been elected to Congress in 1896 and had served for many years under the Republican administrations of Theodore Roosevelt and William Howard Taft as the ranking minority member of the House Committee on the District of Columbia. I had also become friendly with Judson C. Welliver, John Snure, and Fred A. Walker of the *Washington Times*. These three had helped set up as early as 1907 the daily luncheon at the Willard, the group which had been christened the "Doughnut Cabinet." It was from these three also that I had got an insight into the affairs of the District that had whetted my interest and helped determine my habit of inquiring into municipal and local government affairs during my trips into foreign lands as a member of the staff of the Frederic J. Haskin Syndicate. In the presidential election of 1912, Welliver, Snure, and Walker had been Bull Moosers and supporters of "T. R."—Theodore Roosevelt—while Woolley, Newman, and I were supporters of Woodrow Wilson. Newman had been dropped from the *Washington Times* and had joined the United Press. Woolley had been the second in command under Josephus Daniels of the publicity section of the Democratic National Committee during that campaign. Newman had covered Mr. Wilson during the campaign and after his election had been assigned to stay with the president-elect until after the inauguration; he therefore had been stationed at Trenton and had accompanied Mr. Wilson to Bermuda. I had known Mr. Wilson since 1906. Mr. Woolley and I had joined in recommending to the incoming administration the appointment of Newman and Siddons as commissioners.

My wife and I spent the early months of 1914 in the British Isles and had intended to go on to the Continent for the summer. We had been called back by illness in her family and in mine and by a slump in the sales by the Haskin Syndicate. In June, 1914, the newspapers were so much more interested in the Mexican border than they were in European affairs that the market for European newsletters was at an all-time low.

When I got back to Washington in June, Newman told me that the President was considering appointing Commissioner Siddons to an expected vacancy on the District of Columbia Supreme Bench and that he, Newman, had suggested to the President as well as to Joseph P. Tumulty that I succeed Siddons.

I was eager to see the President to tell him some of the things that I had observed in England and Ireland. I was convinced that the Irish situation had got out of control and that internal violence if not outright civil war was at hand. I also was convinced that, if civil war did break out, Germany might strike at France and Belgium while the British forces were tied up in internecine strife.

Through Mr. Tumulty I sought an interview. I saw, the President for about three-quarters of an hour on July 1. Archduke Ferdinand of Austria had been assassinated at Sarajevo on June 28, but that event was not then recognized as the occasion for the beginning of the war. In his conversation with me the President referred to it as one of those incidents which were dangerous enough to precipitate a crisis, but he did not recognize it as *the* critical event. Indeed, it was not until July 5 that the emissary of Count Berchtold, the foreign minister of the Austria-Hungarian Empire, arrived in Berlin to explain to the German government the Viennese desire to use the assassination as an occasion for an ultimatum to Serbia and to present their plan to march into Serbia and force its eventual partition.

Mr. Newman had told me he already had given the President copies of many of my dispatches from Europe, especially those dealing with municipal matters, and both Newman and Tumulty told me that the

President wished to see me about the commissionership. But Mr. Wilson did not once mention the subject.

In the *Evening Star* of July 1, 1914, Bill Price, the White House reporter, commented at length on my visit with the President. The reasons he gave constituted a rather authoritative, if unofficial, announcement of my coming appointment. Why it was that such an announcement was made seven months prior to the day on which I took the oath of office is a story that throws some light on Woodrow Wilson and his methods, his interest in the District of Columbia government, his persistence, and, perhaps some persons would add, the inflexibility of his determination.

During all that long seven months' period no opposition to my nomination was made, at least not publicly, and the event was taken for granted.

But what a seven months it was!

On August 4, the German army invaded Belgium and the World War had begun. On August 6, Mrs. Ellen Axson Wilson died.

Nothing in the President's demeanor on that first day of July had indicated that he was laboring under a great private sorrow. And now he was faced not only with the deprivation of Mrs. Wilson's companionship and a world conflagration of the direst portent but also with the relatively petty concerns that no President can escape, among them the municipal concerns of the District of Columbia.

There was a great deal of opposition to the nomination of Mr. Siddons to the Supreme Court of the District of Columbia. It was that opposition which occasioned the long delay and perhaps also the hardening of Mr. Wilson's persistence. The President had first heard of Siddons when his name was recommended for District commissioner by Robert Wickliffe Woolley and me. Mr. Woolley had written a series of what were then called "muckraking" articles about the real estate lobby and the public utilities lobby in the District of Columbia. He asserted that both lobbies had powerfully affected local legislation and, even more, had dominated the local municipal administration. In the preparation of these articles, Mr. Woolley had talked with my father-in-law, Judge Sims. The judge had opposed many of the legislative measures and had adversely criticized some of the administrative actions of the local government, believing as he did that the scales were all too frequently tipped in favor of the dominant utility and real estate interests. Mr. Woolley had had an even closer tie with Mr. Siddons, then a member of the law firm of Ralston, Siddons and Richardson. Siddons and Sims were regarded by many of the more well-heeled and highly respected citizens of the District of Columbia as dangerous radicals. To that roster had been added the name of Oliver Peck Newman, who in his capacity as an editorial writer on the *Washington Times* had given support to the general opposition to the powers in the District.

Those were the days of attack on "the interests" and counterattack on "the muckrakers." Those were the days when in that particular struggle between "big business" and the "people," between the "interests" and the "common man," no quarter was asked or given. President Wilson immediately after his inauguration made plain his stand on the local situation, just as he had made it equally plain at the Baltimore convention in 1912 and in the campaign against President Taft and former President Roosevelt in the election campaign of that year. The President declined membership in the Chevy Chase Club because he identified it with the social lobby which represented those interests he deemed inimical to the common good. His stand was affirmed when he appointed Oliver Peck Newman and Frederick L. Siddons commissioners of the District of Columbia, knowing that they also were to serve as members ex officio of the Public Utilities Commission.

Mr. Wilson, however, had not known Mr. Siddons personally until after his appointment. In the conferences with the new District commissioners, Mr. Wilson had found himself in rapport with Mr. Siddons. It was the beginning of a friendship which was to endure throughout their lives. Long after Mr. Wilson's illness, long after his retirement from the White House when his doors were closed to so many of his former intimates, and to the very end of his life, it was Justice Siddons who was a frequent caller on S Street. It was Justice Siddons who remained as the close friend with whom Woodrow Wilson could talk not only about the affairs of the world, perhaps, but about literature, poetry, and the stage, about cultural as well as political events of the past.

When, early in 1914, a vacancy on the Supreme Court of the District of Columbia appeared to be imminent, the President intimated to his attorney general that he desired to appoint Mr. Siddons to it. Attorney General James Clark McReynolds did not share Mr. Wilson's opinion.

He believed that there were other lawyers in the District who would better grace the bench. Mr. McReynolds was a conservative. Mr. Siddons was a liberal. However, since Mr. Wilson did not desire to go over the head of a member of his Cabinet, the discussions between him and the attorney general went on for some time. Mr. McReynolds would not yield. Finally, President Wilson nominated Mr. McReynolds to the Supreme Court of the United States and Thomas Watt Gregory to be attorney general. Mr. Gregory took a different view of Mr. Siddons' qualifications and recommended him. The President sent his name to the Senate; opposition developed to the confirmation in a subcommittee of the Senate Judiciary Committee. An objection was placed before the committee based on an allegation that Mr. Richardson, one of Mr. Siddons' business partners, had unethically solicited legal business for his firm. While the matter was still pending before the Judiciary Committee, the Congress adjourned and the nomination lapsed. When the Congress met again in December, the Siddons nomination again was sent to the Senate. After much debate the Judiciary Committee approved the nomination, and the appointment of Mr. Siddons was confirmed on January 18. On January 19 the President sent my name to the Senate. I was confirmed on January 20 without opposition, and on January 26, I at last took the oath of office.

I am quite sure that Mr. Wilson's persistence with respect to my own nomination had nothing in it of the determined quality of his support of Mr. Siddons. I had met the President first in 1906 in Chattanooga, when I was engaged in training his brother, Joseph Ruggles Wilson, to succeed me as state political editor of the *Nashville Banner.* I had seen Woodrow Wilson a few times during the campaign of 1912. My name had been suggested to him as a successor to Mr. Siddons by the then president of the Board of Commissioners, Mr. Oliver P. Newman.

The newspaper reports also noted that I was the son-in-law of Representative Sims of Tennessee, for whom the President had expressed great admiration. Yet the White House reporters were careful to add that Representative Sims had not recommended me. As a matter of fact, my father-in-law was very dubious about my undertaking the position; and, even if he had not been, he was not a man who ever would have made a recommendation for an appointment for a member of his family. Mr. Wilson was particularly grateful to Mr. Sims for his action in respect to the repeal of the law which had given United States vessels preference in the Panama Canal by exempting them from tolls, thus, in the opinion of many, violating our treaty obligations with Great Britain to Panama. Mr. Sims, then the ranking majority member of the House Committee on Interstate and Foreign Commerce, captained the movement for a repeal, and the President had formally acknowledged his gratitude to Mr. Sims. What influence that circumstance had in the President's inclination to appoint me as successor to Mr. Siddons I have no means of knowing. It probably did me no harm.

Yet, I prefer to believe what Mr. Wilson said to me when I went to the White House to thank him for my appointment. He said that he had been interested in what I had written about municipal government in Germany and England.

It should not be forgotten that Woodrow Wilson's arrival in Washington in March, 1913, was looked upon with either faith or fear as marking the end of an era of special privilege. Certainly it was true that up to that time certain persons and cliques had had a preponderant influence in determining many matters of local concern in Washington. While this was also true in other cities, the method of exerting that influence in Washington was different. In other cities it was through the capture and control of the political organizations and processes. In Washington, where there were no elective city positions, it was through the power of the White House. I do not mean to say that these influences were corrupt or that their sole aim was private enrichment. It was simply that they did not take into consideration the "little fellow."

There is no doubt that leading citizens of the District of Columbia were shocked when, in 1913, Mr. Wilson named Newman and Siddons as commissioners. Siddons was a professed single-taxer. Both had manifested a great interest in sociological affairs and were sometimes sneered at as "do-gooders" and "up-lifters," and they were outside the group that had hitherto supplied the municipal government with its executives.

In making his choice of commissioners, President Wilson decided not to ask the advice of a small group of local financial leaders, a sort of Washington "genro," who had advised his predecessors about these appointments. He either chose not to ask the member of the Democratic National Committee for the District of Columbia or forgot to do so.

He did, however, apply his idea of party responsibility. For many years it had been the custom to name one civilian commissioner from the Republican and one from the Democratic party; the third, chosen from the Army, was presumed to be without party. From this precedent Mr. Wilson departed, deciding to choose two Democrats. However, it should be said that the bipartisan appointments for many years had been merely nominal. There were always enough Democrats of the pro-McKinley, pro-Roosevelt, or pro-Taft variety to fill the places under Republican presidents and always enough Cleveland Republicans to satisfy Mr. Cleveland's requirements.

However, in the two-year interval before I succeeded Siddons, the tension of the local atmosphere had diminished. The much-feared "radicals" had not done much damage. True, there had been a revision of real estate values for the purpose of taxation, and many persons had charged the commissioners with excessively increasing the assessment on unused land in an effort to introduce the principle of the single tax. But the issue had not excited much interest either in the town or in the Congress. There was little or no evidence of hoofs and horns in the District Building. The Public Utilities Commission, under the chairmanship of Major Chester Harding, the engineer commissioner, had begun the long process of valuation of the local utility companies in a sober and seemingly fair manner.

Newman and Siddons had proved themselves eager to hear the opinions of the various citizens' organizations. Newman was an outgoing person who made friends in all sorts of circles. Siddons had made some special efforts in the administration of the police department, especially to assure greater respect for civil liberties. But Siddons was a practitioner of his own oft-repeated motto, "Suaviter in modo, fortiter in re"; he acquired new friends and supporters and made few enemies.

Major Harding's successor, Major Kutz, had joined Newman and Siddons in extending the scope of official consultations with organizations of citizens.

When I began my service with Newman and Kutz, I thought it would be three years well spent in further training for my newspaper work. The salary was $5,000 a year, and, while I had been earning considerably more than that, my wife and I faced the financial sacrifice without dismay, little dreaming of the wartime inflation to come.

I could not but be proud of the fact, duly reported in the newspapers —the source being me—that I was the youngest man ever to become a commissioner of the District of Columbia. I am afraid that I was probably puffed up with my new grandeur, but I am grateful that it was accompanied by a compensating sense of obligation and responsibility. My new status came to me with sudden realization that afternoon at about half-past four, when my messenger came in and told my secretary to tell the commissioner that his carriage was ready.

When I got home to Florence Court, my wife was waiting for me. In the enthusiasm of the moment I retailed to her all the glories of the day since she had left me at noon; the doubts and suspicions that impressed me even then did not find immediate vocal expression. I was too full of myself and overwhelmed with the adulation that had been poured out before me.

Bess took the situation in hand. She listened. She was sympathetic. She was lenient. Anybody that bragged on her husband was all right. She liked it. She had shared from her childhood that interest in politics, public affairs, and government that had been my principal concern. Her father had been a member of the Congress since she was twelve years old. He had been on the House Committee on the District of Columbia, and she had shared his interest and mine in municipal problems. Since she and I saw the Newmans three or four times a week and since she also had been a close friend of Judge and Mrs. Siddons and was well acquainted with Major and Mrs. Kutz, she was as well informed as was I about current problems of the municipality. She shared fully in my triumph that day. But she saw beyond that day.

"Brownie," she said after I had finished talking, "you must be careful. You must keep your feet on the ground. Don't get a swelled head, and don't on any account mistake deference for agreement or momentary pretense of agreement for loyalty."

Month after month and year after year, during the six years I was District commissioner, during the three years I was city manager of Petersburg, and during the three years I was city manager of Knoxville, my faithful wife, my guardian angel, never failed, in season and out of season, to remind me of the danger that always besets the prominent man in office: the temptation of committing the unpardonable sin of a public servant—permitting one's self to exhibit the arrogance of office.

Always it was Bess who would tell me, when I became too impatient with adverse criticisms or when I became too intolerant of opposition, that after all I was only an ordinary citizen "dressed with a little brief authority" and that I would be a better public servant if I were humble as a servant and not dictatorial as a Dogberry or a little Caesar.

I was soon to get another lesson from a great teacher. When, as was the custom, I called at the White House, the President received me most cordially. He made it clear at once that he had a very definite sense of responsibility toward the municipal government of the voteless and legislatively unrepresented people of the nation's capital.

"I would like you to understand," he said, in substance, "that under no circumstances do I intend publicly to intervene in any of the affairs of the District of Columbia. I rely on Newman and Kutz and you to administer District affairs, but that does not mean that I am not responsible for the results; and I want to tell you, as I have already told Newman and Kutz, that I expect all of you to feel free to consult me about any matter that in your judgment requires my advice. It would help me a great deal if you would adopt a certain practice that I wish I could get all the members of the Cabinet and others who have official business with me to adopt. Boil down to its elements the proposition that you think I should consider; present it fairly, and then tell me frankly what you think I should do. If you will do that and try to keep it all on one page and send it to me in the mid-morning, I will try to do my part before night. If you send me a great long document full of 'ifs' and 'buts' and 'whereases,' and if you don't let me know exactly what *you* think but try to pass the buck to me entirely, you may never get an answer, and certainly you wouldn't deserve one."

During all my years as District Commissioner, I endeavored not to bother the President with local affairs unless it seemed absolutely necessary. And then I was careful to compress my communication into the standard one-page length. I sent the messages over in mid-morning as he had suggested. And only once did I fail to get a reply in writing before nightfall. On that occasion the letter from the White House came two days later, with an apology from the President for the delay— he had had to consult Paris before making up his mind!

In the same conversation in which he gave me that little lesson in administrative procedure, Mr. Wilson also gave me another in administration, one that was to profit me even more, since it went to the heart of the whole process.

"Let me share with you," said the President, as I recall his words, "something that I have picked up in Trenton and in the White House that I think will not only help you to avoid embarrassment but will also rid you of many unwelcome and importunate visitors. It is this: When any person comes in to see you and you have any reason whatever to suspect that he has come with ulterior motives, that he is either seeking a special privilege for himself or involved in a scheme to make money for himself out of public business, be sure to control the conversation yourself and immediately take high moral ground. The chances are that he will slink out of your office without ever getting up his nerve to say what he came there to say. Better than that, the chances are that he won't come back."

That bit of practical administrative advice I tested almost immediately and found that it worked. It worked so well that, during the years I held administrative office in Washington and elsewhere, I rarely suffered the embarrassment of having to listen either to the pleas of self-seekers or to the so-called smooth approaches of crooks. It also worked in the other direction. It encouraged the distinterested and the community-conscious people to say their say and say it convincingly.

"Take high ground," was Woodrow Wilson's advice to the administrator. I wonder if, when fully explored, those three words do not contain all there is to say about the art of good administration.

CHAPTER II

THE WORK BEGINS

The invitations to speak at meetings all over town came rolling in. I was both sobered and frightened by them. I was a new commissioner, and all program committees of all the citizens' associations and other civic organizations were always on the lookout for speakers. That I had not been too prominent in civic affairs and that my actual appointment had not been accompanied by any particular demonstration of approval on the part of the populace made no difference. I was new and I was the target.

I accepted the first invitation. It was from the Mid City Citizens Association. It came in the form of a personal visit from the president of the association, A. J. Driscoll, a railway post office clerk. A speaker who had been scheduled for a meeting had canceled his appointment, and would I take his place? I would.

That night about eight o'clock, accompanied by my wife, I showed up at the Strong John Thomson School at Twelfth and L streets, N.W. There were the usual preliminaries—the reading of the minutes, the report of the membership committee, and so on—and then I was introduced, "The new commissioner of the District of Columbia." I spoke. I wandered. I rambled. I said too little in too many words. But I did manage, I think, to say, although not succinctly, that my obligation was to all the people, that I considered it a sacred trust, and that I would endeavor to carry out my responsibility with the help of the citizens of the community, organized or unorganized, in a city that had none of the normal outlets for democratic action through elections. Although I did not at that time mention home rule, I was not then convinced that it would be a good thing. On the whole my speech was a success. Mr. Driscoll congratulated me.

But the success of the speech was not measured by that. I was soon suffused with shame. I accidentally heard Mr. Henry P. Blair, president of the Board of Education, say to someone as he walked up the aisle to congratulate me, "This fellow must think he is running for office, the way he is trying to put on an act that he is in favor of all the people."

In all candor I must say I owe a great debt of gratitude to Mr. Blair for that sarcastic comment. It brought me up short. It taught me once and for all to talk about concrete things and to let my crusading enthusiasm show through my plans, actions, and recommendations for specific programs, rather than to attempt to shape my enthusiasm into inspirational recitals.

Another thing I received that night was a lecture from my wife. Bess told me that I had talked too long and that I had repeated myself several times. I put up the best defense I could and stuck by my guns on the necessity of repetition for emphasis. Nevertheless, I took to heart the dressing-down she gave me.

That maiden effort in the Strong John Thomson School was the beginning of speech after speech. Oddly enough, it was the last time I suffered stage fright. Just a few years later I sat on the platform with President Wilson at a great outdoor gathering south of the White House. I was to make the first speech, Secretary of War Newton D. Baker, the second, and the President was to close the program. When I sat down, the President said to me, "Brownlow, weren't you frightened?"

"No, Mr. President," I said.

The President shook his head sadly and said, "I wonder how you do it. Baker tells me he never suffers from stage fright. In all my years, even including my years as a teacher, I never arose in a classroom or elsewhere without my knees shaking. I never have got over stage fright. And here today I am more scared than usual, as I always am when I speak outdoors. I feel as if I were compelled to raise my voice so that I will be heard by the entire human race."

But of course the public speaking was extracurricular, despite the great quantity of it. The work lay in the District Building.

Usually in the commission form of municipal government, which was adopted by many American cities after the initial examples of Galveston and Des Moines in the first decade of the twentieth century, each member of the elected commission of five or seven persons is in direct administrative charge of a particular governmental department.

At the same time each is a member of the collective group known as the "commission," insofar as the municipal government exercises legislative functions.

Not so in the District of Columbia. Here the three commissioners, or at any rate a majority of them, act in concert and are charged with collective responsibility for the executive and administrative work. Their legislative functions are meager, being confined to the enactment of police, health, and other regulations within a narrow range predetermined by the Congress. I believe that in the forty years since I became a commissioner, this legislative function has been somewhat expanded, but it still falls far short of the legislative authority ordinarily possessed by city councils or commissions.

The administrative responsibility rested upon the three commissioners, but not equally. The division of responsibility was predetermined by the Organic Act of 1878, which stated that the engineer commissioner should have primary responsibility for the engineering and public works functions. "Primary responsibility" meant that the heads of departments and agencies of the engineering branch reported directly to the engineer commissioner or one of his assistants assigned from the Army Corps of Engineers. The engineer commissioner would then take his proposed orders and decisions to the board of three as recommendations to be approved. That led in turn to the assignment of other departments as primary responsibilities of each of the two civilian commissioners.

I inherited without change those departments which had been reporting primarily to Commissioner Siddons: the police department, the fire department, the health department, the welfare agencies and board, the then existing recreational agencies, the office of weights and measures, and a few others. This division of initial responsibility was precisely what I liked at the time, because the center of my interest was the impact of municipal government upon the people in their homes, their places of business, and their workshops. That meant to me the police, welfare, health, and educational functions. The public schools were administered by the separate Board of Education, the members of which formerly had been appointed by the District commissioners but now were appointed by the justices of the Supreme Court of the District of Columbia.

Already I had become sufficiently familiar with the internal workings

[20]

of the District government through my close association with Commissioners Siddons, Newman, and Kutz to have made up my mind that when I got to the District Building there was one reform that I would endeavor to make, one I considered essential to efficient operation.

It had been the practice for many, many years for each commissioner to deal separately with every problem that had to be submitted to the entire commission. Each member of the board dictated his recommendation, which was then recorded on the back of a folding jacket that inclosed the file of papers forming the basis for the recommended action. The original file was composed of papers of legal-cap size. The file jacket was folded twice, so that it presented to the eye a surface three by eight inches. On this narrow jacket-back each commissioner in turn would record his indorsement—approval, disapproval, or a request for additional information. If he even so much as desired to ask a question, he recorded it in writing on the jacket. That meant that, if there was not instant agreement, and frequently there was not, additional sheets had to be pasted on the jacket. During my first few weeks I struggled with this absurdly inefficient scheme. I had to act upon matters that had been pending for weeks and even months, and I ran across jackets with commissioners' indorsements which unfolded to the length of ten or twelve feet.

I had been on the job but a week or two when I asked Newman to call a meeting of the three commissioners in his office. At that meeting I proposed a radical procedural reform: that the commissioners meet twice a week, or oftener if necessary, as a board at a board meeting, each commissioner with his recommendations written out on a flat sheet; that the secretary of the board be present to take minutes on the action of the board on each recommendation; and that the old-fashioned folder-file system be abandoned and vertical files substituted as soon as an appropriation for them could be obtained from the Congress. Newman agreed at once; in fact I already had talked it over with him. Kutz demurred on the ground that in the case of disagreement the files would not show the grounds for disagreement, since the minutes would record only the final vote. My counter to that was that any commissioner, if he so desired, could insist on a recording of any difference of opinion and that there were very few actual disagreements in the long jacketed indorsements I had read; most of the delays were the result only of inquiries. If we were together the questions could be either answered immediately or deferred until the next meeting, when the necessary information would be forthcoming.

Dr. Tindale, the secretary, objected as strongly as his gentle nature and deprecatory manner would permit. He said that it would upset the work of years, that no one would be able to trace the considerations that had been involved in the final decision, that it would be difficult to pin responsibility for action, and, most particularly, it was a change, and change was something to be avoided. Dr. Tindale, as able and as devoted a public servant as I ever knew, was elderly. He was cautious. He was meticulously careful and he abhorred change.

Nevertheless, the change was made, and from that time forward the old system was abandoned. The three commissioners began to meet regularly, and eventually the necessary appropriation was obtained and vertical filing cabinets were installed.

At the same time I was learning a great deal about administration from a master of the art, Major Kutz. He didn't lecture me. He didn't tell me directly that I had put my decisions and recommendations on too narrow a base. He didn't reprove me for my impetuosity. He didn't remind me that I was not a newspaperman writing a hot story and trying to make the first edition. He didn't tell me directly that there were some things I ought to look into more carefully and think about longer before I reached my final conclusions. He didn't tell me any of these things, but in every board meeting he gave me a lesson by example. For every recommendation he brought in, he was careful to explain the reasons for his determination. He was careful, when there was a division of opinion among his subordinates, to state each side and then to give in detail the basis upon which he had chosen the one or the other alternative. When I was too hasty, and I frequently was, Kutz sometimes would ask a question, always phrased in tentative form and always asked quietly. It was impossible for me not to answer the question, and frequently that meant that my recommendation had to be carried over until the next board meeting. In the interval, I would seek more facts and frequently change my mind.

As the months went on, it became more and more my habit, when issues were complex, to walk into the engineer commissioner's office and ask Kutz what he thought we should do.

Thus it happened that, during the first months and the first two years of my actual experience as a public administrator, I found a teacher and a mentor, wise, kindly, and sympathetic, in the person of a then major in the Corps of Engineers of the United States Army, a graduate of West Point, a military man with a military mind, who still never permitted for an instant the rigidity of his training to over-come the flexibility of his mind and heart.

While I was absorbing eagerly Major Kutz's lessons in the elements of administration and while I relied upon him more and more for ad-vice, he and I did not always see eye to eye on the question of *what* to do. In fact, on policies Newman and I were very much closer to each other. In politics generally, as well as in the immediate questions of policy determination in the District government, we were practically always in agreement.

In Washington forty-odd years ago, there was an organization known as the Monday Evening Club. It recruited its membership from among those local residents engaged in, or interested in, social work and public health work. While it was made up primarily of local resi-dents, it attracted the attention and attendance of persons in the federal government who were also interested in those problems. It included some members of the Washington Sanitary Housing Corporation, the few people who at that time were interested in housing. The club had ardently supported the slum-clearance measures that were centered in the Alley Dwelling Bill, which had been promoted by the first Mrs. Wilson during the first year of her husband's incumbency in the White House.

Siddons, the ardent single-taxer who had addressed himself to the slum problem, had been president of the Monday Evening Club. So had Newman and I. The club secretary had been another young news-paperman, Raymond W. Pullman.

When Newman and Siddons first were appointed, the newspapers quite naturally mentioned that each had been a president of the Mon-day Evening Club. That didn't attract much attention at the time; but when Siddons' nomination to the court came up and the White House simultaneously announced that I would be appointed to succeed him, the fact that a third former president of the Monday Evening Club was to be District commissioner created quite a stir. Many persons on the Hill, including the chairman of the House Committee on the District of Columbia, had the notion that the Monday Evening Club was a sort of Tammany Hall, that it was seizing power in the District in order to gobble up all the jobs. Others took up the same idea. The Monday Evening Club, so ran the gossip, intended to fill all the offices, even at the cost of flouting the Democratic National committeeman, the local Democratic committee, and also the Democratic members of the Congress. Here was a pretty how-do-you-do.

It so happened that Siddons and I at the time of our appointments also were members of the ancient and honorable scientific organization known as the Cosmos Club and that Newman soon was to be admitted to its ranks. Even the Cosmos Club was dragged into the rumors.

Matters were brought to a head by conditions in the police department, conditions which Newman and I felt called for a change. For many years Richard Sylvester had held the title of major and superintendent of police. He was in many ways an excellent police official. He stood high among the police chiefs of the country, and he had the hearty backing of the leading business organizations of the town. But both Newman and I thought that he was too old-fashioned; that he relied too much on the inherent virtues of the night stick; that he was not sufficiently interested in many of the social problems that we believed should be a concern of policemen; that he had not demonstrated a great deal of interest in the problems of juvenile delinquency; and, specifically, that he had resisted efforts to introduce some social hygiene for the control of venereal diseases.

Before I went to the city hall, when the board consisted of Siddons, Newman, and Major Harding, the tolerated red-light district had been closed. There was considerable doubt that Major Sylvester had approved that action, although it had been taken with the entire support and even under the direction of the Congress.

Furthermore, Major Sylvester was ill. The police surgeons told me that in their opinion he would not live more than a few months unless he were relieved of his work. I talked the matter over with him. He told me that he regretted it more than he could say but he felt compelled to ask for retirement. When his retirement, on my recommendation, was approved, I went home that night to find the largest and most gorgeous sheaf of American Beauty roses that I had ever seen. It had been sent to me by Mrs. Sylvester with her thanks, as she wrote on the card, "For saving my husband's life."

Then came the question of whom to put in his place. Newman and

I agreed at once that the man we wanted was Raymond W. Pullman. Pullman had had no police experience. As a reporter he had seen a good deal of police work. As a native of Washington and a product of its public schools, he had an intimate knowledge of the town. After leaving the newspaper business, he went on the staff of Gifford Pinchot at the time of the organization of the United States Forest Service. He was a tall, handsome bachelor with quite a formal and meticulous enunciation, the result of his attempts to overcome a childhood tendency to stammer.

Newman and I decided to take quick action, end the gossip, and appoint him. The matter came up in a board meeting. Major Kutz protested on the ground that we ought to make an appointment from within the police force and that he did not believe in placing the responsibility of the operation of a uniformed force on a lay civilian. He made his opposition clear and stated his reasons for it. The matter went to a vote. Newman and I voted "Aye" for Pullman, Major Kutz voted "No." It was the first time there had been a divided vote on any recommendation of any commissioner since we had instituted the board meetings. It was the last time and therefore the only such divided vote while Newman, Kutz, and I constituted the board.

The appointment hit the town like a bombshell. Some of the reporters upstairs in the municipal building, the ones who covered the doings of the commissioners and most of the departments, knew Pullman and were inclined to like him. The newspapermen who covered the police department were horrified. Some of the ranking members of the uniformed force who had seen Major Sylvester's decline in health and who had hoped for promotions were stunned.

Worst of all, here was the Monday Evening Club again. Yet at the same time there was much greater public support of a revitalization of the police department than Neuman and I had believed existed. Furthermore, from the Senate and the House of Representatives came much more applause than we had ever dreamed of. The members of the two subcommittees on appropriations who had charge of District of Columbia expenditures all seemed delighted. There was a feeling on the Hill that we certainly had not relied upon, because we didn't know it existed, that, so far as the Washington police force was concerned, it was time for a change.

The immediate reaction from the White House was a roar of protest from Mr. Tumulty delivered over the telephone both to Newman and to me. Tumulty said in no uncertain terms that "The White House" should have been consulted before the appointment was made. Of course, I happened to know that Mr. Tumulty had looked forward to backing Police Captain Robert Emmett Doyle of the third precinct for Major Sylvester's place, but, as Tumulty himself had not told me that, I was not supposed to know it.

On the first day of April, 1915, Major Pullman took the oath of office as superintendent of police. Newman, Kutz, and I already had an engagement to call on the President at the White House on the evening of that day. We were to take with us Conrad H. Syme, the corporation counsel, and also Charles F. Nesbitt, superintendent of insurance. Justice Siddons also was invited to be present. Shortly after the Tumulty explosion, the President himself telephoned to me and suggested that I bring Major Pullman with us that evening, as he would like very much to get acquainted with the new chief of police and perhaps would have something to say to him.

The delegation from the District Building arrived at the White House at eight o'clock and was welcomed by the President in his study on the second floor. Mr. Wilson was at that time still a widower, and he probably had arranged the conference not only because he wanted to talk about the District of Columbia affairs but because he was lonely. He was extremely gracious to Major Pullman, whom he had not known except as a member of his press conferences.

Siddons came in a little later and got the heartiest of greetings.

"Mr. Justice," asked the President, "are you getting accustomed to that black gown or would you prefer a scarlet robe and a full-bottomed wig?"

Siddons flushed a little, as he frequently did when someone made reference to his English birth and ancestry. Mr. Wilson seemed to enjoy teasing him and pursued the subject by telling us how often he had noticed Mr. Siddons' remarkable resemblance to that portrait of his distinguished great-grandmother, Mrs. Sarah Siddons, as the Tragic Muse, which hung in the gallery of Dulwich College in London.

Turning to the business of the evening, he asked Newman what he thought was the most important task now facing the District government. Newman responded that it undoubtedly was the conduct of the valuation proceedings in the Public Utilities Commission. Mr. Wilson's response was the following advice:

"In considering the problems of a public utility remember that the rights of the public must be protected but that none of the rights of the owners of the public utility properties may be invaded. Hold the scale in balance between the public interest and the private interest with scrupulous exactitude."

He asked us if we had read a recent article that appeared in the *Wall Street Journal,* suggested that we look up a series of articles that had appeared a few months earlier in the *Economist* of London, referred to some pronouncements of democratic doctrine by Jeremy Bentham, and settled back in his chair, apparently ready to spend the evening in similar discussion. Still talking about Bentham, the President arose from his desk to turn to a bookcase to get a book. Judge Siddons, always correct and meticulous in his manners, rose as the President rose. His elbow accidently jostled the kerosene student lamp on the President's desk and almost turned it over. There was a flurry of excitement. Major Pullman picked up a rug from the floor to throw it over the desk to smother the flames, but fortunately only the green glass shade was broken and there was no blaze. All of us, including the President, were frightened. Poor Siddons was in an agony of contrition.

The President did not particularly help him out when, after the agitation had subsided, he said, "Mr. Justice Siddons, the British burned this building once. Are you trying to do it again?"

An usher came in to repair the damage; an electric light was substituted for the kerosene lamp that the President had preferred for its soft light, which he said was more agreeable than any electric illumination; and the company sat down again.

Still teasing Siddons, the President said, "You know it wouldn't be very patriotic even of an Englishman to start burning the White House over again by using this particular desk for kindling wood. This desk was made of oak from the timbers of Admiral Nelson's ship 'Victory,' which he commanded in the Battle of Trafalgar and on which he died."

Queen Victoria had presented it to President Buchanan as a token of her appreciation of the White House's hospitality to her son, the Prince of Wales, during his visit in 1859.

That reminded the President of a story, which reminded him of another. He told two or three anecdotes. Syme came in with an anecdote. Newman, a very prince of raconteurs, told one or two. The room was full of laughter.

And then the President took over again with his favorite sport of quoting limericks. He gave us half a dozen. He asked us for others. All thought of business disappeared. Whatever worries he may have had about the European war were forgotten. It was an evening of sheer fun.

But it could not last. A little after eleven o'clock the secretary of state, William Jennings Bryan, came in. He apologized for the interruption but said that he had an urgent message in relation to the Mexican border problem.

The President bade us goodbye, saying, "Well, gentlemen, you see I must again go to work for Mr. Bryan."

Up to that time he had not mentioned anything particularly that he had to say to the new chief of police. As we all stood with him and Mr. Bryan shaking hands to say goodbye, Major Pullman was the last in line. To him the President said, as I recall his words, and in the hearing of all of us:

"Major Pullman, you are taking up a most important work. In connection with it, I have but one thing to say and that is to urge you to stamp out special privilege in the administration of the law. I do not know what my driver does that is wrong, but I do know that when a bicycle or a motorcycle policeman gets near enough to see that it is a White House car he disappears from the scene. I want you to tell your men that White House cars must obey the traffic regulations just the same as any other cars. And another thing, I am told that the police permit certain highly placed persons to put their carriages and automobiles ahead of others waiting at the gates of the White House on the occasion of the large receptions here. I want that stopped. If there is any creature on earth I despise it is a man who, by reason of his wealth or his social position or his official standing, seeks to disregard with impunity the police regulations and the local ordinances by which society keeps its processes in order."

This speech was not only significant of Mr. Wilson's attitude toward the essential principles of government but had a train of consequences. In the first place, the speech prospered in the ear of him to whom it was spoken, for Major Pullman held precisely the same ideas. In the next place, it made Major Pullman feel, as it did us commissioners, that we would have the backing necessary to carry through such a policy.

The Work Begins

The next day, Major Pullman, who had barely turned thirty years old and was looked at askance by his veteran corps of hard-boiled cops, assembled all the inspectors and captains of police. He told them that everybody was equal before the law and referred directly to the White House cars to illustrate a statement that all drivers of automobiles must obey the traffic rules.

As was to be expected, the police promptly put the matter to a test. The very next morning they arrested a White House chauffeur who was driving Mr. Tumulty from his home to the White House. Mr. Tumulty protested most vigorously to me. I told him I could do nothing. If the driver was not guilty, let him go to the court and tell the judge. The driver was found guilty; the fine was paid. During the next few days other White House car drivers were arrested. Miss Margaret Wilson and Mrs. McAdoo, the President's daughters, and Miss Helen Bones, the President's cousin who lived at the White House, were passengers. Almost everybody's car coming out of the White House was stopped except the President's own.

A committee of newspapermen from the White House, my former colleagues, came to me to protest. They said that Mr. Wilson would never forgive such interference with members of his family and that I must stop the fool thing Pullman was doing or I would be kicked out of the commissionership. I replied only that the White House drivers ought to obey the laws. My newspaper friends went away shaking sorrowful heads.

But Miss Margaret Wilson telephoned Mr. Newman and me nearly every day to tell us gleefully how much her father was enjoying the test to which the policemen were putting the new chief of police. "Every night at dinner," said Miss Wilson, "Father comes in with the same question, 'Who's been pinched today?'"

Newman, who saw the President more frequently than I did because he often played golf with him at the Washington Golf and Country Club, told me that the President was highly amused by the whole circumstance and was delighted that Major Pullman was standing to his guns.

Then there was another consequence. Several newspapers, none of them Washington newspapers, however, began to print gossip stories that Pullman had been appointed chief of police of Washington solely for the reason that he was engaged to Margaret Wilson; and the President had ordered Newman, Kutz, and me to give him a job.

We knew that President Wilson instantly and furiously resented any gossip about the women in his family. This new development disturbed both Newman and me. We knew that Major Pullman had never so much as met Miss Wilson and that it would be useless for us to issue a denial, for that would only add fuel to the fires of gossip.

Fortunately, the story was ended within a very few days. I was walking through Peacock Alley at the Willard Hotel with Major Pullman. Without warning we met Miss Wilson. I stopped to speak to her and, of course, to introduce Major Pullman.

"How delighted I am to meet for the first time the man to whom I am engaged to be married," said Miss Wilson.

Pullman was greatly embarrassed, but just at that moment up came Arthur J. Sinnott, the Washington correspondent of the *Newark Evening News*. Miss Wilson turned to greet him.

"Mr. Sinnott," she said, "this is a wonderful occasion for me. I have just met for the first time in my life the man that the newspapers say I have been engaged to for many months. I don't think anything like that has ever happened before."

Arthur Sinnott did the rest and gossip's tale was dead.

CHAPTER III

LEARNING THE JOB

My attitudes were changing rapidly. From my earliest boyhood, in my constant preoccupation with politics and political parties, I inclined to the view that the only necessary qualification for a public position was that the candidate be honest and that he get the job. I felt that those who agreed with me in politics and were members of my political party were, by that very token, better qualified than those who belonged to a different political party to fill almost any position in government—local, state, or national. In retrospect it is not a little frightening to me even now to remember that I then held the belief that any public office could be successfully administered by any honest and intelligent person and that no particular preparation was needed, that no special skills were required. I was dangerously near to holding the view later expressed by President Harding, "After all, government is a simple thing."

Of course, I was not quite so simple as to believe that some of the positions in municipal government did not require professional equipment. I knew that the corporation counsel and his assistants should be lawyers, that the health department required men with medical training, and that the engineering positions demanded engineering skills. However, even in these professional positions I thought that any lawyer, any doctor, any engineer, would be competent to undertake any task imposed by public position. I then had little or no notion of the fact that members of these professions also would require special skills and particular orientation if they were successfully to undertake the tasks imposed by the obligations and responsibilities of public administration.

One part of that particular attitude concerning qualifications for a public position I was not to change. That was the idea that the person should be a man of good will, devoted to the general good. Indeed, during the six years I was commissioner and later, I became ever more deeply convinced that good will and concern with the public interest still remain the primary characteristics of the successful administrator in government.

In that respect I was greatly impressed and influenced by the attitude of the corporation counsel, the chief of the legal branch of the District government, who had been chosen by Newman and Siddons. He was Conrad H. Syme, a lawyer of course, a West Virginian, a quick-motioned person with tousled hair, a perpetually belligerent personality, a sharp tongue, and a biting wit. Those who knew him soon discovered that his bark was much worse than his bite. Actually he possessed a characteristic attitude of good will and a high degree of devotion to his responsible duties.

I remember Connie Syme telling me at the "Doughnut Cabinet" table only a week after he had assumed his duties that he had in that week an odd and curious experience.

"Heretofore," he said, "in all the years I have been at the bar, I have held it to be my chief duty and principal concern to be faithful in my relationship with my clients and vigilant in the protection of their interests. I have had a fairly good practice and a good many clients, but during the last week I have experienced a new and startling feeling. Every time I go out on the street, I am struck with the fact that every person I see on the sidewalk, every person I see in the streetcar, every person I see in the stores, all these people, every one of them, is my client. It is a realization that has sunk in upon my consciousness and my conscience that it is my duty to be vigilant in the protection of the interest of all the people of Washington."

That was an attitude that I admired, and one that I had assumed in advance would be mine also. But as a matter of fact it was not borne in on me with any great force until after I had assumed the responsibilities of my official position. It was not until after I had begun the new work that this overpowering sense of responsibility to the general public, to the public interest, struck me with forcible conviction. I had expected to find conflicting interests, individual citizens, organizations of citizens, special organizations of businessmen and professional persons who would urge upon me actions consonant with their special interests and particular desires. I had not known how difficult it would be sometimes to adjust these special interests to my idea, or perhaps I should say my ideal, of serving the general interests, the whole people. That was a task never completely mastered—one that was increasingly difficult as I learned more and more about my job.

It didn't take very long for me to realize that I was profoundly ignorant of many of the processes of administration that manifested themselves in different types of paper work. I fear that at first I was impatient with all the detail—as a newspaper reporter would be likely to be, considering his training. But I was soon convinced not only of the usefulness of such detail but of the fact that it was necessary for me to understand the intricacies and to learn to discriminate between those things that would promote accuracy of information and facilitate communication and those that had been continued simply as traditions and sometimes multiplied the work even if originally they had met a genuine need.

I didn't know anything about public administration aside from the journalistic interest in its product.

Fortunately, I found in the District Building veteran administrators, some of whom were not only masters in the theory but exemplars in the practice. One such was Dr. William C. Woodward, the District health officer. He was a physician and a lawyer, and to those two professional skills he added another: he was one of the most capable administrators and department managers it has ever been my good fortune to meet. Also, he was a superlatively good teacher, and this was of even more benefit to me. Some of the best-equipped departmental managers in the District Building outside the health department had been chosen for their positions because at one time they had worked in that department under Dr. Woodward and had benefited by his tutelage. Dr. Woodward was kindly and patient to his students, whether those in the medical colleges, those under his instruction in legal jurisprudence, or those he regarded as members of his staff. He was equally kindly to his superiors, for he had had long experience educating relatively ignorant commissioners of the District of Columbia who had been appointed to supervise his department and its work. Underneath the smiling and kindly exterior, however, there was a will of steel and a set of standards of official conduct as inflexible as a pillar of granite.

The United States Public Health Service at that time was endeavoring through some of its principal officers to persuade state and local health departments to expand their activities. Most of the local health establishments had been set up on the theory that they were the guardians of sanitation and of prevention of communicable diseases but that they had nothing whatever to do with any branch of medicine save the preventive. If prevention failed, if despite the best efforts of enforcing the sanitary codes and fending off epidemics, disease struck, then its treatment was not within the province of the health department but fell rather upon the patient himself and his private physician or upon the welfare organizations, public and private, the hospitals, and the charities.

Dr. Woodward was a product of the sanitation school. He was in that field the strictest of the strict, and he did not desire to go further. Nonetheless, I was inclined to follow some of the suggestions for experimentation made in the Public Health Service. An instance soon arose when I wished to promote a venereal disease clinic under the aegis of municipal government. Dr. Woodward and his assistant, Dr. Fowler, firmly opposed the step. I hoped to bring in from time to time persons from the United States Public Health Service to make special surveys and recommendations in the field. Dr. Woodward did not agree.

Yet, despite these differences of opinion, he became my principal mentor in the procedural details of organization and methods. He was my instructor in the value of statistical data and a convincing advocate of basing recommendations upon accurate information, which he held could be obtained only by prompt reporting and the most rapid communication. I have never ceased to be grateful for his instruction.

My interest in the health department, despite my yielding to Dr. Woodward's resistance to expanding its scope, did result at once in my persuading my fellow commissioners to add to its facilities in their estimates for the next year's budget; and, when the budget was adopted by Congress, I was proud indeed that the appropriation for the health department showed an increase of a little more than 50 per cent.

The welfare agencies of the District of Columbia also covered a field in which I long had had a journalistic as well as a personal interest. There was no separate department of public welfare under the commissioners at that time. The principal agency was the Board of Charities composed of persons appointed by the President with the advice and consent of the Senate. Its administrative head was the secretary of the board. However, since the board's budget estimates came to the commissioners and its expenditures were controlled by the regular District establishment, in actual practice the secretary of the Board of Charities reported to me more promptly and more frequently than he did to the board to which he owed his first and formal allegiance. Then, also, there was a Board of Children's Guardians, which was responsible for welfare work with the juveniles who were public wards. The board necessarily maintained constant relationships with the police department, with the then newly established juvenile court, with the health department, and with the Board of Charities. There were other independent boards, such as those which managed the Columbia Lying-in Hospital, which was not entirely governmentally controlled, and a few others. I had come to know most of the people on these boards and on their staffs quite well during the years I had been a member of the Monday Evening Club, and among them were many of my close personal friends.

My wife had a special interest in children's work, and, as a fellow member of the Monday Evening Club, she also had made many friends among the staffs of the public agencies in this field. At the same time, both my wife and I were well acquainted with the private agencies in this field, such as the Associated Charities and the Instructive Visiting Nurses Association.

I was ignorant about their procedures of internal administration, and I was soon to find out that I had much to learn. Here again I was fortunate in finding, not only in the District Building itself but among the members of the various boards and among the ranks of the private agencies, individuals who were capable instructors.

The secretary of the Board of Charities was George S. Wilson, a canny Scot who had been educated in Scotland and England and was inspired by the lofty ideals of the mid-nineteenth-century English reformers and littérateurs. He had a passionate interest in the unfortunate and underprivileged, but as an administrator he watched every penny.

The Board of Charities was at that time headed by John Joy Edson, a banker who had been appointed to the position for many successive terms by several presidents and who had repeatedly declined offers to serve on the Board of Commissioners. Mr. Edson was looked up to as the leading citizen of Washington. He was a leader in the business community, a conservative banker who was outstanding among his fellows, a devoted churchman (he was a Swedenborgian), and at the head and front of practically all the community service movements. Another member of the board at that time was Father William J. Kerby of the faculty of the Catholic University of America, a man I also had known through his interest in community services and welfare work in the Monday Evening Club. Still another was Rev. John van Schaick, pastor of the Universalist Church, sometime president of the Monday Evening Club and a fellow member of the Cosmos Club.

As a result of Mr. Edson's zeal for prison reform and his humanitarian faith in the amelioration of prison discipline as a means of rehabilitation, the Congress had been persuaded to permit the District government to embark on what was then a radical experiment in penology: the establishment at Occoquan—twenty-odd miles south of Washington in Virginia—of a new workhouse which was characterized first of all by the fact that it would have no barricading walls, no barred windows, no locked doors. To the workhouse were transferred prisoners sentenced to the District of Columbia jail for periods up to one year—misdemeanants, principally. The new workhouse had been built by the prisoners themselves from lumber they had sawed from trees felled on the site; the chimneys and the few brick buildings had been erected by the prisoners from bricks they had made from clay dug in the workhouse grounds. The experiment actually was in its third year when I came to the District Building. It had been so successful that the Congress had authorized the construction, on a nearby plot of ground at Lorton, of a reformatory to which prisoners convicted of felonies and sentenced to the federal penitentiary at Atlanta could be transferred. The reformatory at Lorton was in the process of being built when I took up my responsibilities.

What passed for a city hospital at that time was a disgrace. It was called the Washington Asylum and Jail and was housed in a brick building erected in 1810 as an almshouse. It was supplemented by a great many temporary wooden buildings, some of which had been thrown up in a great hurry to serve as hospitals for wounded and sick soldiers during the Civil War. The commissioners had been endeavoring for years to persuade the Congress to make an appropriation sufficient to build and equip a modern city hospital, but thus far they had failed. To continue that effort was one of my principal jobs.

Yet, much as I was interested in prison reform, as great as was my devotion to the need for improving the institutions caring for delinquent children as well as for the aged and infirm, I had little idea what would be necessary for managing such institutions efficiently and economically while insuring that they fulfilled their primary humanitarian and social purposes. These things I was yet to learn.

Another source of information and experience was my colleague Oliver Peck Newman, who had shared my journalistic interest in all these subjects but who, during his two years as District commissioner, had also learned a great deal about how to get things done, how to manage things, and how necessary it was to obtain sufficient, accurate information upon which to base appeals to the committees of the Congress which held the purse strings.

All these principal concerns for which I had primary responsibility—police and fire departments, the health department, and the welfare agencies—I soon discovered had vital cross-relations with the engineering department, the finance department, and the legal department. And here again I discovered my ignorance of administrative procedures and the differing emphases, if not the differing values, placed upon certain types of paper work.

The engineering knowledge which seemed to me necessary for my own work I acquired almost entirely through the process of osmosis. My intimate relationship with Major Kutz was my primary source of information. He not only permitted but encouraged direct dealing between his engineers and the civilian departments with common concerns. Thus we were able to maintain rather direct communication between the police and the highway departments, the health department and the water and sewer departments, and between the welfare department and the office of the architect and the divisions of building, plumbing, and electrical inspection.

The division of refuse collection and disposal crosscut many of the departments, and here again I was permitted to talk directly with the responsible division heads without being compelled to go through channels whenever it seemed desirable to me to seek information.

The fiscal information I needed came by edict from the office of the auditor of the District of Columbia. The auditor, Alonzo Tweedale, and his principal assistant, Daniel J. Donovan, were not only first-class accountants but also first-class accounting lawyers. The scheme of their organization and the methods they employed had been time-tested, and they were not to be trifled with. While they reported primarily to Newman, I was permitted also to talk with them directly and to ask them questions. In the beginning months of my training they gave me the answers, and it was not until later that I felt sufficiently confident of myself to make suggestions for improvement. Another division was that of the purchasing officer who controlled all purchases not only for the police and health departments but also for the public schools and the huge housekeeping necessities of the welfare institutions.

It didn't take me very long to find out that I would be compelled to give greater attention to those departments which had the most direct contact with individual citizens. That inevitably made the police department a prime problem. Not only do the police have a great number of contacts throughout the year with citizens, but in all too many instances the contact is, to say the least, not highly appreciated by the individual concerned. The policeman in his round of daily duties frequently is compelled to interfere, and, to the discomfort of the top administrator, the individual thus interfered with will find a great many other citizens in the community who will sympathize with him.

When the fireman goes out to fight a fire, he finds that, with the occasional exception of a pyromaniac, perhaps, the crowd is on his side. It is true that the policeman who detects a murderer, arrests a holdup man, or performs some heroic feat of rescue will gain applause. But a policeman enforcing parking regulations or speed regulations rarely draws a gallery of cheering citizens to his support.

While, as I have said, there was no formal civil service arrangement at the disposal of the District commissioners in the recruiting or promoting of District employees, the commissioners in self-defense had set up certain standards for the uniformed forces—the police and fire departments—which involved physical, written, and oral examinations given by senior members of the two departments. In general all these examinations, however, emphasized brawn rather than brain. Even worse than that, perhaps, was the effect of the low salaries, the long hours, and the unsatisfactory working conditions, which effectively prevented the recruitment of policemen and firemen able to handle some of the more difficult problems they would face.

The defect, however, had within it some elements of self-correction. The very fact that the police officer did have on his beat scores of daily contacts with citizens brought out and developed innate capacities that were not readily revealed by the written examinations or the tests of scholastic experience then ordinarily employed. The result was that a great 'many of the low-paid, hard-working, overburdened members of the police force had demonstrated in the course of their work superior mental qualities that enabled them to profit from the experience gained in their daily work.

However, I believed, and my colleagues agreed with me, that the department had suffered from too much dependence upon traditionalism. That was one of the reasons that Mr. Newman and I had taken the bold step of appointing a chief of police from outside the department.

The new chief, Major Raymond W. Pullman, not only had to meet the severe test that his subordinates put him to with his first order of "no favoritism in the enforcement of traffic regulations"; his subordinates also were dubious about his lack of experience, his youth, and, for that matter, even his enthusiasm. A policeman of long years of experience is likely to develop certain cynical attitudes toward life in general and more especially toward those persons who think that a law on the statute books or an ordinance duly passed and recorded will be self-enforcing unless there is some absence of zeal or skill in the police department. Too often the policeman finds entirely too many persons who act as if any violation of any law is the fault not of the lawbreaker but of the law enforcer.

Major Pullman's task and therefore mine—and, in the last degree, that of all three of the commissioners—was not made easier by the fact that we at once instituted an intensive survey of what had been going on; some rumors had reached us indicating either maladministration or laxity in the department.

There undoubtedly had been instances of corrupt collusion in the toleration of the red-light district, which had, as I have said, been abolished—collusion not only with the persons who had managed the now-forbidden establishments but also with the owners of the property and with some highly respected business concerns which supplied the goods purchased by those establishments. We also discovered that occasionally it was difficult not to believe that some particular gambling establishments had enjoyed police protection, which was not given for nothing.

There were even more easily detected instances of gross favoritism. Mr. John R. McLean, who was then publisher and owner of the *Washington Post,* maintained two residences in the District of Columbia: a town house on McPherson Square and a large country estate in what was then a rural suburban section. This estate, "Friendship," long ago swallowed up in a housing development, was protected by three private watchmen. Those three were regular members of the metropolitan police force and were paid regular salaries by the District government, but their duties were supervised by Mr. McLean. They were not even put to the trouble of reporting to police headquarters or to one of the precincts. Their checks were sent to them through Mr. McLean or through one of his secretaries. That was a piece of rank favoritism and easy to stop; but it was not extensively publicized and certainly did not win many friends among the members of Mr. McLean's entourage.

It was more difficult to run down some of the cases in which members of the police department, we had reason to suspect, were actually in cahoots with thieves. One day Mr. Frank L. Ball, the commonwealth's attorney of Alexandria County (now Arlington County), Virginia, came to tell me that he had discovered in his bailiwick a thieves' fence operated in conjunction with the kindly ministrations of a captain of our District police force. The precinct headquarters he commanded was very close to one end of a bridge across the Potomac. The thieves' den and fence were just over the river in Virginia.

Charges were filed by Major Pullman against this police captain. He was tried under the regular system of a police trial board with this difference: up to that time a police trial board always had been composed of one inspector and two captains; shortly before this trial, on my recommendation, the composition of the trial board had been changed to consist of one inspector, one captain, and one assistant corporation counsel as chairman. The police captain was found guilty. The commissioners upheld the verdict, and he was dismissed from the force. This was the first time in the history of the department, so far as I could learn, and certainly the first time in recent years that an officer of the department of the rank of lieutenant, captain, or inspector ever had been found guilty by a police trial board.

A great many citizens, even some organizations of citizens, appealed to me to modify the verdict. Sometimes in my interviews with these advocates of mercy it developed that this particular captain had been very kind to the advocate in question. The chief of police and I stood our ground. We were upheld by the full board, and an effort to get the case into the courts was unsuccessful.

This case had, at least for several years thereafter, a salutary effect on discipline in the department. It gave courage to those honest members who felt themselves and the whole department disgraced by a departure of any fellow member from the path of rectitude and thereby enabled us much more easily to get the information necessary to discipline the minority of the members of the force who, for one reason or another, went astray.

Major Pullman set about with great intelligence and vigor to improve the police work of Washington as he found it. One of his first tasks was to reorganize the system of communications and reporting. A police telegraph system had been in existence for many years with the familiar call boxes on the street corners and at the telephone switchboard exchange in the municipal building. The American Telephone and Telegraph Company had just perfected its mechanical arrangements for conference circuits, and one of the first, if not the very first, installed was that connected with the District Building switchboard and the police telegraph system, so that it was possible for the chief to get the captains of the twelve precincts, the chief of detectives, and any other person, up to thirty people, on the conference circuit simultaneously. This device had an immediate effect of raising the morale of the department, especially when added to the demonstration that the administration meant what it said when it issued an order for no special favors.

Another feature of Major Pullman's work was his intensive effort to educate the public, especially children, about the police officer in the community. This required a systematic propaganda campaign to persuade thoughtless mothers not to frighten their children by threatening to call a cop. The core of that campaign was to try to teach every child that the policeman was his best friend. A police sergeant with a gift of gab, William S. Shelby, and a police private possessed of great skill with a crayon, Richard Mansfield, were sent into the public schools to speak and to make chalk talks. The almost instantaneously favorable response to this campaign in the schools astonished us.

We were much concerned with some of the other difficulties that came about as a result of the abolition of the red-light district. As a

matter of fact, our investigation showed that there was little or nothing
to the fears of those who believed that the closing of the red-light
section would scatter the business of commercial prostitution throughout the residential sections of the city. We found plenty of such scat-
tering, but, to the astonishment of even some of the veteran members
of the police department, that dispersal had happened long before the
tolerated quarter was closed.

We did find, however, that the business of dealing with delinquent
girls required a special study and a method of work that seemed to us
to be beyond the capabilities of the ordinary policeman. For that reason
I decided, with the support of Major Pullman and the approval of my
colleagues, to establish the Women's Bureau of the Police Department.
This required the consent of the Congress and the appropriation of
funds. To obtain those appropriations required the better part of two
years, but in 1917 the money was voted, and in September, 1918, the
first women's bureau of any police department in the United States
was inaugurated in my office by the swearing in of Mrs. Marian C.
Spingarn as detective sergeant. By that time the war was nearly over,
and the problem of delinquent girls in Washington had increased
tremendously under war conditions. Mrs. Spingarn was the wife of a
former district attorney of New York and a trained social worker. We
turned over to her the task of recruitment, and a few weeks later two
other women, Mrs. Mina C. Van Winkle and Mrs. Leola King, were
appointed privates. Mrs. Van Winkle was a graduate of a New York
school of social work. Mrs. King was a registered nurse.

The commissioners then transferred to the new women's bureau the
supervision of the House of Detention, which was an institution in
which women arrested for crimes were detained and which also served
as a receiving home for juvenile delinquents.

We soon discovered that policewomen not only were successful in
dealing with problems of women and girls but also were very much
better than men in some types of detective work, particularly that
extremely difficult task of locating and arresting shoplifters. Putting
women on the police force was not accomplished without trouble or
opposition. Some citizens said that it was an insult to American woman-
hood. Others believed, or said they believed, that our purpose was
solely to trap the unwary male. Greatly to our astonishment, even some
of the social workers of the community with whom Mr. Newman,

Major Pullman, and I had been well acquainted in our work as officers of the Monday Evening Club were violently opposed not only to our employing women as police officers but also to our attempt to recruit trained social workers for those jobs. In that dim and distant day many social workers associated the very word "police" with all that was repressive, evil, and corrupt.

We actually put one of the policewomen on the corner to direct traffic at the time when the police roster was low and it was almost impossible to employ any man at all. That was widely considered an outrage. But it proved to be one of the important revolutions in police systems throughout the country; and its value today is no longer even questioned.

CHAPTER IV

COUNTERESPIONAGE AS A
SIDE LINE

World War I began with the invasion of Belgium by Germany in August, 1914, but certainly the United States and the American people did not at first realize how this country and its citizens would be affected. The war waxed in fury and widened in extent, and, during my time and Major Pullman's time, it was to involve the police department as well as the other branches of the municipal government of the District of Columbia in many ways. We were destined to experience the mobilization of the American Expeditionary Force; we were to deal with German and Austrian spies and saboteurs. We were to help in our modest way in the task of establishing counterespionage in a country until then completely innocent of the machinery required for such purposes. We were to have to deal with the severe strains put upon the capital city by an unprecedented influx of men and women workers, military and civilian, required for the national military effort; and then, in the aftermath of the war, we were to cope with a severe and tragic race riot and an imminent police strike.

Truly, Mr. W. S. Gilbert was quite correct when he penned the immortal words, "A policeman's lot is not a happy one." Fortunately, in 1914 we didn't know of the troubles yet to come.

To say the government of the United States and that of its national capital were unprepared for the impact of the great war that began in August, 1914, is to make an understatement that plunges almost to the nadir of discourse. I have no doubt that in the departments of the Army and Navy there was a cadre of organization for intelligence services, but in the civilian departments there was none at all. In the Treasury Department there was the Secret Service, which had the primary function of enforcing the laws against counterfeiting and against internal revenue violations by running down moonshiners and illicit tobacco peddlers. The Secret Service also had a small detail assigned to the White House for the protection of the President. The State Department had no means whatever for dealing with espionage or sabotage. In the Department of Justice there was the recently established Federal Bureau of Investigation, the FBI, but its principal, almost its only, duty was the detection of frauds against the public land laws, under a scheme which had been originated by President Theodore Roosevelt as a part of his conservation program. The metropolitan police of the District of Columbia, for which I had primary responsibility, was in charge of a detail of police officers who guarded and policed the White House. The Capitol had its own police force, the members of which were chosen by patronage only, and there were separate systems of park police and an anomalous Department of Agriculture police.

At the very beginning of World War I, when rumors began to be circulated of undue activity in this country on the part of the warring European powers, the State Department borrowed from the Secret Service in the Treasury one lone operator, Mr. William Nye. The chief of the FBI was Mr. A. Bruce Bielaski. I had first met him when I was a newspaper reporter looking into the land fraud cases, chiefly from Nebraska and the Dakotas, under the urging of a special assistant attorney general, Colonel John S. Moseby, a famous former Confederate partisan ranger.

Mr. Bielaski was a product of the public schools of Washington. He and his sister, later Mrs. Ruth Bielaski Shipley, had gone to grade school and later to Eastern High School with my wife. Also with them, and in the same classes with my wife, was Chief of Police Raymond W. Pullman. In my days as a newspaper reporter I had become very well acquainted with several members of the Treasury Secret Service.

All these personal acquaintances led to confidential conversations when, almost immediately after Major Pullman assumed office in April, 1915, very disturbing news of attempted or planned sabotage began to reach us. The Secret Service had assigned two or three operatives to the Port of New York, and they began to detect evidence of interference with United States shipments of war materials and other things to Britain and France.

It didn't take very long to trace the source of some of these attempted interferences to the German and Austro-Hungarian consulates, to the officers of German business establishments, and, indeed, to the offices of the military and naval attachés of the Imperial German Embassy in Washington.

Most of the principal agencies concerned with counterespionage had small staffs; indeed, Bill Nye had not one single assistant at the beginning. The State and Justice departments turned over a portion of these antisabotage and counterespionage problems to the metropolitan police department of the District of Columbia.

It should be recalled, as it is difficult these days to recall, that at the beginning of World War I, although President Wilson had asked the citizens of this country to be neutral in thought as well as in deed, there was strong pro-German sentiment in various parts of the United States, just as there was strong pro-British and pro-French sentiment. Most Americans were neutral in deed. Very few were neutral in thought. The pro-German sentiment prevailed among many citizens of German or Austrian ancestry and also, to a very large extent, among those of Irish ancestry, especially the violent partisans of home rule or even of independence for Ireland who, animated by motives more anti-British than pro-German, arrived by a different route at the same goal.

Two young women of German parentage, who were skilled stenographers accustomed to the use of either English or German in their work and who were also violently pro-German, sought and found employment as stenographers at the German Embassy. To be for Germany against France and England was one thing; but to find the Germans actually plotting sabotage in the United States was quite another matter. To be a German-American in sentiment was quite all right; but the hyphen was a dividing mark which found its two wings not always in exact balance. The two girls took their lunch one bright day and sat down on a bench in McPherson Square to eat it. They talked over their problem. They decided that they were more American than German, so they went to the police. They told Major Pullman their story and said they were going back to the embassy and resign. Major Pullman prevailed upon them to stay where they were and, if possible, to give the police as many carbon copies as they could. They stayed on the job and we got the carbon copies. The aid of persons in similar positions who found their sentimental attachment to the land of their ancestors overwhelmed by their American patriotism helped in the defeat of hundreds of schemes of major and minor sabotage.

Counterespionage as a Side Line

Captain Franz von Papen was the German military attaché; Captain Boy-Ed was the naval attaché. One or the other of them rented an old three-story house on Fourteenth Street, just south of Thomas Circle and not very far from the German Embassy, and installed in it a group of pro-German Americans, all of them women, most of them young and personable. These lovely ladies were employed as lobbyists and encouraged in every possible way to make as many contacts as possible with Americans highly placed in the executive department and in the Congress.

We knew all about it in advance, and this was the first and only case, to my knowledge, in which, in a responsible position in police administration, I employed or even so much as condoned wire-tapping. Before the house was redecorated and occupied, we had its telephones tapped. Then we employed three stenographers, each working eight hours a day, and we recorded all the incoming and outgoing conversations. The typed reports went several times a day to Major Pullman and very frequently to me. This gave us some excellent leads as to just what was going on, but these leads were often of the kind that would take us far, far afield from the legitimate sphere of police administration. Therefore, we turned them over as we received them to the Secret Service, to the FBI, and to the State Department, each of which, of course, was busily engaged in expanding its activities. Long before the entry of the United States into the war in April, 1917, the federal agencies had expanded to the point where they were fully capable of taking over the task, and the metropolitan police department bowed out of its intriguing but uncomfortable task.

The ladies in the house on Fourteenth Street did not confine their activities absolutely to assignments from the German Embassy, and sometimes for some of them there would be dull days. One of them, a young and very pretty girl from Mississippi—altogether the moonlight-and-magnolia type—met a bachelor who was employed in a fairly responsible governmental position. This bachelor was a very good friend of mine and also of Major Pullman. He had more than once been my guest at the "Doughnut Cabinet" table in the Willard.

Major Pullman brought me one morning the transcript of the telephone conversations at the house on Fourteenth Street. The young lady had made a date to have dinner with our bachelor friend. She had told him that she was visiting with a great-aunt who was a demon chaperon and would not permit her beau to come to the house; therefore she must meet him outside. This time the date was for seven o'clock in the evening at the corner of Fourteenth and K streets.

Shortly thereafter, Captain Boy-Ed called her and assigned her to go to dinner at the Purple Iris Inn that night, where she was to manage to meet a certain senator who would be in the party. She tried desperately over and over again to reach our friend by telephone. He was not in his office. He was not in his apartment. He was not to be found.

So Pullman suggested to me that we keep the engagement. Shortly before seven the chief and I strolled up Fourteenth Street, loafed along the side of Franklin Park and ran into our friend at the appointed hour at the appointed corner. We were in a chatty mood. I talked long. I told long stories. Pullman, who sometimes stammered, stammered through two or three longish tales. Our friend look up the street and down the street and across the street. Of course he didn't know that we knew that she would not come. We kept him on the griddle for a long, long time until it struck us both that we were inflicting unconstitutionally cruel and unusual punishment; and we left him.

More than a year later I met this gentleman at Fifteenth and G streets a day or two after the United States had declared war on Germany. He was highly indignant. He said it was an absolutely crazy thing to go into a war utterly unprepared; that we had no army and no navy and not a scintilla of an intelligence service. That was a little more than I could take, so I came back with, "I believe you know Miss So-and-So."

He stared blankly. I said, "You probably haven't any notion that she is a German secret agent and that through you we have been feeding misleading information about the state of our preparedness to the German naval attaché for months."

His jaw dropped. He walked away without a word, and thereafter, whenever he saw me coming down the street, he always crossed to avoid seeing me. Once or twice I cornered him and tried to talk with him, but he was always evasive.

Even though the District police force was soon relieved of responsibility for intelligence work of this type, it continued as a matter of course to co-operate with the federal officials and thus was frequently called upon for special services.

One morning the British ambassador, Sir Cecil Spring-Rice, came to see me. It was rather unusual for an ambassador to come to the District Building to call on a District commissioner, but of course I received him instantly. He said:

"Mr. Commissioner, I have come to see you because I know that you have supervision of the police department, and I have something that I would like to report. It seemed to me wise not to involve the Department of State in this matter, which is one that I consider solely of interest to the municipal police. You know, of course, that the British Embassy occupies the building at the corner of Connecticut Avenue and N Street. Perhaps you have noticed that adjoining it on the north is a row of four-story red brick buildings. The one next door to the embassy has been vacant for a long time. A few weeks ago it was purchased by a physician, Dr. So-and-So, who moved into it promptly and has installed not only his office but a small infirmary. Beds have been provided for many of the rooms, and he has a staff of one or two physicians and four or five nurses.

"Shortly after the house was occupied, members of the embassy staff heard suspicious sounds in the cellar. It soon became evident that somebody from the house next door was apparently driving a tunnel into the basement of the embassy. I cannot help suspecting that somebody is trying to get in, probably with the idea of finding important secret papers. There are no such papers in the embassy. Everything that would be of the slightest use to an enemy or anything that would be of the slightest value to anyone seeking secret war information has been removed to my cottage in Cleveland Park. I am not particularly disturbed about what is going on, but I thought that you and the chief of police might like to know.

"I shall not communicate this matter to the State Department, nor do I expect you to say that you will do anything about it; nor, if you do, do I expect you to make any report to me or to any member of my staff concerning the matter. I merely called because I was under the impression that you would be interested. Good morning."

That was that. I immediately got hold of Major Pullman and told him the story. Within an hour or two we had ascertained that the physician who had bought the house next to the British Embassy was an elderly impecunious physician of German birth who had maintained a small practice in the southwest part of the city for a good many years; also that he apparently had come into considerable funds; that he had purchased the house and paid cash for it; and all the equipment that he had installed for the infirmary had been paid for in cash; and that the two assistant physicians and the four or five nurses all were regularly licensed physicians or registered nurses and that all of them were of German-American lineage.

Then the question was, What to do? As Pullman and I sat talking about it, a young newspaper friend of ours, Stuart Price, walked in. "What's the news?" he asked.

"Stuart," I responded, "we have one of the best stories that you ever heard in your life, but we can tell it to you only if you give us your solemn word of honor that you will not tell it to anybody, much less write it or print it."

That not only excited his curiosity but raised his blood to the boiling point. He protested and protested but after a long while he discovered we were adamant. His curiosity got the better of his journalistic devotion, and he gave us his word. We told him the tale. Then Pullman said: "Stuart, you are the one man that I believe is able to get into that house and find out what is going on. It is up to you."

Stuart lived across the Potomac in Alexandria and drove to work in Washington in his Model T Ford, something in that day and time that itself was a manifestation of adventurous spirit and great courage. He left my office, went out and got in his Ford, and decided that this would be a good time—it was around four o'clock in the afternoon—to "case the joint." He drove up to Connecticut Avenue, around Dupont Circle, and came back down Connecticut. As luck would have it, just at the corner of N Street, directly in front of the embassy, he choked his engine. He got out to crank it; but he had advanced the spark too far. The engine backfired and broke his right wrist.

We had established a constant fixed-post police guard outside each of the embassies of the belligerent powers. The policeman on duty there knew Price and came out to help him. The car was shoved around into the side street. It would be impossible, of course, for Stuart to drive home.

"Here," said Stuart, "is a doctor's office. This is the place to get my arm set."

He went in. The doctor was there. The doctor set his arm. Since it was impossible to get home, he asked to telephone his wife. He told her that the doctor had an infirmary in the house, and he would spend the night there. He was put to bed properly with physicians and nurses in attendance.

About three o'clock in the morning, when everything was quiet, he awoke. With his right arm in a sling and with a flashlight in his left hand his only weapon, he walked down three flights of stairs into the basement. There he found four individuals engaged in digging a tunnel in the south wall of the basement aimed at, of course, the British Embassy. They had cut almost through the party wall into the basement. Throwing his flashlight on the men at work, Stuart uttered one sentence: "Boys, that will be about all!"

Without a word he walked back upstairs and went to bed. The next day his wife came for him.

Stuart reported to Pullman, and within a week or two the infirmary was vacated. The beds were moved out; the physicians and nurses dispersed; and the house was put on the market.

There were other instances of similar interest. At that time the Austro-Hungarian Embassy occupied a building at Connecticut Avenue and N Street directly across from the British Embassy. It was built on a triangular lot and occupied the ground running through from Connecticut Avenue to Eighteenth Street. On the Eighteenth Street side there was a carriage entrance which gave access to the front door of the embassy from a driveway protected by a porte-cochere. Next door to the north there was a four-story apartment house which ran all the way from Connecticut Avenue through to Eighteenth Street. That meant that the windows of the apartments at the rear of the building on the southwest side overlooked the porte-cochere and driveway into the Austro-Hungarian Embassy.

One morning shortly after nine o'clock a man came in and told my secretary that he had something he must tell the commissioner at once. He declined to give his name, but he was so urgent that my secretary let him in. He told me his name and said that he and his wife occupied an apartment on the third story of the apartment house overlooking the driveway into the Austro-Hungarian Embassy.

"About four o'clock this morning," he said, "my wife, who is a semi-invalid and who was awake, thought she heard shots in the building next door. She awakened me and I went to the window. I saw two men bring a limp body of another man out of the embassy door and put it in the back seat of an automobile. Then the two men got into the car and drove away. Of course I can't say positively, but I cannot help believing that the man was dead. I thought the police ought to know, but I do not want to get mixed up in anything that may have something to do with this war."

I was much puzzled. I telephoned Major Pullman, who had not yet come in, and left word for him to come to see me as soon as he got to the office.

In a few minutes two other callers came. One was a middle-aged woman with her ten-year-old granddaughter. They told me that they lived on the second floor of that apartment house, that both of them had gone to the window, that both of them had seen the limp body of a man they believed was dead carried out of the embassy by two men. The body was put in the back of the car and the two men drove it away.

I did not know what to do. Pullman made discreet inquiries in the neighborhood and among the attachés of the British and French embassies. They knew nothing. If it was one of their agents who was shot and killed, they cared not to let us know about it. If only one person had reported the tale to me, I would not have believed it, but, with the corroboration from the grandmother and the granddaughter, I have always believed that early that morning some secret agent of the Allied Powers was discovered or some agent of the Central Powers was found to be disloyal and that a summary sentence of death had been carried out.

However, with all Pullman's and my own fringe connections with the problem of espionage, it was our duty, of course, to turn over information to the federal authorities; and after the first few months we knew nothing of the ends of the stories or to what use the information had been put. It so happened that Major Pullman and I were never absolutely sure that we had seen a genuine German spy except in one case, and that, oddly enough, came after the United States had entered the war; but again we never knew the end of the story.

When the United States entered the war early in April, 1917, the Allied Powers each at once sent a special mission to Washington. The first to arrive was the British mission. It was headed by Mr. Arthur J. Balfour and was composed of a group of distinguished statesmen and military officers. They came on a British war vessel directly up the Potomac to Washington. Major Pullman and I were at the Navy Yard to welcome the delegation and to see to it that they were comfortably taken care of in motor cars for their trips to their destinations.

One man in particular we met at the Navy Yard dock that morning was General Bethell, the chief of the British Army Intelligence Service. Major Pullman was in uniform and, as soon as he was introduced, General Bethell said he would like to have an interview at once. An appointment was made for that afternoon in Major Pullman's office. Pullman indicated that I, as the commissioner who supervised the police, also would be present. All this was very early in the morning, and we got back to our offices about ten o'clock. There Major Pullman found something unusual. It was a young man who had been picked up by a precinct detective in the fourth precinct on a charge of stealing a cornet from a fellow roomer in an obscure rooming house. He had been arrested on a warrant sworn out by the landlady and taken to the precinct station. There the briefest examination of his baggage, which consisted of one large suitcase, resulted in his being taken at once to the chief's office.

The person arrested was a strikingly handsome youth with pink cheeks and very fair hair who spoke English with what we considered to be a marked Oxford accent. The landlady who had sworn out the warrant said that the young man had come to her house about ten days before, had paid for his room in advance, and had asked her as a special favor to prepare meals for him, which she did only occasionally for her tenants, and that during the ten days he had never left the house. She had another tenant who was struggling to learn to play the cornet. A few days before, she had heard the cornet being played during the daytime. She had assumed that her cornet-playing tenant was home for some reason, and she had remarked on how much better he was in his playing.

Then the student of the cornet came to her and said that his instrument was missing. The cornet was found. The arrest followed. The young man's suitcase was opened and he was taken to Major Pullman's office. Major Pullman sent for me. We, together with the chief of detectives and one or two others, interviewed him. He was very candid. He said that he was an agent of the German government, that he had come to Washington, that in the flurry of activity that brought the United States into war he had lost contact with his principals, that he knew that he would have to conserve his funds and so had sought out a cheap rooming house. He did not dare go out either day or night and found the time hanging heavy on his hands. He had heard somebody practicing on a cornet. In his loneliness he had got into the habit of going into the other man's room, which was unlocked, borrowing the cornet to while away the time and then putting it back before the cornet student came back home. Last night he forgot to replace the cornet. Its owner complained to the landlady. The landlady had sworn out the warrant, and here he was.

The focus of our interest in questioning him was his suitcase. It had a false bottom which divided it into two approximately equal compartments. In one was a complete outfit of women's clothes. In the other was an excellent selection of men's clothes and haberdashery. Immediately off the office of the chief of police was a bathroom. Major Pullman told our prisoner to take the suitcase, go into the bathroom, and make the change which, as indicated by his baggage, he was prepared to make. He disappeared into the bathroom, which had no other exit. In a few minutes the door opened and out came a strikingly beautiful blonde young woman.

Our prisoner told us that when he had come to the United States after two or three years in schools and one year at Oxford, he had gone to Minnesota, where he had some relatives. When the war came on he thought it his duty to do something for Germany, and he decided it would be a good thing if he could get into the Canadian Army. He crossed the border, enlisted in the Canadian Army and found himself at a training camp in England not far from London. From there he took French leave and found his way to a German secret agent in London. He was very hazy in his replies to our questions of how he could find this man so easily. The agent had equipped him with a false American passport, and he had come back to this country to do what he could for the German cause. He had instructions to report to certain German agents in New York, Baltimore, and Washington. He had no contact with the German Embassy at all.

His ability to masquerade as a woman, he told us, was acquired in amateur theatricals. He seemingly was candid, but he said that on account of personal loyalties he could not disclose anything about any of his contacts.

Knowing that General Bethell was coming in that afternoon, we decided to keep him under guard in the chief's office. When General

Bethell came about three-thirty, Pullman and I told him the story, and he asked to see the young man, who was brought in dressed in men's clothing, the outfit he had worn at the time of his arrest.

Instantly General Bethell rose from his chair, walked over, threw back the young man's coat, took a fountain pen out of the young man's vest pocket, walked back to Pullman's desk, opened the pen, and took from it a coil of paper.

"This," said General Bethell, "contains his credentials. He is a trained secret agent of the German Army. He has been in training since he was fourteen or fifteen years old, and I don't think you had better put any reliance whatever in the tale he has told you about his travels and his conduct. I think we probably know much more about it already than he is willing to tell."

We kept the young man safe and sound that night. I consulted the State Department and the War Department, and the next day we turned him over to General Bethell. That was the last I ever heard of the case of the only genuine German spy I ever met.

CHAPTER V

THE COUNTRY GOES TO WAR

When in early April, 1917, the United States entered the war, it was immediately evident that the personnel of the Board of Commissioners would be changed. Mr. Baker, the secretary of war, told me that the Army would soon require the services of Major Kutz.

Mr. Newman, the president of the board, had had two years at West Point in his youth before he stubbed his toe on a mathematics examination, and he was eager to go into active service. When Mr. Baker suggested to him that he enter one of the officers' training camps then being set up, Newman immediately took leave from the District government.

Thus, in April, 1917, I was made acting president of the Board of Commissioners. Major Kutz resigned in July to go overseas with the American Expeditionary Force. He was succeeded by Brigadier General John G. D. Knight, retired. General Knight was a man of commanding presence, outstanding ability, and great charm. However, he was elderly and his health was not good. He at once told me that he would rely on my judgment about many matters in municipal government, reserving to himself the initiative only in the engineering department. Very soon he was deprived of all but one of his assistant engineer commissioners, the others being called into active service. With Mr. Newman absent, General Knight began to consult me even more intimately on matters affecting the engineering department than had his predecessor, Major Kutz. As a result the Board of Commissioners became in a sense a one-man show with me at the controls. This experience, albeit only *en passant*, proved in later years to be of incalculable value to me as an introduction to my work as a city manager and later as a sole executive in other fields.

In October, 1917, the President appointed W. Gwynne Gardiner to replace Mr. Newman, and I was formally elected president of the Board of Commissioners.

Our efforts to fit the work of the police department into the related community services, while contributing to my own education, were destined to be interrupted and confused but not entirely defeated by international and national developments. The direct effect on the government of the District of Columbia of events that concerned only indirectly the municipal institutions of other American cities was vividly demonstrated when the United States declared war on Germany and the other Central Powers.

In the first place, there was the necessity of creating a great military establishment in a nation which, except for the ephemeral and relatively small war with Spain, had been at peace since the Civil War. President Wilson almost immediately after the declaration of war realized that the American armed forces could not be recruited by the volunteer method. He told the Congress that he would support conscription and called on that body to enact the necessary measures.

Conscription had been the most unpopular feature of the Civil War, both in the Union and in the Confederacy. Conscription had not been dreamed of in the war with Spain. Conscription had not been enacted even in the embattled nation of Great Britain.

The judge advocate general of the Army, General Enoch Crowder, an able lawyer as well as a brilliant administrator, was set to the task of preparing the new draft law. In deference to the prejudices against the word "conscription" or even "draft," the phrase "selective service" was adopted in the hope that it would make this radical change in American military methods more palatable to congressmen and to the public. A division of the Department of the Interior had just been moved into its new building, leaving vacant a handsome but ancient structure which long before the Civil War had housed the Post Office Department and later the General Land Office. That building was turned over to General Crowder.

It was decided that the armed forces would come directly under the national government and would compose a national army. This was a complete reversal of American policy; even during the Civil War troops had been recruited primarily by the states under the effective control of the governors. There were, of course, the units of the National Guard in each of the states as well as in the District of Columbia, which could be called into the national service by the President but which were administered by the states. To make this radical change more acceptable, it was decided that the administration of the Selective Service Act, with its direct impact on the persons to be drafted, would be intrusted to the governors of the states acting under the uniform provisions of federal law. Since there was no governor in the District of Columbia, the president of the Board of Commissioners was given the title of governor for the purposes of the enforcement of the Selective Service law and was authorized to designate an adjutant general under whose immediate direction the same system provided for all the states would be effective in the District of Columbia.

Since, if the act were to be passed as written, as eventually it was, I would be a governor, and since I was in Washington and quite handy, General Crowder asked me to come over to see him. He asked me if I would help draft the detailed regulations and the necessary forms on the assumption that the bill as submitted would be enacted into law. Of course I consented.

General Crowder took me into a room adjoining his and introduced me to Captain Hugh S. Johnson. Captain Johnson was a West Pointer who had recently completed a course in a law school and had been admitted to the bar. That was my introduction to the man who later was General Johnson and, still later, head of the National Recovery Administration, the man who was destined to be known to all the world as "Old Iron Pants."

When General Crowder had left, Captain Johnson asked, "Do you know the public printer?"

I did. He was Cornelius Ford.

"Do you know anybody high up in the Post Office Department who has control of the mails?"

I did. His name was Otto Praeger, second assistant postmaster general.

"Do you think these men are patriots?"

I said I thought they were.

"Do you think they would risk going to the penitentiary by anticipating appropriations not yet made in the interest of winning the war?"

I was quite sure of it.

"Do you know a good lawyer here in Washington with sense enough to keep his mouth shut?"

I recommended James Easby-Smith.

"Will this lawyer friend of yours work nights?"

I said I was quite sure he would.

"Let's go," said Captain Johnson.

We went first to the Government Printing Office and found Mr. Ford. "We don't know how long it will take to get the Selective Service Act through Congress, but we have to be ready," Captain Johnson told him. "This will mean printing an enormous number of blanks and forms for which, of course, no appropriation is authorized. However, if we wait until the act passes and then wait for an appropriation, the recruiting of the army may be delayed for months. Are you willing to take a chance? You know, if the law doesn't pass and you do spend all this money, you may go to the penitentiary." Mr. Ford agreed to take the risk.

At the Post Office Department I explained the situation to my old newspaper friend, Otto Praeger.

"If we get these blanks printed, will you undertake to get them through the mails and into the hands of the sheriffs of all the counties in the United States?" asked Captain Johnson. "In my opinion it would be fatal to wait until the act passes and then still further to wait for an appropriation." He warned Mr. Praeger that he too would be running a chance of being sent to prison. Mr. Praeger accepted the chance.

From there we went to Mr. Easby-Smith's office, to which I had telephoned for an appointment. Captain Johnson told him the story of our arrangements thus far. "Now we have got to design the forms and blanks," he continued. "Where do you live?"

Mr. Easby-Smith said that he lived on the 1700 block of Q Street and that he was willing to work through the night. By this time it was after five o'clock in the afternoon. We arranged that the three of us would meet at Mr. Easby-Smith's house at seven.

I went home to dinner and told my wife that I would have to work practically all night. Easby-Smith may have got some dinner. I doubt very much if Captain Johnson did. At any rate we met at seven, went into the dining room, cleared the table for work, and sat down with yellow pads and sheets of white paper. Around midnight we raided the icebox. At eight o'clock the next morning when we stopped, the blank forms, the draft cards, and all the paraphernalia for the paper work of the Selective Service System were drafted. The next two or three days the three of us spent practically all our waking hours perfecting the forms, checking them to see that there were no contradictions, eliminating ambiguities, and making them as simple, as direct, and as foolproof as we had the wit or command of language to do.

General Crowder was busily engaged in recruiting the staff which he was so brilliantly to administer. Almost the first thing that happened was that Captain Johnson became Major Johnson.

All our material went to Cornelius Ford, the public printer, and the Government Printing Office, then, as ever, accustomed to secrecy, was set to work.

At last, on May 18, 1917, the Selective Service Act was signed by the President. The President summoned Secretary Baker, Secretary Daniels, and General Crowder to come to the White House. General Crowder took Hugh Johnson with him.

"How soon do you think you can get the machinery for the enforcement of the act under way?" asked the President.

The secretary of war referred the question to the judge advocate general who probably knew a great deal more about it than he was willing to admit. General Crowder referred the question to Major Johnson.

"Mr. President," the major answered, "the blanks and forms have been prepared, they have been printed, and they are now in the hands of the sheriffs of every county in the United States except those in Hawaii and Alaska. The machinery is ready."

There followed a pretense, at any rate, of astonishment on the part of General Crowder, genuine surprise on the part of the Secretary of War and of the Navy, and a greatly pleased and almost awed response from the President. Then and there it was decided to set the registration day uniformly throughout the United States for June 5—just a little over two weeks from the time the bill had been signed by the President. That gave but scant time to me, acting in the capacity of governor, to choose an adjutant general and get ready the machinery for the enforcement of the Selective Service law in the District.

I chose Daniel J. Donovan, then secretary of the Board of Commissioners, a position to which Newman, Kutz, and I had promoted him from his old place as deputy auditor, which he had held for many years. Donovan was an energetic and hard-working man who in his many years of service in the auditor's office had come to know intimately every department and agency of the District government and its relationships with the Congress, the several executive departments, and the many organizations of citizens in the city. I put him into uniform, pinned oak leaves on his shoulders, and made him Major Donovan.

The work began under the general superintendence of Major Donovan with material assistance from Major Kutz and the engineering department, the school board, the police department, and many persons from various divisions of the city government who were pressed into service.

The first step was to divide the territory of the District of Columbia into precincts. Since its inhabitants were voteless and there were no recognized boundaries except for the eleven police precincts, which were too large, this meant cutting up the territory of the city into new units. All the other cities and counties of the country had either voting precincts or school districts that could be adopted as registration precincts, but in Washington we had to begin at the beginning.

This done, we covered the District with huge posters (which of course were reproduced by the daily newspapers) carrying a map of the new precincts and detailed descriptions of their boundaries. The poster also contained a reproduction of the registration card with explicit instructions on how its twelve questions were to be answered.

Nothing like this had ever happened before in the history of the United States. There was some anxiety, which turned out to be wholly unnecessary, that in some parts of the country there would be resistance in the form of mass refusal to register or the like. Actually the machinery operated with amazing efficiency in every part of the country, including the national capital.

By coincidence—it certainly was not by contrivance—the United Confederate Veterans had arranged to hold their annual reunion in Washington in June, 1917. It was the first time the Confederate Veterans ever had invaded the capital of the United States. And it also was the first time that the Confederate Veterans looked forward to being greeted by the President of the United States. Mr. Wilson had agreed to deliver a welcoming address on June 5, long before that day had been selected as registration day and, indeed, long before the United States had entered the war.

It so happened that this particular assembly of ex-rebel soldiers had a personal interest for me. Among those coming to Washington for the reunion were two men from my father's old company, the former captains Buchanan and Black, both of whom had known both my parents. They were physicians. I looked forward with the keenest pleasure to seeing them, as did my father-in-law, Representative Sims, who knew them both quite well. They were residents of his congressional district.

The President was to make his address of welcome to the former Confederates at the opening session of the reunion at eleven o'clock in the morning. The old-timers wouldn't go into the hall. They waited outside to see the President arrive. That made it necessary for the President to wait for some fifteen minutes before walking out on the stage, and, of course, I was with him.

As we waited, I told the President that the registration was proceeding in an orderly fashion and also that I had asked John Joy Edson, whom I had selected to be chairman of the District Board of Appeals, whether he would not put on his Grand Army of the Republic uniform and ride with me and my freshly uniformed adjutant general to as many of the registration places as we could reach in an afternoon's drive. I asked Mr. Wilson if he would approve my asking my father's two comrades-in-arms, Dr. Buchanan and Dr. Black, to go with us in their gray Confederate uniforms.

The President thought it was an excellent idea and said in substance, "I'll tell you, Brownlow, what to do. When you get through bring them to the White House. They won't know Washington and they won't know where you are going. Just bring them up and I'll be ready to greet them in the Blue Room."

I said, "Very well, Mr. President, but Mr. Edson and Major Donovan will know very well where we are bound."

"Let them in on the secret then, but don't let the two old men know."

We toured the city. The presence of the Grand Army uniform and the two Confederate uniforms roused a great deal of interest and not a little applause among the crowds at every registration place.

But the great climax to me was when it was over, when the chauffeur swept the car into the driveway at the White House, and the two old men realized where they were going.

The President was ready. Tea was offered. I don't remember that any was drunk. I doubt it. But I do remember Mr. Wilson's gracious reception, and I do remember that Mr. Edson in blue, Dr. Buchanan and Dr. Black in gray, all three dissolved in tears.

It was a touching and dramatic symbolization of a reunion of the sections of the country.

The machinery of the Selective Service began to grind. The drafted men from the District of Columbia were assembled at the Union Station by each local board when it met its quota, and all were shipped to Camp Meade in Maryland for their training. With only a few exceptions, I was present every night and, in my capacity as governor, inducted these men into the Army of the United States.

We had excellent and most efficient administration by the unpaid volunteer members of the local boards and by the volunteer medical examiners; very few of the men chosen in the District and sent to Camp Meade were rejected for physical reasons or, for that matter, for any other reason. The job was well done, thanks to the competent supervision and utter devotion of my adjutant general, Major Donovan.

However, once in a while, there was a slip-up. One night when I went to the induction ceremony and walked down the ranks of the seventy-five or eighty men being inducted, I could not help noticing a colored man who presumably had been sent in by one of the local boards. He attracted my notice because he had lost the thumb and forefinger on his right hand. I stopped and asked him, "What local board do you come from?"

He told me. I turned to the representative of that particular board. He denied that he had sent the maimed man in. But there had been some sort of a slip and the man had received a red card, which was the signal for him to report for induction.

I said, "Stand aside."

"No, sir," he said, "I got a red card and I'm going. If I don't go, I'll be sent to the penitentiary. You can't keep me out. I'm going. I've got a red card."

"But," I protested, "they don't want a man in the Army with no right forefinger and thumb. You couldn't shoot a gun. There is no need of your going over to Camp Meade. Those doctors over there will send you right back, which will not only cause you a lot of trouble and a lot of expense but will force us to go through all the work of getting you cleared and out of the Army."

He said, "No, Mister, you are wrong. I am going tonight and the doctors over at Camp Meade are not going to send me back."

"Why in the world do you think that, when you have no thumb or forefinger on your right hand?"

"I don't think it, Mister. I just know. When I get over there and tell them officers that for fourteen years I've been the head meat cook at the Maryland Club of Baltimore, they are not going to send me back."

He went. He did not come back.

With Major Donovan's help I went on to organize the District's territory into eleven sections, each to be presided over, as prescribed by law, by a draft board of three persons. These people, of course, were to serve without compensation, as were the five people on the District-wide Board of Appeals. We recruited also volunteers for clerical work, volunteers for motor transport, and, over and above all, a volunteer corps of medical examiners. There was no difficulty in getting the volunteer services.

It was necessary in a city that had no election machinery and no recognized permanent subdivisions to take some care to ascertain that the members we appointed to the local boards actually were residents of the particular districts they were to serve. While it took some time, we succeeded in recruiting not only five leading citizens for membership on the Board of Appeals, headed by John Joy Edson, but also thirty-three able and dedicated men to serve on the local boards.

It was, on the whole, a rewarding experience, but it added a tremendous burden to the already heavy load that I was carrying and compelled me to learn how to delegate more and more detailed work to my subordinates. It taught me how to maintain over-all supervision without going into too much detail and helped me learn the lesson of communication and co-ordination with departments and agencies of the government, District and federal, at the horizontal level.

CHAPTER VI

PROBLEMS MULTIPLY

As the war went on and the town grew more and more crowded, the demands for services of all sorts increased. Inflation soared, and things became more and more difficult for the municipal government. One lesson, which was a tough one but nevertheless contributed a good deal to my understanding of the way in which administrative problems sometimes are confused by political sentiments, might appropriately be called "the case of the garbage can." In the District at that time there were three systems of refuse disposal. The District government collected separately trash, garbage, and ashes from individual houses. Apartment houses having more than twelve habitations, and hotels, were required to attend to their own collection and disposal. The ashes and cinders were dumped. The trash was taken to a municipally owned and operated recovery plant, where the usable paper, tin cans, rags, etc., were recovered and the rest burned. The garbage was sent to a reduction plant some twenty-odd miles down the Potomac River in Virginia, where it was treated to recover the grease and other valuable components in a privately owned plant operated by a private contractor.

Collections became more and more difficult as the labor scarcity made it hard to hire drivers and collectors under the wage scale fixed by Congress eighteen months in advance; and the commissioners, at the beginning at any rate, were allowed no flexibility whatever. At the same time, the garbage contractor, a very able businessman and a highly competent engineer, was getting into more and more difficulty. He was an honorable man who continued to carry on his work under the contract even at a great and growing daily loss.

The commissioners employed a consulting engineer, Irwin S. Osborn of Columbus, Ohio, to make a survey of the refuse collection and disposal system of the District. It was from this survey that I first got the notion of using the garbage can as an index of the sociological characteristics of different sections of an urban community. We discovered that, in the parts of the city inhabited by the wealthy and well-to-do, the garbage was quite valuable. More food was thrown away and therefore the grease content was greater, making the reduction method worthwhile. The trash in the higher-income communities, however, was of very poor grade. At the trash recovery station, rags were the most valuable commodity, tin cans were next, and paper was of least account. The well-to-do homes showed up heavy on paper, low on tin, and almost nil on rags. The explanation was, of course, that the well-to-do people didn't wear out their clothes but usually gave them to servants or passed them on in some other way. It followed that in the poorer sections of the city the garbage was hardly worth collecting because food was not thrown away and there was little or no grease, but the trash was rich in rags and tin.

In other cities, I very frequently looked into matters not only of income but of nutrition, gaining sociological insights into the quality of neighborhoods simply by going around and lifting the lids of the garbage cans. If there were many tin cans and some rags, it was quite evident that here was a community with income trouble and probably with a high disability from illnesses caused by malnutrition.

Things went along from bad to worse until at last Mr. Harrison Stidham, the contractor, having exhausted his resources because of the losses on the garbage reduction plant, threw up the contract. It was up to the District to take care of its own garbage.

On the basis of the survey, Mr. James W. Paxton, who had the title of superintendent of street cleaning but who actually was the head of the entire refuse collection and disposal agency, prepared an estimate for an emergency deficiency appropriation which would enable the District to take over the reduction plant and carry on. I took the estimate to the House Committee on Appropriations' special subcommittee that was considering deficiency estimates. The chairman of both the committee and the subcommittee was my old friend Swagar Sherley, of Louisville, Kentucky. The two other Democratic members were John J. Fitzgerald of Brooklyn, who later was to become chairman of the whole committee, and Thomas U. Sisson of Mississippi. The two Republicans were Joseph G. Cannon, "Uncle Joe," the former speaker of the House, and William S. Vare, a representative from Philadelphia, who was well known as the Republican boss of that city and who had made a fortune reckoned in the millions of dollars as the garbage and trash contractor for Philadelphia.

As soon as I had presented the estimate, Uncle Joe pulled his feet off the table and slammed down his estimate book. "How far do you think you are going to try to lead us into this business of socialism?" he barked.

"There is not one bit of use coming up here and asking us in time of war to permit you to start off the District government on a lot of socialistic experimentation," added Mr. Sherley, throwing his pencil down on the table.

Mr. Sisson and Mr. Fitzgerald were absent.

"We will not consider this item under any circumstances," announced the chairman. "It is now twelve o'clock and we will take off thirty minutes for lunch. When we come back you can continue with the rest of your estimates. This one is dead."

I had not expected an easy time but neither had I expected an absolute, ultimate turn-down before I had had a chance to explain my position. As I started to walk out of the room, Mr. Vare said *sotto voce,* "Go to lunch with me."

I took with me my package of papers, and, at the table in the House restaurant, Mr. Vare asked to see the estimate.

I handed it over to him and with it the survey of the District and the memorandum supporting the estimate prepared by our own superintendent of street cleaning. He glanced through them.

"I'd like to read these carefully," he said. "So you go back to the hearing and say nothing more about this until I get there. It will take me twenty or thirty minutes. And when I come, I will get you your appropriation."

I was amazed but grateful. I went back into the hearing room. Nothing was said about that particular matter, and at the end of a half-hour in came Mr. Vare. At the first pause he addressed Mr. Sherley.

"Mr. Chairman, as some of you know, I know something about this business of garbage and trash. I have been in it for years. I have studied these papers carefully. The survey is excellent. The recommendations are sound. The appropriation is needed, and, when we go into executive

[67]

session, I shall do everything I can to convince you that this is not a socialistic scheme at all but something which has come up as a result of wartime conditions. It absolutely must be done."

Sherley seemed startled and Uncle Joe bewildered, but nothing more was said. After a few more minutes, I had completed my work and got up to leave. On the way out Mr. Vare said, "I will telephone you as soon as I get the news."

Two or three hours later that afternoon, Mr. Vare showed up in my office. "I didn't use the telephone," he said, "because I have something to say to you. You've got your appropriation all right, but I just wanted to tell you that the reason I came down here instead of telephoning you is that I have just been downstairs and have hired your director of refuse disposal away from you. You pay him $3,800 a year. I am giving him $10,000 a year. Get yourself a new superintendent.

"And furthermore if you ever tell anybody in Philadelphia that it was I who got this appropriation for you for this socialistic garbage-reduction scheme, I will not only call you a liar but I will prove it."

And so ended happily my one adventure with Big Bill Vare, the Republican boss of Philadelphia, who saved the day for me, although he did deprive the District of the services of an excellent civil servant.

Even earlier in the war these same pressures at one time had practically put the sewage system of the District out of business. The District had a large station that pumped sewage from the city's system under the Anacostia River to a treatment works and an outfall at Blue Plains at the southernmost tip of the District. The men who operated the pumping station were paid salaries ranging from $900 down to $540 a year. The impact of the higher costs of food and the high rate of employment set up a very difficult problem for us. The Congress had appropriated $100,000,000 to be spent at the discretion of the President of the United States without regard to specific appropriations. It was absolutely vital that we keep the sewage system going; so I went to President Wilson and asked him for a sufficient amount of money from his free fund—I think I asked only for $8,000 at that particular time. It was not difficult to justify my request, and the President granted it.

What astonished me was that he took out of his desk a book and a package of forms, made the necessary requisitions in his own handwriting, and entered the transaction with his own pen in his own account book. I suppose I lifted my eyebrows. At any rate, Mr. Wilson looked up at me with a smile and said, "I am doing this myself because, as soon as the war is over, there will be investigating committees in the Congress who will ask all sorts of questions about how I spent this hundred million dollars. They will have my answer in my own handwriting."

Whether or not in the stress of events he continued that particular system of holographic bookkeeping I do not know. At any rate he began that way.

In the summer of 1917, Dr. William C. Woodward, who had been health officer of the District of Columbia for more than a score of years, resigned to become health commissioner of the city of Boston. The health officer's salary in the District was only $4,000 a year, and Dr. Woodward was attracted to Boston not only by a $10,000 salary but also by what he considered to be a great opportunity. The mayor of Boston who persuaded Dr. Woodward to leave the District was Andrew J. Peters, who had served for several terms in the Congress and was well acquainted with the District government and with Dr. Woodward.

Early in September I had a telegram from Dr. Woodward saying that several cases of what then was known as the Spanish flu had occurred in Boston; that neither he nor anybody else in Boston knew what to do about it; that he was afraid it would be particularly severe if it reached Washington on account of the terrific overcrowding in the capital and he thought the commissioners ought at once to make the new disease reportable. This was done at the next meeting.

On the afternoon of the morning the commission issued its order to the physicians of the District to report any case of the disease, whether actually diagnosed or merely suspected, I was called to the Metropolitan Hotel by the manager, who said that my cousin, William B. Vaught of Greensboro, North Carolina, had arrived in the city about midnight the night before and was extremely ill. He had not seen a physician. I asked Dr. Fowler, the health officer whom I had appointed to succeed Dr. Woodward, to go with me to the hotel. We found Mr. Vaught very seriously ill, and Dr. Fowler had no doubt that this was a case of the flu. He himself as a physician reported to himself as health officer the first case of the so-called Spanish flu in the District.

In the next two or three days the reports mounted rapidly. Within less than ten days the reporting system utterly broke down. Every physician had too many cases, and there were not enough physicians in the city to begin to care for the thousands who were stricken. My colleagues, Mr. Gardiner and General Knight, were ill. I was forced to carry on the District government with the able assistance of Captain J. J. Loving, an assistant engineer commissioner.

Dr. Fowler became my chief aide. Every agency and division of the District government was impressed into the work. The attendance at schools dropped so much that the school boards were persuaded to close the schools for the time being. We closed the theaters, the moving-picture houses, and even the churches, and for a few days all mercantile houses except grocery and drugstores. We established four or five nursing centers in schoolhouses in different sections of the town, manned by volunteers and served by volunteer motor corps drivers, all of which were operated in co-operation with the Red Cross, the Visiting Nurses' Association, and the Medical Society of the District of Columbia. So many of the physicians were ill that soon our volunteer nursing service and medical service could not cope with the demand.

Seven or eight months earlier the commissioners had made a survey of the traffic situation and had drawn up a plan for staggering the opening and closing hours of government offices. These recommendations I had sent to the President. They had been discussed in the Cabinet and turned over to the secretary of the treasury, William G. McAdoo. Mr. McAdoo, after taking counsel with some of his cabinet colleagues, had decided to do nothing about it. Now, in the crisis of the epidemic, with more than half the operators of streetcars stricken, the situation became almost chaotic. I took a copy of the recommendations to Mr. McAdoo. With a characteristic shower of expletives he demanded to know why this hadn't been done long before. I am afraid even in that crisis I took a little grim pleasure in telling him the recommendations had been on his desk for at least six or seven months. Now, however, they were put into effect at once. But despite all we could do, things got worse.

At last it seemed that we had come to the end of our resources. There was a dreadful Saturday. Through the White House I succeeded in enlisting the co-operation of all departments and agencies of the government, and an arrangement was made for a high-level meeting of the office of the War Industries Board on Sunday morning to be presided over by Judge Edwin B. Parker, who was the principal deputy of Bernard Baruch, chairman of the War Industries Board.

On Saturday my task was to mobilize all the resources of the city. I got the figures on the number of dead in coffins but unburied in cemeteries because of the lack of grave-diggers. I obtained the approximate figures on the number of dead lying in houses for which there were no coffins available. I assembled from the cemeteries the immediate requirements for the number of grave-diggers and got all the information I could on available medical and nursing personnel. Fortunately, every person who had come to Washington to do war work had been required to list emergency skills, and thus we were able to assemble by midnight that night a list of everybody in the government who had had nursing experience as well as those who had formerly practiced medicine.

Every hospital bed in town was filled. One of the largest, George Washington University Hospital, had every bed filled and not a single nurse on duty.

I canvassed all the department stores, furniture stores, and the like and asked them to send representatives to the Sunday morning meeting with information as to available beds, bedding, and other equipment necessary for emergency hospital use. All the undertakers were told to be present. We also invited representatives of the contractors' association, the building-trades unions, and merchants', manufacturers', and citizens' organizations.

On Sunday morning at nine o'clock we met in Judge Parker's office. There were perhaps 100 or 125 persons there. I reported my dire statistics.

Judge Parker and his assistants had been making a survey of the federal resources. One division of the Army had just moved out of a large temporary building at Eighteenth Street and Virginia Avenue. Judge Parker told the assistant secretary of war that we would take it over. The representatives of the contractors and the unions were told to get the building ready by erecting ramps so that the two upper floors could be utilized for hospital purposes without necessitating the use of the interior stairways. There were, of course, no elevators. The merchants were told to assemble seven hundred units of bedding. The surgeon general of the Army was placed in charge of setting up the hospital. The task of assembling the necessary number of nurses and physicians was delegated as a joint effort to the district health officer, the United States Public Health Service, and the Army and Navy medical officers.

For some unexplained reason the Marine Corps base at Quantico had suffered very little from the epidemic, and a sufficient number of marines were ordered to Washington by Secretary Daniels and assigned to the cemeteries to dig graves.

Then Judge Parker brought into play the knowledge and the absolute power of the War Industry Board. It was discovered that there were two carloads of coffins in the Potomac railroad yards consigned to Pittsburgh. These were commandeered and the coffins sent to the city hospital. There already had been many complaints of profiteering in the sale of coffins. It was decided to consign all coffins to the health officer of the District, no matter to whom they were being shipped, and he was put in charge of their sale at a fixed price.

Also in the Potomac railroad yards we found a complete hotel-kitchen outfit consigned to some point in Georgia and a complete laundry plant destined for some point in Texas. The kitchen and the laundry machinery were commandeered and ordered delivered at once to the new emergency hospital.

And thus, by the co-operation of local and federal administrative officers acting for the moment with absolute power, a completely equipped seven-hundred-bed hospital was opened at eight o'clock that Sunday night, staffed by at least a skeleton corps of physicians and nurses.

All night long the ambulances ran. All night long the volunteer motor corps operated. The drivers dropped out from time to time but new drivers were found and at two o'clock on Monday morning every one of the seven hundred beds in that new hospital was occupied.

All day long on Monday the coffins were distributed, the graves were dug, and the victims were buried.

My wife had been in bed two or three days. We had got a physician, but while he was asking about her symptoms he collapsed. It was not until Wednesday that I came down. My telephone at home was ringing constantly. Our faithful maid escaped the disease and was able to answer the telephone throughout the day and far into the night. The night I collapsed I had just been to the telephone. A girl had called to say that she and three other girls had a room together, that two of the girls were dead, another was dying, and she was the only one not stricken; would I please get some help there. I managed to get the police department, and it found someone to go to that house. When the policeman got there, there were four dead girls in the room.

Fortunately for me, my case was not very severe, and I was in the house only two or three days. I am sure that both my wife and I owed our survival to the ministrations of one of the policewomen who had formerly been a trained nurse. She not only waited on us but also took charge of handling that constantly ringing telephone and undertook to discharge a large part of my administrative work for me.

The worst was over. The deaths decreased. The cases decreased. While we had to continue for several weeks to operate the complicated emergency machinery we had set up, the end finally came. The plague lasted from September 21 to November 4.

No one will ever know the number of cases in the District. No one will ever know the number who died, but approximate figures as we collected them a few weeks later showed the number of cases actually reported as 35,000 and the deaths as 3,500, a fatality of 10 per cent. But there were thousands of cases unreported and hundreds of certificates issued showing deaths attributed to other causes resulting from complications following the influenza.

CHAPTER VII

WOMAN SUFFRAGE

From 1912 when the National American Woman's Suffrage Association established its headquarters in Washington until the ratification of the Nineteenth Amendment in 1920 there was hardly a day when the issue of Votes for Women was not in the papers and hardly a day when the problem was not brought to my attention.

From my earliest childhood I had been an ardent advocate of votes for women. I had written editorials about it in the *Dallas County Record* as early as 1894. My mother, whose avid interest in politics was a part of her daily life, had thoroughly indoctrinated me. Susan B. Anthony, Elizabeth Cady Stanton, and Lucretia Mott were among the heroines in my Valhalla many years before I myself was old enough to vote.

In 1912 the National American Woman's Suffrage Association, headed by Mrs. Carrie Chapman Catt, who had succeeded Dr. Anna Howard Shaw, leased a house on Rhode Island Avenue as a base from which to conduct its campaign. Very shortly thereafter Miss Alice Paul and a group of younger women established within the national association the Congressional Union, which was to devote itself to the Congress while the national association carried on its campaign for the suffrage in the several states. The Congressional Union set up headquarters in a building at Fifteenth and F streets and began to canvass the town for members, men as well as women. Raymond W. Pullman and I were among the first to call on Miss Paul at the new headquarters to inscribe our names and pay our dues as members of the Congressional Union. It was later, after I became District commissioner and appointed Mr. Pullman chief of police, that our difficulties with Miss Paul began.

On March 3, 1913, the general public discovered that Miss Paul and

her followers were not loath to use militant tactics. A group of followers got embroiled in a bad traffic situation on Pennsylvania Avenue
when they attempted to anticipate the next day's inaugural celebration
with a demonstration. The police handled the situation very badly.
None of the women marchers was seriously injured, but the clash
among the marchers, large crowds of sightseers, and the police snarled
up traffic and created a sensation.

Miss Paul was an American of a Quaker family. She had done her
graduate university work in Germany, and she had spent a good deal
of time in England, where she had participated with Mrs. Emeline
Pankhurst in the activities of the militant English suffragettes.

In England she had absorbed a political theory that was sound enough
in British practice but hardly fitted into the American constitutional
system. She held that the party in power could and should be held
responsible for any action within the framework of the federal government, including the process of amending the Constitution. This theory
did not apply in the United States because a two-thirds majority of
both houses of the Congress is required to submit a proposed constitutional amendment to the states for ratification. Since the creation of
political parties in the United States, no party had ever at any time had
control of two-thirds of both houses. But this fact had no effect whatever on Miss Paul. She insisted from the moment of Mr. Wilson's
inauguration that, as the leader of the majority party, he should be held
responsible for the submission of the suffrage amendment.

Mrs. Catt and the officials of the national association did not agree,
and the difference of opinion led to the separation of the Congressional
Union from the national association. Miss Paul and her followers
established the Woman's party.

President Wilson at the beginning of his administration was, I believe, quite firmly opposed to the woman-suffrage amendment. He
based his opposition on his theory that changes in the suffrage should
be made by the states and that woman's suffrage should be achieved
gradually by state action. Later, however, Mr. Wilson changed his
mind and during the greater part of his presidency heartily favored
the proposed amendment.

The Woman's party moved its headquarters into a house on Madison
Place facing Lafayette Square, the old Cameron mansion which had

been occupied by Senator Mark Hanna, and from that advantageous location began a very active and militant campaign.

My personal relations with the national association became more intimate. Mrs. Brownlow became the president of the local woman-suffrage organization which worked in close co-operation with the national association at its Rhode Island Avenue headquarters. I was in frequent consultation with Mrs. Catt, with Dr. Anna Howard Shaw, with Mrs. Maude Wood Park, who was the principal lobbyist for the association on the Hill, and with Mrs. Helen Gardener, who was the diplomatic representative of the association at the White House and was among the principal officers of the executive branch.

It wasn't long after Major Pullman and I had taken over the responsibility for the police that the Woman's party began to picket the White House, marching up and down in all kinds of weather carrying their banners inscribed with "Votes for Women!" This militancy gradually increased its tempo and led me into the only serious disagreement with President Wilson that I had during my six years as District commissioner. This disagreement was sharp, face-to-face, and fully fought out.

The suffragettes had been picketing the White House for some nine months in the hope of arrest and martyrdom—a hope they frankly expressed to the police authorities. Mr. Wilson did not want them arrested, and I did not want to arrest them. But, after we entered the war, conditions because such that Major Pullman felt obligated to arrest them to protect them from the mobs who resented the insulting inscriptions on their banners; and this feeling on Major Pullman's part was supported by an ultimatum from the suffragettes themselves threatening the use of firearms if we *did not* arrest them.

During the months the suffragettes were picketing the White House there were many discussions, and on the whole everybody agreed that the President's policy of ignoring the pickets (except to send them hot tea and warm bricks for their feet on cold days) was the best policy. The whole matter of woman suffrage was receiving intensified study; but the fact that the President worked so cordially and intimately with the leaders of the National American Woman Suffrage Association, Dr. Shaw, Mrs. Catt, Mrs. Park, and Mrs. Gardener, infuriated the leaders of the Woman's party—Miss Paul and others. Miss Paul, in her contacts with Mrs. Pankhurst, had developed an appetite for jails and hunger strikes, and she had from her German schooling a bias unfavorable to our entrance into the war. She herself, I think, referred this bias to the pacificism inherited from her Quaker ancestors, but to the disinterested observer the pacifism of Alice Paul was of infinitesimal dimensions.

The foreign war missions from Britain, France, and Russia were arriving, and the suffragettes informed the visitors by their banners that Mr. Wilson was a worse tyrant than the Kaiser and told the Russians of the Kerensky regime that Mr. Wilson was a more autocratic tsar than any Romanoff. The clerks who poured out of the government office buildings tore down the banners. The women defended them. The result was a riot every afternoon; and that riot, so we were told by the Allies, was interpreted in the newspapers of the Central Powers as a pro-German uprising.

I talked with several of the members of the Cabinet about the matter. I did not talk with Mr. McAdoo because of his family relation to the President. I did not talk with Mr. Tumulty because I intended to take the full responsibility for what I was about to do, one way or another. I did not talk to the President because I did not wish to involve him in the consequences and because I had been advised by him not to give the militant suffragettes any additional publicity. I found that every man high in the government with whom I talked except Secretary of War Newton D. Baker thought the women ought to be arrested, or in some way taken off the street in front of the White House—that the daily riots ought to be stopped. Without my knowing it, on the day when the matter became acute because of the riot in which the "Kaiser Wilson" banner was torn down, Mr. McAdoo, Mr. Tumulty, and Admiral Grayson, at breakfast at the Grayson home, demanded of Major Pullman that the police "do something."

But arrest meant publicity, a fine and more publicity, refusal to pay the fine and more publicity, jail in lieu of a fine and more publicity, a hunger strike and more publicity—martyrdom. Many of the women in the movement were sincerely convinced that by such tactics women would get the suffrage sooner. Some of the leaders, I am quite sure, thought that by such tactics they could postpone suffrage until there was a Republican Congress.

The arrests were made (the women knew they were to be made and sent some specially prominent women into the picket line that day); the fines were imposed; payment was refused; and the women were sent to jail to be removed, according to the usual routine, to the work-house at Occoquan, the model institution without barricaded walls, palisades, cells, locks, or bars.

Among the prisoners were Mrs. J. A. H. Hopkins of New Jersey, a friend of Mr. Wilson, and Miss Doris Stevens, then a friend of Dudley Field Malone, collector of the Port of New York and a friend of Mr. Wilson.

After the arrests had been made on July 15, 1917, but before the trial of July 17 at which the women were fined, Mr. Malone came to me at my home with a protest loud and long and told me that he had seen the President; but apparently the President had not expressed his opinion of the arrests to Mr. Malone.

The women were taken to Occoquan, and the President almost instantly pardoned them. Then he sent for me. I went to the White House about three o'clock on the afternoon of July 19.

Mr. Wilson was highly indignant. He told me that we had made a fearful blunder, that we never ought to have indulged these women in their desire for arrest and martyrdom, and that he had pardoned them and wanted that to end it. I was obliged to tell him that the women had refused to accept his pardon. He was more indignant than ever when he found that they were still in prison despite his pardon, and his temper was not improved when I told him that the attorney general, Thomas Watt Gregory, had ruled that a pardon wasn't an effective pardon until it was accepted. Later, Mr. Malone persuaded the women to accept the pardon.

Mr. Wilson let me know in very plain terms that he disapproved of the arrests. I told him that I had acted with great reluctance, that I agreed entirely with him about the utter undesirability of giving these women their accolade of martyrdom, that I furthermore believed their antics were delaying the grant of suffrage, and so on. I also told him that I was responsible for peace and order on the streets of the capital, that the nation was at war, that these riots were being misconstrued in Europe, and that, while my resignation was his for the asking, I could not continue to hold my position and fail to accept full responsibility for policing the city.

At the end he asked me not to make any further arrests until after notifying him, making it plain that he would never consent and that he wished to be advised if I, knowing his dissent, nevertheless intended to take further action.

I do not recall whether it was the very next day or two or three days later that a particularly belligerent group of pickets in front of the White House began to belabor members of the crowds with the staffs of their banners. That precipitated another near-riot. I called the President on the telephone. He was not in his office. But after a few minutes delay I got through to him and said, in substance:

"Mr. President, I have decided on my own responsibility that I must order the arrest of the pickets, since their riotous behavior has become worse instead of better. I shall act on my own responsibility."

There were a few seconds of silence and then the President said, with more sorrow than anger in his voice, "The blood be on your head!"

Thereafter we pursued a policy of attempting to keep the peace, not arresting the pickets until they, or at least some of them, had taken positive action. Once in Occoquan they began to imitate what the British suffragettes had found effective as a publicity scheme, the hunger strike.

In the beginning we did some forced feeding, but later the District government began also to imitate the British, and, as soon as the strike had persisted for a certain length of time, we let the prisoners go, sometimes practically having to use force to eject them. It was our edition of the cat-and-mouse procedure that had been set up in England by the home secretary in charge of police, Mr. Winston Churchill.

The difficulty of handling the recalcitrant prisoners at Occoquan finally compelled us to remove them to the jail in the District of Columbia. Here they discovered a new high in nuisance value. They took turns throughout the day and night screaming and yowling. Pretty soon we had another difficulty on our hands. The people held in jail for trial and the convicted felons awaiting sentence and transfer to the Atlanta penitentiary, an assorted crew of holdup men, burglars, and murderers, went on strike.

"We want sleep," they pleaded. "We want sleep."

Now it so happened that before the Congress had approved the proposal for the open-country workhouse at Occoquan, it had appropriated money for a new workhouse in Washington, which had been built on a plot of ground near the District jail. It was a tall brick building with an interior cell-block of typical jail construction arranged so that all the prisoners could be locked in their cells by a mechanism operated by one man. The windows were very high, some fourteen or fifteen feet from the floor, and the cell-block was surrounded by a wide corridor. It had never been used as a prison. At this time it was full of models, gadgets, and contraptions stored by the Patent Office.

Also, the building was so far away from any other building that no noise of which the human voice is capable could be heard in any other building, save perhaps the little cottage nearby in which from time to time we entertained Mr. John Early, our peripatetic leper.

I went to Mr. Franklin K. Lane, the secretary of the interior, communicated to him my purpose, and got his consent to move the models into another warehouse. When they were all moved out, the interior of the discarded but never used workhouse was freshly painted; the empty cells were furnished with new beds and brand new bedding, mattresses, pillows, sheets, blankets, and so on; and we prepared to receive there the next bunch of suffragettes to be arrested.

And this is where I finally resorted to what may have been regarded as unconstitutional means, as in some minds it might have been considered a cruel and unusual punishment. I installed in one of the corridors two gas stoves. I employed six women cooks so that each stove could be manned in eight-hour shifts around the clock.

Then the prisoners came. As I recall now, there were some twenty or thirty of them in the first group that we received in our newly furnished, newly painted establishment. The locking mechanism was so fixed that it was impossible to close a cell door, much less to lock it. The inmates could choose any cell they liked and could roam around the corridor as long as they liked, and if they so desired they could walk out the front door into the free air. Then came the cruel and unusual part of my strategy. Of course the women at once went on a hunger strike and refused to eat. But I kept those cooks busy day and night frying ham.

I was convinced that the fragrance of frying ham was the greatest stimulus to appetite known to man. It was terribly hard on the women. And of course there was no waste because there were several hundred prisoners in the adjoining jail, and we could use all the ham the cooks could fry. This went on for a while until at long last one morning about three o'clock some of the prisoners said they wanted to see the jailer, Mr. Peak. He was awakened and came over to the workhouse. They said they wanted to leave and would like him to get a conveyance. He said he would be very delighted to furnish them transportation. They said they wanted to go to their headquarters building. They also said they couldn't possibly get home, and there was nothing in their headquarters to serve as bedding. They asked to take blankets and pillows, the very blankets and pillows—brand new—that they had been denouncing as verminous. Mr. Peak obliged. They left.

That was the last of the battle of the suffragettes. Actually during all this time I continued my close contact with the National American Woman's Suffrage Association and especially with Mrs. Maude Wood Park, who was the head of its lobbying crew in the capital. Time and time again we were convinced—that is, Mrs. Park and I were convinced, as were many of the friends of suffrage in the Congress—that the militant suffragettes, for reasons one could only surmise, actually were attempting to delay the vote on the submission of the amendment.

When the amendment came up for action in the House of Representatives, my father-in-law, an ardent supporter of the votes-for-women cause, had suffered a severe accident the day before. In a fall on the ice he had broken his shoulder. He refused to have the shoulder set, and, despite very great physical suffering, he attended the session of the House. He refused to accept medical ministration and furnished the one vote that meant the two-thirds majority for the submission of the amendment so far as the House of Representatives was concerned.

The amendment went to the Senate. When it seemed by a count of polls that there was a sufficient number of favorable votes to furnish the required two-thirds majority, the suffragettes would stage another demonstration, perhaps burning the President in effigy or something like that, and that sensation would alienate one or two wavering senators. The test would have to be postponed. However, at last the Senate did act favorably, and the fight then was transferred to the various state legislatures. In the end, in August, 1920, the Tennessee state legislature ratified the amendment and by that action, three-fourths of the states having ratified, the Woman's Suffrage Amendment became the Nineteenth Amendment to the Constitution.

The Woman's party still claims that by its militant tactics it brought about this constitutional change. I am convinced that many of the women then were quite sincere, and I believe that now nearly all of them actually believe that their strategy and tactics, their militancy, prevailed upon a reluctant President and Congress. However, I am equally convinced that they are wrong and that women were given the vote because of the wise and statesmanlike leadership of Mrs. Catt, Dr. Shaw, Mrs. Park, Mrs. Gardener, and other leaders of the National American Woman's Suffrage Association.

CHAPTER VIII

THE POLICE UNION

The summer of 1919 was crowded, excited, and not a little mad. The demobilization of the armies was accompanied by the remobilization of the parties; the economic and industrial solidarity of the war was splitting into fractions and factions that heaped bitterness on the shamefaced memory of their days of partnership; the exaltation of common sacrifice was giving way to the sordid search for the main chance; the descent to normalcy had begun.

The unrest in the country was reflected in the threatened strike of the railway shopmen, the steel workers, and many other labor organizations. National prohibition had been enacted and the date for its effectiveness was coming on apace. Union labor was supposed to be opposed to prohibition.

When the American Federation of Labor met at Atlantic City in July, 1919, a petition for a charter for a police union to be affiliated with the AF of L was considered favorably. For a dozen years or more such petitions had been uniformly turned down. Now, the policy of the great labor organization was reversed. By the middle of August some thirty-seven charters for police unions had been granted.

In Washington the police union had the support of Mr. McLean, a millionaire publisher but not always an ardent labor partisan, and was advised by Mr. McLean's attorney, a very expensive lawyer, Mr. Wilton J. Lambert.

I heard something about the Policemen's Association changing its name to Police Union, but as the association had been going for seventeen or eighteen years, I did not at first consider the matter of much importance. This was early in August. (It may be necessary to say here that I was friendly to labor and not at all alarmed by the mere word "union.")

Then I heard vague rumors that all the police departments of all the cities were to be unionized and that they would refuse to enforce the prohibition laws. That, I thought, was just part of the crazy talk of the times.

In the weeks immediately preceding these events, the need of police protection in cities had been powerfully demonstrated by the series of race riots that had swept over the country. In Washington these riots began with a few sporadic encounters between Negroes and uniformed men presumed to be ex-service men. I have always believed that these white ex-service men were frauds, paid to provoke the trouble they began. But unfortunately I cannot prove that.

It is an indisputable fact, however, that the *Washington Post* on Monday, July 21, carried an alarming article with inflammatory headlines announcing that the ex-servicemen would gather that night at a certain place for the purpose of cleaning up the Negroes.

That night the race riot swept over Washington. If it had not been for the good work of police and soldiers who kept the large mobs from contact, the city would have been a shambles. During the week the race riots in Chicago and Knoxville followed, and the month of July ended with a feeling of apprehension and disturbance.

One day the mayor of Detroit, James Couzens, later a senator from Michigan, came to Washington. He had been police commissioner and as such had formed a very close friendship with Major Pullman, whom he greatly admired. He told Major Pullman and me that the police-union matter was a serious national threat to the integrity of government and that he had got wind of the purpose in Detroit and had prevented the formation of the union.

I had Major Pullman investigate, and to our astonishment we found not only that Mr. Couzens was correct in his idea that the unionization was a threat to take over governmental functions but that in Washington the vicious forces fighting the police department were seemingly in direct charge of the unionization, a surprising thing in view of the past attitudes of some of the leaders of these forces toward labor unions.

I went at once to President Wilson (it was on August 20) and told him what I had learned. Without the slightest hesitation he told me that in his opinion this movement must be stopped at once. He instructed me first to proceed with all possible vigor to make arrangements for the protection of the town in case the police should strike and then to forbid the policemen's staying in an affiliated union.

The next day I prepared a statement of the policy of the commissioners which I took to the President. Mr. Wilson made one or two verbal alterations and then gave me the paper with his approval. Because it did have his approval, word for word, I set it out here in full:

August 22, 1919

The Commissioners of the District of Columbia at a Board Meeting held on this date announce the adoption of the following statement of policy:

"The Commissioners, after careful consideration of the whole question of the organization of a policemen's union affiliated with any other labor organization, have reached the conclusion that they must take the necessary steps to assure entire and complete independence of the Police Department.

"They approve heartily of the principle of collective bargaining and they welcome the organization of members of the Police Force for purposes of collective representation, mutual support and organized effort to increase their salaries or improve their working conditions.

"They must, however, withhold their consent from any project to connect such an organization of members of the police department with any other labor organization.

"The fact that the Policemen's union is bound by a 'no-strike' provision is an earnest of the intention of its members not to resort to a strike as a weapon of compelling its demands. But if it be affiliated with other organizations which do contemplate the use of the strike in an emergency, every member of the police force who is a member of the union would be liable to the charge, however falsely made, of favoritism in the performance of duty in the event of industrial trouble involving the organization with which it is affiliated.

"Authority, especially here in the National Capital, at all times must be represented by a police force that has no connection with any organization but the constituted agencies of government.

"This decision must not be interpreted to mean that the Commissioners are opposed to labor organizations, nor must it be taken to mean that they are unwilling to meet representatives of any organization of policemen. It is only what it purports to be—a statement of the decision of the Commissioners that the organization of policemen, a body of men sworn to enforce the law impartially under all circumstances, must be an organization of policemen and nothing more; that it must not be connected with any other labor organization."

Pursuant to the President's directions, I called on Secretary Baker and, through the War Department, we made ready. Men with good records as military police were taken as they debarked from overseas and sent to Camp Meade, Maryland. There a number of them, three times the number in the Washington police force, were divided into units comparable to our Washington police force, instructed in our police usages, and drilled for duty. When these men had been trained, they were brought into Washington itself, to Camp Meigs, where, with the motor equipment provided, they might take over the police posts, three men for one, in less than half an hour. When all this was ready, I confided what we had done to a man I knew to be a spy for the union. Then the commissioners issued an ultimatum. This order, issued on September 2, had the effect of dismissing from the police force any man who stayed in the union after September 7. While the President did not see the text, I had told him of its purport before it was issued, and I talked with him about it the next day, so that I know he approved of it.

In the meantime I had been in touch with the mayors of Boston, Buffalo, New York, and perhaps some other cities, as well as with Mayor Couzens of Detroit. Police Commissioner Curtis of Boston had issued an order forbidding the affiliated police union on August 12, ten days before our first proclamation, but little attention was paid to it at the time, at least outside of Boston.

In our proclamation of August 22 we had assumed, on information given by policemen, that the new police-union charter had a no-strike clause, but this we discovered was not true, and when we issued the ultimatum of September 2, we knew that the strike was a threat of the new police union. Major Pullman went to Boston to see Mayor Peters and Commissioner Curtis, but Mr. Curtis did not seem to appreciate the danger of the situation.

In the meantime other things were afoot in Washington. The President announced that he was going to take the issue of the League of Nations to the country. On Labor Day, September 1, he went to a baseball game between the police force and the Home Defense League. I sat with him and we discussed the police-union matter. I told him of the precautions against a strike that we had taken and of our intention to issue the ultimatum the next day.

The order to quit the police union was issued on September 2. On September 3 the President left for the West. On September 4 the policemen's union applied for an injunction to restrain the commissioners from enforcing the get-out-of-the-union order, and on September 5 the court granted a temporary injunction and fixed a hearing for September 11.

On September 9 the Boston police went on strike. The resultant disorder changed the whole face of the police-union question. The *Washington Post,* and I think the other Washington newspapers, had demanded that the President remove me from office because I had opposed the police union. Some of the correspondents, notably David Lawrence, had said that it was known that I had had several conversations with the President, and that it was inconceivable that my stand did not have his approval. Nevertheless, I was attacked from many angles and my dismissal generally demanded.

The Boston strike changed that.

On September 10 Mayor Peters seized the reins in Boston and the restoration of order was begun. On September 11, I received a telegram from Mr. Tumulty reading as follows: "The President suggests the great advisability of postponing any issue regarding the police situation until after the forthcoming industrial conference at Washington and hopes the postponement can be effected."

At an utter loss to understand that message, which was most prominently displayed in the *Washington Post* before I ever received it, I could do nothing but instruct the corporation counsel to appear before the court and ask a postponement of the proceedings to vacate the injunction.

Later in the day I read other messages from the President to Mr. Gompers, head of the American Federation of Labor, urging the steel workers not to take action on their threatened strike until after the industrial conference the President had called for October. I then concluded that Mr. Wilson was trying to prevent the steel strike and could not call upon Mr. Gompers to interfere there with good grace unless he, too, agreed without urging that his own labor dispute, so to speak, be postponed until after the conference.

But, for the time, the message was taken to be a repudiation of me and my policy toward the police union. A week earlier such an apparent repudiation would have been welcomed for its own sake, for then I had been the cruel taskmaster who was denying to policemen the common rights of man. But the situation now was different.

That afternoon I went on the floor of the Senate and was immediately surrounded by Republican senators. "Will you resign?" they asked excitedly. They would back me up. They would see me through. Resign and make it an issue was the tenor of the advice.

But I knew what they did not, that Woodrow Wilson had advised me all along and fully approved my course; and I was certain that he had not changed nor deserted.

The news of the interpretation of the Tumulty telegram reached the President in the West, and at Helena on September 11 Mr. Wilson interrupted his speech to say that there would be no more police strikes in the United States if he could help it. This speech was interpreted by David Lawrence as a complete vindication of my course. (I say "I" and "my" because I had direct charge of the police force at the time and made all the dispositions. My colleague General Kutz agreed with me at all points. My colleague Mr. Gardiner did not agree and had his negative vote recorded but withheld from the public. Mr. Gardiner's signature to the proclamation was *pro forma.*)

On September 13 General Pershing reached Washington with the vanguard of the victorious army. On that same day in Seattle, Woodrow Wilson met his first alarmingly hostile audience made up of labor men. During the week the Macon, Georgia, police defied orders to get out of the union, and the police-union matter was a matter of moment in thirty-seven cities. Boston was becoming quiet under the volunteer police force and the governor and the police commissioner were saying that the strikers would never be taken back.

On September 17 the First Division paraded in Washington, led by General Pershing and reviewed by Vice-President Thomas R. Marshall.

On September 18 the Senate Committee on the District of Columbia met to consider the police matter, and I was called before it. The hearings, which began with intimations that I should resign and "show up Wilson" ended abruptly when I read aloud a telegram I had received the night before. It read:

I hope you understood my brief telegram of the other day. I am quite willing that you should tell the Senate Committee that my position in my conversations with you was exactly the same as I have expressed recently in speeches here in the west, and, of course, I am as desirous as you are of dealing with the police force in the most just and generous way, but I think any association of the police force of the Capital City, or any great city, whose object is to bring pressure upon the public or the community, such as will endanger the public peace or embarrass the maintenance of good order, should in no case be countenanced or permitted.

This telegram came from Dunsmuir, California, and was signed "Woodrow Wilson."

The increase in pay for policemen which Major Pullman had urged and the commissioners had repeatedly recommended to the Congress was put through, and when the bill finally passed, a provision of it forbade the unionization of the police.

Later, when a Democratic candidate for governor of Massachusetts hinted at sympathy for the striking policemen, Mr. Wilson sent a telegram supporting the candidacy of the Republican nominee, Calvin Coolidge. But as I saw it at the time, Mr. Coolidge took his position after the event, and not before it. Mr. Wilson took his position before the event, when it was unpopular. That he supported Mr. Coolidge later was to me proof of Mr. Wilson's disinterested and impartial attitude. Here Mr. Wilson manifested his faith in the organization of municipal services as a governmental function, superior to every consideration of private policy or partisan politics.

CHAPTER IX

PUBLIC UTILITIES COMMISSION

Very shortly after Mr. Wilson was inaugurated President, the confused state of the regulation of public utilities in the District of Columbia was brought into focus by Senator Robert M. La Follette of Wisconsin, in consultation with Mr. Wilson. He introduced and piloted through the Congress, with the help in the House of Representatives of my father-in-law, Judge Sims of Tennessee, a bill establishing a Public Utilities Commission for the District of Columbia. This commission was to consist of three members, ex officio the commissioners of the District of Columbia.

Among the more important features of the bill was the grant of authority to the new commission to control the sale of stocks, the issuance of bonds, and the emission of other securities by the several public utilities in the District. Along with this negative authority was granted the positive authority to fix rates. The rates determined were to be based upon a physical valuation of the property of the several utilities, which in turn was to be preceded by separate findings of the physical value of the properties as measured by original cost, reproduction cost new, and reproduction cost less depreciation, each of these elements to be given due weight in the final finding of a fair valuation to serve as a base for the rates to be charged to the consumers.

The District Public Utilities Commission was set up before I went on the board by Major Chester L. Harding, the engineer commissioner. When he was relieved by Major Kutz, Major Kutz became the chairman. Under Major Harding's regime the intricate business of the physical valuation was begun. Experts were employed. Staffs of engineers were set to work to find the reproduction value. Staffs of accountants were set to work to determine the original value. Engineering and accounting staffs were asked to act together on the problem of depreciation.

Not until after I had become a member of the commission, still under the chairmanship of Major Kutz, were the preliminary reports of the engineering and accounting staffs received. That meant that the commission had to hold hearings at which the several utilities, each of which had employed staffs of both engineering and accounting experts of its own, would present their estimates and comment on ours. And, quite naturally, each of the staffs of the utilities was backed and supported by an able group of attorneys.

This may sound quite simple. What it meant, however, was the review of literally millions of words and hundreds of thousands of figures. All three commissioners sat in at the hearings, which usually occupied four or five full afternoons every week.

There were four principal utility companies in the District then: the Washington Railway and Electric Company, which operated one of the two streetcar systems in the District, and its wholly owned subsidiary, the Potomac Electric Power Company, which was the only electric power utility; the Capital Traction Company, which operated the other competing street-railway system and for which it generated its own electric power; the Washington Gas Light Company and its wholly owned subsidiary, the Georgetown Gas Light Company; and the Chesapeake and Potomac Telephone Company, which was affiliated with the American Telephone and Telegraph Company.

Each of these utilities had its own battery of lawyers, its own staff of accountants, its own force of engineers. No one of the reports of the experts of any of the utilities was even in remote agreement with any other, much less with those made by our own staff. The commission had assigned the corporation counsel of the District of Columbia to be the counsel of the Utilities Commission, an assignment which effectively removed him from any but the most important of his ordinary duties as corporation counsel for the District.

The long, dreary hours, the fiercely contested step-by-step reports, the examination and the cross-examinations of our experts and of their experts in the end were recorded in many millions of words reproduced in typewritten and mimeographed documents.

This long and tedious process, which was wearing upon not only the members of the commission and its staff but also the staffs of the public utilities' companies, was interrupted in mid-stream by the entry of the United States into the war, the disappearance of Major Kutz and Major Newman, the appointment to the commission of General Knight and Mr. Gardiner, and the necessity of having two new members of the commission read all the records. All this meant more hearings and more delays and compelled us to put off the whole complicated business until after the war. President Wilson took over all the telephone and telegraph companies of the nation and turned them over to Postmaster General Albert Sydney Burleson for operation very soon after he had seized all the railroads of the country and intrusted their operation to William Gibbs McAdoo, the secretary of the treasury.

At long last the war was over. General Knight was ill. His place as a District commissioner could be taken from day to day by the assistant commissioner, Captain Loving of the Corps of Engineers, who by this time had been promoted to the rank of colonel. But the Public Utilities Law did not permit him to participate in the activities of the Public Utilities Commission. Moreover, I knew that Colonel Loving's idea of the control of public utilities was about as far removed from mine as it possibly could be. It was evident from his conversations after he had succeeded Colonel Schley, another assistant engineer commissioner, that he was inclined to accept the utilities' side of practically every argument. I was not.

Kutz, by this time a brigadier general, had come back from France and was in command at Fort Humphrey, now Fort Belvoir, the engineer post a few miles south of Washington on the Potomac.

One day I went over to see Secretary of War Newton D. Baker. I interrupted him at a time when he was extremely busy, and I detected that in spite of our long friendship he was a little bit annoyed by my insistence upon an interview. He asked me to cut it as short as possible.

In reply I said, "The reason I am here is precisely that. I want to cut it short."

"What do you want to cut short?"

"When you used to be city attorney," I replied, "in Cleveland under Tom Johnson, you and Tom had your troubles with utilities. Every time a new party primary or a new election came up, you would have to go through a fight first in the Democratic primary, then through the election. Sometimes your Republican rivals would win and you would have to wait a year and sometimes two years for a chance to get your

[92]

wagon back on the road. Now, I am in the same situation. But I don't have to wait for a primary. I don't have to go through an election. All I have to do is to persuade you to help me cut it short. All I need you to do is to write a half-dozen words on a sheet of paper."

"What do you mean?" he asked.

"I mean," I replied, "if you will bring Kutz back here, then two members of the Utilities Commission will have heard all the record, and we can cut the whole business short where we were forced to leave off by the war. Otherwise, you will have two new members of the Public Utilities Commission and all those millions of words and figures will have to be gone all over again."

"But that will mean," he demurred, "that I will have to go over the head of the chief of engineers."

"I know perfectly well that is what it means," I replied, "but I still want you to write those few words."

"What do you want me to write?"

"I want you to write a note to General Black, chief of engineers, telling him that the President desires that he recommend General Charles Willauer Kutz to be appointed the engineer commissioner of the District of Columbia, and that will put Kutz back on the Public Utilities Commission."

"But the President hasn't told me any such thing."

"That is up to you."

After a pause, after looking around, after asking me to sit down (I had remained standing), he said, "I have to go over to the White House now about another matter."

Later that afternoon Mr. Baker telephoned me that General Black had recommended, and he had transmitted the recommendation to the President, that General Kutz be reassigned to his old position as District commissioner.

I shall never forget the concerned, puzzled, and frustrated look on the face of one of the presidents of one of the utilities when he came into my office later that afternoon and I told him that Kutz would be back.

Kutz again was made chairman of the Public Utilities Commission. The cases were reopened. The hearings might have dragged out much more than they actually did had the new member, Mr. Gardiner, so desired. But for reasons of his own, he elected to attend very few of the hearings; and, therefore, it was relatively easy to deny the motions of the attorneys for the utilities for completely new hearings, *ab initio*. In time we made our decisions, Kutz and I in agreement, Gardiner in dissent. We found, as the law required, in each case the original cost, the reproduction cost new, and the reproduction cost new less depreciation. But in relating either one of these three elements to our final valuation for rate-making purposes we were as vague and as opaque and as un-understandable as the Supreme Court ever had been able to make itself on all valuation cases that hitherto had reached it.

All the utilities in the District of Columbia, as a matter of course, appealed our decision to the Supreme Court of the District of Columbia (now the District Court). The Supreme Court of the District approved in every one of the cases the findings of our commission.

Only one of the four utilities elected to appeal from the decision of the District Supreme Court to the Court of Appeals, as each of them had, of course, the right to do. That one was the Washington Railway and Electric Company on behalf of itself and its wholly owned subsidiary, the Potomac Electric Power Company.

In the Court of Appeals the decision of the Supreme Court of the District was reversed by a margin of two to one for reasons too legally esoteric for me to analyze. Nevertheless, I have always taken a little bit of personal pride in the fact that the dissenting justice of the Court of Appeals, the one who upheld our valuation, was Constantine J. Smyth, who in his earlier days as attorney general of the state of Nebraska was the very Smyth whose name appeared in the case of *Smyth* vs. *Ames,* one of the ruling cases in the whole history of public utility regulation.

Then we, the Public Utilities Commission, appealed to the Supreme Court of the United States. That august body declined to take jurisdiction, and the case went back to the District Supreme Court, where our valuation was necessarily amended in accordance with the findings of the Court of Appeals.

Despite the fact that, particularly in the case of the Washington Railway and Electric Company, valuation was set at a figure considerably higher than our commission had found, a rate base had been established. In all subsequent valuations, so far as I know, and in all subsequent rate cases in the District of Columbia, the Public Utilities Commission, now differently composed, has used as its base the figure we originally determined plus the amendments, the alterations decreed by the Court of Appeals, and all later additions at their actual original cost.

Probably that is the reason that the exceedingly prosperous Potomac Electric Power Company, now divorced from the traction business, greatly expanded and serving a community of an enormously greater population, still has one of the lowest rate schedules of any privately owned electric power utility in any urban community comparable in population and area to the metropolitan District of Columbia with its Maryland and Virginia suburbs.

CHAPTER X

I LEAVE WASHINGTON

In the spring of 1920, the state of my personal finances became a matter of pressing concern. Prices had been greatly affected by the war, and my salary of $5,000 a year had not been enough to meet my absolutely necessary costs of living. My few thousand dollars in savings had finally disappeared. I had sold my Liberty Bonds at a considerable discount and borrowed on my life insurance policies to meet day-to-day expenses. It was inevitable that I was forced either to think of some way to supplement my income or to get a better job.

During this time, I had several very attractive offers in journalism at considerably larger salaries than I ever had enjoyed in my newspaper days. Some of them were very tempting, but I had no stomach for the business. I had become so deeply interested in government, especially in its administrative aspects, that I did not like to leave the field.

I was also deterred from accepting any of the newspaper jobs because I was eager to stay on the commission and with General Kutz until we had completed a project which we had tentatively started before the United States entered the war. In 1919 it could be completed because the Congress had passed the appropriate legislation. The project was the preparation of a zoning ordinance for the District of Columbia. It was, I believe, the second comprehensive zoning ordinance ever adopted in the United States.

The extent of the utility of citizens' organizations was never more clearly demonstrated to me than in the preparation of this ordinance. We employed as our chief planner Mr. Harland Bartholomew of St. Louis, who had done some excellent preparatory work along the same line in his own city. He set up the framework of the zoning ordinance. It so radically affected the real property in the District and was in itself such a radical interference with the rights of landowners as they had previously been interpreted and accepted that Kutz and I decided we would do everything possible to take the community fully into our confidence and to enlist the help of the citizens generally.

Three basic maps were compiled: one for the control of property uses, another to control the height of buildings, and the third to limit the area of the lot on which buildings could be built. These three maps —use, height, and area—were reproduced by the hundreds. We divided the District into 175 local areas and got out a map showing their boundaries. This was more necessary in Washington than it would be in most other cities because there were no election precincts, and the only other divisions at hand were the police precincts, which were too large.

With Mr. Bartholomew and his staff, we went over every single determination of use, height, and area. General Kutz spent two hours each morning traversing every street in the area that we were supposed to take up the next day. I spent two hours late every afternoon doing the same thing. Thus it came about that during the commissioners' consideration, we covered every foot of open street or roadway in the District and also the undeveloped areas. We then tried not only to project a new street plan but also to suggest the best uses to which these undeveloped areas could be put.

Citizens were assembled in schoolhouses, churches, or other public buildings in each of the districts. Either Kutz, a representative of the Bartholomew staff, or I took the maps and explained them to the citizens in these gatherings and asked for suggestions, which we then considered at night meetings.

In another room in the District Building the Zoning Committee of the Board of Trade was similarly at work each night under the leadership of its chairman, Edwin C. Graham, later president of the Hamilton National Bank and a director of the Federal Reserve Bank of Richmond. About eleven o'clock each evening he and his fellow workers joined with Kutz and me and our staff, and we made the final determinations.

After all this had been done, we issued other maps radically changed from the previous ones, especially with respect to use. Then, as the act of Congress required, we held a series of open hearings at which representatives of citizens' organizations and other groups, as well as individuals, could make their comments. After all this the final zoning maps were approved and the ordinance written.

It was early in the life of zoning in this country. We made many mistakes, but not until 1954 did the community sufficiently recognize our errors or the changed character of the District and begin to revise that zoning ordinance. I doubt very much whether any city in the country where the normal electoral processes go on and where the heads of the city government are elected by the people ever undertook such an intensive program for inducing citizen participation or such careful consideration of citizen suggestions.

With the zoning ordinance out of the way, it seemed to me that I must do something about my financial situation. Every time I thought about it I was influenced by a consideration that had been revolving in the back of my mind for four or five years. In 1913, soon after Siddons and Newman were appointed to the commission and the President and Mrs. Wilson were so much concerned with community organization in the District, I had been in touch with a man named Edward J. Ward, who was considered an expert in the establishment of community centers and in the encouragement of recreational facilities. He was a frequent guest at the "Doughnut Cabinet" table. He was an earnest crusading soul with the flamboyant manner, the vocabulary, and the forensic flair of an evangelist. He whooped it up at meetings, and he was able to persuade people in the meetings to whoop it up for him.

I had never heard of the National Municipal League. Ward told me about it because the league had published his book, *The Social Center.* Among the other books published by the National Municipal League, I found one entitled, *The City Manager,* by Harry Aubrey Toulmin, Jr. I read it, and it interested me even though I didn't think it a very good book. It stressed principally the electoral and political side of the newly launched council-manager system and was oddly deficient in its treatment of administration.

Nevertheless, I talked it over with my wife frequently, and we agreed that if I got a chance when I left the District Building I would try my wings in this new profession.

During the war I had been invited to Petersburg, Virginia, to make a speech in a Liberty Loan drive. Adjoining the city of Petersburg was one of the great training camps for World War I, Camp Lee. Petersburg was much excited by the war, and its people demonstrated a fervent patriotic interest in what was going on. The editor and publisher of the two Petersburg newspapers, Walter Edward Harris, had been my close friend in my early days in Washington when he was the correspondent for the *Richmond Times-Dispatch*. Mr. Harris had suggested that I be invited to speak at a great Liberty Loan rally. And, partly because the invitation came through him, I accepted.

The meeting was held in the Petersburg High School auditorium. All its 1,700 seats were filled. I made my speech, and a young Petersburger in the uniform of a captain followed me in a most eloquent direct appeal for the sale of the bonds. For the time being that was all I heard of Petersburg.

But in the spring of 1920 Petersburg adopted the council-manager plan of government. It held an election and chose five men as members of the city council. The council was on the prowl for a manager. A merchant, Louis A. Rosenstock, suggested my name to the mayor who had been chosen by the council—Samuel W. Zimmer, who was the young captain that had spoken with me on the same platform in the Liberty Loan drive. Mr. Zimmer came to Washington and, as I later discovered, talked to a good many of the leading citizens of the town. He went back to Petersburg, consulted the other members of the council, and then came again to Washington to talk with me and to offer me the position subject only to my meeting his colleagues in Petersburg.

The council was prepared to pay a salary of $10,000. This was exactly twice as much as I was earning. The District, a city then of 450,000 people, could pay but $5,000. Here, however, was a city of 30,000 which would pay $10,000. Although, as it turned out, I was not fully prepared for all the elements of the task, I had had six years of municipal government, and I was imbued with the notion that municipal administration was the most important activity in which one could engage. I took the job.

On August 24, 1920, I sent my resignation to the President; and two weeks later I went to Petersburg.

The Washington to which I bade goodbye in 1920 is not at all the Washington of today. In common with all other American cities, the national capital in the last thirty-five years has witnessed and struggled with profound changes. It also has been shaken by the impact of the additional problems imposed upon it as a capital city. It has become now the principal diplomatic capital of the Western world, and it is the seat of the greatest national governmental, military, and economic power in the world.

As if these problems were not enough, it also continues to suffer because of its archaic, awkward system of local government. It is still ruled by a city council composed of 96 senators and 435 members of the House of Representatives. Its administrative management is still intrusted in the main to a three-man board of commissioners. As I have observed events from outside the municipal building, the commissioners during the thirty-five years since I left have found it increasingly difficult to get an adequate response to the problems of the city from the Congress and its committees. The national and necessary business of the Congress has increased in size and complexity. There has been even less time for the parochial affairs of the District.

During the six years I was a District commissioner, I found myself changing many of my views. At the beginning of my tour of duty I was not at all persuaded that the government of the city should be devolved upon its residents through home rule. At the end of my term I was a convinced believer in home rule by a locally elected, democratically controlled local government. As late as 1917, I wrote to President Wilson telling something about the then nascent revival of the home-rule sentiment of the District, expressing my doubts and asking his advice. That advice was promptly given, and it consisted simply of his statement that he thought it would be the wiser course for the commissioners to refrain from participation one way or the other in the discussion.

What persuaded me to change my mind on the home-rule question was the fact that it already was becoming increasingly difficult to get action from the Congress. Because the membership of the Congress was overwhelmingly rural in background, it was frequently impossible to get the necessary legislation or the required appropriations of funds to enable the District to keep up with the constantly increasing demands of American urban life.

For instance, at the very beginning of the establishment of public playgrounds, we were stopped when a member of the Congress in an important and determining position of power exclaimed that it was idiotic to hire persons to teach children to play.

"God taught children to play!" was his final comment.

While that particular obstacle was overcome by argument and persuasion, it always was difficult to persuade men who had lived their whole lives on farms or in small rural villages not only to appreciate the desirable changes that should be made in municipal housekeeping but also not to resist those that seemed absolutely necessary.

For years before my time, for example, the commissioners had endeavored to get funds to build a city hospital. What then served the District was an old almshouse, a three-story structure, which had been built in 1810 under the autonomous government of the old city of Washington that had existed from the beginning of the nineteenth century until after the Civil War. That particular building was then the psychiatric ward of the hospital. The other parts of the institution devoted to hospital care were a group of originally flimsy and by my time decrepit wooden buildings erected as hospitals for the sick and wounded Union soldiers during the Civil War.

Occasionally an appropriation for a new modern hospital would carry through one house of Congress only to fail in the other.

Just at the close of World War I, I was able to persuade the House Appropriations Committee to include an item for the beginning of a city hospital. When the appropriation bill went to the Senate the prospects were gloomy. It seemed expedient to me to substitute political strategy for factual arguments.

During the last several years of the Republican administrations before Wilson, the chairman of the Senate Committee on the District of Columbia had been Senator Jacob H. Gallinger of New Hampshire. Senator Gallinger was a practicing physician before he came to the Senate, and he always liked to be called Dr. Gallinger. He was retiring from the Senate, and the end of his term was approaching. Relying upon the clublike spirit of the Senate, I suggested that the new hospital be named Gallinger Hospital in honor of the great physician who had done so much for the District of Columbia.

And that is the way I got the appropriation for the Gallinger Hospital. Time went on. Dr. Gallinger was forgotten. The reason for giving his name to the hospital was forgotten, and in 1953 Congress wisely changed its name to "General Hospital for the District of Columbia."

My views about other matters more fundamental and much more important also changed a great deal during my six years as commissioner of the District of Columbia. I am sure, as I look back now, that I came into that position still convinced that what was most needed to meet my views of greater service to the people was the election of the right persons to proper legislative bodies and the enactment of laws which would require a more liberal approach to the problems of urban peoples. Six years later I was inclined to believe that an enlightened, informed public administration was the basic requirement of better living for all citizens, great and small.

PART II

PETERSBURG, KNOXVILLE, RADBURN, AND CHICAGO

CHAPTER XI

MY INTRODUCTION TO
PETERSBURG

Petersburg, Virginia, is an old town—by American standards a very old town—steeped in history and tradition. What is history and what is tradition might perhaps be differentiated by meticulous research, but it would have little effect on the mores of the people. They devoutly believe in all their traditions and consequently are influenced in their daily lives by what they believe—not by what has been proved true.

According to their tradition, Petersburg was founded by one Peter Jones, who came up the James River from Jamestown and up its tributary to the falls of the Appomattox in 1619 to set up a trading post. According to older tales, King Powhatan and his daughter, the Princess Pocahontas, had one of their several seats on an island in the Appomattox River that is part of Petersburg and still is known as Pocahontas Island.

By the beginning of the eighteenth century, Petersburg was a flourishing market town and tobacco port, and by the middle of that century it was large enough to send a contingent of troops to the French and Indian War. Long before the Revolutionary War it had had a race track, several flourishing inns, and even a theater to which the players from Williamsburg were accustomed to come every spring for the month of May.

When the Revolutionary War came, Petersburg was a commercial center. One of the tobacco-auction warehouses still in use was partially built in 1776. During the Revolution, Petersburg was occupied by the British troops. It was the scene of a siege and a battle which resulted in the defeat of the British and the death of General Phillips, their commander.

The town sent an organized militia company into the War of 1812. It contributed its quota to the war with Mexico. And in the great Civil War it was the site of the longest of the long sieges in which Lee and the Confederates resisted the assaults of Grant and the Federal troops. It lasted from June 9, 1864, until April 2, 1865. The fall of Petersburg plainly foreshadowed the fall of the Confederacy at Appomattox Court House a week later.

In my day there were still a great many Confederate veterans in the town, and the A. P. Hill Camp of the United Confederate Veterans was one of its principal organizations, as were both the United Daughters of the Confederacy and the Sons of Confederate Veterans. Many of the families of Petersburg lived in houses that had been built by their grandparents or even their great-grandparents, and many more traced their ancestry back to Jamestown itself.

Petersburg was proud of its past and often seemed reluctant to change its ways. In 1920 it was a city of 30,000 people living conservative lives, along conservative lines, devoutly attending its many churches and upholding high standards of honor and conduct.

The revolutionary political change, which was the reason for my being there in September, 1920, was a direct result of the impact of yet another war, World War I.

A few miles to the east of Petersburg had been established Camp Lee, where thousands of men were trained. This had had a tremendous effect on the placid paths of peace in Petersburg. The town was crowded with the wives and other relatives of men in camp. The community facilities were unable to meet the demands. The camp followers swarmed into the city's highways and byways, and even the inevitable accompanying spurt to business hardly seemed to compensate for the upset. Overcrowding at the respectable levels and vice at the lower levels stirred the citizenry as it had not been stirred since Lee's surrender. A bureau of municipal research was set up under Colonel LeRoy Hodges. A group of church people and others interested in the few small welfare organizations had got together a fund and had had a survey made of the social facilities by a New York welfare-consulting firm. The municipal research reports and the welfare institutional survey added great force to the movement to take advantage of the act of the Virginia legislature permitting cities, by a vote of their people, to adopt any one of three optional forms of municipal government. One of these was the council-manager plan.

My Introduction to Petersburg

On Monday, August 23, a dull, gray day, I alighted from the Seaboard Airline train at Petersburg's Dunlop Street Station. I was eager and thrilled by the challenge of an entry into a new profession, but a little uneasy. I feared that I would find it difficult (as indeed I was to find it) to reduce my idea of the scale of municipal housekeeping from that which befitted the capital city of the United States with almost half a million people to the requirements of a small city of thirty thousand.

I was met by Mr. Selwyn Hoag. Mr. Hoag was a young man, an employee of the Petersburg Savings and Insurance Company, one of the leading banks of the town. He was a skilful guide, but he exhibited none of the fervor of the hometown booster. He took me to backstreets that were unpaved or, if paved at all, full of chuckholes. He took me through Guarantee Street, where on my right I found the great high school and on my left, after a thin screen of respectable houses on the front of the main street, a series of dismal hovels perched precariously on the edge of a deep ditch which separated them from the narrow roadway over which our Ford was traveling. He took me through Gill Street, narrow, unpaved, deep in dust that would, I knew, be quickly transformed into mud when it rained. The street was lined on either side by houses in various states of disrepair, inhabited, as it was easy to see, by Negro people. He looped me around through alleys and backstreets, through the slums from one end of the town to the other, and only then, when I had seen all the slums that one could see from a moving motorcar, did he drive on the well-paved streets to show me the good houses, many of them beautiful houses, the fine churches, and the substantial buildings that housed either industry in the outlying circuits or commerce in the center of the city.

It was a sobering excursion. It put me on my toes. Here under the ministrations of my good guide I sensed at once that there was much that needed to be done that I could not hope to do, but there was also the insistent challenge that there was much that perhaps could be done and more than enough to bring out the best that was in me.

Mr. Hoag delivered me to an office where I met Mr. Zimmer, who in turn introduced me to his four colleagues: Thomas Jefferson Meredith, a machinist; Grover Cleveland Wright, a banker; Wallace M. Rucker, a proprietor of a department store; and William H. Willcox, the proprietor of a furniture store. Mr. Meredith was the oldest, a man in his sixties. Mr. Rucker was in his late forties. Messrs. Zimmer, Wright, and Willcox were all in their early thirties, and I was within six days of becoming forty-one.

Mr. Zimmer had told his colleagues what he had learned about me and my administration in Washington, but each of them asked me a good many questions, and the interview lasted until shortly after twelve o'clock. Then the job was formally offered to me and I formally accepted it.

Mr. Zimmer telephoned to my friend the editor and publisher of the morning newspaper, Walter Edward Harris, and asked him to come over. The councilmen told him that he was at liberty to announce my appointment. I had said that I would endeavor to come to Petersburg to take over not later than September 15.

When I returned to Washington, I had no opportunity to see President Wilson, who was ill. I discussed the situation with Mr. Tumulty, and on the Tuesday after Labor Day, I announced to the newspapers that I had resigned as commissioner of the District of Columbia, effective September 15.

On September 16, Mrs. Brownlow and I left for Petersburg. We were met at the Atlantic Coastline station by Mayor Zimmer, Councilman Willcox, and a large delegation of citizens representing the Chamber of Commerce, the Ministerial Association, the Community Council (which had just come into existence), and many other local organizations. To the accompaniment of a trial run of the fire department's equipment and with considerable fanfare, we were conducted to the Petersburg Hotel, where we were met by Mr. and Mrs. Walter Edward Harris and where we established our temporary residence.

That afternoon, accompanied by the mayor and Mr. Willcox, I went to the courthouse, there to address the assembled heads of city departments and other important city employees.

I told them that it was my purpose to continue them in their several positions and, insofar as possible, to make no change in the personnel of the city's employees, so long as they were rendering efficient service and were giving loyal co-operation to their fellow workers. I told them that I would spend the next few days getting acquainted with them and their work and that for some time they need expect no innovations and no upsets.

It was an unusual situation, since the council had just conferred upon me complete and absolute authority over the personnel of the entire city government with only a few exceptions. The exceptions were the school board and its employees, the auditor who, under the new charter, was to be elected by the council itself, and the several city officials elected by the direct vote of the people—the city treasurer, the collector of taxes, the city sergeant, the revenue commissioner, and the clerk of the courts—these being constitutional officers in Virginia.

Having that authority in that absolute degree, I desired above everything else to allay unnecessary apprehension and to maintain the best possible services.

Two days later there was to be a huge picnic at Swift Creek, a few miles north of town, which was to be attended by members of the Chamber of Commerce, the Rotary Club, and the city council and by city officials and many others.

This type of picnic, which was called a "Brunswick Stew," was new to me. Since long before daybreak huge iron kettles had been simmering with a savory concoction of chicken, green corn, lima beans, peppers, and what not (there should have been squirrel meat, too, but that seemed to have been too hard to come by), all a-cooking under the direction and immediate supervision of a particular character who was always master of ceremonies of any outdoor event held in or near Petersburg. He was Cap Stewart, a big man with a kindly and benign countenance. Cap was a close friend of most of the leading citizens of the community, and among them, it might have been remarked, he numbered not a few ministers of the gospel and not a few pillars of the church who were teetotalers and ardent advocates of the strict enforcement of the prohibition laws. These people never seemed even to notice what later some of us suspected: that Cap on occasion, for a good friend, might possibly contrive to find somewhere a vial of spiritus frumenti.

I had driven out to the barbecue with Mr. Harris. With the skill of an experienced journalist he began to fill me in on the personalities with whom I would be engaged in the council, among the city officials, and all around the town. I asked him to try at the barbecue to throw me together with some of the heads of the city departments.

Cap Stewart's "Brunswick Stew" was an excellent introduction to sociability, and Harris proved adroit, so that in this informal setting I had my first private conversation with Robert D. Budd, the city engineer, with Dr. Robert A. Martin, the health officer, and with Edwin P. Goodwyn, who under the old government had served as clerk of the committees. There also I met William M. Martin, the secretary of the Chamber of Commerce, and it was Billy Martin who offered me a suite of offices in the headquarters of the Chamber of Commerce on the top floor of the most imposing office building in the town, which also had the advantage of being almost directly across the street from the courthouse. There were others also from the city government and, of course, many citizens whom I had not had any chance to meet. Harris with his thumbnail sketches was priceless as an introducer. One could almost see the relaxation of tensions and the beginning of a concert of welcome to me as a person, not either as the devil or as a *deus ex machina,* the symbols in the minds of many of that bloodless and mechanized creature, the city manager.

Virginia is unique among the states in that every first-class city in the Old Dominion is an independent unit of government and not a part of any administrative county. A city government in Virginia carries on all the functions and bears all the responsibilities of a county. Each one has a judge—in Petersburg called "Judge of the Hustings Court"—elected by the legislature, a clerk of the courts elected by the people, a city sergeant who in a county would be called a sheriff and who also is the jailer, a commissioner of revenue who is the tax assessor and the collector of taxes, and a city treasurer, all elected by the people but serving only the city.

In those circumstances lay the fact that all other municipal functions were presumed to be directed from the courthouse. That venerable and I daresay beautiful building on its second floor had a courtroom, while the ground floor was devoted to the municipal establishment—the city treasurer's office on the left, the city auditor's on the right, and in the rear across the width of the building, the council chambers. Nearby on the courthouse hill was the jail, a part of it apparently underground, showing only a low brick structure. On the other side of the courthouse were two low brick buildings. The judge and the clerk of the courts had their offices in one, in which the clerk carried on all the functions of court clerk, recorder of deeds, and registrar of wills. In the other were the offices of the commissioner of revenue and the collector of taxes. Nearby there was a two-story wooden building which, so tradition said, had been built about 1730 to house the first medical college in

Virginia. The courthouse itself, with its imposing granite façade, its elaborate steeple, its clock, and its statue of Justice, had been built in 1835; and thus it was that the courthouse hill was a municipal center. I had explored it externally but had postponed any closer inspection until I felt I was more firmly set in my environment.

On Sunday after the "Brunswick Stew," I went to the Washington Street Methodist Church. Somewhere along the line I had picked up even that early an invitation to speak at a Sunday school at the Old Street Presbyterian Church on Sunday afternoon. Mr. Goodwyn, clerk of committees, volunteered to drive me out there. I had no notion at that moment what a sacrifice it must have been to Mr. Goodwyn to give up his Sunday afternoon at the Elk's Club and his game of poker to take me to a Sunday school meeting.

The old church was only a mission, the building a small wooden structure which the congregation almost filled. I am sure that never before, and I hope never since, have I made a talk that was so ill-suited to the occasion, the audience, or the setting. The regular attendants at that particular mission Sunday school were mainly women and children with a few men from the immediate neighborhood, in which years and years before there had flourished cotton mills and silk-throwing mills. Now practically all the industries had been abandoned, and in their wake they had left a poverty-stricken, dilapidated neighborhood. But that Sunday afternoon the attendance was swelled not only by Mr. Goodwyn but, although I did not then know him, by an individual who had been one of the leaders of the opposition to the establishment of the new form of government, and by some other politicians of that general section of the city who had taken one side or the other in the recent referendum. I am very much afraid I spoke to them and not to the children; but I could comfort myself then only by surmising, as I still do, that most of the regular attendants were entirely accustomed to the ministration of speakers who talked about something they did not fully understand.

Afterward I walked with Mr. Goodwyn and the opposition political leader, Joshua Wheary, across the street to Mr. Wheary's home. The car that had brought us had gone about its business, and Mr. Goodwyn was depending upon his colleague the city engineer, Mr. Budd, to come to get us. We waited. After two hours Mr. Budd arrived driving a Ford, the only passenger automobile owned by the city. It belonged, of course, to the engineering department. He apologized for being late but said he had had trouble with the car. I, at any rate, forgave him, and Goodwyn and I got in. It was late, already nearly dark. Mr. Goodwyn was visibly nervous. I, not being acquainted either with Mr. Budd or his chariot, was calm enough. Mr. Budd said he would like to take me to see a certain engineering project. I assented. It was at the bottom of a hill and it was necessary to double back. Mr. Budd said that there was no second gear on his Ford and the only way he could climb a hill was to climb it backward. I have never been so absolutely astonished, nor, I must confess, more thoroughly frightened. He put on an enormous amount of gas, stepped on the reverse, and we zigzagged up that hill over a rough dirt road with Goodwyn and me clinging on for dear life.

It was a real introduction to Bob Budd, one of the most engaging and delightful human beings I have ever known, one of the best city engineers I ever met, but one full of quirks and foibles, whose immediate conduct in any particular circumstance was as unpredictable as the wind.

The next day I settled myself at a desk in a corner of the Chamber of Commerce offices, began to find my way to the particular soda fountain where the leading citizens gathered for their half-past nine or ten o'clock Coca-Cola, took up the time of two or three real estate agents in house-hunting, and looked around. I knew that I had not yet met a certain test that was due to come on Tuesday.

That test was the weekly luncheon of the Rotary Club, where I would be expected to speak. There the measure would be taken of my capacity to consume the type of foods served by women of the several churches; there I would be subjected to the test of my ability to withstand community singing, in which I was painfully aware that I could never join; and there I would make my first speech before some fifty or sixty of the principal men of the town. It was an inescapable ordeal.

In the auditorium of the Young Men's Christian Association that afternoon (for the lunch was served at two o'clock, the customary hour in Petersburg for the midday meal), I was careful, or at least I tried to be, not to promise too much. I was careful not to seem to be afraid or appalled. I tried to express confidence in myself while at the same time calling on them and their fellow citizens for day-to-day, week-in-and-week-out support, without which neither the council that they had elected nor the manager that the council had chosen could possibly succeed.

The rest of the afternoon I spent with Mr. Harris going to the stores, banks, and business establishments. At the end of that day, whether it was justified or not, I thought that it had been a day well spent, that I had made progress, and that on the morrow I would be ready at last to tackle my job.

At the Rotary Club meeting in the YMCA I was overwhelmed by the warmth of my welcoming reception. I could not but be profoundly affected by the evident sincerity of this group of principal citizens as they individually and collectively tendered me their support and aid. Nor could I but be sobered and most seriously concerned by their great expectations. As is so often the case in any type of governmental reform, especially one that follows a stirring campaign, many people are led to expect a miracle in the field where miracles never come to pass. Thanking them for their welcome and promising them to do all that I could within my power and within the framework of the policies to be established by the council and the financial and physical resources of the city, I attempted also to warn them that not all would be smooth sailing and that not everything they hoped for could be accomplished. However, on that occasion, as is usual under such circumstances, they barely heard my warning, but they took my promises neat.

When I left Petersburg, a little more than three years later, I was able to say at another luncheon of the Rotary Club, this one given to tell me goodbye, that during all my time in Petersburg that club and its members had never once failed to support the policies adopted by the city council and had never once wavered in its help to me in administering the work of the municipality, and that even where there had been, as was inevitable, differences of opinion with respect to detail, there had not been at any time any but the most friendly and cordial personal relationships.

That first Rotary Club meeting in Petersburg was a good omen and a favorable augury for what I was about to try to do.

The immediate significance to me and my work of the influence of the deep-seated local traditions was plain. I would have little or no chance of success unless I endeavored to identify myself with the community and its history. Friendliness and informality had pervaded

the municipal government as well as the other community organizations to the extent that they were so informal as to be lacking in order.
The very first time I went to the courthouse unaccompanied, I saw
on the steps, leaning against one of the granite columns, a policeman.
I knew he was a policeman because he had on a blue uniform and
carried a policeman's club and revolver. The jacket of his uniform was
unbuttoned. He was smoking a cigar, and the whole effect was crowned
by his headpiece, a black derby hat. He nodded to me genially. I introduced myself as the new city manager. He grasped my hand and said
he was very glad to meet me, that he had heard a lot about me. He
did not stand erect. He did not throw away his cigar. He did not so
much as approach the attitude of the salute that for six long years I
had been accustomed to receive from any policeman I met.

I had been told that there was a vacancy in the position of chief of
police and that the little direction that the police force had had of
late had been supplied by one of the committees of the council. In
that minute I saw it would be folly for me to go too rapidly. I would
first have to find out what I could about how things had been done.
I then would have to do all I could to make myself, as rapidly and as
unobtrusively as possible, into an accepted Petersburger, and then, and
only then, would I be able to introduce order, discipline, and managerial direction into the municipal government.

The first thing was to find a place to live, a quest in which I was
joined by Mrs. Brownlow. The various real estate agencies had been
trying to sell us a house but had agreed upon one thing only: there was
not a suitable house nor indeed any vacant house within the city limits
of Petersburg. Very nice houses ranging from quite modest ones in
Colonial Heights across the Appomattox River to very handsome ones
in a new suburb called Walnut Hills were offered for sale. There was
nothing for rent in any suburb, and I was assured that there was no
house to rent in Petersburg. The price of the houses in Walnut Hills
was high, for the inflation of World War I and the wartime boom in
Petersburg had not yet deflated.

I knew, or thought I knew—at least I felt it in my bones—that while
everything might seem friendly and beautiful now, the town would
not tolerate a city manager who didn't live within the boundaries of
the city. My hunch was confirmed when I made my opinion known to
various people who were helping me find a place. Even the real estate

agents who wanted to sell their houses couldn't conceal from me the fact that they secretly approved my attitude.

Finally I found not a completely vacant house but a two-story frame duplex. The lower floor was occupied by the manager of the gas company; the upper floor was vacant. The floor plan was not good but the building was relatively new. It was clean. And my wife and I could find nothing better.

This humble house was on Harrison Street. Its front windows opened directly on the end of a short street only one block long leading from the principal street of the town. Harrison Street itself was in the main occupied by very old houses, some of them not in the best state of repair and some of them, at the upper end of the street, occupied by Negroes. Down the street a little way was a tobacco-stripping factory. The press announced our choice of residence some time before it was possible to bring our furniture and belongings down from Washington.

It was almost instantly apparent that, by and large, almost all the people I or my wife met heartily approved the modesty of our choice. One could almost overhear them saying, "Well, the new city manager does not intend to put on highfalutin airs." And, indeed, newspaper reporters and others told me that that was exactly what they were hearing around the town.

The reporters were asking me constantly what I was going to do about the city, what departments heads I was planning to keep, what ones I was going to dismiss, and the like. They had perforce to be content with what I repeated every day, that I would make no decisions and certainly no changes until after I had had time to acquaint myself thoroughly with the situation as it stood.

We were extremely fortunate in not having to deal with any organized politically partisan or factional opposition. There was little activity in local politics and almost no partisanship. Practically everybody who voted, voted the Democratic ticket. The Democratic nominees for local office were elected without question or opposition, and the relatively few Republicans in the city contented themselves with voting for their presidential electors and sometimes for governor and state offices, but participated in Democratic primaries and supported Democratic candidates for the local elective offices.

It is not to be taken, however, that there was not some latent opposition in the town to the new government. That latent opposition occasionally made itself vocal. One morning about two o'clock a terrific rain was beating upon the city. It was so heavy against the windows of our home and on the roof, accompanied as it was by hail, that I was wide awake. The telephone rang. I went to it.

A woman's voice asked, "Are you the city manager?"

I said, "Yes."

She said, "Well, there has been a dead cat lying in the front of my house for the last three days, and the city has done nothing about it."

"Madam," I asked, "where do you live?"

She gave me an address less than a block away from my house.

"Madam," I said, "did you telephone to the city stables about it?"

"I did not."

"Did you telephone the police about the dead cat?"

"I did not!"

"Did you call the health department?"

"I did nothing of the kind."

"Well, Madam, I am very sorry. It is very late and it is raining very hard, but I can assure you that I will have someone there the first thing in the morning to remove the dead cat."

"That's exactly the trouble," she shouted back. "This heavy rain has washed that dead cat down the sewer and now I never will know how long this new-fangled city government neglects its business."

CHAPTER XII

A REORGANIZATION OF THE CITY

The first thing I wanted to find out was how the city stood financially. The members of the council who had employed me didn't know. I had heard enough about the auditor to know that his reputation in the town was that of a demoniac Cerberus who under no circumstances would pay a bill or a claim against the city unless there was an adequate appropriation by the council for the particular purpose. He was German B. Gill, a Confederate veteran who had served in Forrest's cavalry—and he didn't know how the city stood either. His bookkeeping was of the single-entry type. He had no notion of the outstanding obligations and indeed he could not have been expected to know much about them. The city had no budget.

It was instantly apparent that the first necessary reform that I would institute would be a budget system, a modernized accounting system, and a central purchasing office. I assembled the heads of all the departments, talked to them about my plans, employed a certified public accountant's firm of national reputation, and set the machinery to work.

The city engineer had a one-room office in the old McGee Building, the use of the famous city car, and the assistance of one rodman and one Negro laborer. He supervised the superintendent of streets, although he had no authority over him.

The superintendent of streets, whose name was William T. Mulcaha, had at his disposal a considerable working force. It put in three days a week on street-repair work, street-cleaning, and the like, and the other three days on collecting garbage and other refuse. A few years before, the city had built a modern and efficient incinerator. However, the street-laboring force under Mr. Mulcaha was under the direction of the Street Committee of the council and the incinerator was under the control of the Health Committee of the council. The Street Com-

[117]

mittee successfully opposed the enactment of an ordinance which would require the separation of various kinds of refuse, with the result that garbage, trash, ashes, and cinders were intermingled. The Health Committee refused to accept at its incinerator such a mess of things, on the ground that no incinerator could be expected to burn ashes and cinders. This dispute had not been resolved; the incinerator stood idle and the dumps were most smelly. This seemed to me a relatively simple problem. I got the engineer, Robert D. Budd, the health officer, Robert A. Martin, and Mr. Mulcaha together to talk it over.

It was decided to recommend to the council an ordinance requiring the separation of ashes and incombustible material from other types of refuse and to divide Mr. Mulcaha's working force in half, with one section to work on street-cleaning and street repairs all the time and the other to work on the collecting and disposal of refuse. We divided the city into two zones, and the refuse was to be collected on alternate days from each zone. The council promptly passed the ordinance. While the newspapers carried the details, I didn't think that was sufficient notice, and so I had the requirements of the ordinance printed in simplified terms and the penalties for disobedience set out in bold-face type. These notices I had printed on heavy paper and delivered to every household and to every business establishment in the town by a policeman. Then I set up an engineering department, put Mr. Mulcaha under Mr. Budd, transferred the incinerator to the engineering department, and began an orderly attack on the neglected street repairs.

All around Petersburg there were deposits of gravelly clay, which Mr. Budd had developed into an admirable low-cost paving material. The scheme was to take this gravel with its clay binder directly from the gravel banks, spread it on the streets, roll it with a steam roller, known to everybody in those days as a willipus-wallipus, and then treat it with a binder of oil. This gave the appearance of an asphalt pavement and could be laid at a cost of less than one-tenth the price of standard asphalt on a concrete base. However, it had some defects. Whenever the surface suffered a slight abrasion, the traffic and the rainfall would combine to dig into it a neat, round pothole. When there were a sufficient number of potholes so that they could not be avoided by even a weaving motorcar, the going got very rough. The custom was to wait until a street was nearly impassable, and then the council would pass a specific special ordinance with a specific appropriation for the repair of that particular street.

It occurred to me that it would be much cheaper to keep the potholes from developing. It put that problem up to Budd and "Monkeyhead," as Mr. Mulcaha was called. Very soon they had a mule and a man and a wagon loaded with a quantity of gravel, a barrel of oil, and a heating kettle, all of which could stop the formations of potholes. That one device so cheaply operated ended the pothole nuisance. However, at the end of two or three years these gravel roads would begin to wave and roll and it was necessary then to resume the old rebuilding operation which had been in good use for many years.

The immediate attention I paid to the repair of the streets paid off handsomely in dividends of public gratitude and support, even if the great majority of the town was somewhat startled by the procedure I used. The first streets I treated were the worst streets, the slum streets, principally those in the Negro districts of the town. One day a man who had once been a member of the council and of its Street Committee telephoned me. He said that this new program was wonderful, but nothing had been done to the street in front of his house. I told him I would look into it. "Mr. Manager," he said, "I am willing to do anything within reason to get my street repaired. If I have to, I will get some burned cork and black my face."

I created a new position of executive secretary and to it appointed Edwin P. Goodwyn, who had been clerk of committees and who had in his memory a better record of the general obligations of the city than existed anywhere on paper. While the accountants were devising an accounting system and installing it and while I was busy at work on a budgetary scheme, I made the executive secretary the central purchasing agent for the city and also imposed upon him the task of the care of public buildings and public property. Then, as the accounting system progressed, I issued the necessary orders that no purchase should be made nor any obligation incurred except through the office of the executive secretary and that he could issue no purchase order until the auditor had been notified and the appropriation account obligated. Theretofore all the auditor had had was the cash balance in any appropriation account. He had had no notion of the obligations incurred against it. Thus, in just a few weeks' time the picture began to clear, and the balances left in the several appropriations made by the old council began to show themselves as actual available balances rather than as mere cash balances.

This enabled me to get a very good picture of the finances of the city, and at last, when the work was completed, I found that the city had a deficit for the year of about $50,000.

And here I got into my first difficulty in the town. I gave the figures to the newspapers. Of course I used the word "deficit" in its budgetary meaning of the difference between the anticipated tax revenues and the authorized appropriations. Some of the people thought that I meant that the old council had made away with $50,000. I received an indignant delegation headed by a distinguished man, Robert B. Gilliam, a highly esteemed lawyer and a Confederate veteran who had served as mayor of the city for the previous four years. With him were several former aldermen and councilmen.

Fortunately, what looked like the beginning of a political storm proved to be easily averted. I seized the occasion to talk to them about the problems as I had found them and described in detail the steps I had taken to solve them. I kept them for two hours while I explained the budget system, the central purchasing system, the new accounting system. I was successful in winning them over to enthusiastic support of the new program. As they went about the town and on the streets, and as they were met by inquiries, sometimes indignant, of their friends and associates on what many people had considered a reflection on their honor and their honesty, they proved to be my most effective advocates. It was they who told the town that what I was doing on the fiscal front was what ought to have been done years before.

One extremely interesting fiscal fact was turned up by Haskin and Sells, the accountants I had employed to set up the new system. Not once during all the years after the Civil War had the city neglected to pay the stated annual allotment into the sinking fund for the redemption of the bonded debt. All bonds that had been issued up to that time and, indeed, all through my administration were term bonds. The ordinances authorizing the issuing of the bonds always had set up a percentage standard for payments into the sinking fund. The astonishing discovery was that the sinking fund was too fat. Many of the annual payments had been set at as much as 6 per cent. The fund had been carefully administered and conserved. The demon auditor had seen to that, and, when he died (as he did early in my administration, to be succeeded by his assistant, Forrest Tucker), the sacredness of the sinking fund was absolute. On the basis of the report of the certified public accountants, we found that we could cut the annual payments into the sinking funds by $10,000 a year and yet have more in the fund than would be necessary to retire every outstanding bond issue at its maturity.

That meant that for eleven years in the future the payment into the sinking fund could be reduced by the amount of my salary. Thus it came about that by modernizing the accounting system I was able to save in my first year the full amount of my salary for a period of eleven years.

Dr. Robert A. Martin had served as health officer of Petersburg for two decades. He had relatively little to work with. His office occupied one large room in the old McGee Building, where he was assisted by a vital-statistics clerk and a bacteriologist. There also existed under him a venereal disease clinic, which had been installed during the time of Camp Lee. For many years Dr. Martin had been a member of the American Public Health Association and had maintained close and friendly relations with the United States Public Health Service. He had a program worked out in his mind for the improvement of his department, and a most intelligent program it was. I adopted it at once, almost *in toto,* and week by week on Tuesday nights when the council met I began to seek authority for its execution.

The principal feature of the plan was the establishment of a health center. No suitable building was owned by the city, but the council approved my plan to lease a commodious residence on a downtown street which was rapidly turning commercial. Here the health officer was installed along with an assistant, whose employment had been authorized by the council. Here we moved the bacteriologist, the vital-statistics section, and the venereal disease clinic, and here we set up a new unit, a well-baby clinic, and initiated an attack on the problem of infant mortality. The council on my recommendation adopted the standard milk ordinance which had recently been recommended to the cities of the country by the United States Public Health Service, and the employment of milk inspectors was authorized. This unit was also established in the center. Then we invited to the center some private health organizations, among them the Kings' Daughters, an Episcopal church organization which for many years had employed a nurse to help in dealing with tuberculosis. The Petersburg chapter of the American Red Cross came also. We employed additional public health nurses and benefited greatly and promptly by the co-operation given to our new health center by both the state and federal governments.

Among many other activities, we initiated a complete tubercular survey of the town, taking the reported cases and deaths from tuberculosis as a basis and then bringing into the clinic for examination every person we could find who had had either a familial or a domiciliary contact with a case of tuberculosis within the last decade. We did not have at that time the X-ray and other equipment now available for such a survey, but we did succeed in discovering a number of unrecognized and incipient cases. Perhaps the most beneficial effect of the survey was the education of the public to the tubercular problem, which prepared the ground for our intensive publicity campaign for better health controls and especially for better nutritional habits.

The well-baby clinic operated by the health officer in co-operation with the local chapter of the Red Cross turned out quite a different story statistically. The infant mortality rates, that is the number of deaths per thousand births, was reduced in the very first year of operation from 139 to 104. Among the white people the rate was decreased from 97 to 85, while among the Negro people there was a startling reduction from 210 to 126.

As a part of the campaign to reduce the infant mortality throughout the country, the Children's Bureau in Washington, then headed by Miss Julia Lathrop, had prepared a model ordinance for the licensing and control of midwives. Miss Lathrop sent me a copy of the ordinance, which had been developed but recently. It made as a condition for granting of the license an examination to be conducted by the health officer. The council, at my suggestion, adopted the ordinance but postponed its effective date for three months in order that the health department might set up a training school. The Children's Bureau supplied the city with model examination schemes and also with texts prepared for a training school. There were then forty-one midwives practicing in Petersburg, all but two or three of them Negroes. The school was started at the health center. The midwives were told to come and each of them was given a copy of the textbook. The difficulty was that more than half of them were illiterate.

One of the sections of the text was concerned with the care of prematurely born babies. It contained instructions for the building of home-made incubators, complete with drawings and illustrations. One morning Dr. Martin and Miss Ada Beaumont, the nurse, came into my office with a protest. They said that the training school for midwives was a terrible waste of time, that the women couldn't read or write, that the health officer and the nurses already knew who were the good midwives and who were the poor ones, and that there was no sense in going along with the program. To support their objections, they showed me the section of the book on the construction of home-made incubators.

I told them that perhaps they were right but I had promised Miss Lathrop in Washington that we would go through with the training school and would report the results directly to her, since she was very eager to know what happened in the field when her new program of control of midwives was put into effect. They shook their heads sadly and left.

When the training school was over, the examinations were held and twelve of the midwives passed muster and were duly licensed. Dr. Martin told me that they were the twelve that he and Miss Beaumont would have licensed if I hadn't forced him to go on with the school.

Then one day a few weeks later two excited persons burst into my office. They were Dr. Martin and Miss Beaumont.

Dr. Martin said, "Get in my car and come with us immediately."

I tried to get out of them what it was all about but they said, "No, we want to show you. We do not want to tell you."

I stopped everything and got in the car, and Miss Beaumont drove us to Pocahontas Island, which was just about the worst slum then left in Petersburg. There they took me to a little house, and there was the oldest one of the newly licensed midwives, one who had never learned to read or write. But she could see pictures. There in bed was the old midwife's granddaughter and by the bed was a home-made incubator. It consisted of a carton which had once contained packages of Quaker Oats. The necessary heat was furnished by a kerosene lantern. In that incubator lay a seven-month-term baby.

No one could have been more delighted than the health officer, the nurse, or the midwife-great-grandmother, unless, indeed, it was I. Twenty-five years later I got a letter from Atlanta from a graduate of the medical school of Spelman College. She wrote to me to thank me for establishing that school for midwives, which had enabled her great-grandmother, the old midwife, to save her life when she was prematurely born, a life she was determined to devote to the healing art.

While the bacteriologist in the health department had been making routine examinations of samples of the water from the city waterworks for many years, there were other sources of water used in the city which had theretofore not been subjected to examination. At once we made a routine examination of the springs and wells used locally in various parts of the city. Some of these we found contaminated, and we closed them.

One case was that of a spring in Central Park. Central Park, which originally had been known as Poplar Lawn, was situated in the very center of the very best residential district of the city. The waters of Poplar Lawn Spring had been reputed for two centuries to have medicinal qualities of high curative value for any number of diseases. Every day people from all over the town and some from outside the city were wont to come to the spring with their bottles and jugs and take home the water to drink in order to cure their many illnesses.

The bacteriological examination showed that the waters of the spring were polluted. It was no wonder, since it stood on the banks of Lieutenant Run, a stream that ran diagonally across the park and was paralleled by a sanitary sewer. Dr. Martin, Mr. Budd, and I held a consultation. We decided on a scheme to remove the potential danger to health in a manner that would not stir up a community ruckus.

We went in one morning about one o'clock, deflected the spring water into the sewer and hooked the spring outlet up with the chlorinated water supply of the city. The last time I heard anything about Poplar Lawn Spring some of the faithful were still bringing their bottles and their jugs to be filled with its life-giving waters. There was nothing in the newspapers; there was no public outcry; and the people who lived around the park, when they saw the disturbance of the earth the next morning after our midnight raid, simply assumed that the city had been repairing a broken sewer line.

However, some of our attempts at improvement did not get by so smoothly or successfully. One of the earliest tasks we undertook was to pave Wythe Street, which ran from the main street of the city, Sycamore, to Main Street in Blandford and was the route taken by most of the funerals of the persons to be buried in Blandford Cemetery.

It was paved with cobblestones, it carried a streetcar line, and it was uneven in width. It ran downgrade to a crossing of Lieutenant Run and then up sharply toward Blandford. To pave it required straightening the lines on both sides, adjusting the width, and also adjusting the vertical curves. At the eastern end, nearest the cemetery, the old street lines converged into a funnel. It was necessary, to adjust the width of the street, to cut off a triangular strip of ground on one side or the other. The newspapers carried a map of the proposed improvement.

Then the storm struck. Representatives of the Daughters of the American Revolution and other patriotic societies descended upon me in force. They said that the very piece of land that we were about to dig into should be preserved because it was the resting place of the bodies of the patriot Continental soldiers who fell in the course of Lafayette's assault on Lord Cornwallis in the Battle of Petersburg in the Revolutionary War.

I sent for Mr. Budd. It was soon apparent that it made no difference which side of the street we cut. The protestants were perfectly willing that we cut on the other side, because they said the bodies buried there were those of the British soldiers who fell in the Revolutionary battle.

A few days later when the work was actually under way a most agitated City Engineer Budd appeared in my office. He had with him several handfuls of metal. They were belt buckles and buttons identifying not only Virginia troops but troops from Maryland, Delaware, and New Jersey.

I told him to keep quiet. Later that day Mr. Budd suggested that he would like under the cover of darkness to do a little experimental digging on the other side of the road. I not only said "All right" but said I would go with him. The experimental digging was undertaken shortly after midnight and there we found the belt buckles and the buttons of the troops of His Majesty George III. It was too late to change sides of the street. There was nothing to do but to keep the secret, which I suspect until this moment has never been revealed.

At the very beginning of my service in Petersburg, I was faced with a perplexing problem with respect to the police force. There was a vacancy in the position of chief, and it did not seem to me that I could discover in the force anybody then prepared to fill the job. The fire department was fairly well organized and equipped and, although the fire chief was quite old, his assistant was young, vigorous, and intelligent. I decided to recommend to the council the establishment of a department of public safety at the head of which I could place a qualified man as director and under him co-ordinate the services of the two uniformed forces. The department would also take over the problem of building, electrical, and plumbing inspection. Having gained the council's consent, I actually offered the position to two or three residents of Petersburg whom I believed to be qualified, but they all declined.

One day Mr. A. M. Pennybacker, the secretary of the Young Men's Christian Association and a leading member of the recently organized Community Council, came to tell me that his brother-in-law, John Otey Walker, who had been a major in the American Expeditionary Force and who after the armistice had joined General Goethal's import and export concern in New York, was out of a job because of the collapse of General Goethal's corporation, a victim of the postwar depression of 1921. He said that he had advised Major Walker to come to see me and to apply for the vacant post of director of public safety. Major Walker came. I interviewed him. I considered him to be qualified and appointed him.

Walker came to Petersburg and assumed his new station, and we began to lay out plans for the improvement of the police and fire services. For the time being he took direct personal command of the police force. We decided to give some of the men of both forces more intensive professional training than they ever had had an opportunity to take. The assistant fire chief and one of the firemen we sent to the New York City Fire Department Training School, and we likewise sent two men of the police department to the New York City Police Training School, through an arrangement that I made with my friend Colonel Arthur Woods, then police commissioner of New York.

One of the first things Major Walker did was to take over personally the task of drilling the police force, which had about fifty members, and to insist on proper uniforms, proper dress, and proper posture. The men responded with enthusiasm to this innovation and it soon was apparent that they had more pride in their work than before. Also about that time the Civil Service Assembly, an organization of civil service officials in the United States and Canada, was undertaking to elaborate a series of tests for police officers. I had participated to some extent in this endeavor when I was District commissioner, and when the tests were ready I was given the first opportunity to try them out.

I had decided to establish in Petersburg, as I already had done in Washington, a women's bureau. There were two vacancies in the ranks of the privates authorized by the council. I asked Lieutenant Mina C. Van Winkle, the head of the Washington Women's Bureau, to come to Petersburg to talk over the proposed innovation, which literally was a revolutionary one, with the women's clubs and church groups. She found a ready and even an enthusiastic response. Thereupon I appointed two women privates, Mrs. Minnie Rowland, a white woman who had been extraordinarily successful in doing church-group social work among delinquent girls, and Mrs. Lizzie Forbes, a Negro who also had been successful in voluntary social work for church groups among the people of her race.

To appoint a Negro to the police force in Petersburg at that time was chancy business. It had not been so very long in the memories of Petersburgers since 1884, when for the first time after the Civil War the city government was captured by the Democrats, an all-Negro police force dismissed, and an all-white police force appointed.

Foreseeing possible unfavorable reactions, Mrs. Brownlow and I prepared the way by talking with Walter Edward Harris, the editor of the local newspapers, and, more than that, by assembling an advisory committee of the leading women of the town who were to co-operate with the newly established Women's Bureau.

The day that Mrs. Rowland and Mrs. Forbes were sworn in as members of the police force, this committee of the most prominent ladies in the town, women high in social rank and representatives of the oldest and wealthiest families, came to the police headquarters, where they were photographed with Mrs. Rowland and Mrs. Forbes. The Petersburg papers at that time had few facilities for running illustrations, but that particular photograph was sent to Richmond; a cut was made, and it appeared in the Petersburg papers.

After that public display of high social approval, not one word of protest was uttered in sufficiently loud tones for me or Major Walker to hear it.

The vacancies in the police force having been filled, the men having been drilled and their morale enhanced, Major Walker decided the time had come to apply the Civil Service Assembly testing technique. Every incumbent of the force, fifty in all, including Major Walker, took the examination. The results were sent to Princeton to be scored. Major Walker himself came out at the head of the list. But very, very closely behind him was Mrs. Lizzie Forbes, the only Negro on the force, and, as one of the cops later remarked, "a woman at that!"

A few of the pieces of fire department equipment were horse-drawn, steam-pumping engines. In the former administration, the city had desired to substitute motor equipment, but the great motor pumpers were too expensive. Major Walker and I decided to retire the horses but to keep the steam engines, substituting for the beautiful fire horses not-so-beautiful Fordson tractors. It worked and it saved money. A routine fire inspection service was also installed. Some of the firemen in rotation were assigned to inspect premises and, over a period of several months, covered every structure in the city. This led to a general cleanup of basements and the destruction of many small outbuildings and resulted in a very marked drop in fire losses and also in an enormously improved morale among the firemen.

One major difficulty with respect to the police department was that it had too few men, yet it was evident that it would be extremely difficult for the city to afford any considerable increase in the force. That led Major Walker to study how to improve its efficiency. A number of men were necessarily assigned to the detective force, the non-uniformed staff of the department whose work was so essential to peace and order. Among these men we discovered considerable skills and native talent, the application of which was greatly improved by the instruction the men received in the New York City Police Training School. The traffic situation, already becoming complex, was aggravated by the necessity of control occasioned by the presence of railroad tracks running through the town, particularly at a point where the traffic on Route 1 from New York to Miami had to be guided. The parking problem already was showing its ugly head, and these things necessitated the assignment of several men to traffic duty.

Major Walker then came up with a novel plan for the patrol. It was simply to mount the patrolmen in Ford cars so that the entire city could be under patrol instead of the very small portion the force was able to cover by foot patrol. Of course that was long before the day of radio-controlled cars, but even then the council was persuaded to accept my recommendation and furnish the money for the requisite number of cars. The result of the motorcar patrol was an almost instantaneous drop in complaints of petty thievery and disorderly and noise-making disturbances in back streets and alleys. So far as I know it was the first completely motorized police force in the country.

Of course in those days the principal police problem anywhere was bootlegging. We made many arrests. We got many convictions, but still the illicit trade in alcoholic beverages continued. There was one particular place where it hurt and hurt deep. For months and months the police kept their eyes peeled on an old residential building diagonally across the street from police headquarters. Time and time again, perfectly sober persons were seen to go into the house and a few hours later to come out reeling. The judge was prompt in issuing search warrants. The house was searched, but nothing was found.

Then one day Mrs. Forbes, the Negro policewoman, came in with a tale. She had arrested a young Negro girl for shoplifting and had discovered that the girl was half-tight. She had asked her where she got her liquor. The girl had said she got it from a truck driver who supplied the liquor to the house across the street from the police station.

"But," said Mrs. Forbes, "we have searched that house dozens of times and never found the liquor."

"Oh," said the girl, "on the stair landing going up to the second floor you turn on the gas jet and the liquor will flow. My friend the truck driver pours it into a chute in the house around the corner and up the hill, four doors away."

We got another search warrant. The gas jet was a faucet from which flowed white mule corn liquor. After more search warrants and more exploration we found a long copper trough leading from a copper tank in the rear of a house four doors away and up the hill, some thirty feet higher than the level of the stair landing.

The destruction of that easily operated blind tiger may not have done very much to stop the flow of moonshine into the city of Petersburg, but it certainly relieved the feelings of the police department from top to bottom. It was not, perhaps, that every member of the police force was so much concerned with the suppression of the illicit liquor trade, but all were eager to stop the tittering and giggling about the house across the street.

That the method of resolving municipal problems merely by enlisting highly skilled and efficient personnel is not infallible was made clear to me by another incident. By this time I had come to believe that no city manager anywhere could possibly have a more efficient and better-qualified staff than I had in Petersburg. The purchasing agent and custodian of public property was alert, dedicated to his duty, and seemingly possessed of inexhaustible energy. The city engineer was the best city engineer I ever met. The director of public safety was industrious, skilful, inventive, completely devoted to his work. On one occasion an old Negro came into the headquarters of the police and demanded to see Major Walker. The sergeant on duty tried to deflect him to the chief of police.

"No, Boss," he said, "I've got to see the top man. I am in bad trouble."

After this had gone on for some time, Major Walker said, "Have him come in. I will talk to him."

The old man got into Walker's office and said, "I'm in trouble."

"What trouble?"

"My horse fell in the well."

"Is he dead?"

"Yes, I think he is dead. There is a lot of water in there and all you can see is the heels of his hind legs sticking up out of the water."

Just at that juncture, into Major Walker's office came the city engineer, Mr. Budd, and the executive secretary, Mr. Goodwyn. Major Walker repeated to them the story of the old man's difficulties. They found out from him that the well was on property on Halifax Street at the extreme edge of the city limits. The three high officers decided to go out and see about the trouble. They invited the old man to go with them, piled into the engineer's car, and went out to Halifax Street. There in the rear of a residence, the last one on the street before it faded into Dinwiddie County, was a well. The well had had a wooden covering. The wood had rotted. The horse had stepped up onto the platform, had broken through, and had dived head downward into the water. Only his hind heels showed.

What to do?

The three chiefs of departments put their heads together. The purchasing agent moved in first. He said, "We have got to get the horse out of the well. I'll go call up the two hide-and-tallow concerns and see if they will come out and take the horse out for his hide and carcass."

Goodwyn disappeared to find a telephone at a nearby drugstore. After a while he returned crestfallen. Neither of the concerns would undertake the task. Private enterprise having failed, there was nothing left but for the government to come in. The city engineer took over. He made a rapid calculation of the cost of erecting a gin pole, block and tackle, and the like and estimated the engineering cost of taking the dead body of the horse out of the well. It ran up to a considerable figure. That he presented to his colleagues. The cost was too high. Then they turned to the old man and said, "The horse is dead. We don't think we can get him out of here. Don't you think the best idea would be just to fill up the well and bury him there?"

The old man sadly and dejectedly nodded his head and said, "I guess that is all we can do."

Close by, Mr. Mulcaha, with a gang of street laborers, was engaged with a steam shovel in excavating gravel and clay from a nearby bank and loading it into six-ton Mack trucks for dispatch to a street-rebuilding job. Mr. Budd called him and explained the situation. Two panels of the fence were let down, and in just a few minutes truckloads of earth had gone into the well, the platform had been taken away, and a little rounded mound of clay and gravel had been patted down over the grave of the horse.

Then, turning to the old man, Major Walker said, "We are very sorry for you and for the horse, but this looked like the only thing we could do, since the horse was already dead."

"Yes sir, yes sir, Boss, I guess it was the only thing you could do, but I can't help wondering what Mrs. Ferguson is going to say when she gets home tomorrow."

"Who is Mrs. Ferguson?" asked all three public administrators in one breath.

"She is the lady what owns the well."

It wasn't long until the city manager received an unexpected, unscheduled, and unappointed delegation of three of his most trusted and devoted department heads.

It happened that I knew Mrs. Ferguson. She had been trying to get city water out to her house for some time without putting up the deposit that the city ordinance required in such cases—a deposit that would be reimbursed to her by crediting it to her ensuing water bills until the water bills had absorbed the amount. She was unwilling to obey the ordinance. She had gone away. According to the old man, she was due back in Petersburg the next morning. The city engineer received along with my commiseration a peremptory order: "See to it, even if you have to work all night, that when Mrs. Ferguson gets back tomorrow morning she will have water and a sewer laid on."

Three better men had never dealt with an administrative problem, but no one of them had extended his curiosity far enough to ask the single question: "Whose well is it?"

What early became a problem of great importance to me and of even deeper concern to my wife was the almost total lack of any facilities for public welfare work in Petersburg. With Mrs. Brownlow's help, I began immediately to see what could be devised or improvised to make up for this deficiency. I was encouraged from the very beginning by the knowledge that the community already had sensed the difficulty. Just before I came to Petersburg a survey had been made by a New York organization, and as a result a community council was organized in the very week of my advent, and I was chosen a member of that council.

Under the aegis of the Community Council, various informal arrangements were set up to try to solve the difficulty. The first was the organization of a family service agency, which was called, for convenience and because the title was well known, the Associated Charities. It was some time, however, before any funds could be provided for a trained family service worker, and so the very first thing we did was to set up a confidential exchange. Through the Community Council we persuaded agencies such as the Red Cross, the Kings' Daughters of the Episcopal Church, the Salvation Army, and the charitable committees of most of the principal churches of the town, to report to the confidential exchange the names of their clients and the amounts of relief given to them. This exchange we established in the health center. Many of the churches were utterly astonished to discover that some of their clients were not nearly so needy as they had pretended and some of the recipients were on the list of as many as five or six different churches and agencies. That discovery alone (which from experience Mrs. Brownlow and I had confidently anticipated) made it possible to raise sufficient funds by public subscription and by an additional appropriation from the council to employ a most efficient secretary, who carried on until a trained family caseworker could be found.

Very shortly after our arrival in Petersburg, Mrs. Brownlow was appointed a member of the State Children's Code Commission by Governor Westmoreland Davis. That commission set to work to modernize the public welfare machinery of the state. The men and women who were appointed to it were devoted and industrious persons. Their work terminated in a report recommending to the governor and to the legislature twenty-one different statutes. With the hearty support of both houses of the legislature, eighteen of these recommendations were enacted into statutes and signed by the succeeding governor, E. Lee Trinkle.

One of them set up the State Department of Public Welfare to be headed by a commissioner to be appointed by the governor. It was to take over the functions formerly delegated to the State Board of Charities and Corrections and various other agencies. There also was provision for the establishment in the cities and counties of local departments of public welfare and, furthermore, a provision for united action by cities and counties in the field of institutional care for the indigent and diseased and also for misdemeanants.

As soon as this authority was granted by the state, the Petersburg City Council set up a department of public welfare. Neither the financial resources of the city nor the local needs indicated the desirability of appointing a full-time person to the position, so, instead, the council authorized the city manager to act in the capacity of director of public welfare.

The reorganization of the state welfare functions gave the newly created State Department of Public Welfare and its director, who now was to report directly to the governor of the state and not, as under the old law, to the Board of Charities, a much greater degree of control over, supervision of, and influence upon the welfare functions throughout the state. It centered in one man the executive responsibility for all the welfare functions of the state, including the institutional supervision of state hospitals for the mentally ill; for all prisons, from the state penitentiary down to and including the county and city jails; and for the organization of community services for relief. The secretary of the State Board of Charities and Correction had had some responsibility for local correctional institutions, but it was confined essentially to inspectional visits.

The secretary of the old State Board of Charities and Correction had been Dr. James T. Mastin. I had known Dr. Mastin in Washington before I came to Petersburg and had a most favorable opinion of his wisdom, his humanity, and his diplomatic skill.

One day shortly after I became city manager of Petersburg a young man came into my office and said he was an assistant to Dr. Mastin. He also said that he had come over to Petersburg to inspect the jail. Now the jail was a correctional and penal institution wholly under the direction of the city sergeant and jailer, an elected official who was not subject in any way whatever to the control of the city manager.

I asked the young man what he thought of the Petersburg jail. He was a personable young man. His face was illuminated by a charming smile. He spoke smoothly and rapidly. He skilfully evaded a reply to my question until I had repeated it three times.

Then when at last I forced him to answer, he began to tell me that the Petersburg jail was a very good jail. Unfortunately I accepted his reply as an absolute opinion, not at all sensing the fact that he was offering an opinion of its relative position among other jails in Virginia. I exploded.

"Young man," I said, "I don't know who you are and I don't even know your name because I didn't quite get it when Miss Bird [Miss Mary H. Bird, my most efficient secretary] gave it to me, but one thing I do know: if you are the inspector of jails and prisons for the State Board of Charities and Correction, you are utterly and absolutely incompetent and totally unfit for your job."

The young man rose and said, "Thank you, sir. My name is Frank Bane."

That was the beginning of a beautiful friendship which was to endure through four decades of close and intimate association in many fields of public administration.

Under my newly acquired capacity not only as a city manager but as a director of public welfare and in what I assumed to be my capacity as a community leader, it seemed to me that one of the greatest lacks was in the field of recreation. A great unused tract of land, which had been acquired by the city before the Civil War as a watershed for its water supply, had within it some practically unspoiled earthworks, which had been thrown up in the engineering school of the Confederacy under General Beauregard. Its discovery led me to engage upon a rapid, even a radical, development of public recreational facilities.

The tract of land comprised about seven hundred acres without a

Louis Brownlow, July, 1914

PARADE IN HONOR OF THE SOLDIERS OF THE DISTRICT OF COLUMBIA, 1917

Left to right: Louis Brownlow, Commissioner of the District of Columbia; William F. Gude, President of the Board of Trade, District of Columbia; unidentified man; Woodrow Wilson; Robert Harper, President of the Chamber of Commerce, District of

KNOXVILLE CABINET, 1926

Left to right: Louis Brownlow, City Manager; Major John O. Walker, Director of Public Safety; John C. Borden, Director of Finance; Alexander Harris, Director of Public Service; Frank Bane, Director of Public Welfare; William H. Peters, Director of Law.

MR. AND MRS. BROWNLOW ABOARD SHIP

CHARLES E. MERRIAM   FRANK O. LOWDEN   BEARDSLEY RUML

road or any other access except a few faintly outlined footpaths. It was used, so far as I could find out, only as a hideaway for an occasional moonshine still. With its hilly terrain, with its lake which had long been abandoned as a water supply, with its great trees and its wide open spaces, it seemed to me an ideal spot for the development of a park.

One afternoon my wife and I, with Mr. and Mrs. Budd, "surveyed" it—laid out automobile drives and foot walks and envisaged a swimming pool.

The question came: How to finance its development? The town had no golf and country club. It needed one. I proposed a country club and suggested that the city sell enough land for a club to pay for the development of the park with a swimming lake, tennis courts, baseball diamonds, and a series of paths and roads. The council approved. The club was organized. The real estate deal was made. I was active in the development of the new club as well as the park and found adequate support for both schemes.

Once Mr. Budd's and my plan for the creation of the park around the old Willcox reservoir was approved, there remained but one thing to do. Mr. Budd, being an engineer, mildly suggested that the park be named for General P. G. T. Beauregard, who was in charge of military engineer's training school in 1861 and under whose command the earthworks so excellently preserved in the tract of land were built. However, it didn't seem to Mayor Zimmer and the other members of the council, nor did it to me, that there was sufficient identification of Petersburg with General Beauregard. In Petersburg, where the Confederacy had met its final defeat, there was almost no other possible choice of a name but that of General Robert E. Lee.

I also was mindful of the great need for recreation for the small fry. In the center of town, Central Park, or Poplar Lawn, had been given to the city by the Bolling family in memory of the Petersburg contingent of troops sent to the second war of independence, the War of 1812. There was a West End Park in a poorer section close to the city's great landholdings—the fair grounds and the almshouse gardens and fields, and then also there was a tract of land in Blandford, which we discovered had been given to the city as a park as early as 1810 but which never had been put to use.

I had become very much interested in the training of young men for municipal administration, an educational effort which then was largely centered in New York under the direction of the National Institute for Public Administration, which had founded and was maintaining a training school for municipal administrators and particularly, with the assistance of the National Municipal League, for budding city managers. At the head of that school was Dr. Charles A. Beard, who, just about the time I went to Petersburg, had turned over the direction of the school to Luther H. Gulick, who was assisted not only by the members of his own staff but also by William E. Mosher. Dr. Mosher in particular had not only had a very great influence on the curriculum of the school but had insisted upon recruiting young men who were willing and financially able to undertake approximately one year of uncompensated work in the offices of the city managers or in municipal research bureaus scattered over the country. Dr. Mosher recommended to me one such student. The young man had received a degree in mechanical engineering from Stevens Institute, had been in the air force toward the end of World War I, and was willing, so Dr. Mosher said, to come and spend a year in Petersburg to assist me in my administrative work. The title that Dr. Mosher chose for him was "student assistant to the city manager." The young man came to join me and immediately began to prove his worth. He had been indoctrinated in the theories of economy and efficiency. He was determined to be economical and immediately put into effect one of his efforts at saving money. The first thing he started to save on was typewriter ribbons. At the very beginning, at the end of a memorandum, he signed himself, "The Student Assistant to the City Manager." That wore out an awful lot of typewriter ribbons. So, strictly in the interest of economy, he dropped the word "student," and then later, further pursuing his ideal and mindful of his training, he dropped "to the." That left him signing himself "Assistant City Manager." That particular designation did not make a tremendous hit with the rest of my staff.

However, the young man demonstrated his ability and skill and devotion in many other respects. He introduced order into my office. He revised and improved the reporting scheme which I had established, and by which the heads of various departments kept me informed through daily and weekly and monthly reports of their activities. I had been content to make my reports to the council and to the people through newspaper articles. He, without interfering with my plans, reviewed and reported textually to the council and to the public in formal reports what the city had been doing.

More importantly, however, the young man demonstrated that he was greatly interested in children. I therefore assigned to him the job of organizing the playground system for the city.

I mention him particularly, not only because of the great service he rendered to Petersburg and to the city manager at that time, but also because of some of his subsequent career and the effect that my contact with him had on some details of the future training for public administration. He left me to become head of a municipal research bureau of the Newark Chamber of Commerce. While he was in Newark, he went frequently to New York. And there he met Ruth Brownlow, my niece, the daughter of my elder brother. He married her. His name is John B. Blandford, Jr., a name writ large in the annals of public administration in this and in other countries. My kinship to him I have always called "nepotism ex post facto."

Later, when I had become city manager of Knoxville and the training school in New York had been moved to Syracuse University, again on the nomination of Dr. Mosher I accepted in my office a graduate of his school for a year's free service to complete his training. I told Dr. Mosher about the resentment that the implication of "assistant city manager" had caused, so we decided to call the new student an "apprentice." That too was most unfortunate. It gave the impression to the heads of departments and to the staff of the city that he was just a young fellow who came along with the plumber to be sent back for the tools. Then again, while I still was in Knoxville, I took another graduate from the Maxwell School at Syracuse University, presided over by Dr. Mosher, and again there was some difficulty about the title to give him. In Knoxville the city managed a city hospital, and therefore the city council was entirely accustomed to the use of the word "interne," so for that young man we invented the title "interne in public administration," which, so far as I can discover, was its first use in that sense in the country.

To carry on my program, I tried to keep in as close touch as possible with the general public. That meant that I was continually making speeches at all sorts of club meetings, in the churches, to the parent-teachers' clubs, to women's clubs, and the like. But most of all, as was quite natural considering my former profession, I relied upon the newspapers. The editor of the two newspapers (reduced to one by a consolidation of the morning *Index-Appeal* with the *Evening Progress* into the *Progress Index* during my time in Petersburg), my old friend Walter Edward Harris, I saw every day. The reporters I naturally saw each day. I tried insofar as possible to tell them and, through them, the public not only what was going on at the moment but what plans were being made for the future. About the forward program, it was not always possible to be either specific or candid, since many things of that nature were necessarily subject to higher approval, sometimes by the city council and sometimes by the council in concert with other groups. Also, sometimes their nature was such that premature announcement would not only prove disappointing but might tend to prevent their initiation.

Occasionally, I attempted to extend my program of public information even further. For instance, at the end of the first full year when the new systems were installed and all the primary organizational machinery was set up, I prepared a detailed budget which I submitted to the City Council and asked for an intensive review and tentative approval, with the idea that the council actually would not vote the budget until it had contrived a budget exposition on a large scale.

The City Council met every Tuesday night. The newspapermen were always there, of course. Sometimes a few individuals came when some problem in which they were particularly interested was on the agenda, but the general public was but sparsely represented. Considering the annual budget to be a program of work for the year, a program involving a commitment of the funds and the taxpayers' contributions, the mayor and council issued an invitation to the general public to come to a special meeting of the council to be held in the auditorium of the high school. At that meeting the tax rate for the new year, as well as the detailed particular appropriations, was to be announced. Many publicity devices were employed to drum up attendance, and the council evoked the co-operation of many, many organizations to that end.

When the night of the special council meeting came, the high school auditorium, seating 1,700 persons, was crowded. The mayor called the meeting to order and then asked me as city manager to submit the annual budget. That I did, not only by setting up the estimates of the revenues for the year—the proposed appropriations for the year in dollars and cents—but also by explaining, or attempting to explain, in every part of the budget, the program of work to be undertaken by the city, which would be paid for out of the budget allowances.

The mayor had told me that almost the only serious adverse criticism he had heard of the new administration was the high salary paid to the city manager. On that account I felt justified in including some extra-budgetary figures that covered the expenditures for those local governmental units which were not subject to the council but to the officers who were elected by the people. Some of these were fee officers. I had obtained from the state capital in Richmond the amount of their remuneration. My salary was $10,000. When I read the report and showed that the city sergeant and jailer and the clerk of the courts received annual remuneration considerably greater than my salary, there were gasps of astonishment from all over the auditorium. These elected officers were all seated on the stage with the members of the council. They had not been apprised of what I was about to do. Perhaps it was unfair of me to make such a public revelation, but it at least had the effect, for the rest of the time I was in Petersburg, of relieving the mayor and the other members of the council of that particular criticism.

The undertaking of a program of capital improvements to be financed by bond issues required a great deal of work by the city administration and most careful consideration by the council, but in my estimation it also demanded a very wide and thorough exposition before the public. This was undertaken not only by newspaper articles but by attendance at many group meetings with intensive explanations not only by the mayor and me but by Mr. Budd, the engineer, Dr. Martin, the health officer, and others. What actually was undertaken was a conservative program of permanent street-paving to cover principal arterial and supporting highways, the construction of two new schoolhouses for Negro pupils, and the extension of the water and sewer system to serve practically all the city.

However, the greatest single need in the town was a new bridge over the Appomattox River. Petersburg, being on the national highway, Route 1, with no provision for a bypass, carried already in the early 1920's a very heavy traffic burden along two of its principal streets and then northward across the Appomattox. There it crossed a low-level wooden bridge, which by any account must be rated as utterly inadequate.

The council directed me to undertake negotiations for the erection of a new bridge. That was no light task. It required not only consent but a division of the cost of construction among several agencies: the city, the state highway department of Virginia, the Norfolk and Western Railroad, the Atlantic Coastline Railroad, the Richmond and Petersburg Interurban and Electric System, and (at least as far as consent was concerned) the United States government, which had general control of the bridges. In addition, in Petersburg, which was at the head of navigation of the Appomattox River, the federal government not only had control of port and harbor facilities but incidentally owned directly certain parcels of land that would be needed for the footings.

These negotiations were begun very shortly after I took office. They continued until almost the very hour of my departure, although I did stay in Petersburg until after the bridge had been designed and put under contract and its construction begun. It was finished and dedicated after I left. Nothing I ever attempted was more difficult and, by the same token, nothing I ever accomplished was more successful, if measured only by the then prevailing standards of transit, transport, transportation, traffic, and intergovernmental interco-operation of the early 1920's.

CHAPTER XIII

ORGANIZATIONAL WORK BEGINS

Among the experiences I had in Petersburg were my contacts with professional and jurisdictional organizations in the field of public administration.

My appointment as city manager of Petersburg in September, 1920, brought me at once welcoming letters and telephone calls from other city managers in Virginia, each of whom offered to help me in any way he could. Two of these invitations were so phrased that I accepted them immediately. I went to Norfolk to see Charles E. Ashburner. Mr. Ashburner, an English-born engineer who had made an outstanding record in railroad work, had been appointed "general manager" of Staunton, Virginia, in 1908, thus becoming the first city manager in the United States. Later, he had served as manager of Springfield, Ohio, and now was back in Virginia as manager of Norfolk. Ashburner was fully conscious of his general responsibility as a pioneer in municipal management and was greatly interested in the extension of the new profession, as well as being, I suspect, quite eager to make a careful inspection of each new recruit as soon as he could. He gave me a great deal of useful advice about my relationships with the "constitutional" elected officials of the city and much good guidance about state offices I would find myself dealing with and the particular persons who probably would be most helpful. I also went to Lynchburg to see the manager there, Edward A. Beck. Petersburg and Lynchburg had about the same population, just a little over 30,000 each. Lynchburg was a much richer town. Its industrial workers had a higher wage level and the city itself was wealthier and in many respects more progressive. I at once acceded to Beck's suggestion that we establish cost accounting procedures in the field of public works and make monthly exchanges of our experiences. The two towns, while of the same population, were entirely different in other respects. The topography of Petersburg was generally level, its drainage problem simple, and its street and highway pattern relatively regular, whereas Lynchburg was a hilly, almost mountainous town with sharp and sudden changes in levels that made public works more expensive to construct and more costly to maintain. Our monthly exchange of cost data was not designed as a dollars and cents contest between the two places but rather as a device to measure, if possible, the differentiations imposed by topography as well as by variant economic factors. Every water main laid, every sewer trench dug, every street paved, every street cleaned, every truckload of garbage and trash collected, so it turned out, always cost more in Lynchburg than it did in Petersburg. It was a good thing that Lynchburg was wealthier, since its taxpayers were compelled eternally to pay the extra topographical tax.

The exchange of information with these and other city managers of Virginia was so immediately helpful that I decided at once to attend the meeting of the national City Managers' Association in Cincinnati to seek further enlightenment. The association met in mid-November, just two months after I had taken office in Petersburg and before I had had the time or opportunity to organize my work. At the meeting in Cincinnati, which was attended by some half-dozen other Virginia managers, I found the exchange of information, although at that time very largely centered in the engineering functions of the city, exceedingly helpful. The Cincinnati meeting had a total attendance of only about 40 of the 157 managers then in the country. Practically every person in attendance participated in the informal discussions. I profited so much from these talks that I resolved to do all I could to keep in touch with the association and with as many similar organizations as possible.

In August of the next year, 1921, I went to Norfolk to attend a meeting of the Virginia League of Municipalities. Its membership embraced not only city managers but mayors and members of city councils of the cities governed by the mayor-council form of government, and also mayors and other officials of the small towns of the state. The organization, by tradition, was headed by a president representing one of the larger cities of the state, selected for a term of one year, and a secretary, also changed annually but selected from one of the smaller cities or towns. It had no headquarters and offered no continuing services but confined its activities to an annual meeting.

On the last day of the session I found to my astonishment that I had been chosen president. I immediately asked to be heard. I thanked the members of the league for the honor conferred upon me, but at the same time I ventured to ask them to empower me to select a permanent secretary and establish permanent headquarters in Richmond, which would be available throughout the year for service to all members. Through it there would be a continuous exchange of information, and it would represent the views and interests of the cities before the appropriate state officers and the legislature. I told the members that if they felt that the time had not yet come for such a permanent organization, I would be forced respectfully to decline the honor they had conferred upon me. A considerable discussion followed, at the end of which it was unanimously agreed not to elect a secretary but to leave that choice to me and to authorize me, if I found it possible, to set up permanent headquarters.

Actually it took nearly all the year of my incumbency to put my proposition into effect. Toward the end I found, in the person of a young lawyer who was a graduate of the University of Virginia and of the Harvard Law School, a man who was imbued with a great desire to do his share in public service. He was willing to take over this particular task without salary, to set up the headquarters of the league in his own office, to help raise sufficient funds from increased dues imposed upon the members, and in other ways to enable the league to establish a permanent seat. He was Morton L. Wallerstein, who, while pursuing a successful career at the bar, for many years carried on the work of the secretariat of the Virginia league. After he turned it over to his successor, he continued to serve as its counsel and legal representative.

That was my first experience in setting up an organization of public administrators, an experience which later was to be repeated again and again over a period of many, many years.

Later in the summer of 1921, after I had become president of the Virginia league, I went with Mrs. Brownlow and several other Petersburg citizens interested in public welfare to the State Conference of Social Work held at Charlottesville. In that session I contrived to extend my acquaintance with municipal, county, and state officials and representatives of voluntary agencies interested in social work and public welfare, as also did Mrs. Brownlow, who was advancing her work as a member of the State Children's Code Commission. These acquaintanceships put us in personal touch and in a position to exchange information and experiences not only with a wider group of specialized officials but also with the representatives of many volunteer welfare agencies and citizens' groups, such as the League of Women Voters, which, though newly organized, was then extremely active, especially in state affairs.

More than that, my attendance at that conference in Charlottesville greatly intensified my feeling that the work of municipal management could be most rapidly advanced by organizing closer contacts among the several cities. So strongly did I feel that this was necessary that I asked the City Council at city expense to send Dr. Martin, the health officer, to a conference of state and provincial health officers to be held in Washington. He had been invited to it—an exceptional honor, since very few municipal health officers had been asked. Then, I proposed that the council permit me to take the city engineer, Mr. Budd, and the executive secretary and purchasing agent, Mr. Goodwyn, with me to a meeting of the City Managers' Association to be held in Chicago in the autumn.

Up to that time the officials of Petersburg, in common with those of many cities, had seemed to regard a trip to an annual convention as only a junketing joy ride at the taxpayers' expense. Dr. Martin didn't think so, because for some years he had been attending these conferences of top health officers of the United States and Canada at his own expense, but I suspect that Mr. Budd and Mr. Goodwyn thought that my principal purpose was to give them a little vacation.

When they got to Chicago, however, they learned better. The city managers' convention even at that early day was essentially a working body; and these two gentlemen found themselves hard at work putting in slightly longer hours than were required by their duties in Petersburg.

In Chicago I made bold not only to engage in the informal interplay among the managers and find out the results of their experiences in their several towns but to venture some tentative philosophical conclusions. The result, together with the leadership of others both within and without the new profession, was that the members took themselves and the problems of their municipalities more seriously and tackled the questions raised in a framework much broader than a mere discussion of the techniques of public works or of accounting or what not.

From as early as 1915 under the administration of an able secretary, Harrison Gray Otis, then city manager of Beaufort, South Carolina, the association had been publishing its annual proceedings and occasional bulletins, sometimes printed, sometimes mimeographed. In 1919 it had begun the publication of a monthly journal called the *City Managers' Magazine,* a title not long thereafter changed to *Public Management.*

In the autumn of 1922 the City Managers' Association was to meet in Kansas City. I put in my appearance and took an active part in the proceedings. There were just 55 managers present out of a total of about 281 then in the country. Here there developed a cleavage among the members which manifested itself in the discussion of various city problems but was much more evident in corridor and lobby conversations. Many of the earlier city managers, especially those who had taken upon themselves the burden of organizing the profession, had been trained as civil engineers. Some of them apparently believed that the city-manager profession should be confined to engineers. Others, despite their engineering background, were in complete disagreement. This difference of opinion about the future of the profession was put to the test when the Committee on Nominations brought in two names to be voted upon for the office of president. One was an engineer, Edwin J. Fort, city manager of Niagara Falls, New York, and the other was Louis Brownlow, non-engineer, city manager of Petersburg, Virginia.

The vote was taken. I was elected. I had received twenty-five votes. Mr. Fort had received twenty-four votes.

It must not be assumed, however, that this vote of 25 to 24 was strictly an engineer versus a non-engineer vote. At that time, of the fifty-odd members, about forty were civil engineers, and there was merely a handful of us non-engineers.

The secretariat had moved with Mr. Otis as he moved from the city managership in Beaufort, South Carolina, to Auburn, Maine, and then to New York, where he was with the Institute of Public Administration. But when he became city manager of Clarksburg, West Virginia, Mr. Otis resigned and the secretariat passed to Paul B. Wilcox, private secretary to C. M. Osborn, city manager of East Cleveland, Ohio, and president of the association. Hence, as the secretariat was moved, the journal was issued from a different city; and there was no permanent office or center for its activities.

After the ballot for president had been announced, I arose to thank the members. Acknowledging with gratitude the overwhelming majority by which I had been elected, a majority of one, I said, "If you will authorize me to select a permanent secretary, to establish permanent headquarters, and to undertake the beginnings of some plan for the better financing of the association, I will be delighted to accept the honor you have conferred upon me. If you think that the time has not yet come to take such a step, I will gladly relinquish the office and ask you to select someone to serve in my stead."

A quite lively discussion followed; but in the end there was unanimous agreement, and I was given the authority to proceed with my plan. This is exactly what had happened the year before in the Virginia League of Municipalities. I had not anticipated that the same problem would arise so soon on a national scale, nor, indeed, had I any notion that the opportunity to press a decision would come to me in that wider field.

I already was acquainted with Mr. John G. Stutz, the secretary of the League of Kansas Municipalities, which had its headquarters at the University of Kansas at Lawrence. I asked Mr. Stutz if he would undertake the position of secretary and help to establish permanent headquarters. He accepted, subject to the will of the university. I telephoned the president of the university. He agreed. I submitted the fact of the agreement to the members of the association. They agreed. And so the permanent headquarters of the City Managers' Association was established in Lawrence, Kansas.

A little later I made a journey to Lawrence to help Mr. Stutz set up the new office and to arrange to keep in the closest possible touch with him by correspondence. Contracts were to be let for the printing of the magazine. Ways and means had to be found for engaging the necessary clerical help (most of which we wangled for free out of the students in the university), and plans had to be laid for persuading members of the association to agree to an increase in dues, for the solicitation of advertising in the magazine and yearbook and for attempting to get other financial help.

Organizational Work Begins

A few months later, when I found it inconvenient to go to Lawrence, Mr. Stutz came to Petersburg. There we spent several days attempting to solve the extremely difficult problems which we had encountered. In the course of these conversations, Mr. Stutz, who was a graduate of the University of Chicago, suggested to me that we attempt to enlist the aid of Dr. Charles E. Merriam of the Political Science Department of the University of Chicago, who had been Mr. Stutz's teacher and who was greatly interested in the problems of municipal government. I had followed at a great distance Merriam's unsuccessful campaign as the Republican nominee for the mayoralty of Chicago against Carter Harrison in 1911, and I had high esteem for his approach to the problems of municipal reform.

Stutz and I decided to draft a memorandum in which we would seek the help of some philanthropic foundation in establishing a national centralized bureau of municipal research to be set up near some university and in the same headquarters as the City Managers' Association. We wrote an outline of a memorandum to be sent to Dr. Merriam. Mr. Stutz took it back to Kansas, wrote the first draft of the memorandum, and sent it to me. I rewrote it and sent it back to him. After several such exchanges we brought it to final form, and Mr. Stutz transmitted it to Dr. Merriam, a man whom I had never met.

That was the beginning of what later was to develop into the Public Administration Clearing House and the agglomeration of organizations of public officials that was destined to be centered adjacent to the campus of the University of Chicago. But of the subsequent developments arising from that small beginning I shall tell much more later on.

One incident that Mr. Stutz's visit to Petersburg brought about I cannot neglect to record. Mr. Stutz was Kansas born, a stalwart Republican in party politics, and an intellectual descendant of the violent pre–Civil War dissensions out of which arose the popular term "Bleeding Kansas." As I took him around Petersburg, I could see that the evident pride of the Petersburgers in their part in the southern side of the Civil War disturbed as well as astonished him. I am afraid I began to tease him a little. He could hardly bring himself to reconcile what even I had to say about the Confederacy with what he believed from convictions which had been intense since his childhood. Noticing this, I saved for the very end of my sight-seeing trip with him one particular

[147]

thing. I actually drove through Bollingbrook Street several times without telling my visitor the object of my quest.

The stage had not set itself. At last it did. I stopped the car. I asked Stutz to look across the street. There in a window of an old house sat an old man knitting a sock.

"Stutz," I asked, "do you see that old man?"

"Sure," he said. "Isn't it odd to see a man knitting?"

"Well," I said, "this old man sits in the window most of the time. He is always knitting. He sits where he can look out at the townspeople who pass by. He has a very remarkable history, and he stands very high in the estimation of the Petersburg people."

"Who is he?" asked Stutz.

"He is Sergeant McChance," I said. "He was a sergeant in the United States Army before the Civil War. He is the man who actually sprung the trap and hanged John Brown of Osawatomie."

Stutz was speechless. At first he was plainly incredulous. At last when I convinced him that I was telling the truth, he had but one thing to say, "To think that *I* should ever live to see *that* man!"

At the Kansas City meeting it had been decided to hold the next session of the City Managers' Association in Washington. When, a few hours later, I was elected president, that prospect seemed to me to be most agreeable. Working as I did throughout the year with the newly established headquarters in Lawrence, I looked forward with pleasure to presiding over the convention when it met in my old home town. The commissioners of the District of Columbia were most hospitable, as was the then existing City Club, and quite elaborate arrangements were made on behalf of the host city and its neighbor, Alexandria, Virginia, where Wilder M. Rich was city manager. The convention was to meet in mid-November. By the time that month came around I already had resigned as city manager of Petersburg and had accepted the appointment as city manager of Knoxville, Tennessee, but I was not to go to Knoxville until mid-December. The number of city managers in the country had increased to 284 and the attendance at the convention had risen to 127, but only 61 of them were actually managers.

The commissioners of the District of Columbia had arranged for many trips of inspection to various municipal works in the District, as had the city manager of Alexandria in behalf of his town. Luncheons and dinners were tendered the delegates by various service clubs on both sides of the river. In fact, there was so much entertainment that at my initiative the association decided thereafter to curtail as much as possible its purely social activities. This was hard to do, for the next year we were destined for Canada. Nevertheless, the restrictions adopted that year have endured until the present day; when the city managers *meet,* they *work,* and, by division of time, when they *play,* they play.

A highlight of that convention was the reception at the White House by the President of the United States, Calvin Coolidge. Every attendant at the meeting was told that he would be admitted to the White House by virtue of the name badge that he was to wear upon his lapel. I was shown first into the President's office. I stood at the President's left. The delegates came in. As each one passed I announced his name to the President and the President shook hands with him. When all the 126 had passed by and each had been duly introduced, the President turned to me and said, "Brownlow, I thought these city managers were not politicians."

"Well, I think, Mr. President," I replied, "that they are not politicians in the ordinary sense, since none of them has been elected to office. The managers are presumed to serve without respect to their partisan party affiliations."

"Well," he came back, "anyhow, *you* are a politician."

"Why do you say that, Mr. President?"

"Because you knew the name of every one of those men who passed by here and pronounced it out loud to me, and that is proof that you are not only a politician but a good one!"

Turning directly toward the President, I picked up my coat lapel, pushed my badge forward with my thumb, and said, "Mr. President, I can read."

"Oh," was his sole reply.

CHAPTER XIV

A PROPOSAL FOR ADVANCEMENT

In 1922 and 1923 there was a great upsurge of interest in the problems of municipal government that found expression in many different parts of the country. One manifestation of this phenomenon was the rapidly increasing attention to the then relatively new and quite novel council-manager form of city government. When I was elected president of the City Managers' Association the event was given considerable publicity by the newspapers throughout the country. During the succeeding year the reorganizaiton of the association contributed no little to this increasing interest. During the next twelve months many visitors came to Petersburg, some of them interested because of a desire to enter the city-manager profession, some of them trying to find out whether or not it would be adaptable to their own particular home towns, some of them merely curious, and a good many of them journalists preparing to write articles about it.

The immediate publicity following my election as president of the association also was marked by special articles in newspapers in Virginia, since I was a Virginia city manager, and in Tennessee, where I had a wide acquaintanceship especially among my old newspaper friends. A few days after I returned from Kansas City to Petersburg, I received a letter from Wiley Morgan, the managing editor of the *Knoxville Sentinel,* telling me something that I had learned already through the newspapers and from my friends in Knoxville, that his city was considering the adoption of the new form of government and that a committee already was at work drafting a new charter. The purpose of his letter was to ask me to write an article for the *Sentinel* about my experiences in Petersburg.

I already had had one or two inquiries as to whether or not I would be willing to come to Knoxville to make some speeches on the subject.

A Proposal for Advancement

Since these hints were not in the form of actual invitations, my only reply was that I was very greatly interested in the movement and would be glad to do what I could. I did not commit myself to any particular action.

Certainly it was not then in my mind that I would go to Knoxville as its first city manager. According to what I learned from the newspapers and from a few friends who wrote to me, the municipal affairs of Knoxville were in a sorry state. The city, which for years had had an ordinary mayor-council form of government, in 1912 had adopted the commission form that was then looked upon favorably as an advanced municipal reform. Under that system it had abolished its wards and was governed by a commission of five persons elected at large, one of whom served as mayor. Acting together, the five constituted the legislative branch, the executive and administrative functions being divided among the five acting as individuals.

During the previous year the *Knoxville News,* a newly established Scripps-Howard newspaper edited by Edward J. Meeman, had exposed a scandalous state of affairs in the Knoxville General Hospital, a municipal institution. A series of articles written by a brilliant reporter, Nathan White, had brought into focus the inefficiency of the city government and had convinced many citizens that it not only was incompetent but corrupt as well. Occasionally I would see one of these articles, but I was far too busy to keep up with the progress of the investigations. Indeed, Mr. Stutz, the secretary of the City Managers' Association, had found that it was impossible for him, even with the help of a volunteer staff of students from the University of Kansas, to begin to read and keep abreast of the many investigations that were going on in different parts of the country or even with the progress of the campaigns for the adoption of the council-manager system.

Knoxville at that time had three newspapers. The morning paper was the *Journal and Tribune,* a direct descendant of the *Knoxville Whig,* which had been established and edited by my father's cousin William Gannaway Brownlow, the famous "Fighting Parson" Brownlow, before the Civil War and which had been the journalistic vehicle of his vehement support of the Union and his intransigent attacks upon secessionists. Indeed, the editor of the *Journal and Tribune* was still William Rule, a venerable octogenarian, who had had his first newspaper experience under the editorship of Parson Brownlow. Its managing editor was William M. Clemens, with whom I had formed a close personal friendship at the time I was a reporter on the *Nashville Banner* and he had a similar position on the *Memphis Scimitar*. Billy Clemens was one of the first of my Knoxville friends to begin to correspond with me about the municipal situation there.

The older of the two afternoon papers was the *Knoxville Sentinel,* whose managing editor, Wiley L. Morgan, I had known very well during my Tennessee political days when the *Sentinel* was owned by George F. Milton, Sr. At that time I had been the Washington correspondent of the *Sentinel,* and by virtue of my by-line, my name had been fairly well known in Knoxville.

All these factors conspired to promote special attention in Knoxville to anything that appeared in the newspapers or magazines concerning my administration of municipal management in Petersburg. For these reasons, although I did not know it at the time, many of the Knoxville citizens who were engaged in the endeavor to change the form of government in their city had me in mind as a possible city manager.

The agitation in Knoxville resulted in the passage by the legislature of an enabling act providing for the establishment of three commissions, one to draft a charter along the lines of the mayor-council form; one a charter for the commission form; and one a charter for the council-manager form of government. These three charters were then to be submitted to a referendum of the people, and there was an implied and even an expressed commitment of the representatives and senators from Knox County to ask the state legislature to adopt the particular charter which had attracted the support of the greater number of citizens of Knoxville.

When the election came in March, 1923, the council-manager charter obtained an absolute majority of the whole number voting; the aldermanic charter was next; the commission charter was at the bottom of the poll, a circumstance due in part to the fact that most of the leaders supporting the retention of the commission form of government and the commissioners themselves had, toward the end of the campaign, transferred their support to the aldermanic system in the hope of defeating the manager form.

The Tennessee legislature did enact the council-manager charter, and an election for a new council of eleven members, five at large and six from districts, was held in Knoxville. The elements that had supported the new charter put up a ticket under the name of the People's Ticket. The opponents ran a full slate of candidates on another ticket. Ten of the men named on the People's Ticket were elected, five from the city at large and one from each of the five districts; one candidate on the People's Ticket from one district was defeated. The sole opposition man elected was Lee Monday. He was the only man elected whom I had known before. I had met him once or twice briefly when I was in Knoxville as a newspaperman and was in contact with his brother, Monroe Monday, who was a leading Republican politician of the state. In retrospect there is a tinge of irony in the fact that among the eleven men who chose me to be city manager, the only one I had known before soon became my implacable enemy.

As soon as the election was over, the stream of correspondence from Knoxville opened up again. I was told that two members of the council-elect had been selected as a committee to go to Washington and to Petersburg to investigate my record.

I was invited to come to Knoxville. That invitation came just as I was about to leave for Roanoke, Virginia, for a conference with the officials of the Norfolk and Western Railroad to prepare for advertising for bids for the bridge across the Appomattox River, which was the number one improvement project in Petersburg at the time. This invitation came from Captain Mitchell Long, who had been the campaign manager for the People's Ticket. I told him I could arrange to come directly from Roanoke but that it would be impossible for me to stay in Knoxville more than one day. I was met on my arrival in Knoxville early in the morning by Captain Long and taken to the Civic Building, which housed the offices of the Board of Commerce and had been the headquarters of the People's Ticket campaign. There I met nine of the eleven members of the council. The mayor designate, Ben A. Morton, and another member of the council, Dr. A. D. Albright, were out of the city.

The questioning was led by the vice-mayor, William M. Fulton, by Captain Long, and by Mr. Toms. The questions fell under two heads. The first concerned the names that I, as president of the City Managers' Association, could recommend as persons competent to fill the position of city manager of Knoxville. I responded with several names. The other series of questions was directed almost entirely to what I thought should be the attitude of a city manager toward his relations to the city council, especially in making appointments to positions in the city government.

To this line of questions, I replied that in my opinion the council should be responsible for the over-all policy of the city; it should receive and review the reports of the manager; it should take full responsibility for the adoption of the budget after receiving the recommendations of the manager. But, I said, the manager himself should be solely responsible for all the appointments he made in every instance, except where the law required appointment by civil service procedures. Toward the end of the interview the question of partisan politics was raised, and I responded that a city manager ought not under any circumstances to be motivated by partisan or factional politics and that if he were, it would be the duty of the council to dismiss him. Not one word was said to me in the whole interview about whether or not I would be interested in the position, nor did Vice-Mayor Fulton and his fellow councilman Rush Hazen, who had been appointed to the committee to look into my record in Washington and Petersburg, say anything to me about their forthcoming journey.

At the end of the interview, I was told that the city was dreadfully in debt, that nobody quite knew the amount but that the charter gave the city council the authority to fund all the floating indebtedness by a bond issue which would not have to be submitted to a referendum.

I took the train back to Roanoke, for I had not completed my work there, and two days later was at home in Petersburg, where I received a letter from Lee Monday. "After you left," he wrote, "we talked it over and there is no doubt that you are it. Pack your bag and get ready to move to Knoxville." Mr. Monday went on to intimate that he was the leader of the pro-Brownlow faction in the council and that he was quite sure that he and I would be able to work together closely.

I was back in Knoxville on October 12. The council had taken office on October 1. It had chosen a businessman, Howell J. Davis, as temporary city manager. It had appointed Ernest Keller, a member of the council, to work with Mr. Davis on the attempt to analyze the floating debt, to gather in the outstanding bills and claims against the city, to undertake to verify them, and to discover as far as they could what was the actual financial condition of the city. Alexander Harris, an engineer, had been appointed temporary city engineer and temporary head of the department of public service. M. W. Egerton had been made temporary director of law. Temporary appointments were made to head the departments of public safety, public finance, and public welfare. Fred Ault had been elected treasurer and city clerk, a position which the charter provided should be filled by the council rather than by the manager. All these things were explained to me; the council told me that they had unanimously decided to offer me the position at the salary of $15,000.

I accepted, subject to the condition that I would have to complete my work in Petersburg and could not come to Knoxville until December 15. On the other hand, I would be glad to do what I could in the interim for Knoxville; especially I would be glad to inquire into the bond-market situation in New York and make tentative arrangements for the flotation of a bond issue to fund the floating debt, as was provided by the council. The next day, back in Petersburg, I submitted my resignation and the newspapers in Knoxville announced my appointment.

Here I was, at the end of a little more than three years' service in Petersburg, ready to take the next step, a step which I considered to be both upward and onward in my career in the city-manager profession.

The public expression of regret by many leading citizens in Petersburg was heartwarming. Even those regrets were tempered by congratulations on what was conceived to be a promotion for me personally, both professionally and salary-wise, and by frequent expressions of pride in the fact that what Petersburg had done had met with the approval of a larger city in another state.

It is difficult now, thirty-odd years later, for me to recall precisely what went on in my mind which led me to make the change. While the proposed increase in salary from $10,000 to $15,000 had something to do with it, I am sure that I made the decision primarily because I was convinced that I should continue in the profession of municipal management and I thought a promotion from a city of 30,000 to a city of 75,000 constituted a recognition of my professional competence. It is equally clear to my hindsight that I had not sufficiently inquired into the state of things in Knoxville, but my hindsight also informs me that had I asked all the right questions, no one could have answered me because the situation was so chaotic that no member of the council that employed me would have been able to make the right replies.

A Passion for Anonymity

Nobody in Knoxville knew just what a mess the city was in. It is undoubtedly true that later, in Knoxville, I found not only a mess in the city hall but also a strong body of public-minded citizens of great ability who were willing and eager to clean up that mess.

I cannot pretend to myself that I did not already know that it was the natural order of things in Tennessee, and more especially in East Tennessee, to take party, factional, and personal politics not only seriously but screamingly at the top of the collective voice of the citizenry. I suspect that that circumstance constituted some of the challenge which invited me—the challenge to attempt to establish in politics-ridden Tennessee an unpartisan, unpolitical municipal administration.

At any rate, I took the step. And then came the convention of the City Managers' Association in Washington over which I was to preside as president and where my successor was to be elected. And there, in Washington, meeting the largest group of professional city managers ever assembled up to that time, I received from them hearty congratulations. The profession gave me every testimony of its confidence in my administration of the affairs of the association and in the action I had taken in establishing a permanent secretariat at Lawrence, Kansas, and indicated individually and collectively that it considered my translation to Knoxville a recognition of the professional attainments of the association as an association, as well as a personal promotion.

I had come to look upon the manager-council form of government as a usable piece of machinery for the reform and advancing development of municipal government in the United States. I had seen and heard so much of the miasmatic jungles of partisan, factional, and personal politics, of the graft and corruption in city government, that I had come to consider the problem of cleaning up municipal government and introducing economic and efficient methods of management into its conduct as one of the principal problems facing American society.

In the government of the District of Columbia there was little or no graft, no partisan politics, and little factional or personal politics, but the commissioners at the top of the government were compelled to fight a continuous defensive war against the encroachment of partisan patronage drives initiated by members of their city council, the Congress of the United States.

In Petersburg there was no graft and almost no partisan or factional politics. The city was buttressed by the tradition of a century; even personal politics were discouraged, and a career system based on earned merit was the prevailing rule in all matters of personnel. Every movement for increased efficiency and economy in management had met with all but universal public approval.

I was fully aware that in Knoxville, where I was going, the city government had been corrupt, graft-ridden, dominated by political considerations—partisan, factional, and personal—and that the principal motivation for the conduct of the top ranks of the municipal machinery had been private gain for either the public officials or for their favorites in business, banking, and the professions.

I had studied the new charter of Knoxville, which had been drawn up with the advice of many of the leading experts of the country. While it contained some features that I considered to be hampering or at least of doubtful utility, in the main it incorporated what I deemed to be the most advantageous form of organization. The administration of the government was to be left to a manager appointed by the council. That manager was to be responsible for the appointment of all personnel in the city except those reserved to the Civil Service Commission by law or by the charter; all the sections of the city government were divided among five departments, each to be headed by a director; that director was to be appointed by and directly responsible to the manager, and the manager in turn was to be responsible for them to the council.

These notions of mine were widely and generally discussed at the meeting of the convention in Washington and met with almost complete approval. At any rate, there was no vocal dissent to one of these basic ideas: that the manager's administration should be non-political and non-partisan.

What was more important to me was that in my talks in Knoxville on my early visits with members of the council, they too had accepted, apparently wholeheartedly, the basic ideas of the new scheme of government. The plan had been widely discussed throughout the city for the better part of two years, and the provisions of the charter were pretty well known. In fact, at one meeting of the council two weeks after I had accepted the job as manager and six weeks before I actually went to Knoxville to take it over, the new mayor, Ben A. Morton, a businessman, gave a full expression to his conviction about the nature of the new form of government. When the council met on November 2, a citizen addressed the chair and asked that the council order an immediate repaving of a certain street which served his residential neighborhood. To that Mayor Morton made a reply which was taken down stenographically and which appeared in the *Knoxville Sentinel* on that same day. Mayor Morton said:

First, this council is a legislative body only. It has no executive and administrative powers. This is a government of delegated powers. The power of enacting legislation is conferred upon the council alone by the charter. The charter gives the council the power to select and employ the manager, but it stops the administrative authority of the council there.

Executive and administrative powers are conferred upon the city manager by the charter, assisted by the department heads he may appoint. The power to do things, to fix things and to change things is vested in the city manager, and he has the power and authority to delegate authority to subordinates the charter provides for. Outside of enactment of legislation the manager has supreme power. . . .

If any citizen or taxpayer needs relief, or has a complaint, he should go with it first to the head of the department to which matters of the kind have been distributed in the charter. If he fails to get relief there he should go to the next higher head which is the city manager. If he fails to get relief there, he has a right to come before the city council. The council will not attempt to give him his relief. But it will inquire and take cognizance of the operations of the city manager with reference to the case. It will not order the city manager to do the work, or remedy the condition, fix the street, or extend the main. If the case should be serious enough, and should enough dissatisfaction arise with the city manager to determine that he is inefficient, unsatisfactory, and cannot deliver the goods, the council is empowered to dismiss him and select his successor and it would do so should the case warrant it and justify it.

The Mayor's position was summed up by the following illustration:

If a credit man in one of the business establishments with which I am affiliated calls me over the telephone and asks my advice about letting Mr. ———— have $1,000 worth of goods on credit, I say to him: "Mr. Credit Man, if I were you, I might let Mr. ———— have the $1,000 of credit, but if you do, and at the end of the year it is not collected, I will hold you responsible." This is exactly what I mean by delegated authority.

My credit man has the right to let Mr. ———— have the $1,000 of credit, or any other amount he chooses, uninterfered with by me.

Mr. Brownlow is given power to manage the city within the scope of the charter. But in both cases we have the right to deal with results.

A Proposal for Advancement

It is of course the duty of the members of the council to render every helpful assistance to all administrative officers and to citizens generally, cooperating to make the city more livable and pleasant.

I was sure that the task I was about to undertake in Knoxville would be a difficult one. I had no idea at the time how difficult it would be, but I was convinced that I would have the support of the mayor and the council, and I was determined to do all that I could to justify their confidence.

For weal or for woe, I was on the way.

CHAPTER XV

KNOXVILLE IN 1923

I went to Knoxville in that highly individualistic era in the history of the United States when the citizenry was keeping cool with Coolidge, when the all but complete isolation of the United States among the nations of the world was taken for granted, when there was not a cloud on the economic horizon, and when everybody agreed that what was needed was bigger and better business, bigger communities, and bigger and better cities—all to the end that each individual might have a bigger and better home and a bigger and better bank account and could look forward confidently to a bigger and better job. That is, that might be the attitude of the particular group in which one found one's self; but it was modified by the supervening doctrine of individualism. The thing to do was to get as far ahead as one could, joining others engaged in a similar line of endeavor only for mutual protection and for both defensive and offensive action against other groups.

On the other hand, East Tennesseans in general, and Knoxvillians in particular, were conscious of their obligations not only to members of their immediate families but to their kin of even distant degrees of consanguinity, and they likewise were aware of their duty to their neighbors. Ever ready to help anyone in distress or in need, if only that person was someone personally known to him, the individualistic Knoxvillian was inclined to be skeptical (as indeed are most of the members of the human race) when asked to contribute in an organized way to unknown and distant beneficiaries of almost any cause. The exception probably was the support given to missionary societies, but the rule was proved by the public attitude toward any sort of welfare or medical assistance which depended for its support on taxation. The same intense devotion to the principle of individualistic liberty extended to the realm of ordinary law enforcement. The mountains were not far away, and, indeed, the mountain spirit still survived among the descendants of the mountaineers who made up such a large proportion of the population of the city. In the mountains sometimes quarrels were settled by lethal violence. The family feuds had carried on the clan warfare inherited from the Scotch ancestors of the mountain families.

And when it came to minor police action, such as traffic control or parking regulations or things of that sort—the interference with individual freedom on the part of a policeman acting under the collective authority of a municipal ordinance—that was something hardly to be borne by the free spirit of man!

"Montani semper liberi," the motto adopted by the freedom-loving people of mountainous West Virginia when it split from the parent state over the issue of slavery and loyalty to the Union, was equally apposite to the mountainous sections of Kentucky and Tennessee, and Knoxville was veritably the center and the capital of the conservative, loyal, freedom-loving, individualistic province of East Tennessee.

Knoxville in 1923 was a far different city from what it is today. Then, although the Aluminum Company of America had begun its great work at Alcoa near neighboring Maryville, there was no atomic energy plant at Oak Ridge; there was no Tennessee Valley Authority; the Tennessee River had not been converted into a chain of lakes; there was no abundance of cheap electric power; there was no Smoky Mountain National Park; the University of Tennessee had not yet begun its remarkable expansion; there were no airplanes; there was no radio station; there was no television; and there were not even paved highways connecting the city with other cities of the state.

The city was, like most cities in those days, practically self-sufficient in government. It of course depended upon the countryside for its trade; it drew upon the neighboring coal-mining and metallurgical background of East Tennessee; it had its agricultural hinterland. But its connection with them was largely by railroad, and it deemed itself a city set apart, as much as did ever a walled city of ancient or medieval times. Its schools, it is true, received some small help in the way of grants-in-aid from the state, but otherwise it had no direct connection with state government and, with the exception of the post office, none with the federal government that affected the daily lives of its citizens.

Knoxville had grown rapidly. It had a population in 1900, when I first knew it, of 32,637; in 1910, 36,346; in 1920, three years before I went there as city manager, 77,818; and it was calculated to have 85,000 to 100,000 when I got there. Its industries were varied; they included textile mills, ironworks, manufacture of electrical appliances and thermodynamic contrivances, and its own great natural resource of marble quarries. Its population was overwhelmingly white and almost 100 per cent native. Its traditions were rooted deeply in the history of the mountainous part of the state. Its population had been overwhelmingly for the Union during the Civil War, and it all but completely shared the conservative and Republican tradition of the eastern part of the state.

Here, however, there was a slight difference. The city of Knoxville itself was frequently and even usually Democratic in politics while Knox County was practically always Republican. The county had been Federalist when it first organized in 1796. It had been anti-Jefferson during the Jeffersonian epoch; it had been Whig during the Jackson era; it had been loyal to the Union when the rest of the state was secessionist and Confederate; it had been conservative when the Republican party nationally was radical; and later it had been loyally Republican.

The corruption that permeated politics and government in the tragic era following the Civil War had affected all three levels of government: federal, state, and local. The reform movements in government that followed that tragic era had for the most part their springs in the federal government, which by the beginning of the twentieth century was happily purged of the grosser manifestations of corruption. Many of the state governments followed suit. But in those days the municipal governments were most important, carried on more public enterprises, and more closely affected the citizenry. It was in them that graft and corrupt practices were most manifest and most harmful. Therefore, it was in the cities that the reform movement originating at the turn of the century found its most active expression. And one such movement had resulted in the revolutionary new charter of Knoxville.

Knoxville was like most other American cities—a mixture of handsome residential districts, of undistinguished two-story houses and one-story bungalows where families of moderate income lived, and of some ghastly slums inhabited by the lower-paid factory workers. But not even the ugliness of many of the buildings and the undistinguished character of the business and financial districts could blank out the sheer beauty of the physical surroundings. The city was built on both banks of the Tennessee River, predominantly on the north, and on most days one could look southward and see the crest of the Great Smoky Mountains. Even within the city there were high hills and deep-cut valleys that always presented something of natural beauty on which the eye could rest.

Many a Knoxvillian was heard to boast that he was an "East Tennessee Jew." That meant that he was proud of the fact that he was a hard bargainer. It sometimes meant that he was boasting of the fact that he was a sharp trader. The word "cute" was applied admiringly to one who had a reputation for turning a quick corner in a deal. Indeed, it was said boastingly that in East Tennessee no Jew and few Scots could survive. Once I heard it said as an addendum that there was once an Armenian who set up shop in Maryville, but he soon starved to death.

I went to Knoxville as a Tennessean. All three newspapers so described me. Everybody so considered me because my parents were Tennesseans, and I had had my beginnings in daily newspaper work in Nashville. I suspect that I agreed, although once in a while I would justify my skeptic curiosity by proclaiming my Missouri nativity.

From my newspaper experience in Tennessee I had learned that public office there was regarded not so much as a public trust but as a private privilege within the province of political patronage. My distant cousin Walter P. Brownlow was for years the Republican boss of Tennessee in an era when the White House was always occupied by a Republican. He was recognized by all Tennesseans from the mountains on the east to the Mississippi River on the west as one of the greatest dispensers of federal patronage of his time. But even Walter was wont to regret the rapacity of Tennessee appetites for jobs as recompense for political activity. He was fond of quoting the old saying "Every job I get for a man nets me one ingrate and twelve enemies."

Virginia was different. In the county adjoining Petersburg there was a surveyor who was the son of a surveyor, who was the son of a surveyor, reaching back well into the seventeenth century. There were political offices in Petersburg filled by the election at the polls, but except in the rarest instance these incumbents always were renominated by the Democratic party without opposition and always were reelected. In the capitol at Richmond, where the governor could serve but four years and was ineligible for re-election, the appointive officers kept on through administration after administration, through factional change after factional change; but, of course, for many decades the nomenclature of the political party at the head of the state had not changed.

In Tennessee the habit was to change practically everybody after every election. I knew that my chief difficulty would center in the matter of appointments.

In my interviews with the members of the council in Knoxville, I made it very plain that I would assume the sole responsibility for the appointments to be made by the city manager. I extracted from the members of the council before I accepted the position the promise that no one of them would make recommendations for appointment. At the same time, I told them I would feel free to ask their opinion.

"You gentlemen may think it odd," I said to them, "that anybody in the city of Knoxville will be quite free to come to me with a recommendation of anybody he thinks fit for any position that may or may not be vacant, except the eleven men who have chosen me to be the city manager.

"You may take this as pretty hard," I went on, "thus to be the only eleven persons in Knoxville deprived of the privilege of recommending persons for office, but if you are anything like the members of the council in Petersburg, or members of councils in other cities where the manager has taken the same stand, you will presently discover that God in his goodness has sent down to you from heaven the greatest gift that any man holding a political position can ever receive—a solid silver, gold-crested, blown in the bottle, genuine, unbreakable, and incontestable alibi."

I got a laugh and I got the promises. But to many minds it was just a piece of smooth politics.

On my first official visit to Knoxville in mid-October, I talked with the acting city manager, Mr. Davis, with Mr. Ernest Keller, the member of the council who had been assigned to work with him on the city's financial situation, and with Mr. Egerton, the acting law director. They told me that the city in the year before had operated in such an extravagant manner as to leave a deficit of more than two million dollars. As a matter of fact, even according to the antiquated bookkeeping system then in vogue, which took no account of obligations incurred, the income had been two million dollars and expenditures four million dollars. On the very last day of the commission form of government, the commission entered into contracts involving almost a half-million dollars.

All this, Mr. Davis and his colleagues said, would mean that under the authority given by the new charter to fund the floating debt of the city, it would be necessary to issue at least two million dollars in bonds. They also told me that the authenticated claims that were coming in indicated that a great amount of money would be involved in the unrecorded obligations and actual purchases made under the old system, in which each of the five commissioners and many of their subordinates were authorized to buy almost whatever they liked at almost any price, with no record kept of the purchase or the obligation incurred, and no accounting possible until the bills actually turned up. Even then, they were not recorded until there was money enough to pay them. It was worse than I thought. The situation seemed to require immediate attention, and yet I was loath to leave Petersburg until I had fulfilled my obligations there, especially until I had got under contract the Appomattox bridge.

I compromised by saying that I would come back to Knoxville as frequently as I could for short stays during the interim and that I would appreciate it if Mr. Davis and the other temporary executive officers would keep me informed of the progress of things. I also subscribed to the three daily newspapers and for the next two months, while my principal interest was in Petersburg, I had a finger in the pie in faraway Knoxville.

My public statements in Knoxville when my appointment was announced were limited to two or three brief interviews with the newspapers, in which I was able successfully to parry most of the detailed inquiries. I said that it was quite evident that the first task I would undertake when I came to Knoxville would be the modernization of the accounting and purchasing system; that I would not make up my mind about filling any position for which I would be responsible until I had had time to make a careful survey of the situation, and that I would not give any attention whatever to applications for positions until I actually had taken over the job.

A week or two later I went back to Knoxville to help Mr. Davis work out a budget. Since the fiscal year began on the first of October, when the new form of government was put into effect, it was absolutely necessary that some type of temporary budget be set up and approved. It was clear that the city would be compelled to raise money by the sale of tax-anticipation notes. While the fiscal year began in October, tax collections were not due until the following March, and no penalty for non-payment of taxes was attached until the following September, so that an eleven-month lag made temporary financing in anticipation of taxes mandatory. In the year before, so I was told, tax-anticipation notes had been sold for $900,000 at an interest rate of 6 per cent plus a $22,000 commission. I thought that absurd and said so and undertook to go at once to New York to see what could be done.

The council, during the next week, authorized the sale of $900,000 in tax-anticipation notes, and I went to New York from Petersburg to negotiate their sale. I was fairly well acquainted in those days with the municipal bond market and had friendly relationships with the Guaranty Trust Company, the Bankers Trust Company, the Chemical National Bank, and several other banking houses. Without any difficulty, I sold the $900,000 note issue at $4\frac{1}{4}$ per cent (which was then the Federal Reserve Bank discount rate) and as a matter of course I paid no commission to anybody. The only cost to the city of Knoxville was my expenses for the trip to New York. While on the market, I made some tentative negotiations for the sale of a much larger issue of what I thought would be approximately $2 million in refunding bonds.

The announcement of this piece of financing, when reported in Knoxville, elicited a most favorable response from the council, the newspapers, and the public and no doubt greatly aided me in my long-distance dealings with Knoxville.

I also was apprised of the litigation between the city and the Southern Railway over the cost of a viaduct which had been constructed several years before. The case had been up and down in both state and federal courts for several years. I stopped in Washington to see Mr. Fairfax Harrison, the president of the Southern Railway, and in the course of a half-hour we decided that it was not very economical for either the city or the railroad to continue to pile up court costs and that we would settle the case on a fifty-fifty basis. Because of the state of the litigation that arrangement had, for the time being, to be kept in absolute confidence.

Every time I went back to Knoxville I discovered something new and something more disturbing. One thing that struck me immediately was the lack of physical facilities for the city administration. The city hall occupied the second floor above the city market. The market occupied the ground floor of a long, two-story red-brick structure surrounded on all four sides by narrow streets. The streets on the long axis were more than half taken up by farmers' market wagons, and the congestion was terrific. The clamor was intense and the atmosphere certainly uncongenial for the transaction of administrative business. Access to the upstairs was difficult, not only because of the traffic, but also because of the bad arrangement of the offices. There was a council chamber called the Market Hall large enough to seat several hundred persons. It served not only for meetings of the city fathers but for political meetings, civic gatherings, and what not. There was the police court presided over by an elected police judge. There was the headquarters of the police department presided over by the chief of police. There was also the office of the auditor, in which was established the bookkeeping and the accounting division of the city government, operating under an archaic system but with a large complement of clerks. There was an office for the city engineer, but most of his staff was established elsewhere at the city stables. At one end of the building there were two small offices which theretofore had been occupied by the auditor and his assistant. Neither the mayor nor any one of the commissioners under the commission government had had an office in the city hall, nor indeed any office at all except in his own place of business. There was no place for the city manager to sit. The two small offices had been taken over by the acting city manager, Mr. Davis, and his colleague from the council, Mr. Keller. These two would be assigned to me when I got to Knoxville.

The offices all were crowded. The windows were dirty, the floors were not clean, and there was an appalling lack of office equipment. But these things were as nothing compared to the almost utter lack of records or files. On every visit I made to Knoxville I found the temporary executives increasingly worried about that situation. If there had been records, they either had not been filed or had been so negligently filed that it was impossible to keep track of them.

While the temporary heads were concerned for the moment with fiscal problems, Mr. Egerton on one of my visits took me into the police department to introduce me to Chief of Police Haynes. I was more than astonished—I was dumbfounded—to find that the police chief had no filing cabinet, only spindle files set around helter-skelter on the tops of the few tables and desks. Moreover, the police department had no type- writing machine, no clerk, and no office equipment whatever. Chief Haynes told me that when he got a letter from a chief of police in some other city the best he could do was to go to some neighboring business house or office, carry with him a few sheets of department stationery, and beg the office force of the business institution to answer the letter for him. He was ashamed to do all his correspondence in longhand.

There were five departments of the city government, but no one of them had a head save for the temporary appointments that had been made by the acting city manager, Howell Davis. The reports that I got from these temporary heads and the visits I made to various offices of the city convinced me that one of the first things it would be necessary for me to do would be to find competent men to fill the directorships of the five departments, or my managerial job would be impossible.

There was plenty of trouble. In the waterworks there was at work one horizontal reciprocating steam pump with a capacity of fifteen mil- lion gallons a day. There were two other pumps, stream centrifugals, one with a daily capacity of ten million gallons and one of six million, but neither had turned over for five or six years. The daily consumption of water was around twelve-and-a-half million gallons, and that one fifteen-million-gallon pump was the sole source of supply.

I went to see it. There on the water cylinder on the low-pressure side, a domed structure of perhaps ten or twelve feet in height and five or six feet in diameter, was a crack from the bottom upward about six feet long—a crack one could stick one's thumb in, and that crack was stuffed with gunny sacks. That was all that kept Knoxville from being a catastrophically waterless, devastated town of nearly ninety thousand persons!

Somehow or other I had thought that smallpox had been conquered, but in Knoxville, a day or two after I had assumed office, I found that we had six or seven hundred smallpox cases in the pesthouse. Not one word of that had been in the newspapers because it had been agreed many years before between the newspapers and the business organiza- tions that a smallpox scare would be bad for business. Therefore, al- though the smallpox cases had been reported and the victims were taken to the pesthouse—an institution which lived up to its name in many more ways than one—nobody knew anything about it. Knoxville had had no compulsory vaccination, in fact hardly any vaccinations at all.

The situation at the city hospital was alarming. It had been the scandal about the conduct of the hospital that had caused the revolution resulting in the new charter, the installation of the manager form of government, and the relegation of the professional politicians who had theretofore administered the city. Here the superintendent, a former foreman in a plow factory, told me that he was still able to get credit for food but that the drughouses had stopped the city's credit and that the hospital was not able to purchase so much as a pound of sulphuric ether on credit. When it or similar drug supplies were needed, either the patient or the individual physician had to put up the cash for them to enable the superintendent to make the purchase. That was typical of the credit-standing of the city, despite the fact that the new charter had authorized the funding of the floating debt and that the new council had already authorized the issuance of $3,750,000 refunding bonds to pay the outstanding claims against the city government, almost twice as great a floating debt as had been anticipated.

Obviously my first task was to get help. Fortunately the temporarily appointed heads of the Department of Service, under which the public works and water system was operated, and the Department of Law were excellent. It didn't take me long to determine to keep Alexander Harris at the head of the Service Department and M. W. Egerton at the head of the Law Department. In the Department of Finance, the temporary head was Michael J. Coen, who had been with the city for many years. He was universally trusted and respected for his skill in accountancy and for his personal integrity, but I soon came to the conclusion that he did not have sufficient drive or force to serve as a permanent head of the department. The fact was that he had kept accurate account of all the monies collected by the city and all the expenditures made by the city, and it was not his fault that the accounting system was so antiquated. There was not even a proper current record of the dates on which interest was due to be deposited in the New York banks against the maturing coupons of outstanding bonds. Mr. Coen, of course, knew the dates, and it had been his habit to report to the commissioner in charge of finance; but ordinarily nothing was done about it until the city was in default, and then there was a hurried conference of the commissioners, a quick loan at the bank, a commitment for a juicy commission, and a remittance to New York. While the coupons eventually were paid, the credit of the city suffered. The accuracy of Mr. Coen's accountancy, moreover, so far as receipts and expenditures were concerned, was attested by the reports of certified public accountants who usually made an annual audit, received in January or February after the close of the previous fiscal year on September 30, at an annual expense to the city of from thirty to forty thousand dollars.

I talked to many of the principal businessmen, bankers, and other citizens and, indeed, asked for suggestions from everybody in the city except the mayor and his ten colleagues on the city council. It was clear to me that I would have to maintain my determination to make my own appointments and be responsible for my own choice of personnel. I also was very desirous of finding local persons to fill these directorships if I could, although at the same time I reserved in my own mind my freedom of action to go anywhere in the country to find the persons I wanted.

For finance director, I finally persuaded John C. Borden, a Knoxville resident then employed by the comptroller of currency as a national bank examiner, to resign his position and become director of finance.

The sorry situation in the health department and in the hospital required, in my opinion, an exceptionally strong man with practical administrative experience for director of public welfare. Here, after looking over a great many local persons, I chose Frank Bane, then state commissioner of public welfare of Virginia. I had known him since my earliest days in Petersburg, when he was an assistant to the secretary of the State Board of Charities and Correction. Both Mrs. Brownlow and I had worked with him in the reorganization of the Virginia state government when the Board of Charities was converted into the State Department of Welfare.

But the first appointment that I actually made was that of director of public safety. The situation in the police department was to my mind appalling. I had no doubt about the integrity and ability of the chief of police, but it was very evident that he had little actual control over his force and that the political interference he had experienced under the commission form of government had deprived him of the necessary authority. Here, knowing the sensitiveness of the police department to all things municipal, I turned to a man who had worked under me and whom I knew to be able, honest, and above all, an excellent administrator.

I announced the appointment of Major John O. Walker, director of public safety of Petersburg, to the position of director of public safety of Knoxville. Major Walker had come to Knoxville to see me. I had explained to him the great difficulties he would encounter but persuaded him to take the job. When the appointment was announced in the newspapers, neither the mayor nor any member of the council had known that the appointment was to be made. Within a few minutes after the newspaper containing the announcement reached the street, my telephone began to ring. Even some members of the council asked me who was Walker and why? But none actually protested. It was evident, however, that I had shocked some of them. The fact that none of them had known of the appointment shocked a great many of the citizens. Despite all the public statements that had been made by the mayor and by me, many persons still could not credit the fact that a city manager actually would make an important appointment without consulting his council. Of course in my opinion, given the tradition of Knoxville politics, if I had consulted the council either severally or collectively, I would have run the grave risk of sacrificing my independence of action and would have undermined my authority, which was vitally required to restore orderly government in such a disorderly situation.

However, what was a shock to some elements of the community gave a thrill to other elements. The three newspapers, which had been supporting the change of government, were literally entranced to discover that I meant what I said when I came to Knoxville and announced that if I took the position I would take it only on the condition of the literal interpretation of the freedom of the manager from political pressures, solicitations, or trades.

It was not until the end of March that all the directorships were filled and my managerial team was complete. It was high time. Now it was up to me to tackle in an orderly way the complex problems of the city that I had theretofore necessarily dealt with only as emergencies demanded.

CHAPTER XVI

STRAIGHTENING THINGS OUT

Even before I left Petersburg, I had employed a firm of certified public accountants, Scott, Charnley and Company, of Charlotte, North Carolina, to set up an accounting system for Knoxville which would give me without undue delay the data that I felt I would need to do my job properly. In addition to the necessity of installing good accounting practices, I demanded a system that would give me prompt and accurate reports that could be keyed in with the control necessary to maintain a sound, efficient, and economical purchasing system. It was in the irregularities of purchasing that the city had suffered most. Such irregularities had permitted if not encouraged the corruption, carelessness, and inefficiency that had brought the municipality to the verge of bankruptcy.

The system which I devised and which was set up by the certified public accountants was designed to give me full and complete data with never more than twenty-four hours' delay. Actually it was a very simple system.

The hurriedly made budget adopted by the council in its first few days of the fiscal year, which began on October 1, was rearranged, although not actually revised, to be geared into a code system of account numbers, the appropriations to be subjected to quarterly allocations to be adjusted to monthly work reports. Purchases, payrolls, contract payments, and other obligations of the city were to be charged to appropriate budget items in advance of expenditures. That enabled the director of finance to give me by eleven o'clock every morning a complete picture of the state of the budget—the obligations against each item, each departmental appropriation, the expenditures actually made, the balance available for additional obligations, and the actual cash balance in dollars and cents unexpended and unobligated. And with that, the same data on capital, contractual, and other non-budgetary items.

The same daily report set up the receipts by the city treasury of taxes and other items paid in and the balances to be anticipated as of the previous day and cumulatively for the fiscal year.

These daily reports were inserted in a large loose-leaf binder and exposed on a table in my office for the inspection of anyone who cared to see them—a citizen visitor, any employee of the city, the newspaper reporters, or anybody else.

In addition to this system, I arranged for an independent audit by a certified public accountant. It was not a pre-audit, but it was a daily cumulative audit in which were reviewed the transactions of the previous day. Exceptions by the auditor came to me immediately, and when adjustments or reconciliations were required, they were made at once. That meant that by the third or fourth day of each month I had a complete audit of the previous month; and at the end of the fiscal year, within a week, a certified audit of the previous year's business. Theretofore, the annual audit usually had been turned in to the commissioners three to five months after the end of the fiscal year, and in the last year of the old government it had cost $40,000. I made the arrangement for the continuous audit and immediate reports at a cost of less than $10,000 a year.

Shortly after Mr. Borden became director of finance, he and I agreed upon the appointment of Wiley W. Thomas to be purchasing agent. The system we set up required that for all but very small emergency purchases the purchasing agent solicited bids and gave the order to the lowest bidder. Careful records were made of the bids received and the awards made. These were kept on a visible Cardex file in duplicate, one set remaining in the office of the purchasing officer, and the other set exposed in an open corridor where it could be examined by any person at any time during office hours by a mere flip of the cards. If, for instance, someone was interested in the city's purchase of brooms, all he had to do was to pull out the "B" drawer, flip the card under the title "Brooms," and see there every purchase of brooms made during the year, from whom the purchase was made, at what price, and also all the other bids made by any prospective vendor of brooms.

To fit into this system, purchase orders were made in quintuplicate: one copy was retained in the purchasing office; one went to the department of finance to be entered as an obligation against the appropriation and to receive certification that funds were available in the proper appropriation of the budget to meet the expenditure; a third copy, after that certification and award was made, went to the auditor, a fourth to the city manager, and a fifth copy, also certified, went to the vendor. I did not myself see any of the purchase orders until the day after they had been awarded, cleared, and certified. However, every morning I went through all the purchase orders of the previous day, and, if anything seemed to me to require more information or my comment, I would indorse the order in green ink. It was not very long until I discovered that, not only in the purchasing office in the finance department but in all the other departments of the city, a note from the manager's office in green ink got instant attention. In fact it was not long before I began to hear little tales of how, when there was an argument in any department about what ought to be done, one of the favorite comments was, "Look out, or you will get a letter in green ink!"

There was a particular problem concerning the administration of the purchasing office which stemmed directly from the language of the new charter. The charter forbade the city from purchasing anything from any member of the council or from any corporation in which any member of the council had any interest as a stockholder, officer, employee, or otherwise. That limitation, which of course had seemed very wise to the charter commission in view of the history of the past four or five years, actually worked out as an inconvenient handicap. For instance, there were two large flour mills in Knoxville. In one of them Mayor Ben A. Morton was a stockholder and actually exercised control. In the other the majority stock was owned by William Peters, another member of the council. That meant that for the use of Knoxville's institutions we could not buy flour in Knoxville except at retail prices. Of course the retail prices were higher than the prices we could command by purchases direct from the mills, so we turned to Chattanooga or Johnson City or some other place for our purchases of flour, a circumstance which caused no little comment not only in Knoxville but in the cities from which we solicited bids.

Then also the mayor, Mr. Morton, was the principal stockholder in one of the largest wholesale grocery stores in the town, while another member of the council, Rush S. Hazen, was stockholder in another wholesale grocery establishment. That meant that we could not even ask those establishments to bid. This, however, worked out pretty well. Mr. Thomas, the purchasing agent, when he got bids for grocery supplies soon formed the habit of checking the prices with the wholesale establishments which were barred by law from bidding. And I must say that occasionally I made that particular check myself after the purchase orders had been made.

In the last previous years of the city's operations the expenditures had run to nearly $4 million. The floating debt of the city was ascertained by mid-summer to have been over a million dollars more than had been anticipated, and actually ran to over $4.5 million. The previous administration had had authority to fund this floating debt and had actually issued $2 million in bonds to do so, but none of that money had been applied to the debt. Therefore, during the year I arranged for the sale of $3,870,000 in bonds to fund the open debt, and claims to the amount of $300,000 were rejected as representing duplicate payments or in some instances claims for goods and services which actually had not been received or rendered.

The new accounting, contract, and purchasing systems equipped me with the necessary machinery to control effectively all the city's expenditures and, on the other side of the budget, to be currently informed on revenues and other income. The income control was particularly valuable for the water revenues, the fees received at the city hospital, the fines assessed in the police court, and the like—miscellaneous forms of revenue which theretofore had been reported at irregular intervals and without any immediate auditorial supervision. The revenues from these sources soon began to amount to more than had been estimated in that very quick and hurried budget that the new council had passed when it first took office, in the preparation of which I had assisted in one of my visits to Knoxville some weeks before I actually took over the manager's job.

In addition to the handicap in the matter of purchasing from concerns in which members of the council had any interest, the charter also contained another limitation also evidently inserted because of the difficulties in which the city had been placed by the old administration. Just as purchasing had been a matter of favoritism, so also the city had had the habit of letting contracts for public works and then, after the work was done and the bills were due, facing the community with an election for bond issues to meet the city's obligations. Therefore the new charter contained a provision that no contractual obligation should be entered into until after the bond issue had been approved by the people, the entire issue sold, and the money put in the bank. This meant that when we entered upon a great improvement program for a new waterworks or for new school buildings, etc., something more than $2 million worth of bonds had to be approved and sold and the proceeds deposited in the banks. The normal and proper procedure, of course, would have been, after the bonds were approved by the people in a referendum, to issue them only as they were needed to make payments on the contracts.

While this feature of the charter was a protective one, and one easily understood by anybody who looked over the past record of the city, it did mean that there would be large amounts of money lying idle. Up to that time no bank in the city of Knoxville had ever paid any interest on city deposits. That meant that the feature of the charter intended to protect the city's interest would actually work out as a bonanza for the banks.

When I arranged for the sale of the bond issues, I asked the banks in New York what interest they would pay on deposits if I left the cash in New York. I got several bids there. Then I approached a bank in Chattanooga and found that it would pay me 4¼ per cent on deposits of the bond money against withdrawals of sixty-day periods, this being the interest the bonds would carry and also the then prevailing rediscount rate of the Federal Reserve Banks. Then I asked the presidents of the five banks in Knoxville to meet in my office. I told them that the charter compelled me to sell the entire bond issue at one time, that there would, therefore, be large amounts of money on deposit in the banks, that I had approached bankers in other cities, that one bank had agreed to take the entire amount and pay the city 4¼ per cent interest on deposits—the same rates carried by the bonds. But, of course, I added, I would prefer to keep the money in Knoxville, and as I knew all the banks there were rediscounting paper with the Federal Reserve System, I thought they ought to be willing to pay the city the interest. The five men looked at each other. Some of their Adam's apples rose and fell. It was to some of them a bitter dose, because they had looked forward to a free ride on that amount of money, assuming that I would distribute the deposits equally among the five banks, as I had been doing with daily balances. But, of course, they all accepted my proposition, and thus the city was saved any expense on account of the extraordinary provision of the charter. The city would pay 4¼ per cent interest on the bonds, but it would receive the same interest from the banks until the money was actually required for expenditures.

One feature of the new financial and purchasing system that I installed was that the city paid its bills promptly. Since no purchase order or contractual debt was entered into unless the money was on hand to pay for it, the payments were prompt. One might think that this would be considered an advantage, but that was not always so. For instance, Fred Ault, the treasurer and clerk of the council, arranged in advance, as he was compelled to do by the new accounting system, for a sufficient amount of money to pay the judges and clerks of an election that was held. The judges and clerks, after it was ascertained who they were and that they actually served, were told to come in to the city hall on a certain day to get their checks. When they got there, the checks were all written out, and sufficient identification of the person was all that was necessary before the check was handed over. The judges and clerks went out on the courthouse lawn. They got their heads together. They whined and whimpered. Mr. Ault told me they were out under a big tree, and I suggested that he go out and find out what was the matter with them. After an hour he came back and said they felt that they had been cheated and deprived of one of the principal pleasures of life. Many of them had been judges and clerks before, and always they had had to come down to the city hall on the day of payment, find that there was no money for them, then make out vouchers, then frequently come back four or five times before they got their money. All of this gave these persons, many of them elderly and more or less retired, several trips to town and an opportunity to damn the government and to raise Cain generally with the city. To come merely to present personal identification and get their checks had deprived them of what they considered to be the rights of free American and East Tennessee citizens.

The newly installed procedures of purchasing not only produced some amusing incidents but also redounded to my benefit by giving me a reputation as a hard trader. The charter had concentrated all the purchasing for the city in the department of finance, including purchases and contracts made by the school board and the board of library trustees. The schools and the library were particularly resistant to the new scheme of things since neither their personnel nor their administrative procedures were under the manager. No doubt some of the other departments would have resisted if they had been in a position to question my authority. For instance, the superintendent of schools said that we could order only one particular kind of floor oil—oil to be applied to the floors to keep down dust. The purchasing agent under my instructions got specifications from the Bureau of Standards in Washington and found that a better floor oil could be purchased in barrel lots for less than one-fourth the cost of the product demanded by the school authorities, which was packaged in gallon cans. The school superintendent protested to me. I suggested that he take five or six rooms, apply the floor oil that the school had been using in one, the one that the purchasing agent had chosen in another, and two or three other oils on which bids had been received in the others. If that was done, I told him, I would see to it that the oil chosen by the school authorities would be purchased. It was done. The first choice after inspection by the school people was the cheapest oil—the one which the purchasing agent had rated number one. The one the school people liked the least was the high-priced one that they had been using. That settled the row so far as the schools were concerned.

As in most cities, there was a paving contractor who for many years had managed to get all or nearly all the paving contracts. The first time I advertised for bids, the specifications were drawn up by Alexander Harris, the director of public service and the city engineer, in accordance with the best practices we had been able to observe and were checked against the standard specifications used in the District of Columbia. That meant that, as was usual in those days, bids were made for natural Trinidad asphalt, oil asphalt, and, since we were in that part of the country, Kentucky rock asphalt. Always the natural Trinidad asphalt cost twelve or fourteen cents more per yard.

Two or three days before the bids were to be opened, the Knoxville contractor, who had the reputation of having very close relations indeed with the former commission government, came to see me. He said he was worried by the fact that he had seen in the newspapers that I thought that oil asphalt was just as good as Trinidad asphalt, and he wanted to know how that could be.

"Well," I said, "even admitting that the natural asphalt is better, what is to keep you from giving us natural asphalt, with our facilities here in Knoxville, by the simple process of taking a medicine dropper and putting one drop of natural asphalt in an 8,000-gallon tank car of oil asphalt?"

"I gotcha," he said. "It will be straight oil and not fake natural."

Then he said, "There is something else I want to know. Who gets the split?"

"There will be no split," was my reply.

When the bids were opened, this contractor's proposition was to lay the pavements according to the specifications at a little less than half the price per yard that he had charged and collected from the previous city administration.

There was also the difficult problem of buying fire hose. The fire chief, like most of his brethren, preferred one particular brand of hose. I had no doubt that that particular brand was in some ways superior to most of the others. But when I inserted in the specifications a notice that one of every ten lengths of hose would be selected at random and sent to the Bureau of Standards in Washington for testing, the prices tumbled.

At a later time when I was purchasing nearly a million dollars' worth of cast-iron pipe for a new water system, I knew that I was dickering in a field where it was very usual for all the bidders to submit identical bids. Also, Knoxville was about halfway between Lynchburg, Virginia, and Birmingham, Alabama, two of the principal cast-iron pipe foundries. In this case I announced in a letter to prospective bidders sent to each of the cast-iron pipe foundries in the United States a list of all the names to whom the prospectus was being sent. The list included cast-iron pipe manufacturers in Belgium and Sweden. And that little gambit had a favorable effect on cast-iron prices—that is, favorable to the city. Because of these and many other similar instances, my reputation as a hard trader was improved, bringing me a great deal of praise from a citizenry dominated by a community notion that such a reputation represented a high meed of praise.

In the heart of the city, very close to the business district, there was an elementary school of twelve classrooms. One morning shortly after midnight fire was discovered, and, by the time the fire department came on the scene, it was out of control. The building was completely destroyed. The charter permitted the issue of up to $200,000 in bonds without referendum to replace burned or otherwise destroyed city buildings. The insurance on the building amounted to $52,000. The city owned on the main business street a small two-story building in which had been housed the offices of the water department.

Also in the heart of the city, but some distance away from the principal retail and business center, there had been a state institution, a school for the deaf. A few years earlier that had been moved to a new installation a few miles away from the city, and the old school had been sold by the state to a group of Knoxville citizens for $400,000.

There was, then, in the heart of Knoxville a nine-acre park surrounded by a masonry wall on which stood the original deaf-and-dumb asylum erected in 1835 and designed by the great Philadelphia architect William Strickland. To that had been added from time to time wings which included twenty-two classrooms, a large assembly hall, and a gymnasium. Also in the same park was another well-constructed building and several nondescript structures. Here, then, was almost a perfect site for a city hall.

The owners of the property asked $600,000 to sell it to the city. The newspapers and citizens' organizations highly approved of its purchase for a city hall and indeed put a good deal of pressure on me to recommend its acquisition to the council.

I dickered and dickered. At last, like a good East Tennessee trader, I offered to give them $452,000, which was the purchase price plus interest at 6 per cent for the eighteen months they had held the property, plus 6 per cent profit. I stuck to my offer, and at last it was accepted.

To find the $452,000, the city council issued $200,000 in emergency bonds, sold the lot on which the burned school had stood for $85,000, sold the old waterworks office building for $75,000, collected from fire insurance policies $22,000, and then applied savings already accumulated from expenditures in the amount of $70,000, making up the $452,000. It was a good deal and widely recognized as such.

Then we squeezed the budget just a little more and found enough money to rehabilitate the original old asylum building for the city hall, turned the school buildings over to the school board, and devoted the other large brick building on the grounds to the department of welfare and the health office.

It was about that time that businessmen and others that I began to meet began calling me not only a hard trader but added to that another encomium. They said I was a hard horse-trader.

At any rate, out of the deal the city got a commodious city hall, and we were able to move all the city departments into it with the exception of the police department, which was then permitted to expand its crowded quarters in the second story of Market Hall.

Knoxville had had for many years as its health officer Dr. Cockrane, a practicing physician who carried the responsibilities of health officer for a very meager compensation and with almost no clerical help. Actually, the health department was responsible for little more than the registration of births and deaths; a bureau of vital statistics with only two clerks was set up to meet the demands of the state health department. The doctor had no proper laboratory facilities and no control over the water system, and, with only one inspector, he was able to do very little about milk control. From time to time when the water got too bad he used to issue appeals to the people to boil their drinking water. He had been given almost no money, almost no help, and, being a man of high personal and professional integrity, he welcomed any change. Particularly, he himself did not want to continue in office.

On one of my visits to New York, while I was still in Petersburg on a bond-selling errand, I found myself unexpectedly with a little more than two hours before my train for Petersburg would leave the Pennsylvania Station in New York. At 330 Seventh Avenue, near the station, there was, I knew, the office of the American Public Health Association, of which I was a fellow. In the same building I knew I would find many other organizations in the field of public health and hospital administration. I spent two hours in that building, and while I was there I found the names of two or three likely prospects for health officer, two or three for supervising public health nurses, and seven or eight for public health nurses. I went away with a good deal of armament to pursue my effort to persuade Frank Bane, the Virginia state director of welfare, to come to Knoxville.

If those organizations had not been grouped in one building, I am sure I would have frittered away the two hours and would not have undertaken the task of chasing all around New York to see each of them. It was an important lesson to me in the value of propinquity in the grouping of independent autonomous organizations not working as an integrated or articulated whole but bound together by an interest in common or related fields of activity.

After Bane decided to come with me, he and I selected a Dr. Haygood of the Georgia State Health Department to be health officer of Knoxville. Bane's department was to be responsible for the health officer, for the administration of the hospital, for the meager public recreational facilities then existing, as well as for the detention home for delinquent girls, the pesthouse, and two or three other such institutions.

We asked and got help from the state health department and from the United States Public Health Service and submitted to the council a standard milk inspection ordinance, an ordinance providing for compulsory vaccination for smallpox, an ordinance for the licensing of midwives, and various other standard public health regulatory ordinances, all in preparation for getting a modern health department under way.

An immediate task in the welfare field was the reorganization of the Knoxville General Hospital, a fountain of scandal and a very monument of inefficiency. Both Bane and I had known in Richmond a hospital administrator, Miss Rosa van Vort, who for several years had made a specialty of taking over the management of hospitals that were in trouble, straightening them out, helping to discover a competent superintendent, and leaving for another such job—a veritable female Hercules in her accomplishment of task after task of cleaning out Augean stables. She had just completed one such reorganization job when we persuaded her to come to Knoxville. She tackled the job fearlessly, and with the backing that she received from Mr. Bane and from a majority, but by no means all, of the members of the medical faculty she soon had the institution cleaned up not only physically but administratively and medically.

Alexander Harris, the director of public service, had perhaps the most difficult task of all. The streets and roads of the city needed attention. The streets that were paved were in relatively good condition, but there had been a minimum of maintenance of them, and the greater mileage of the streets that were unpaved, improved only by macadam or in some cases utterly unimproved, were in bad shape. The planning of the city's water and sewers had been hit and miss. There was little relation between the incidental sewage jobs that had been done and no relation at all between storm sewers and sanitary sewers. The outfalls in the sanitary sewers flowed directly into the Tennessee River, and its capacity was often limited indeed. Many parts of the city, including those of the best residential districts, had no sanitary sewage whatever but depended entirely on cesspools.

My experience with the problems of water and sewer had been exclusively in Washington and Petersburg. Both those cities, one in 1876, the other in 1884, had had a great sanitary engineer, Rudolph Herring, make a complete plan envisaging the city fifty years in the future. Knoxville had had no plan at all, and I for one was shocked by the helter-skelter, higgledy-piggledy situation.

To make matters worse, the outgoing government either had kept no blueprints of the existing system or had destroyed them before the new council came in. We did not know where the water mains were. We did not know where the sewers were. We did not know actually the precise location of the force mains that went from the pumping station at the river level up to the height where the filtration plant and the principal reservoir stood. We could trace accurately but with great difficulty the lines of the cast-iron water pipes with magnetic instruments, but that gave us precise information about neither the diameter of the pipes nor, more particularly, the location of valves. When it came to terra-cotta or concrete sewers, the only way to discover them was to dig in.

Mr. Harris tackled the relatively uncomplicated road maintenance problem with great vigor and soon solved it, temporarily at any rate, greatly to the satisfaction of the expressed public opinion. However, the immediate pressing danger to Knoxville, not as a municipal corporation, perhaps, but as the home of eighty or ninety thousand human beings was the touch-and-go problem of the water system. The pumping machinery was not only inadequate but, as I have indicated, in momentary danger of complete failure. There had been agitation for several years for a new water plant, but nothing had been done about it. Again I turned to a man whose qualifications were personally known to me. I suggested Colonel Frederick W. Albert, who had been assistant superintendent of the waterworks in the District of Columbia and who had later been in charge of the water and sewage system of our principal installations made in France for the American Expeditionary Force in World War I. Mr. Harris had looked into the qualifications of a great many persons, and, while I left the choice up to him, he agreed with me that Colonel Albert was the man for the job. We persuaded him to come, and he was installed in the Department of Public Service as the superintendent of waterworks.

Almost immediately, then, we employed the services of a consulting engineering firm, Alvord and Burdick of Chicago, to draw up plans for a new water system, including a complete new pumping and intake system and a radical revision of the circulation and distribution system for the whole city.

The administration of the waterworks was not entirely a physical job, however, as Mr. Harris and Colonel Albert soon discovered. There had been a great deal of maladministration. For instance, in many places the meters, supposed to measure the water used by large industrial concerns, had been bypassed. This was true in one or two large manufacturing establishments, one or two large laundries, and particularly in a recreation park maintained by the street-railway system, where there was a beautiful lake presumed to be fed by mountain springs. One such "mountain spring" was an unmetered, unvalved, four-inch pipe connected to the city water system, which brought in, of course, no revenue at all. Some of these "leaks," which totaled considerably more than a million gallons of water a day, we cut off, and in some instances we collected back water rents. There was no way to measure the water that had been fraudulently bypassed around the meter, but in several cases I simply made an estimate, presented a bill, accepted a check, and made no fuss about it. Perhaps from some points of view it would have been better if I had exposed these water cheaters, but there was no possible way to prove in a court of law how much water had been taken or whether or not it had been done wilfully. I thought it better to take the cash and let the credit go.

Mr. Harris did not hesitate to break with the tradition of the town and do a great deal of work on force account, especially in street maintenance and water and sewer maintenance, that theretofore had always been done by contract. This enabled the city to save a great deal of money not only by reducing the actual cost but by permitting immediate repairs and constant routine maintenance, which would have been impossible under the contract system with the restrictions placed upon the procedure for advertising for bids, receiving proposals, and the like.

Major Walker, at the head of the police and fire departments, also immediately introduced schemes for modernization based on his experience and on the information obtained from other cities. The fire department, as a matter of fact, was very well managed under a chief named Sam Boyd, and in that respect there was little to be done except to improve the flow of information, to regularize routine reporting upward to the director of public safety, to the city manager, and through him to the City Council.

In the police department there was a great deal to be done. Records, if kept, were inadequate and disorganized. The members of the force, which was under civil service, were for the most part immediately responsive to the improved direction and responded to the new spirit of leadership, although it was exercised directly through the same chief. While the recruitment of members of the force was subject to the civil service commission, that body had almost no machinery for its task of selecting persons. On the other hand, it was almost impossible to dismiss a policeman for inefficiency or incompetence once he was on the force. This sometimes was not as bad as it sounds. For instance, we had a detective who unquestionably was the best homicide man that Major Walker and I had ever known. He was a civil service employee. He had, however, one slight handicap: he had never learned to read or to write. But he was a keen observer and had a marvelous memory, and more frequently than not he got his man.

A part of my job of top management was that of keeping the council and, for that matter, the public informed. I kept in close touch with all five directors of departments. I had staff conferences at least once a week, which were promptly dubbed "cabinet meetings" by the reporters. This I did largely because I wanted the heads of departments to keep in touch with each other and partly because it seemed to be the thing to do according to what I read in such journals as were available which touched on administrative problems. Actually, however, my doubts about the utility of such staff conferences soon were strengthened. It was evident that the directors of welfare and safety were not entirely interested in the problems of the director of finance, and the director of finance was not completely entranced by the reports that were coming in from the department of public service. While I continued the weekly meetings, I found it more profitable to my problems of top management to see each one of the directors at least twice or three times a week, separately and alone.

Also, I stepped up my activity of making notes with my green ink on their individual daily and weekly written reports. I also discovered another scheme: I myself would read through all the available journals in the field of municipal administration and send them to the director of the department concerned, with a green-ink notation, asking the director after he had read the piece to talk with me about it. That not only kept me in close touch with the director and his department, but it also enabled me to keep track of how closely the department was keeping up with events in other cities.

That was the internal job of co-ordination.

The external job of my office was first, of course, to live up to my primary responsibility to report to the council. This I did by installing a system of regular reports that went to the clerk of the council and through him to the council at its regular meetings, which were held every alternate Tuesday, and at many special meetings that were called by the mayor.

The other external job was to keep the public fully informed through the medium of the newspapers. I saw a reporter from each of the three newspapers every day. There was one morning paper, and its representative called in the afternoon. There were two afternoon papers, and the rivalry between them was such that under no circumstances would both reporters see me at the same time. Each was avid for a scoop. Each was so jealous that I had every morning to watch my step to see that I did not favor one against the other. However, if one reporter elicited information only by questioning me I did not tip off his rival on the subject.

When my wife Bess and I first got to Knoxville, I told her that I had a great desire to go up to Rogersville, a town in Hawkins County in East Tennessee, to see an ancient distant cousin of mine, Frank Amis, who at that time was the oldest living alumnus of Princeton University. I had heard ever since my childhood that he lived in the oldest inhabited house in Tennessee, a house built by one of the pioneers that came over the mountains from Virginia to set up one of the first of what later became known as the Wautauga settlements. These settlements later became the core of the short-lived state of Franklin, which attempted to secede from North Carolina and which still later became the state of Tennessee.

Our arrival in Knoxville was in mid-December. The winter was bad, the weather miserable, and during the winter I saw in the newspaper that Frank Amis had died.

When spring came, the weather was good; the roads were passable. Bess and I drove up to Rogersville and went out to see Miss Anne Amis, Frank's eldest daughter. There she lived in the oldest house in Tennesseee. Its foundation was an octagonal stone structure pierced by portholes or rifle ports—in short, the foundation was a fort erected for defense against the Indians. The superstructure was of wood. No change had been made in the essential features of the building since the late eighteenth century. Miss Anne Amis' brother, she said, was then the city engineer of Charleston, South Carolina. She pronounced her name "A-mee." She was, as I was also, a descendant of the Amis family of Manikin Town on the James River above Richmond, one of the settlements of the Huguenot refugees who fled France after the revocation of the Edict of Nantes in 1688.

Miss Amis was a most agreeable person. She showed us a grandfather clock that had been brought over the mountains on horseback, rifles and powder horns that antedated the Revolution, and several other mementos of the time when East Tennessee was not quite certainly a part of western North Carolina, not quite certainly the state of Franklin, not quite certainly a part of the Aaron Burr empire of Blennerhasset, which was to be backed by Spanish and French imperial authority.

Now it so happened that both my wife and I were descended from Paris Sims. We had heard tales of how the four brothers of the Sims family had emigrated from Alexandria, Virginia, into the western counties of North Carolina. Some members of the family had looked through the records in the counties of western North Carolina but could find no trace of them. No one of these searchers seemed to have thought at the time that what is now the state of Tennessee then constituted, in the view of the authorities of North Carolina, the western counties of that state. Here Miss Amis brought out an old ledger. It contained the accounts carried on by her ancester, also Frank Amis. He had established an advanced trading post of the Wautauga settlements. He had built a dam across the river. It furnished the power to run a gristmill. He had a distillery. He had a blacksmith shop. He maintained an establishment for the exchange of goods. He was a wholesaler. He was a retailer. And here this ledger contained accounts of the Amis business from the year 1781 down to and including 1784. At first the accounts were kept in pounds, shillings, and pence. Later they were turned into eagles, dollars, dimes, cents, and mills. The accountant seemed to be utterly innocent of the advantages of the decimal system, so he continued to add the amounts recorded precisely in five separate lined columns and translate them each into the next higher denomination as he had done under the English system.

In this book, Bess and I discovered the accounts of William, James, John, and Paris Sims, our long-lost ancestors. This place, then definitely in those western counties of North Carolina, had become Tennessee.

My wife's father, Judge Sims, as he usually was called, was an ardent prohibitionist. At that particular moment he was visiting us in our home in Knoxville with his wife, the former Nancy Kittrell, my wife's beautiful mother. It was with the greatest hilarity that we discovered that while William, John, and James Sims had their accounts charged with all sorts of things from bacon and flour to plows and axes, Paris Sims, our ancestor, at that time evidently a bachelor, for a period of three years also had run up his account with the Amis establishment, and outside of a few charges for the shoeing of his horse, every charge was for whiskey.

CHAPTER XVII

THE BATTLE ROYAL

There were eleven members of the City Council in Knoxville. Only one of them was articulate. The mayor, Ben Morton, could be extremely cogent in conversation with one person at a time, but he seemed to lose his voice almost entirely when he had to stand up to speak or when there were more than three or four persons in the group to which he addressed himself. Dr. Albright, the druggist who had political ambitions but who had never been admitted into the inner circles of either party or any faction of either party in Knox County, could speak at length, but he too was inhibited by the assumption of a standing posture. He could talk but he could not make a speech.

Only Lee Monday, the opposition, the one member of the council who had been elected by the old guard, the only man chosen at the polls who had not been on the People's Ticket, from which every identifiable politician had been excepted, could speak. He in turn represented only one of the six districts, and that district was the then sparsely populated South Knoxville, the portion of the city that lay to the south of the Tennessee River, where little streams came into the great river from little valleys separated by high hills—almost mountain ranges. Many of those ridges were exploited as marble quarries. South Knoxville was inhabited almost exclusively by native white persons of long mountain lineage. With one or two exceptions it had no rich people. It had no Negroes. It was truly mountain, East Tennessee, native American—and "Native American" in the sense that those two words once were used as the official appellation of a political party that in popular parlance and even among its own members gloried in the name of "Know-Nothing."

Lee Monday had an elder brother, a man I had known for many

years, a leader in the Republican party, a wealthy man, a bachelor, a man who patronized the best tailors and who had brought out of his East Tennessee mountaineer origin a great native wit, which he had sublimated into *savoir-faire*.

His brother Lee had none of that. He was a hillbilly and he gloried in it. He was a roughneck and he knew it. He dressed the part and looked it. He was an orator in the good old mountaineer fashion, and he knew that too. Most of the time nearly every council meeting was taken up by his oratorical displays. It was frequently difficult to understand exactly what he was talking about, but one knew, whatever the words, he instinctively was talking for the South Knoxvillians against all and sundry. He was the representative of his district and he was the representative of his clan, the East Tennesseans. He was representative of that top-of-the-voice screamology of East Tennessee mountain politics, and rarely in either his speeches in the council or in the diatribes which my ears suffered when he called at my office did he ever depart from his own clear consciousness of his place in the scheme of things. He never failed to tell me, "Remember young fellow, I am an East Tennessee Jew."

One Tuesday morning when the council was meeting in the old Market Hall he arose and attacked the manager, demanded that the council discipline me, and intimated that they should dismiss me for plunging the city into debt.

The basis for this particular attack was fantastic, but nevertheless it was effective in placing him at once at the head of the opposition to the new administration.

The fiscal year in Knoxville began on October 1. The tax abstract was not received from the county assessor until the following March, and tax collections were not due to begin until June. There was no penalty for non-payment of taxes until the following September. In effect, the city was compelled to carry on for eleven months of its fiscal year very largely on money borrowed in anticipation of taxes. This situation had been aggravated over a long period of years by the action of the state legislature on a motion that the legislative delegations from Knox County would introduce once every four or six years. They would get a bill passed postponing the time of attaching penalties for overdue taxes for at least a month. This always was represented as a scheme to relieve the poor, tax-burdened citizens of the community.

What it actually resulted in, of course, was a continued profit to the banks for advancing money. In the last few years of the old administration, the rate had been uniformly 6 per cent plus commission.

Even before I went to Knoxville, I had negotiated the sale of tax-anticipation notes worth $900,000 at the unprecedentedly low rate (that is, for Knoxville) of $4\frac{1}{4}$ per cent. Later I had sold another $600,000 at the unheard-of low rate (so far as Knoxville was concerned) of $3\frac{3}{4}$ per cent. Even the $3\frac{3}{4}$ per cent I had succeeded in reducing by leaving the bulk of the funds obtained from the sale with the Chemical National Bank of New York, where it was subject to monthly withdrawals and earned 1 per cent interest, so that the cost to the city actually was reduced to a little more than $2\frac{3}{4}$ per cent per annum.

Mr. Monday arose and said that I had been there but three months and had plunged the city in debt to the extent of two million dollars. The mayor and the astonished members of the council asked, in effect, "How come?" He pointed out the fact that I had been borrowing money in the New York banks and part of it I had left in New York. In the course of the attack he did admit that it wasn't two million dollars but only a million and a half. The members of the council and the director of law patiently tried to explain to him that this was the usual practice. His reply to that was that the city owes the money, therefore the manager has plunged the city into debt.

This all was accompanied by a harangue, a pounding of the table, and a show of indignation that clearly indicated that the opposition had opened fire. Actually, he made no particular allegations of any misconduct on my part, or of anything that any of the department heads had done, or of anything that had been done by other members of the council.

The reaction of the public seemed to be nothing more than stunned surprise. All the newspapers pointed out the fallacy of his charges and went into great detail to show how the management thus far had exercised a great many tax-saving economies in practically every branch of the government. For the time being very little public support was attracted to the opposition, but it was evident that it was merely the opening gun in a big battle.

That battle was to be fought not in Knoxville but in the state capital in Nashville. The time was approaching when the Republican and Democratic parties would make their nominations for members of the

House of Representatives and the Senate, to be voted upon in the general election in November.

Ordinarily, the Republican candidates were the only ones that had any chance to win in the regular elections, and therefore only the Republican party paid very much attention to the primary election. A citizens' committee was formed which announced that it would demand of every candidate for nomination to the state legislature a pledge to keep faith with the new charter and resist every effort to repeal or amend it. This soon developed into a pitched battle between the citizens' committee for the maintenance of the charter, on the one hand, and the regular Republican party organization, on the other. When the primary results came in, the five candidates for the House of Representatives who had pledged their support for the maintenance of the new form of government were nominated, but the candidate for the Senate who had given that pledge was defeated, by a margin of eleven votes, by a man who already had served several terms in the legislature and who was recognized as one of the principal leaders of the Republican party in the county.

The Democratic party then had its innings. It decided to make only a token opposition to the five Republican candidates for the House of Representatives and to concentrate its full strength on the opposition to the Senate nominee. Only once or twice in the long history of Knox County had a Democrat been elected to the state Senate from that county. In the following November, on the sole issue of the maintenance of the council-manager form of government, the Democrat defeated the Republican. The effect was to throw back the political battle from the state arena to its proper place in Knoxville, the city most concerned. But in Knoxville the opposition was strengthened; it had discovered that it would have to fight its battles at home. Mr. Monday kept up his harangues, invented a new bogie for almost every council meeting, and demolished it with vigor.

And in the meantime I went on, assured of the support of the other ten members of the council. Nevertheless, it was not long until I sensed that some members of the council were extremely restive, and some of them tended to resent the fact that I made public in advance, through the newspapers, every considered and final recommendation that I was to make to the council. That meant that occasionally the other ten members of the council would meet, usually at the home of one, to talk about what should be done. One member of the council made a motion to expel Mr. Monday. That measure was firmly supported by two of the newspapers and as firmly opposed by another. It was a question upon which I had to be neutral, but in the end it seemed to me wiser counsels prevailed when the motion to expel him from the council was not pressed to a vote. If it had been, undoubtedly he would have been expelled, and he probably would have gone to court. He would have won the case, and, even if he hadn't won, he would have been promoted from the position of public nuisance to that of people's martyr. In the meantime I went on with my tasks.

The axis around which the political affairs of the community whirled was not so much the courthouse, which was the stronghold of the organized Republicans, nor the city hall, which was sometimes presumed to be the headquarters of the citizens' groups, but the sidewalk in front of the Farragut Hotel at Gay and Clinch streets and the coffee shop in the hotel. Here, toward noon, little groups of persons met and talked. Nearly always one or two members of the council were to be found there. Sometimes one or more of my directors would be engaged in these street-corner conversations, particularly Mr. Bane and Mr. Egerton.

While I went to lunch at that hotel practically every day, I always evaded the street-corner conferences and dived immediately through the lobby into the main dining room, where I sat at a table reserved for members of the Rotary Club.

However, during all the struggle for the nomination and election of the delegates for the state legislature, I scrupulously avoided any contact whatever with the organized group that was conducting the campaign for those candidates pledged to maintain the integrity of the charter. I avoided being drawn into conversations, even private conversations, about the forthcoming political fight. It sometimes was difficult to find a way to parry the supercharged questions that were shot at me three times a day by the reporters of the three newspapers, but I managed fairly well and succeeded in preventing any public statement in any meeting or gathering or in the newspapers. I was holding strictly to my line that my business was management of the city's business subject to the control of the council and that I would adhere without variation to my rule not to be involved in any way with political contests—factional, partisan, or otherwise.

By June it became evident that we were collecting considerably more taxes than would be necessary to meet the budget expenditures for the year. I decided that I would recommend to the council a refund of 10 per cent on taxes for the year. This was to be accomplished by remitting the refund to those who had already paid their taxes and by reducing the tax bills by the same amount for those who had not yet paid. This amounted to a 10 per cent tax dividend.

I went over the whole matter with the director of law, then with my other directors. For the first time, I consulted the mayor individually without at the same time going to his colleagues in the council. He agreed with me that in view of the situation it would be wiser to announce to the newspapers the recommendation I intended to present to the council rather than to make the recommendation in a council meeting, where it would be certain to stir up a stormy one-man opposition.

I wrote a brief formal recommendation to the council and gave it to the reporters for the two afternoon newspapers.

The morning paper, which was a staunch supporter of the new system, promptly went on the street with a one-sheet extra. The corner of Gay and Clinch was agog. A tax dividend was something never before heard of. I was utterly astonished at the reaction and much more astonished when not only the Knoxville newspapers but the Associated Press and the United Press circulated the story by wire.

What I intended was a demonstration of efficient management and economical administration. What I actually did was far more than that. It was a political master stroke, and it was so hailed. Members of the opposition began to deride my insistence that I was not a politician; and in the subsequent election, they tended to credit the tax dividend for the victory of the council-manager forces and for the defeat of those who wanted to repeal the charter in the next legislature. And, by the same token, the dividend intensified the political opposition and shifted the center of its attack from the council to me personally.

Bringing in Miss van Vort from Richmond as the new superintendent of the hospital had been the capstone to my importation of Walker and Bane to be directors. Wherever I went, and almost wherever any of those people went, we were certain to be greeted by someone whistling "Carry Me Back to Old Virginia," and in almost no time at all Walker, Bane, and I were hearing that tune from friend and foe alike.

The Battle Royal

I had made the announcement of my settlement of the Southern Railway lawsuit to the reporter for the morning paper. This was in accordance with my practice of apportioning as equally as possible important city news between the morning paper and the two afternoon papers. One of the reporters for the *Knoxville Sentinel* who had asked me dozens of times about the Southern Railway matter became infuriated because I hadn't saved the news for him. He found among the opposition a businessman who was willing and anxious to go after me. The businessman put up the money, the reporter furnished the know-how, and they at once started a weekly newspaper called the *Free Press,* a four-page affair which was devoted exclusively to denunciation of me.

I was called King Louis I. The new city hall was called Buckingham Palace. Just why the French and English royal families and palaces got so intertwined in this affair, I do not know. The *Free Press* came out every week at first. It pretended to print no news except attacks on the city manager, the directors of the departments, the members of the council. In so doing it played up every complaint, legitimate or illegitimate, on the part of any employee of the city. Any rumor that would reflect on the city government was fanned into a full-scale article. All the traditional tricks of invective, of barbed jest, of partisan perverted polemics that had been the tradition in East Tennessee from Revolutionary days were employed.

Personally it didn't affect me very much because I never read it. I did hear a great deal about it, of course, and people told me things that were in it; but I thought I would be more comfortable if I ignored it.

Knoxville was cursed with the nuisance of two telephone systems. There was the Bell system called the "Old Telephone" and the Peoples' Telephone Company called the "New Telephone." In accordance with my notion that administrative officials of the city should be available at all times, I had had both telephones installed in my home, as did all my directors and their principal assistants. At times when one of the *Free Press* stories was attracting a great deal of attention, my wife and I would be the recipients of special visitations. One telephone or the other would ring every thirty minutes throughout the night. I did not dare to fail to answer them. Sometimes this would go on for as long as a week. Sometimes, when I answered the phone, the person at the other end would curse me, sometimes laugh, but more often there was nothing but silence. My wife and I were deprived of sleep and our lives were made miserable in our home. Some of the directors, particularly Major Walker at the head of the police department, was subjected to similar treatment. Rarely did these conspirators in nuisance bother the members of the council, although occasionally they paid their nocturnal respects to the mayor. There was nothing to do but to go on.

Another election was coming up. The council had called a special referendum election on the issuance of bonds for a new water plant. The plans had been carefully prepared, adequately published, and fully discussed in the council. The council had made one change to include a reservoir on the south side of the river in Mr. Monday's bailiwick, although the engineers did not deem it necessary. The opposition attempted to rally its forces against the bond issue, predicting enormous increases in the water rates, attacking the engineering plans, and so on. Nevertheless, when the election came, the bond issue carried by a vote of ten to one, and we proceeded at once to make the plans for the new installation.

Then the *Free Press* converted itself into a daily; the opposition forces began a more intensive campaign, and eventually the terms of the charter itself were invoked for a recall of five of the six district members of the council. Another campaign and another election were on the way.

Despite the 10 per cent tax refund, which amounted to nearly $400,000, and despite extended activities in practically every department, the city ended its first fiscal year under the new order with a surplus of $216,000. The new budget was drawn up in accordance with the experience of the first year, and the city began its operations with the necessity for tax-anticipation note sales somewhat reduced by this very surplus.

However, the following March, when the county assessor finished his work and sent us the tax abstract, we were appalled. He had made such severe reductions in the assessments that it was evident that we were faced with a deficit. The county assessor, Frank L. West, simply announced, "The city manager gave a tax dividend last year; *I'm* giving one this year." The fact that the city hall dividend had applied to every taxpayer equally and that the county assessor's so-called tax dividend favored particular taxpayers was conveniently ignored.

The Battle Royal

The summer of 1925 was a very busy one around "Buckingham Palace." We were building a new water plant; we were building several new schoolhouses and additions to other schools; we were paving streets and getting health and hospital services into full swing; and as the organization shook down and the machinery got in better running order, there was relatively little trouble in keeping things co-ordinated, working together, and being responsive to top management so far as internal affairs were concerned. The political sniping continued, but for a time its principal expression was found in the *Free Press,* and there were fewer and fewer battles inside the council.

Late in August I became ill—quite ill. It was diagnosed as an intestinal flu of a particularly virulent type, which had claimed many victims in the Knoxville area that summer and fall and was usually known by the local title of "devil's grippe."

But here it was the time of year when the new budget must be prepared to be submitted to the council. Even with the most rigorous economies, we were ending the year with a deficit of $150,000 instead of a surplus of over $200,000 as the year before, all because of the cut in the assessments—and the new budget had to be contrived to meet increasing demands, as far as possibly could be managed, with a prospect of a diminishing revenue.

I was too ill to go to the office. The directors of the departments came to me and I, lying on a day bed in the living room, tried with their help to prepare the budget which had to be submitted and adopted by the first day of the fiscal year, October 1. The directors and my secretarial force did everything they could to help me, but the effort I made was too much for me in my weakened condition. As soon as the budget was presented to the council—and I did manage to attend that crucial session—I decided to take a vacation.

I had had an invitation to attend the ceremonies of the dedication of the Appomattox Bridge at Petersburg, to which I had given so much time and thought when I was manager of that Virginia city. I decided to spend a week in Washington and then to go to Petersburg for that ceremony, to take the rest of another week, and then to come back to Knoxville. My wife and I started to drive to Washington from Knoxville. In those days on a long drive we used to spell each other every hundred miles. I started out driving and drove for perhaps fifty miles when I turned the wheel over to my wife. I was not able again to drive. We took three days getting to Washington, and when we got there we went to the apartment of Judge and Mrs. Sims, my wife's parents, and there I fell into bed. Thence I went to Johns Hopkins Hospital in Baltimore, where the physicians kept me all but incommunicado for almost two months.

The council had asked Mr. Howell Davis to serve as acting city manager during my illness. When I returned, I attempted to take up my task again. I had lost some forty pounds. I had to have all my clothes refitted, and I spent as little time at the office and as much time at home resting as I possibly could manage.

At this time along came the campaign and election which resulted in the recall of three members of the council and their replacement by enemies of the new form of government. At the same time one of the members of the council, Ernest E. Ailor, joined the opposition. That, with Mr. Monday, then left the council with five anti-manager members and only six favorable members. I kept on at work through the winter and the early spring. The harassments increased. My health did not improve, and in May I again went to Washington and Baltimore and sought medical advice. The result of that consultation was that I was told I would have to quit work for at least two full years—two years that I was to devote to nothing but resting and endeavoring to get well.

In June, I submitted my resignation to the council and with my wife moved back to Washington, where we took an apartment, installed our furniture, and then went to Ocean City, Maryland, to spend the summer at the seaside.

And that was the end of my service in Knoxville. Looking back on my days there, I am conscious of both success and failure. Knoxville was ready for reform and I reformed it. It was not ready for a revolution, but I tried to revolutionize it.

At least one reason for my failure in the more ambitious enterprise—which was the most needed—lies far back in the history of the community.

East Tennessee, of which Knoxville was the principal city, was divided—families, friends, and communities—from almost the first days of its settlement, and that division was more permanently emphasized as the result of the Civil War and its aftermath than it was in any of the border areas. The result was bitter, vindictive, ruthless partisan politics. In fertile soil it flourished like a noxious weed. Politics and elections were games. Political discussion was personal. It centered on personalities, and it was carried on both by sly innuendo and at the top of the voice—screaming invective and insult. The prizes were not only the offices and the opportunities for personal prestige and gain but the "favors" to be dispensed and received. The rule was anything to win; the sin was not in the crime but in being caught. Both sides understood the rules and played for keeps.

During my term of nearly three years, I rarely was on the defensive about policies or programs, and even my choices of personnel were usually commended as far as competency was concerned, but my failure to conform to the political mores and customs of East Tennessee meant constant attack.

CHAPTER XVIII

A FEW REFLECTIONS

I have found in my experience that the political processes in self-governing communities as well as the administrative establishments are greatly influenced and, indeed, in a large degree determined by the traditional thought habits of the people. In Nashville and Louisville, where I had my first look at the city halls, there was an amiable tradition which permitted great lapses from the standards of morality that applied to other institutions in the same cities. Politics was presumed to be an avocation for the voter but a vocation for the professional politician, who was expected to feather his nest.

Gross corruption was a reprehensible thing, but the communities of both Nashville and Louisville recognized something that was called "honest graft." Nobody was shocked if the mayor or some other city official made money on the side by reason of prior knowledge that permitted him to buy stock in a construction company or make a real estate deal in advance of the opening of a new street. In fact, among the more knowledgeable elements of the community, the officials would have been deemed nitwits if they had not profited pecuniarly from the advantages of their positions.

From time to time there were upsurges of protest, and, indeed, it was only shortly after I left Louisville that, because of some particularly flagrant violations of even that amiably flexible code, a revolution took place which was to endure for the better part of a half-century. That revolution took the mayoralty away from the politicians of the "ward-heeler" type and invested it in the wealthier and more aristocratic men of the town—a habit which was clung to for the most part through decade after decade by both the Republican and Democratic parties, which in Louisville frequently succeeded each other.

My own first official experience, of course, was in the District of

Columbia. Here there had been, in this federally controlled enclave, a spectacular history of corruption and graft, which began immediately after the Civil War when the various self-governing municipalities within the District—Washington, Georgetown, and Washington County—were succeeded by the establishment under the authority of the Congress of a territorial form of government with an elective legislature and a governor appointed by the President. That governor, Alexander R. Shepherd, did a great deal for the capital city of Washington. He ruthlessly transferred from the maps and plans avenues, streets, circles, and the like and put them into actual physical being. He paved the muddy streets. He put in sewers. He extended the water system. And also, a plumber by trade, he managed to make a good deal of money out of it. Eventually he fled to Mexico.

The beneficial character of the physical work he did was comparable to that of Tammany chieftains such as Fernando Wood and Boss Tweed in New York. It was the genius of Frederick Law Olmsted which gave New York the plans for Central Park, for instance, but it was the graft of the captains of Tammany that financed it. It was the genius of Thomas Jefferson and Pierre L'Enfant that gave Washington its plan, but it was Governor Shepherd who brought it into its fullest flower. Governor Shepherd's statue stood, as it does today, directly in front of the District Building, where I had my six years of initiation into municipal administration. Frequently it was pointed out as the only statue ever erected to a statesman with his hand out behind him. I am quite sure that this was an unconscious tribute to one facet of his genius by a non-understanding sculptor.

Following the collapse of Governor Shepherd's career, when the still existing commission form of government was established in 1878, neither the climate of opinion, which in the voteless District of Columbia operates only indirectly, nor the increasingly high standards of conduct imposed by the Congress had tolerated outright corruption or graft. There was, of course, favoritism. There was some evidence over the years of the ability of some persons and institutions to have more weight than others in accomplishing municipal improvements. But in my day, as for many years before, there had been no outright graft, there was little or no political partisan patronage in appointments, and the standard of conduct was high. In occasional cases where it was violated, public opinion both among the citizenry and in the Congress was quick to reprehend the defaulter.

Next I went to Petersburg, Virginia, and found there another tradition, an older tradition, a tradition that might almost be called *noblesse oblige*. The local government had always been the business of the best citizens, and the best citizens usually looked upon themselves as and were admitted by others to be aristocrats. However, they were aristocrats who never failed to take into partnership in local affairs all the other and lesser ranks and grades of society, at least all the others except the Negroes, and, even there, while there was no equality, Negro public opinion was sought and to a great degree respected. There had been occasional instances of graft. There had been occasional lapses into corruption, frequently induced by salesmen from the outer world, but the standard was high and anybody caught violating it, or even suspected of violating it, was instantly reprehended. The difficulty there was the lack of the techniques for efficient and economic administration. There was no trouble with dishonesty.

Then I went to Knoxville. There I found an entirely different tradition. The general notion was that politics was crooked, that all politicians were crooked, and that those who were fortunate enough to be elected in the hurly-burly of the violent campaigns that raged through the city and the county and the state were naturally expected to recoup their "expenses" and even a little more from the opportunities given them by public office. That meant that a great many citizens holding to higher standards in their private lives and in their private businesses deemed it almost indecent to engage in politics.

I was there as a result of a revolution. That revolution had taken the form of the ousting of a particularly incompetent and outrageously corrupt commission form of government in favor of the council-manager form of government. The better citizenry turned out, and in the beginning elected all but one of the members of the council. Later, by use of the recall provision in the charter, the political element recouped some of its losses.

Since I left Knoxville, while I have not followed in detail the history of the town, I have been repeatedly assured that, while the old-style politicians came back and while there was some graft and corruption, never at any time has the town sunk to the low level from which it was lifted by that revolutionary political action in the elections of 1922 and 1923.

As a matter of fact, as I have looked into this phase of politics and public administration in many jurisdictions in the United States at both state and local levels, I have become convinced that in all but extremely exceptional instances the level of performance, once raised, never drops back all the way. A permanent net improvement in any local governmental or administrative establishment always follows any markedly intelligent, well-planned advance to higher ground. The frog may slip back as he attempts to climb from the bottom of the well, but at every jump he makes a net gain.

CHAPTER XIX

INTERLUDE

It was June when Bess and I left Knoxville to drive to Washington. The weather was beautiful; the laurel and rhododendron were in bloom in the mountains on either side as we drove up the great valley toward Washington.

The warmth of the farewells of my friends in Knoxville had greatly encouraged me. I was overwhelmed with kindness, with beautiful presents, and with affectionate and, one felt, utterly sincere good wishes for my recovery and for my future.

I had heard the doctors tell me many times that I must stop work. Therefore, I was not absolutely depressed by their pessimistic prognoses. I was accustomed to illness, and I had recovered from more than one bout. At any rate, my innate optimism was not overthrown, and, most fortunately, my wife shared to the full my hopefulness. It was decided that we would rest and let the future take care of itself. We went to Ocean City, Maryland, found ourselves quarters in an old hotel in which the cuisine was of the very best, and there betook ourselves to sun-bathing and surf-bathing.

Once I did a little too much surf-bathing and got a little too far out into a lively crosscurrent. My wife, thoroughly frightened, stood on the boardwalk and saw me struggling as the rip tide drove me toward the pilings of a jetty. Her shouts enlisted the help of two strong, young girl swimmers who came to my aid just as I had taken advantage of an incoming breaker and had landed prone on the beach, exhausted and hardly able to lift my head. When the fright was over, however, the very fact that I was able to make that last great and saving exertion aided materially in restoring my confidence and in bolstering my optimistic outlook.

When the autumn came, we went back to Washington, found ourselves an apartment, installed our goods and chattels which had been shipped from Knoxville, and set ourselves to continuing my period of rest.

By that time it had become more and more difficult for me to do nothing. There was the Cosmos Club and the Press Club, in which to visit with my old friends. There was the Library of Congress, which was in itself an invitation to revisit my old haunts, and as I went about the town and renewed acquaintanceships, getting back into the stream of things, I began to be most impatient to get back to work.

David Lawrence, then the editor and publisher of the *United States Daily,* was continuing to write his own daily syndicated article, which was distributed by Current News Features, Inc., a corporation wholly owned by Mr. Lawrence. Current News Features also marketed a good many other syndicated articles. One day Dave Lawrence called me and asked me to have lunch with him. At the table he suggested that it would be a good idea to try to establish a daily syndicated article on municipal governmental problems. I was greatly intrigued by the notion, but both Lawrence and I agreed that it was a gamble. Most municipal news, as printed in most of the newspapers of the country, was concerned almost exclusively with the particular problems of the particular city in which the newspaper was published. We agreed that it would be difficult to market a daily syndicated article which would of necessity be compelled to generalize; but we declined to believe that it was impossible.

In November Mr. Lawrence launched a campaign to sell a daily article six times a week to as many newspapers as possible. The series was to be published under the general caption, "The City and the Citizen." He and the other members of the staff of the Current News Features succeeded in selling the idea to a few newspapers, and in November and December, I myself visited several cities across the country and succeeded in selling the series to several newspapers.

Publication began in January, 1927. At first the sale was satisfactory, but after a few months the very difficulties that Lawrence and I had anticipated began to multiply.

As the editor of the Oklahoma City *Oklahoman* wrote me, there was not enough interest in municipal affairs in his city, except at election time or during a crime wave or something like that, to keep the citizens' minds on the city, even when only immediate and local affairs were concerned, let alone the generalization of the problems about which I was writing. The newspapers in various parts of the country began to cancel the series, and it was evident by mid-summer that it would not be a success. The last of the two hundred daily articles was released in September, 1927.

The articles were prepared two weeks in advance of publication. Just before the last ones were sent to be mimeographed and distributed, Mr. Will Hogg, a capitalist and oil-producer of Houston, Texas, who had been reading my letters as they were published in the papers, telephoned me from New York to ask if I would go to Houston with him to see whether I might be interested in the job of directing a new organization of civic and community affairs that he was prepared to set up and finance. I joined him on the train from Washington and went with him to Houston. I told him frankly that the syndicated article I was writing would end in a couple of weeks and that I was on the lookout for something to do, preferably in the field of municipal affairs. I spent a week with Mr. Hogg in his luxurious penthouse atop a downtown office building in Houston. He had his finger in a great many pies. He was one of the leading businessmen in Houston. He was in oil. He was a son of Jim Hogg, who had been governor of Texas and with whose history I was very well acquainted, since he had been one of the leaders of the Farmers' Alliance, a Populist, and a revolutionist in the Democratic party in the 1890's. Will Hogg told me that it was his father who had first discovered, by careful attention to the advice of geologists and engineers, that the Texan oil resources were not being sufficiently exploited because of the custom of shallow well-drilling, a custom reinforced by technical difficulties not then conquered and also by the great expense involved in deep drilling. Will Hogg had gone deeper, and the black gold had poured freely into his pockets.

Not only did Will Hogg have his finger in many a pie in Houston affairs, but he didn't like the intrusion of any other fingers. It was easy to see that he was engaged in a business, political, and civic feud with another Houston tycoon named Jesse Jones. In Hogg's penthouse I met Arthur Holcombe, the mayor of Houston, and, more especially, Hugh Potter, a most entertaining real estate man. These were boom times. There was as yet no hint of the oncoming collapse of 1929, and as a part of the big boom many cities, in fact almost all the enterprising cities, were going in for high-class, expensive suburban developments.

One such was River Oaks in Houston, in which Mr. Hogg had a pecuniary as well as a civic interest and of which Mr. Potter was the head. It was Mr. Hogg's purpose to set up a foundation which would have for its principal purpose the encouragement of community activities, of citizen participation in civic affairs, and of a wider interest in municipal government. This he was to call a "forum." To head that forum, he was searching for a man, and he offered the job to me. The salary was to be $25,000 a year. It was to be guaranteed in a five-year contract, and a deposit of $125,000 was to be put in escrow with a trustee to insure the salary even if the board of trustees (another name for Will Hogg) was not pleased with the conduct of affairs and decided to dispense with the services of the director.

I was greatly interested. I was tempted by the generous salary, and I spent several days talking with other prominent citizens, but not with Mr. Jesse Jones. Then also every day or two I got a long-distance telephone message from David Lawrence pressing me to come back to Washington and take a post under him on the *United States Daily*. The salary would be nothing like as great, of course, but he pointed out to me various things that he knew, and that I was beginning to hear, about the difficulties I might meet in the business and social feuds that were raging in Houston. He also did not neglect to talk to me about the climate and other unpleasant circumstances that might surround me in Houston. He urged me before making a decision to come to see him at his summer home at Spring Lake, New Jersey.

As a matter of fact, I did not do any trading. I rejected the Houston offer because I did not think the plan was sound or that it could be carried out. Two of Mr. Hogg's best and closest friends, Mayor Holcombe and Hugh Potter, had, out of their friendship for Mr. Hogg, urged me to take the job, but neither had been enthusiastic about the prospects for his scheme. I told Mr. Hogg that I could not accept because I didn't believe his plan of organization workable. As a matter of fact, I don't believe it was ever executed. I came back to Washington, went to New Jersey, had a long talk with Dave Lawrence, and then went on the staff of the *United States Daily*.

The *United States Daily* was established by David Lawrence to fill a void in the business of reporting to the people of the United States the day-to-day affairs of their federal government. It was set up as a daily newspaper which was to be published without editorial comment and was to be devoted to printing the verbatim texts of the decisions, rules, and judgments of the several departments of the executive branch of the government, the decisions and judgments of the regulatory bodies, and the decisions and opinions of the Supreme Court of the United States. There was then no *Federal Register*. There was then no place where anyone could find all the Executive Orders of the President, or other similar orders, rules, and regulations. Some of them eventually found their way into books published for a particular clientele after the elapse of sometimes several years—the law reports, the public utility reports, and the like. The *United States Daily* was a full-size newspaper, and it required the services of a staff as large or larger than many flourishing daily newspapers of the general-news type.

Mr. Lawrence, who was continuing to write his daily syndicated column, devoted an enormous amount of energy and thought and a considerable amount of money to the experiment. The idea seemed to be so good, the service to be rendered by the paper so useful, that various public spirited men throughout the country subscribed to its capital stock. In particular, one foundation, the Spelman Fund of New York, invested more than a million and a half dollars to support the effort.

Useful as the daily was to lawyers and others particularly interested in the details of the work of the federal government, its circulation never was great. It endeavored to cover, of course, the whole United States, but it found few readers. It had little appeal to general advertisers. Eventually it was forced to cease publication. Out of it, however, and in part to continue to support the fundamental idea behind the plan, Mr. Lawrence started the weekly *United States News,* now the *U.S. News and World Report,* a flourishing and most profitable journal.

My work on the staff was ill defined and amorphous. I was supposed to contribute some general ideas, to assist in promotion, to endeavor to attract interest in municipal and state officials, and to make speeches in different parts of the country. In particular, it was my task to endeavor to persuade specific cities, through their municipal governments or through their trade organizations, to place promotional advertising in the daily, in the hope of attracting a nationwide interest in their several plans for industrial expansion.

That work was alien to my experience, and I am sure that I did a very poor job of it, although I don't think anybody could have made much of a success in that particular field. At any rate, nobody ever did. Still, I kept at the work, and Mr. Lawrence urged me on.

What I got out of the *United States Daily* was of great value to me. I was closely associated with many of its able and brilliant staff members and formed close friendships, many of which still endure.

One day in February of 1928 I went to New York on business for the *United States Daily* and also to attend a meeting of the National Municipal League Council. Quite by chance, I encountered a situation which changed my orientation, put my feet on another path, and determined the direction of my activities for the rest of my life.

CHAPTER XX

RADBURN, THE TOWN FOR
THE MOTOR AGE

The first time I heard of Radburn was one brilliant autumn afternoon in 1927 when I dropped into the United States Chamber of Commerce Building to call on John Ihlder, then the head of its civic development section. Ihlder and I had been interested in the problem of housing for many years. He asked me if I had seen in the *New York World* of that morning an account of the project of a new planned town for the motor age to be built in Bergen County, New Jersey. I had not. Ihlder's copy of the *World* was missing. He sent out to a neighboring newsstand to get another. In it there was the announcement by the City Housing Corporation, a limited dividend company of New York, of its intention to build a garden-city suburb in the borough of Fair Lawn, New Jersey, on the Erie Railroad just east of Paterson, New Jersey. The plans for the new town were an adaptation of the scheme for the garden cities that had been built outside of London by Sir Ebenezer Howard, who was assisted in their planning by Sir Raymond Unwin. These two garden cities, Welwyn and Letchworth, had been described in many of the then current journals dealing with municipal affairs, city planning, and housing. Ihlder, I believe, had visited them. I had not. Ihlder and I also had had a common interest in the usefulness of limited dividend companies for the construction, maintenance, and management of housing for low-income families. In the District of Columbia two such corporations had initiated a successful experiment, developing their work with the aid of the slogan "Philanthropy and five per cent." These housing developments, planned in the 1890's and the early 1900's, had been set up through the initiative of General George N. Sternberg, then the surgeon general of the Army, with the assistance of Dr. George M. Kober, a Washington physician who had joined General Sternberg in the crusade for the pre-

[210]

vention of tuberculosis. Both of them were convinced that bad housing was one of the principal means of the spread of tuberculosis, at that time the most dreaded disease. These two corporations built several housing projects in Washington, and, while the idea did not spread, the buildings that were erected had been successfully managed, well constructed, and well maintained. I learned to know all about them during my six years as a commissioner of the District of Columbia.

Already I had heard something of the New York City Housing Corporation and its construction in the borough of Queens of the model housing development of Sunnyside. That this company, under the leadership of Alexander M. Bing, its president, was now about to embark on a much more ambitious project in the Jersey suburbs was extremely interesting to me. The scheme was for a satellite town planned in its entirety with special reference to the motor age. It was, so the newspaper announcement said, being planned by Clarence S. Stein and Henry Wright, neither of whom I knew except by reputation.

Greatly as I was interested by the announcement, I then had no notion that I would ever have anything to do with the plan. In January, as I learned later, the City Housing Corporation discovered that in the development of the 1,500 acres of land purchased in the truck-farming area of Fair Lawn, many problems of a municipal nature had already come up.

It was one thing to buy the land; it was another thing to make the plans; it was still another thing to attract attention by the slogan "A town for the motor age," and still another to engage the interest of the youngest generation by publicity about how the new town would overflow and destroy uncounted acres of spinach. The site was in a rich truck-farming area, thinly populated, principally by Dutch and English gardeners.

It was, however, from an urban point of view, raw land. There was no water system. There was no sewerage system. There were, in fact, almost none of the services that would have to be provided for a population of even as little density as was planned for. As a result of heading into these and related municipal problems, the counsel of the City Housing Corporation, Charles S. Ascher, went to see Harold W. Dodds, later the president of Princeton University and at that time the executive secretary of the National Municipal League. Mr. Dodds told Ascher that there was to be a meeting of the council of the National

Municipal League in early February, which would be attended by several persons that Mr. Dodds regarded as experts in municipal government. He mentioned my name among others.

I found myself in New York in the first week of February, 1928, on business for the *United States Daily* and took advantage of that fact to arrange to spend the week end at the meeting of the league's council. My intense interest in the municipal government and community organization had impelled me to keep in as close touch as possible with what I then regarded as my former field of activity. Mr. Dodds and Mr. Ascher had arranged a special conference with representatives of the City Housing Corporation and members of the council of the league. This began with a late afternoon session at the Town Hall Club. Mr. Bing, the president of the City Housing Corporation, was unable to attend and Herbert Emmerich, executive vice-president, presided. Present also were Clarence S. Stein and Henry Wright, who expounded from blueprints and lantern slides the proposed scheme for the new town of Radburn. The meeting continued through dinner, and after dinner there was a general discussion of the problems. Among those participating were Richard S. Childs, then president of the National Municipal League; Morris Knowles, a municipal planner; Morris Lambie, then executive secretary of the Minnesota Municipal League; Harold S. Buttenheim, editor of the *American City;* Spaulding Frazier, a New Jersey lawyer specializing in municipal affairs; and others. Mr. Ascher later wrote:

"To those of the City Housing Corporation who had never met this group of people before, it was obvious that Brownlow made far and away the richest contribution to the evening. He was able to bring to bear on question after question a wider experience, a broader background, a deeper philosophy, and more human approach than any of the others. We were dazzled."

When the meeting broke up, Mr. Childs sought me out and told me he had said to Emmerich that he believed I would be eager to get back into some phase of local government or municipal affairs, that he doubted whether I was finding my current work with the *United States Daily* fully satisfying.

At this time the City Housing Corporation was already dealing with the borough, the county, and the state on many important problems requiring basic major decisions concerning Radburn, its plans, and its operation. The officers of the corporation had discovered that the matter of water supply would be much more difficult than they had anticipated. The semirural borough was contemplating a municipal water supply. Should the City Housing Corporation join with it or develop its own? The corporation had employed a firm of engineers to make a report, but that report was entirely too puzzling for them. They had not anticipated that they would have to deal with the state, as well as the county and the municipal government, in endeavoring to find the solution for the problem. Adam Haskell and Mr. Ascher, from the corporation staff, were pretty well acquainted in Fair Lawn by this time, and one or the other of them found himself attending council meetings fairly regularly, getting back to their suburban homes in Westchester County around three or four o'clock in the morning.

They found it futile to present some of the iconoclastic proposals involved in the Radburn plan at a formal meeting of the council, where its members would be forced to act on proposals that they didn't fully understand, in the presence of their own constituents. For that reason Mr. Emmerich and Mr. Ascher proposed to the officers of the corporation that I be approached to see whether or not I would come up and act as a liaison between the corporation and the municipal, county, and state governmental authorities involved.

Shortly after I returned to Washington I had a letter from Mr. Ascher suggesting that I come to New York at the City Housing Corporation's expense to consult with its officers about their problems in New Jersey. On the first day of March, I went to New York and that morning talked at length with Mr. Bing, Mr. Emmerich, and Mr. Ascher.

They asked me whether or not I would be willing to help them work out their governmental relationships. There was a good deal of discussion about a title, and we finally decided that "municipal consultant" was sufficiently descriptive but also sufficiently non-governmental to avoid confusion with the official authorities. A week later I went back to New York and accepted the job. I wound up my connection with the *United States Daily* and Mr. David Lawrence.

My recommendation that I actually live in Fair Lawn and on the site of the Radburn-to-be was accepted, and it was agreed that one of the red stone Dutch colonial houses would be modernized and that Mrs. Brownlow and I literally would live on the job. Early in April, Bess and

I moved to Paterson, New Jersey, and took up temporary quarters in the Alexander Hamilton Hotel.

It took much longer than had been anticipated to modernize the house, although when it was completed it was cozy and charming. It was set on the narrow Fair Lawn Road, which was the principal artery, indeed, the only road traversing the site, on a tract of fifty-odd acres which for the better part of three centuries had been devoted first to farming and then to truck gardening. The house itself had literally been built out of the site. The red stone of which it was constructed had been excavated from the cellar of the house itself, and, indeed, in the yard surrounding it there was a surface outcropping of the same stone. The beams that supported the attic above the two one-story rooms that we were to use as a living room and dining room were hand-hewn from trees that, tradition said, were cut on the site. Some were oak, some were walnut, some were pine, and one was hickory. In the reconstruction, a bathroom and two bedrooms took the place of the old attic; a well was driven; and water and the pertinent plumbing were installed. Even though it was autumn, we began landscaping. In this house we lived happily for more than two years. It was the only free-standing house in which we have ever lived, and this was the only time we ever had an opportunity to indulge in garden culture.

The familiar alternate Tuesday council meetings began again for me. The Board of Commissioners of the District had met twice a week on Tuesdays and Fridays; but in Petersburg and in Knoxville the council meetings were held on alternate Tuesdays. In the undeveloped rural borough there was no city hall, and the council met in a wooden four-room schoolhouse. The council already had purchased an old residence for the purpose of converting it into a city hall, a project that was pursued a little bit at a time. There was a period of nearly two years of actual construction before it was completed, and even then its approaches were unpaved and, after a rain, axle-deep in mud.

The government of the borough was presided over by a popularly elected mayor and six councilmen, none of whom received any compensation. When I first arrived, there were but three paid officials—the clerk of the council, a collector of taxes, and a building inspector. And these three, with the exception of the clerk, were paid on a fee basis. There was no police force, and such police activities as existed were conducted by the county police. There was no water system, sewer system, or health officer.

In 1928 New Jersey had adopted a municipal government act written by Spaulding Frazier, who was the dean of a highly reputable school of law in Newark, which gave full municipal powers to every unit of local government in the state regardless of whether it was known as a borough, a city, a township, or what-not. This grant of full municipal powers had fallen upon Fair Lawn unsolicited, as a gift from heaven, but the mayor and the members of the council had not fully realized it. They had been apprised of the plans for Radburn necessarily, because of the assembling of the land and the sale of truck farms and gardens to the New York corporation, and they all had been shown the scheme for the new town. It didn't take me long to find out that they thought the whole thing a crazy idea that some crazy New Yorkers had been inveigled into financing. The plan of the town was revolutionary, and the city fathers respected it only because it apparently had strong financial backing.

It was, in essence, a plan for building houses around the perimeter of "superblocks," the houses to face, not outward toward the roadways, but inward toward a strip of lawn and sidewalks that led into a park in the center of the superblock. The usual gridiron system of streets and blocks was ignored. Every house was to have its garage, and the motor entrance was the back entrance. The superblocks were to be connected by footways, either under or over the principal streets, so that a pedestrian could walk all over the town without once crossing a roadway or street where he might even so much as see a motor car. This was puzzling enough in itself to the members of the council, but when they were told that this part of the borough would have better lighting and garbage collections, and also playgrounds, swimming pools, and other services not furnished by the borough, that the City Housing Corporation furthermore would assist the borough in building a water plant and sewer system, that the services and amenities not available to other residences of the borough would be paid for by the residents of the new town separately, they were even more puzzled.

The borough officials were not the only ones who were puzzled. I was. I could not make head or tail of the political situation. The mayor and all the members of the council had been nominated and elected as

Republicans, and there were very few Democrats in the borough. What I couldn't understand was the bitter intraparty row.

The mayor was a fire insurance agent who occupied a small wooden office building facing the principal east-west road through the borough. Four members of the council were truck gardeners, three of them Dutch, one of them English-born. One member was the business agent of the street-railwaymen's union in the neighboring city of Paterson, and the other was a laborer who picked up his living by doing odd jobs.

The borough had been settled in the seventeenth century when the Dutch governed that part of the eastern shore of the United States from their capital in New Amsterdam, the area being known as New Netherland. This Dutch immigration had been refreshed in every generation thereafter, and on my arrival I met some immigrants who had been in the United States less than five years. After a while I discovered that Mayor Smith and his faction had behind them the support of Nicholas Kuiken, who was the Republican boss of the borough. His great rival for the party leadership was Jasper Van Hook, then borough clerk. Kuiken and his brother Henry owned and operated a lumber yard. Van Hook was a clerk in the headquarters of the Erie Railroad in Jersey City.

A Republican primary election came along, and there was a furious battle between the two factions, ending in a decisive victory for Kuiken. That meant that Van Hook was to be dropped as city clerk, which didn't affect him very much because just about that time the Erie Railroad moved its general headquarters to Cleveland, Ohio. Van Hook went with it, and later rose to a very high position in the management of the Erie.

One evening after dinner Kuiken stopped by my house and talked about his victories at the primaries. I said, "Mr. Kuiken, I'm puzzled. What is the issue between these factions?"

"Well," he said, "what do you mean 'factions'?"

"You and Van Hook," I said, "are seemingly always at sword's point. In the past he sometimes has controlled the primary election and sometimes you have, and I don't understand what the fuss is all about."

"Well, that's simple," said Mr. Kuiken. "He is a Flakkee and I am a Frisian." This colloquy occurred just as he was taking his leave.

"Please, Mr. Kuiken," I countered, "sit down and tell me what this all means."

Radburn, the Town for the Motor Age

It seemed that a few centuries earlier, when the Spanish were in control of the Low Countries and the Duke of Alva's soldiers were ravaging the country, the Frisians, who lived on the fringe of the northeast coast and its adjacent islands, accused the inhabitants of the island of Overflakkee of treacherously permitting the Spanish soldiers to enter their gates. Ever thereafter, said Mr. Kuiken, no Frisian has ever forgiven a Flakkee.

I had met many different characters in politics—in my native Ozark Mountains of Missouri, in Tennessee, in Kentucky, in England, in Germany, in Egypt, in India, and in China and Japan, not to speak of the Congress of the United States and the councils of Petersburg and Knoxville—but never had I expected to meet the Duke of Alva and a group of sixteenth-century Spanish-Dutch feudists. Here in Fair Lawn that political struggle was still going on, and it was something with which I had perforce to reckon.

However, my relationships with the borough government of Fair Lawn were principally confined to Radburn and the municipal problems which continued to beset the new development. The City Housing Corporation donated a plot of ground to the borough for a water field, underwrote a contract for drilling wells, helped to subsidize the necessary engineering studies and to pay for a very large part of the cost of the primary installation of a water-distribution system. It built at its own expense a sewage system that covered Radburn and its immediate environs but was so designed that it could eventually be incorporated in a borough-wide system. It undertook to pave the roadways and instal the sidewalks within its own borders without expense to the borough. It undertook to plan and erect an eight-grade schoolhouse within the Radburn area, which would, of course, be administered by the school board of the borough and would be open to students in all the adjoining territory. These gift horses were very carefully examined by the council, which, in its joint capacity as the borough veterinarian, looked well into their mouths. Furthermore, there were negotiations with the county authorities, especially with the county highway department, the county police department, and the county health office. And many of these led also to direct negotiations with the state authorities in Trenton. While these activities took a great deal of my time, I also was in close touch with our own engineers and our own construction department. I was of necessity in New York two or three times a week for consultations at the head office of the City Housing Corporation.

Radburn, for a long time after I got there, was a concept, a plan, a blueprint, and when at long last streets were laid, houses were going up, and a shopping center was being erected, Radburn still had no residents. Nobody lived there.

For a good many years theretofore I had had a notion in my mind about community organization. I had seen so many citizens' organizations of one kind and another flounder on the very minor problem of a secretariat. Many of them chose a secretary by ballot, once they found some man or woman willing to undertake the unpaid and thankless task of getting out postcards announcing the next meeting, a person who would receive no credit for this work, but considerable blame for any mishap. My idea was to set up a citizens' association, complete with a secretariat and ready for use by the inhabitants of Radburn when, as, and if there were any. Accompanying this idea was the concern I had felt, in the three cities over which I had presided, that some parts of the cities had received superior municipal services not always proportionate to the amount of taxes they paid. I wanted to implement the Radburn Association by a series of deed restrictions requiring the payment into the Radburn Association of certain fees to establish a fund. Some of the necessary municipal services that would not or could not be provided by the borough would be paid for out of this fund. For instance, the borough had no garbage collection and disposal. This, in the Radburn section of Fair Lawn, the Radburn Association was to pay for. Radburn required a higher standard of street lighting than was prevalent in the semirural borough. Arrangements were made for the borough to pay as much for street lighting as it did in any part of the borough, and the excess was to be paid by the Radburn Association. The borough had no playgrounds. In Radburn swimming pools were to be established, playgrounds were to be provided, a recreation department was to be set up, and all these things were to be paid for by the Radburn Association until such time as the borough was able or willing to take them over. One of the first things we did was to set up a police force, composed of three persons. Uniforms were provided, motorcycles were bought, and yet all the salaries and other expenses were to come from the funds of the Radburn Association.

In order to set up this system, the City Housing Corporation appointed some leading citizens of the county and neighboring New Jersey cities as a board of trustees for the Radburn Association. A deed-restriction manual was drawn up, and its provisions were incorporated in all the deeds that were to be executed when the houses were built and sold. In making up the manual of these deed restrictions, Mr. Ascher and I studied similar setups in many of the high-class subdivisions of the United States, particularly those of Roland Park in Baltimore, Ginter Park in Richmond, and the River Oaks development set up by Hugh Potter in the suburbs of Houston, Texas. Mr. Ascher, a competent and skilled real estate lawyer, did the actual drafting, and I consulted with him on the goals to be aimed at. Of course, the Radburn Association was eventually to be turned over to the residents (as indeed it has been) and was to become a self-governing citizen body that would conduct relations with the borough, county, and state governments, the relations that were then in my charge.

One of the first things that we decided to set up was a community church, and provision was made for it in the Plaza Building, in which were installed the offices of the City Housing Corporation. We persuaded a drugstore, a grocery store, a hardware store, and some other facilities of that type to move into the building. An office was rented to the mayor for the conduct of his insurance business.

As soon as eight or ten families had moved in, I made the first order of business the establishment of the first Radburn Citizens' Association. None of us could then foresee the Great Depression; none of us could foresee that the Radburn plan itself would have to be abandoned. Therefore, since we expected neighborhood citizens' associations all over the place, we dubbed this one "first" and looked forward to the second, third, fourth, etc. The Citizens' Association was, of course, entirely distinct from the Radburn Association, which had a trust relationship set up in the restrictions of the deeds. The Citizens' Association was composed of community residents.

It was astonishing how quickly my notion about the utility of a ready-made secretariat for citizens' activities was demonstrated. In almost no time at all, with the aid of that central office, we had set up not only a community church but a volunteer fire department, a dramatic club, a chess divan, a tennis association, baseball and softball teams, and even a group for the discussion of international affairs under the leadership of Dr. Clyde Eagleton of Columbia University. By the time the

Radburn population had reached fifty it was a well-organized, going community. The whole borough of Fair Lawn at that time had a population of a little over 3,000 persons. It now has more than 30,000 and a council-manager form of government, and the city hall is established in the Plaza Building, while the community and recreational facilities have been moved to a building that the City Housing Corporation then owned—an old Grange hall. Now in the very heart of what was Radburn, which is merely an enclave in Fair Lawn, there stands on Fair Lawn Avenue a telephone-exchange building and the Grange Hall, reminiscent of the time when this was a truly rural community and the Patrons of Husbandry was the dominating and most influential organization in all of Fair Lawn.

My relationships as municipal consultant and community organizer were not limited to Radburn and the borough government of Fair Lawn; I found it expedient to keep in close touch with many other governmental and community affairs in New Jersey. Very soon I was a member of the executive committee of the New Jersey League of Municipalities and of the executive committee of the New Jersey Council of Social Work; not long thereafter I was an advisory committee member for the New Jersey Planning Association. I began to give occasional lectures at Princeton University to the members of Dr. Harold W. Dodds's classes in municipal government. I became a member of an advisory committee for the National Housing Association and an active member of the Snag Club in New York City, which was a group which met in the evenings in the New York City Club under the presidency of Harold S. Buttenheim, the editor of the *American City*, to discuss city planning, housing, social work, and municipal government generally.

Even these activities did not limit the active expression of my interest in municipal and community affairs. And some of these stirrings far afield from Radburn and even from New Jersey were later to determine the course of the rest of my active life.

In 1927, I went to Cincinnati to attend a meeting of the National Municipal League and to give an illustrated lecture on Radburn as a part of the general discussion of the problem of city planning. One afternoon in the lobby of the Sinton Hotel I was introduced by Dr. Charles E. Merriam of the University of Chicago to a man who immediately impressed me as being as expansive in his intellectual range as his body was generously large. I had heard of him before, but I had not met him. He was Beardsley Ruml, then the executive director of the Laura Spelman Rockefeller Memorial Fund. I knew him, of course, through the *United States Daily,* which his foundation was backing, and had heard of him from many of my friends.

That first meeting with Ruml was freighted with much more importance to me than I could possibly have dreamed of. In response to a question he asked me about the National Municipal League's promotion of the council-manager form of government, I launched into a long talk about something that had been stirring in my mind for some years. I told him about the prospectus that John Stutz of Kansas, Dr. Merriam, and I had prepared some time before and had presented to Raymond W. Fosdick, the legal counsel of the Rockefeller Foundation, asking for funds to permit the establishment of an institute of municipal government. In talking with him about it, I laid great stress upon what I thought was a necessary development in the municipal field— the bringing together in a common center of as many of the organizations of officials as possible, so that in their daily work they and their secretaries would be in constant touch with one another.

Mr. Ruml was very much interested, and from that time forward I met him in New York frequently in his offices at 61 Broadway and elsewhere. On the first day of January, 1928, the Laura Spelman Rockefeller Memorial Fund was merged with the Rockefeller Foundation, and in its stead a relatively small foundation—with ten million dollars— called the Spelman Fund of New York was set up. Mr. Ruml became its executive director. Guy Moffett, whom I had come to know very well indeed, became his assistant and later succeeded Ruml in the directorship. Charles E. Merriam became a member of the board and later succeeded Colonel Arthur Woods as its chairman.

Quite naturally, I was continuing my activities in correspondence with the headquarters of the City Managers' Association in Lawrence. When Mr. Stutz organized the American Municipal Association, which was a federation of the then existing state leagues of municipalities, I was on hand in St. Louis for its second meeting.

In the autumn of 1928 I went to the City Managers' Association convention in Asheville, North Carolina, there to give my illustrated lecture about Radburn and to renew my acquaintance and friendships among the city managers. I persuaded Mr. Ruml and Dr. Merriam to attend the meeting in the hope that it might be possible for the Spelman Fund to find a way to make a grant to the City Managers' Association for the improvement of its headquarters. Such a grant already had been made to a municipal administrative service, which was operated in connection with the National Municipal League and had on its board one or two city managers and local officials. Ruml, Merriam, and I labored assiduously at our task. At the same time, the board of directors of the City Managers' Association was dealing with a very difficult matter, and I was invited to sit in with that board. The upshot of it was that Mr. Stutz resigned as executive secretary. The new president, R. W. Rigsby of Charlotte, North Carolina, then appointed me chairman of a committee to choose a successor to Stutz and to find a new headquarters for the Managers' Association. President Rigsby himself and one other manager was put on the committee with me, but the board instructed me that, while I was free to consult the other two members, I was to consider myself a committee of one. In any event, I was to attempt to settle both the problem of the headquarters and of the executive secretary before coming back to the board. At that very moment I decided I would attempt to persuade Clarence E. Ridley to take the job.

Ridley, a former city manager of Bluefield, West Virginia, was at that time the head of a research unit in engineering problems in the Institute of Public Administration, of which Luther Gulick was president, and which had its headquarters at 261 Broadway in New York. It was evident from my conversations with Ruml and Merriam that there was some hope of getting a grant from the Spelman Fund but little chance of its being realized for a year or two.

I went to see Mr. Gulick and persuaded him to permit the headquarters to be moved to New York and housed with the Institute of Public Administration, which would contribute a portion of Mr. Ridley's salary. At the same time, I had asked Dr. Merriam what could be arranged at the University of Chicago. The university found that it could donate space and give an assistant professorship to Mr. Ridley to help pay his salary, and furthermore it had been able to persuade the Julius Rosenwald Fund to make a small grant to the association.

That resulted, after a few weeks, in the choice of Chicago as the headquarters of the City Managers' Association, and the necessary arrangements were made for Mr. Ridley to take over from Mr. Stutz.

At the same time, the Civil Service Assembly of the United States and Canada, through its secretariat, the Bureau of Personnel Administration, had obtained a small grant from the Spelman Fund, and it, too, moved its headquarters into the same building with the City Managers' Association—an old residence formerly occupied by the great sculptor Lorado Taft, on the south side of the Midway facing across that parkway to the campus of the University of Chicago.

Through 1929, as the building of Radburn went on, it soon was apparent that municipal relationships, community activities, and recreational programs, together with the work that I was able to do in the central city of New York, made it imperative to increase my staff. That was done by bringing in Major John O. Walker, who had been my director of public safety in both Petersburg and Knoxville, to serve as my principal assistant. Then also we employed a recreational leader and began to work on the community-services program in earnest.

The very plan of the town, which made it impossible for any dwelling place to be more than a few hundred feet from a park or a playground, intensified the interest of the people, old and young, in working together in community activities. That meant the scheduling of events, the supervision of the little children in the playgrounds, and the handling of the affairs of the Radburn Association.

In those days almost nobody saw the calamity of the Great Depression just around the corner. Radburn, which was essentially a commuting town, was served only by a tiny station on the Erie Railroad, a little box of a wooden house, which also included a post office. The daily commuter travel was confined, before Radburn came, to seven or eight persons. The spinach-growers did not commute. It took some long negotiations to get the necessary permits from the Erie Railroad for the City Housing Corporation to build a handsome stone station, and then it took me not one, not two, but three visits to the Post Office Department in Washington to get a permit to move the post office from the old wooden station to the new stone one—a matter of about 120 feet. Of course, there were long and intricate negotiations with the electric power company, the gas company, and the telephone company for the installation of up-to-date utility services.

It was about this time that Mr. Emmerich calculated that it would have been impossible to reduce the sale price of a $10,000 house by more than $50 even if the land had been given free to the company in the first place. The $2,000 an acre or more that was paid for the land amounted to a very small proportion of the eventual cost. The cost came from the manufacture, so to speak, of finished urban land from raw agricultural land in a short period of time without the benefits that usually accompany such conversion: unaccounted and unaccountable contributions by state, city, and county governments, by schools, by privately owned public utilities, and, frequently, by successive foreclosures of land mortgages. Here the account was all cast up at once, and it was easy to see how much was the actual cost. It was an expensive business.

About that time Clarence S. Stein and Henry Wright, the principal planners of Radburn, found the records of a large brick mansion built in the neighborhood of Boston just before the Revolutionary War. They found that the same mansion could be built in northern New Jersey of the same materials for a little less than the dollar cost of the Boston house, even in 1770. However, that house would have only four walls, a roof, and two floors. It would have had no water supply, no sewage connections, no central heating, no plumbing, no telephone, no gas, and no electricity—all of the things that were unavailable to the Massachusetts Bay Colony builder. What Mr. Stein and Mr. Wright discovered, however, and what had been pointed out to them by the calculations of Mr. Emmerich and Mr. Ascher, was that the abandonment of the checkerboard street system in favor of the design of superblocks and cul-de-sac streets had actually reduced the 1929 cost of roadway-paving, sidewalk-paving, and water and sewer installation by at least one-third.

That is perhaps the reason that the Radburn scheme, adapted and modified to meet many conditions, has had such a tremendous influence on the development of suburban housing projects, not only in the United States but in practically every country in the world. The growth of Radburn was first inhibited and then stopped because of the economic storms accompanying the Great Depression, but, in plan and as an advanced idea in the field of non-intensive housing development, it was a great success.

While I was still in Radburn devoting all my energy and time to the development of Radburn as a housing project and as an advanced experiment in community life, I was compelled to keep up my contacts with many persons and organizations in the whole field of municipal government, and at the same time I was beginning to think more and more about how the whole business of municipal management was merging into the greater and more general task of public management at all levels of government. This thinking also tended to increase the number of contacts I had with people interested in state and federal government and especially with Beardsley Ruml and Guy Moffett of the Spelman Fund.

By the spring of 1930, while optimism still pervaded the business world, the calamity of the Great Depression was making itself more and more felt. The people who had bought houses in Radburn were having great difficulty in meeting their payments. No such thing as the long-term amortizable mortgage was then known in the United States. In order to sell the houses it had been necessary to reduce the cash payment required, and that in turn had necessitated taking larger and larger second and third mortgages.

The difficulties were increasing rapidly, and at the same time more and more efforts were being made to stimulate the construction industry, and more and more skyscrapers were being built in New York. The federal government entered the picture with the Reconstruction Finance Corporation, and many valiant rear-guard battles were fought in the economic field.

The Spelman Fund, looking over the governmental situation, decided that it ought to extend its encouragement of national associations of public officials of various specialties in state and local government. Mr. Ruml began to discuss with me the possibility of setting up a center—not modeled exactly on the project for the institute of municipal government that Stutz, Merriam, and I had worked on a few years earlier—where many organizations of officials could be brought together to gain the advantages of immediate interchange of information and experience.

Mr. Ruml then suggested that the Spelman Fund give me a traveling fellowship to enable me to visit the British Isles and western Europe to look into the problems of housing and how they were being met, and also to visit European organizations in the field of municipal government and public administration generally.

By the late spring of 1930 it was painfully evident that the arrangements for relief of the needy, the whole institution of private and public relief agencies throughout the country, were not sufficient to meet the rapidly increasing demands for food and shelter from the rapidly increasing numbers of the unemployed. The National Conference on Social Work was meeting in Boston at the end of June. The Spelman Fund authorized me to intimate to public welfare officials assembled there that it would be favorably disposed to make a grant if a new organization of public welfare officials was established.

My wife and I took passage on a ship sailing from Boston for Glasgow and went to Boston a week before the date of sailing. There, in concert with several other persons concerned with public welfare problems in different parts of the country, I organized the American Association of Public Welfare Officials. Arrangements were made for it to set up headquarters in Washington, and tentative plans were made to persuade Frank Bane, then the commissioner of public welfare of the state of Virginia, who had been head of my welfare department in Knoxville, to become its executive director. For that purpose he was given a leave of absence by the state.

CHAPTER XXI

EUROPE IN 1930

Boarding the Cunarder "Caledonia" on a late June day bound for Glasgow, my wife and I were happy to be on board ship again. We were delighted to have another chance to visit Europe, which we had not seen since the spring of 1914—before World War I. Both of us looked forward eagerly to seeing the familiar monuments and venerable buildings, the ancient churches, and the hallowed shrines of our European ancestors and to having an intimate look at what the war and the peace had brought.

Actually, my particular mission was of a dual character. The Spelman Fund had given me a traveling fellowship to look into the current state of the efforts to solve the housing problem in European cities and also to study the activities of the organizations of public officials, more particularly those in the field of municipal government, in which I had so long had an active interest.

At the same time, I was engaged in finding out what I could to help the Spelman Fund itself continue its activities in the field of public administration, again with the major emphasis on local and state government.

Already the Spelman Fund had advanced considerably in its program, and for a large part of the time I had been in close touch with its work. By June of 1930 the Spelman Fund already had made grants to various organizations, most of them composed exclusively of public officials. These grants had financed the Bureau of Public Personnel Administration, which was the secretariat of the Civil Service Assembly of the United States and Canada and had headquarters in Chicago, and the Municipal Administration Service, set up in the headquarters of the National Municipal League under the management of a board on which was represented, in addition to the league itself, the American

Municipal Association and the City Managers' Association. The Spelman Fund had influenced the transfer of the headquarters of the City Managers' Association from Lawrence, Kansas, to the vicinity of the campus of the University of Chicago, and it had made a direct grant to the research committee of the City Managers' Association for the purpose of carrying on an experiment in the planning, organization, and installation of schemes for the better management of street sanitation and of refuse and garbage disposal in four cities of differing sizes. It had made a grant for the establishment of central headquarters for the American Legislators' Association, which was composed of delegations chosen by the legislatures of the several states. And it had also promised support to the newly organized American Association of Public Welfare Officials.

In the United States I had been for a number of years in close contact with a good many organizations of public officials, but particularly with the International City Managers' Association. Others with which I had more or less close relations included the American Municipal Association, at that time a federation of state leagues of municipalities, where my contacts had come through Mr. Stutz, the secretary of the City Managers' Association, who was also director of the Kansas League of Municipalities and who organized the national federation. I had been president of the Virginia League of Municipalities and of the Tennessee League of Municipalities and chairman of the executive committee of the New Jersey League of Municipalities. I also had had contact with public officials through organizations not exclusively public in character, such as the Virginia, New Jersey, and Tennessee conferences of social work. I had been president of two of these conferences and chairman of the executive committee of the third. Through them I attended meetings of the National Conference of Social Work, which had kept me in close touch with many public welfare officials. As I have said, I had also helped to organize the new Association of Public Welfare Officials.

Through their journals, I had kept myself informed about the Municipal Finance Officers' Association, the American Society of Municipal Engineers, the Association of Street Sanitation Officials, and others.

Early in the year 1930, serious consideration was being given by the Spelman Fund to the establishment somewhere in the country of a center for as many of the organizations of public officials as might be interested. The Spelman Fund planned to finance it for a period of years, and it wanted to find a sponsor of sufficient prestige to impress public opinion and to facilitate the work of all the organizations that might join the center.

To that end it was decided to ask the Conference of Governors, which was to meet in Salt Lake City, to give its approval to the enterprise. The Spelman Fund decided to send two representatives to lay the proposal before the governors in Salt Lake. The men chosen were Leonard D. White, professor of public administration in the University of Chicago, and David Lawrence, publisher of the *United States Daily,* which, as I have said, was also receiving financial support from the Spelman Fund. Mr. Lawrence arranged to report stenographically the proceedings of the Conference of Governors and to publish the records as a special supplement to the *United States Daily.*

Mr. Ruml and Dr. Merriam of the Spelman Fund board were going to Europe, and I had engaged to meet them in Geneva, where we three together could consider the action of the governors at Salt Lake. Just before taking ship at Boston, I received from Mr. Lawrence a copy of the supplement.

I read it on shipboard. The result was, so far as our plans were concerned, negative. Dr. White and Mr. Lawrence made excellent presentations, and the plan outlined was received with warm approbation, so far as the plan itself was concerned. However, two governors objected to the idea of accepting foundation funds in support of the enterprise. They each expressed the opinion that if such a center were set up under the aegis of the Conference of Governors, the aid to it should come from public funds and not from foundation grants. These two governors were influential men. They made an able presentation of their point of view. They were careful not to extend their objection to any of the organizations of local officials, but they did stand firm in their opinions so far as the Conference of Govenors was concerned. The two governors were Harry G. Leslie, the Republican governor of Indiana, and Franklin D. Roosevelt, the Democratic governor of New York.

That meant that if the center were to be established, and if there were to be a co-ordinated effort in assisting organizations of officials to set up permanent secretariats and establish headquarters, the Spelman Fund would have to find another sponsor.

That also meant that the special supplement of the *United States Daily* carrying the stenographic report of the Conference of Governors would be the first item on the agenda when I met Mr. Ruml and Dr. Merriam at Geneva. I was not particularly discouraged. I had had considerable apprehension concerning the effect the sponsorship of the Conference of Governors might have on some of the organizations of municipal officials. In many states many members were easily persuaded that the state governments were not entirely friendly and were sometimes actually inimical to the interests of the municipal and other local units of government. However, as far as all that was concerned, it could wait until the meeting in Geneva. At the moment I had other fish to fry.

I was to look at the municipal housing situation in Glasgow and Edinburgh and then go to London. Being fresh from Radburn, which had had its initial inspiration in the garden cities sponsored by Sir Ebenezer Howard and Sir Raymond Unwin in England—the garden cities surrounded by green fields—I was bound directly for Letchworth and Welwyn. Actually, Sir Raymond Unwin had been a consultant in the planning of Radburn, and I had become well acquainted with him there. To see the Unwins in Hampstead, London, was one of our first and most delightful visits. There, too, we saw Thomas Adams, who had been one of the principal planning consultants for the regional plan of New York and its environs, into which plan every effort had been made to fit the Radburn scheme. And then there were the planners of the housing estates in the immediate vicinity of London. I met a great many persons, a few of whom I had already known, many whom I knew by reputation, and others whose acquaintance it was both interesting and informative to make.

On the other wing of my quest were the associations of officials. There was in London the National Association of Local Government Officials, established and still presided over by an organizational genius named L. C. Hill, of whom I had heard much. His association was more like a labor union than an unofficial association of public officials such as we knew in the United States, but he was most helpful, and there began a close personal friendship which has continued until this day. Then also there was the Association of Municipal Treasurers, headed by Mr. Arthur Collins, whom I had met both in Canada and

1936

BREAKING GROUND FOR "1313"

Left to right (front row): Robert Redfield, Dean of the Social Sciences, University of Chicago; Louis Brownlow; Robert Maynard Hutchins, President of the University of Chicago; Clarence E. Ridley, Executive Director of the International City Managers' Association; Henry Toll, Director of the Council of State Governments.

AT THE MEETING OF THE INTERNATIONAL INSTITUTE OF ADMINISTRATIVE SCIENCES WARSAW, POLAND, 1936

Left to right: Louis Brownlow; Mohammed Abdullah al-Araby, Professor of Administrative Law, University of Egypt; Leonard D. White; Charles E. Merriam. *Back row:* Guy Moffett; Clifford W. Ham; Frederick Hoehler.

The President's Committee on Administrative Management, 1936–37
Left to right: Luther H. Gulick; Charles E. Merriam; Louis Brownlow

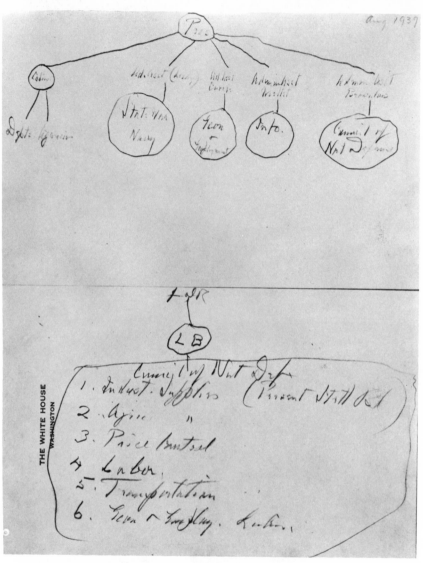

CHARTS DRAWN BY PRESIDENT ROOSEVELT IN AUGUST, 1939

ELIZABETH SIMS BROWNLOW

LOUIS BROWNLOW

in the United States; the Association of County and Borough Officials; and others.

At the top of the list, however, was the Institute of Public Administration. This was an organization, of relatively small membership, concerned with the problems of public administration in both local and central government.

I had heard much from American visitors of the importance of its meetings, and I had read from time to time its journal, *Public Administration*. Bess and I went to Oxford to attend its summer session, which was held in New College. Its technical organization was quite different from that of most of our American associations in that the papers to be discussed were printed in advance and not read at the meeting, an arrangement which gave sufficient time for full discussion, providing the members in attendance had done their homework. This, I discovered, the British were likely to do. I doubted that this technique could be successfully transplanted to the United States.

At that time I knew very few of the men in attendance at Oxford. I did know Mr. Hill and one or two others. My wife and I were the only Americans there, so far as we knew. But at the end of a particularly intense discussion of one of the papers, when a distinguished Englishman had arisen and with a voice of great authority laid down what he considered to be the inescapable conclusion of the whole matter, a young American on the opposite side of the room arose and, in a soft southern accent, drawled a comment which completely devastated the logical foundation of the position that just had been announced as a finality. The chairman seemed puzzled. The whole group was stunned. Whereupon the distinguished man who had just announced his final judgment arose and said,

"Mr. Chairman, I must say that my young friend from the United States has utterly destroyed me. I beg you to withdraw my conclusion and to substitute therefor his wise and logically unassailable opinion."

The meeting at that moment was adjourned for luncheon. Bess and I rushed across the room to congratulate, or at any rate to meet, our fellow countryman. He was a young man just twenty-one years old. He had been a student in several universities in the United States—Texas, Virginia, Michigan, and Princeton. He had done some work in Oxford and in the University of Berlin. He was modest of mien, plump of body, and mild of manner. He was Rowland Egger, who now for many years has been the head of the Bureau of Public Administration of the University of Virginia and frequently has taken leave to work with me and others of my colleagues in the field of public administration, both in the United States and abroad.

There at that meeting in Oxford several other most rewarding friendships were made; some of them endure until this day, and others have been interrupted by death. Among the people we met were Sir Henry N. Bunbury, comptroller general of the General Post Office of Great Britain, who still survives and is one of my closest friends; Mr. I. G. Gibbon—later Sir Gwyllym Gibbon—of the Ministry of Health, with whom I kept in contact throughout his life; and Mr. G. Montagu Harris, of the Association of County Councils, who later became the president of the International Union of Cities; and several others. At any rate, it was the beginning of a close association with what has now become the Royal Institute of Public Administration by grace of Her Majesty the Queen.

We crossed the channel to the Low Countries, visiting in the Netherlands and Belgium the many great municipal housing projects, interviewing Dr. Jonker, the head of the Dutch Union of Cities, and in Brussels finding the two objects of my quest united in the person of Senator Émile Vinck, the vice-president of the Belgian Senate, the chief of the Belgian Public Housing Organization, the secretary of the Belgian Union of Cities, and the secretary-general of the International Union of Cities. He was not only the source of a great deal of valuable information but a veritable powerhouse of inspiration. He had been the secretary-general of the International Union of Cities when it was organized in 1913. He had been the prime mover in its reorganization after the end of World War I in 1918. He was still the dynamic force behind it, and he had literally accomplished miracles, building upon the most meager financial support. He had made bricks without straw.

Also in Belgium I met M. Edmond Lesoir, who was the secretary-general of the International Institute of Administrative Sciences, an organization with which relatively few Americans had had any contact. However, among them was Leonard D. White of the University of Chicago, one of the pioneers in intensive research in the field of public administration as a general discipline.

We went to other capitals, looking at housing projects, meeting the heads of organizations, and looking into their work. This was particularly rewarding in Berlin, where the organization of officials of the larger cities had successfully operated for some decades; and thence on we went to the rendezvous at Geneva.

Mr. Ruml had taken quarters for us at the Hotel Beau Rivage. I was disappointed to find that Dr. Merriam had been delayed and would not be able to meet us there, but would see us later in London.

There were, of course, things to do and see, and Bess and I greatly enjoyed ourselves for the several days while we awaited Mr. Ruml's arrival.

When he came, I gave him the long, printed record of the proceedings at Salt Lake City. That occupied a day of his time. On the next day I gave him, in very great detail, a report of what had happened at Boston in the organization of the Association of Public Welfare Officials and told him of my adventures with, and my comments on, what I had seen of the organizations of municipal officials in Great Britain, the Low Countries, and Germany. I also reported on the discussion of the problems of public administration generally at the conference in Oxford.

One bright and most particular day, Ruml and I had lunch alone together on the terrace of the Beau Rivage. We looked across the lake to where the massif of Mont Blanc had lifted her veil of clouds and stood revealed in all her snowy majesty in the full light of the sun. It was a good lunch. Mr. Ruml, who knew his way around, had ordered a bottle of the best burgundy the excellent cellars of the Beau Rivage could provide.

We discussed the whole program of the proposed center. We discussed the veto of the governors. We discussed the difficulties imposed upon us by the absence of Dr. Merriam. We discussed this obstacle, that difficulty, and the other barrier. And then, with the last two glasses of burgundy, Mr. Ruml announced the decision of the conference.

It was "Let's go. Let's organize the center. Let's set it up. Let us find a suitable sponsor if we can, but if we cannot, let's go ahead."

And that was the birth of Public Administration Clearing House and the decision which determined all the rest of my life.

CHAPTER XXII

ASSEMBLING THE GROUP

In the two or more years preceding the actual organization of the Public Administration Clearing House, my conversations
with Beardsley Ruml of the Spelman Fund and Charles E. Merriam
of the University of Chicago had made clear that one of our principal
purposes was the establishment of a center around which could be
clustered organizations of public officials intimately concerned with the
improvement of the techniques and methodology of governmental
operations.

Some such organizations had been in existence for decades. Most of
the older ones had been built around a particular professional skill or
a particular specialized operation. Among these, the organization of
Public Health Officials had been quite naturally inspired by the professional medical societies and, indeed, had not in the beginning recognized the differentiation between private practice and public administration in medicine. Some, such as the finance officers, had similarly
organized themselves according to the traditions of the professional
accountants. The organizations of public school officials had been set
up on a different basis—that of the competency of teachers as determined by systems of certification. Those systems, operating at first
under purely local auspices and later shaped by statutes enacted by
state legislatures, had approached, because of the mobility of people in
the United States, a nationwide organization responding to a demand
for better and more rapid interstate communications.

Some organizations had been created in response to the demands for
improved statistical information. Thus, the United States Bureau of
the Census as early as 1906 had found that it required better and more
uniform statistical reports on municipal taxes, expenditures, and debt,
and to fill that lack it had encouraged the organization of the Munici-

pal Finance Officers' Association. Likewise, the United States Civil Service Commission, experiencing the difficulties of nationwide operation, found that its contacts with the then relatively few state and local government civil service authorities were extremely tenuous. At the same time, the few state and local authorities that then existed in the personnel field discovered difficulties in obtaining information from the federal government center. Thus it came about, also in 1906, that the United States Civil Service Commission took an active part in organizing the Civil Service Assembly of the United States and Canada. This organization later included the federal and the state, provincial, and local commissions in both countries.

Some other organizations had been attempted in the field of general government. There was an American Municipal League, established at the turn of the century. Having no particular professional or specialized skills to depend upon, it was soon unable to function, largely because of the rapid turnover among the elected officials who were the heads of municipal governments that operated under varying requirements of state constitutions and statutes.

One of the greatest weaknesses of these organizations, many of which did excellent work, was their lack of funds to enable them to establish permanent secretariats. Most of these societies found some dedicated individual to act as secretary, and he, with the backing of his own particular governmental unit, provided the necessary secretarial service for the convening of an annual convention or conference, the development of an annual meeting program, and, sometimes, a report of its proceedings. The principal activity in such cases was the annual convention. There was no means of establishing year-round service, no means of keeping in constant touch with the membership, and no possibility of making current replies to inquiries. And, all too often, the annual meeting was regarded by the public and by many of its attendants as nothing more than a joy-riding junket at the expense of the public treasury.

Mr. Stutz and I, while I was still in Petersburg and Knoxville, had written a memorandum based upon the concept of a national center for organizations in the general field of local government. This we had submitted to Dr. Merriam and had obtained from him many useful suggestions. In 1926, I had presented the memorandum to Raymond W. Fosdick, then counsel for the Rockefeller Foundation. That memorandum contained a request for foundation support for such a center. It was not acted upon. However, Mr. Ruml of the Laura Spelman Rockefeller Memorial Fund, closely associated with the Rockefeller Foundation, knew about it, as of course did Dr. Merriam.

In the lobby of the Sinton Hotel at the 1927 meeting of the National Municipal League in Cincinnati, late one afternoon, I first saw Beardsley Ruml. He had come to look over the league constituents. We talked a little. I found that he was familiar with the proposal for a center that Stutz and I, with Merriam's advice, had made. I was eager, enthusiastic, and, I have no doubt, garrulous in presenting to him my somewhat changed concept of the operations of such a center. At first we had thought of one closely integrated with a university and managed by a board of directors.

By this time I was no longer a city manager. Although I had lost none of my interest in the cause of improvement of municipal government, I had become convinced through my contacts with public health, social welfare, and educational organizations that it would be extremely difficult if not impossible to obtain the adherence of organizations of specialized administrators to any central body.

I told Mr. Ruml of my experience with public health agencies when I was in New York and was about to leave the city managership of Petersburg to take on that of Knoxville. Mr. Ruml knew all about those public health agencies. Each one of them was an independent organization, and their being assembled in one office building had come about because of their recognition of the greater convenience in communication resulting from proximity.

In my speech to Ruml (it was nothing less than a speech), I said that such an integrated institute of local government as we had advocated a few years earlier could be much more successful if it were set up not as a hierarchical membership organization but as a grouping of independent, autonomous societies and associations bound together only by common interests and purposes.

These conclusions, convictions, and notions all were based primarily upon a fundamental theory of government that I had fully accepted. It was that there is and always will be a difference between politics, on the one hand, and administration, on the other, no matter how closely they may be related in a democratic society.

Out of this particular conviction I had developed certain ideas about the organizations in local government. The City Managers' Association, under the practice followed by Mr. Stutz, had replied quite freely to inquiries from citizens all over the country who wanted to know how to obtain the adoption of the council-manager form of government in their particular city. That had brought the association into a political position in certain cities. It had invited the charge that the City Managers' Association was invading the city from outside in order to set up a strange and alien form of government for the sole purpose of obtaining a high-salaried job for one of its members.

At the same time the National Municipal League had been the chief organization promoting the council-manager form. It had issued a model council-manager charter, and, indeed, its principal organizing genius, Richard S. Childs, was the inventor of the council-manager system. When the City Managers' Association moved to Chicago, Mr. Ridley, fully sharing my views, took the position that he would not answer such inquiries but would refer them and their authors in every instance to the National Municipal League. His association took the position that it was interested only in the clearance of information and ideas about the techniques of management.

This led me quite easily and naturally into the belief that insofar as the improvement of municipal government was concerned, there should always be in each particular field two organizations, one of citizens interested in the promotion of reform and political improvement at the polls and before legislative bodies and the other of administrators interested in techniques, methodology, and training.

When, then, Public Administration Clearing House set up its shop in Chicago in 1931, it was by definition devoted to gathering a cluster of organizations primarily, if not solely, concerned with administrative matters.

A very great deal of my time during that first year of 1931 was devoted to the assembling of such a group. It was necessary to try to convince each of the organizations invited to come to Chicago that it might be able to obtain financial help from the Spelman Fund and that coming to a common center would in no wise affect their individual independence or autonomy. In this effort, which was not always as easy as it sounds, I had the invaluable assistance of Guy Moffett of the Spelman Fund, who, with me and sometimes separately from me, visited these organizations and explained to them the basic purposes of the new center.

In the process of organizing the Clearing House itself, I proceeded very slowly. Mr. Robert M. Paige began as my assistant in May. His principal task was to make a survey of organizations of administrators and others in public administration. In the late autumn I appointed as assistant director Charles S. Ascher, with whom I had been intimately associated in New York in the City Housing Corporation, of which he had been general counsel. Ascher was fully apprised of my conception of the nature of the new organization, for I had kept him informed as a personal friend and business associate during the two or three years of conversations that had led up to the establishment of the Clearing House.

So, it came about that in 1932, Public Administration Clearing House actually got under way. Close to it and to the University of Chicago were gathered the International City Managers' Association, the American Public Welfare Association, the American Municipal Association, the Municipal Finance Officers' Association, and also the American Legislators' Association, which was an organization of members of state legislatures devoted to the improvement of the legislative process and sharply divorced from partisan activity—indeed, the purpose of its program was to improve the administrative phases of the legislative process.

Also there was one other organization, the Governmental Research Association. It had been set up several years before by a group of professional persons engaged by privately financed agencies in research and surveys of municipal and state governments. It had had its secretariat in New York near the National Institute of Public Administration. However, the deepening depression had deprived many of its constituent members of their financial support, and the association found it difficult to carry on. I invited it to set up its central offices with the Clearing House. My assistant, Robert M. Paige, was chosen its executive secretary, and it also became a part of the group in 1932.

Thus, in the early part of 1932, I was face to face with several problems: How could the Clearing House, as the focus of the center, be of the greatest possible service to the organizations assembled in Chicago? What could I, from that focal point, do to engage the interest and co-operation of such organizations elsewhere in the United States and abroad? Finally, what was the best way to create the administrative machinery that would give meaning and content to the program indicated by the two words "Clearing House" and make it of service to the advancement of the art and science of "Public Administration"—the other two words? By then I already had had fifteen years looking into the windows of city halls, courthouses, state capitols, and offices of the national governments in the United States and in many countries all over the world. I had had fifteen years inside city halls, looking out onto the world through those same windows. Now the next fifteen years would be spent attempting to do what I could to utilize what I had seen from both sides—looking in and looking out.

What was the beginning of that last sesquidecade? Why did I insist on seeing both sides? What impelled me to try to equate the two views?

It was, I think, that a dream had captured my imagination, a dream that I, in my own way, might contribute as much as I could in my working life to the business of improving the administration of government. It was my dream about what was needed for the advancement of democratic government, about what I conceived to be necessary for the improvement of the welfare of people under whatever form of government and in whatever land they lived—an essentially humanitarian, egalitarian, and libertarian dream.

Despite my deep interest in and great concern with the political processes by which men govern themselves or are governed by others, I became deeply convinced that the methods by which their governments were administered were of great and ever increasing importance. Thus, I began to separate in my mind the political goals of governments—the purposes for which they were set up, the benefits they were expected to produce for their citizens—from the functional and administrative tools and arrangements established to induce and achieve the desired ends.

Early in 1928, I set down some of these thoughts in a paper written for publication but never offered to an editor. In it I limited myself to the province of local government. It has not been revised. It never was finished. It still stands, after nearly three decades, as it was written when I was on the verge of my fiftieth year—the leitmotiv of my mature years. It reads:

"It has seemed to me for a long time that many of us who are genuinely interested in the fundamental problems of municipal government are balked in our efforts to work out solutions not only by the lack of standards of measurement, which we all admit and deplore, but also because we frequently confuse aims with methods; thus giving functional machinery an importance which is merited only by an objective purpose and thus frequently permitting an adventitious exaggeration of the importance of the mere machinery of government to obscure the primary objects sought to be attained.

"That this is true is not surprising, for I think you will agree with me after reflection that the lines of the patterns of the objectives of municipal government crisscross the lines of the patterns of governmental organization, and that simplification of the functional machinery, for which we have been striving, tends rather to intensify this complexity than otherwise.

"Now that we are beginning to address ourselves to the task of measuring government—beginning to set up standards—it seems to me that we ought also to try to clear up the confusion caused by the failure of the functional machinery to coincide with the purposes of local government.

"Let me, then, put up as a target to be shot at the bare bones of a speech that I have been making for the last half-dozen years to rotary clubs and citizens' associations and leagues of women voters and, even, on occasion to high-school students. I have not dared heretofore to expose it to the criticism of the expert.

"Communities organize themselves for the purpose of securing to the individuals who compose them certain commonly desired objectives. These objectives, in the logical order of their relative importance, are:

1. Health
2. Education
3. Facilities for industry, trade and material achievement
4. Opportunities for recreation, cultural development and spiritual growth

"Let us test these four objectives by the desires of an intelligent parent planning for the life of his child. He will wish for that child first of all physical and mental health, for without health he will not be able in full measure to acquire an education, make a living, or live a full life. Given health, and the basic foundation for an education, the parent will wish for his child the facilities for making a living. They will include the physical means of community activity for trade and industry:

traffic and transit within the local area, transportation linking the local community to the fields and mines, the markets and consuming centers of the nation and the world—most of the things that the citizen tax-payer usually considers first, rather than third, in importance in community activities. Given health and education and the means of livelihood and savings, the parent will wish for his child opportunity for play, for cultivation in the higher arts of living, and for growth in spiritual strength.

"If these objectives could be attained in their ideal fulness we would have a community made up of healthy, educated, prosperous people devoting their leisure time to the pursuit of happiness. The ideal is, of course, unattainable; but may not the measure of the success of community organization be the distance advanced toward that goal? May not the measure of common failure be the distance by which that goal is missed?

"But, it may be objected, here is an idealization in terms of community activity that ignores on one side the capacity, purposefulness, fortune, and inevitable mortality of the individual human being; and on the other the influence of national, racial, and world conditions; to say nothing of the inescapable limitations of geography and the impossibility of forfending the natural disasters of flood, earthquake, or tornado.

"To that I say that the community by its organized activities does not ignore these factors. It endeavors ceaselessly to overcome them, postpone them, influence, modify, and mitigate them. The Tokyo building code has an eye for the mitigation of the effects of earthquakes; Dayton rebuilt itself spiritually as well as physically by attempting to prevent a recurrence of its flood disaster; and now we see the levee system of the Mississippi that began with a communal dike at New Orleans, then grew into state systems of levees, and now has expanded to become a national problem in flood control, as local communities, combined by interest in a common danger, more closely united by improved communications, exert an influence on the larger community which is the nation. So, too, the community endeavors to make the individual useful. It tries to help him to improve his capacity, tries to make him purposeful, tries to adjust him to his domestic life, and fights furiously to postpone his inevitable death to the last possible breath, no matter what the pain or the misery of that latter end of life may be.

"Let me repeat, then, that the objectives of community organization are four and that in order of their relative importance they are (1) health; (2) education; (3) facilities for industry, trade, and material achievement; and (4) opportunities for recreation, cultural development, and spiritual growth. Mr. Jefferson wrote it, 'Life, liberty, and the pursuit of happiness,' and nationally we are committed to the credo that for a fair chance in this pursuit 'all men are created equal.'

"Now let us contrast these objects of community organization with the machinery we have set up to help us to attain them.

"Taking first things first, let us consider health.

"If we are thinking in terms of functional machinery, our minds will turn naturally and without hesitation to the health department, that division of the machinery of municipal government which endeavors to safeguard the public health. But if we are thinking in terms of primary objectives, we will remember that the city department of public health as we know it is younger than threescore years and ten, and that many communities even yet have not more than the rudimentary beginnings of such a department, and we will remember, too, that there have been communities, urban communities at that, for centuries. Then we will ask the question, What is the primary health requirement of any human community? The answer is *water*.

"But there is no agreement as to how a community should be supplied with water, or as to how that water should be made safe for the health of those who drink it. The Chinese have been trained to boil the water before they drink it, to make it more palatable with tea leaves, and then to credit the sterilization which came from heat to the magical medicine of tea. In America we prefer to collect a common supply, purify it, and pipe it to whosoever will. But even then we have no universal method of organizing the business; in one city it is a matter for the municipal government and in another for a privately owned and operated public utility corporation.

"The health department, so new to community life if we measure by generations, keeps a watchful eye on that water supply, be it a public or private plant, and looks at it under the microscope and in the test tube and subjects it to all the meticulous ceremony of the laboratory, lest the agency supplying the water fails to keep it pure and wholesome. And if there is no health department, some private society of persons interested in health will of its own motion institute such a watch and ward.

"So we find first of all that the attainment of community objectives is sought through various organizations; the objectives are common—qualitatively—to all communities, and their attainment is intrusted to three types of organizations: (1) government; (2) private corporations operating for profit on the basis of private capital; and (3) private societies operating without profit on the basis of voluntary expression of civic interest. Over and above these three types of organizations, the community still intrusts much of the effort for the attainment of its common objectives to the unorganized activities of the individual.

"To support this, or at least to clarify my view of it, let us go on with health. Ignoring the historic perspective and taking a typical American community of today, let us see to what types of organization the community health is intrusted. The water supply, sewage disposal, and garbage removal are matters of government (although the water supply may be handled by a private company), as is the inspection of milk and other food supplies, the prevention of infection, and so on. The nursing service that means so much to bettered health conditions for the community is partly governmental, some under the health officer and some under the school board; partly corporation, under the life insurance companies and the large industrial corporations; and partly under voluntary societies, as the Instructive Visiting Nurse Society, or the Red Cross. For instruction in hygiene we organize the public, the parochial, and the private school, regiment the pulpit, platform, and press. Does a new danger to health threaten in the form of the automobile? Does not government respond with a traffic policeman; corporate business with posters and prizes for 'safety first' and, representing the voluntary agency, the Chamber of Commerce with its Safety Council?

"All this is but the merest sketch of how the community tries to advance its purpose through its three kinds of civic organizations; above that it tries, ever more and more consciously, to enlist the personal assistance of each individual in attaining this primary objective of health.

"In our recent efforts to measure the results of community effort, and specifically of municipal government, we started by common consent with health work. The ruler had hardly been lifted from the first appraisal form, the ink was not dry on the first toting of a total, before it was apparent that not only governmental but all health agencies would have to be considered in the measurement. 'All health agencies' is an elastic phrase with vague limitations and complex connotations, but it runs all the way from the governmental function of administering toxin-antitoxin for the control of diphtheria and the red-amber-green of the traffic light, through the gamut of corporation and private social agency practice, through the advice of the minatory physician, down to the very private business of precise control of an adequate personal intake of spinach and the matutinal prostration before the muezzin in the tower, the loudspeaker. (I have purposely left out the psychologist, the psychiatrist, and the personnel administrator—mental hygiene is too new and too much confused in the popular mind with an 'inspirational address,' which this very article began by being.)

"Bless me, I began that particular outburst by saying I intended to clarify my views. All right. I have tried to do it by indicating ever so inadequately the tangled complexity of the business.

"Now, if you have the fortitude, let us take but one type of community organization, the municipal government, and see what is the relationship between its functional machinery and the four primary objectives of the community purpose. (I do not mean to imply that there should me any such relation; I am merely trying to find out if there is any.) In the first place I think we will find that the popular will has ordained that government shall not undertake any positive action except as it will advance the community toward the attainment of one of these four objects; but that this public decree has resulted from conscious thought is hardly possible. It has come from the simpler idea that it is not the business of government to try to do what individuals may do for themselves. The confusion in the popular mind about this dividing line has arisen from the invention in the recent past of the artificial individual, the corporation, which is partly private and partly public, partly individual, and partly governmental. That twilight zone obscures some of the lines of the picture I am trying to unveil, but it does not materially affect the final pattern except as to the matter of expense. Then, too, the business is made more complex by reason of the fact that there is an absolute shifting of the dividing line between what a government may do better than an individual and what it may not— a steady shift toward the side of government as electricity and machine tools supplant—and, supplanting, multiply by millions—muscle and the cunning hand.

"So much has thus been delegated to government, that I dare say no citizen of any city in the United States can enumerate the governmental activities of his own municipal government. This means that governmental activities are steadily increasing in number, in scope, and in complexity.

"I am insisting on the recognition of this mazeful labyrinth of complexities, because I must of needs simplify the actual pattern of reality in undertaking, at last, to do what I set out to do, namely, to look at the functional machinery of the typical city government in the light of its purposeful objectives.

"Again, health. It is obvious that the objective of health is a part of the business of the Department of Public Works which instals and operates sewers, cleans the streets, collects and incinerates the garbage; of the Department of Public Service which controls the water supply; of the Department of Public Safety which handles the traffic policemen and inspects the plumbing; of the Department of Law which devises new regulations to meet the new problems that arise from the growing intensity of urban congestion; and of the Department of Education which is responsible for instruction in hygiene, as well as the Department of Public Welfare which includes the Board of Health.

"So we see that every major division of the functional machinery of the local government has a part in striving toward the attainment of the first object—health.

"Let us take the second object—education. The public school system undertakes the major responsibility, but the governmental activity does not end with the public schools. The library system is now almost universally governmental, and its share in the educational effort is a steadily increasing one. As our conception of education changes from the elementary training of children to include the continuing education of the adult, more and more, all the major divisions of the local government take over this and that responsibility that is basically educational. Long before the public schools have admitted the growing child, the health officer has tried to reach him through his mother, and, with pre-school activities of various kinds—governmental, corporation, and those of the voluntary society—the community tries to reach with educational effort the babies whose lives are sought to be devoted to the social ends of the group.

"The third object, which may be summarized as community facilities for making a living, is, oddly enough, not so complex. The government is expected to furnish all the physical facilities which are commonly demanded but the use of which cannot be conveniently charged for at a measured rate—paved streets, bridges, viaducts—all the necessary public ways for privately owned vehicles of every sort and kind. The public utility corporations—sometimes government-owned but treated as a self-sustaining and separate entity—are expected to furnish the means of transit and transportation, telephonic communication, power, gas, and so on. Those promotional and experimental civic endeavors having for their purpose the business improvement of the community are left to the Chamber of Commerce, and to other voluntary societies of citizens. Even here there is no standard of simplification, and each separate community has its own method of dividing the responsibility for these important functions among the three types of community organization.

"So far as the functional machinery of local government goes, again we will find every major division of the municipal organization striving in some fashion to advance the community toward the attainment of this third object. The Department of Public Works here takes the lead, but in some measure all others contribute.

"Indeed, in the popular mind, the utility of the efforts for health and education is measured by the definitive contributions made toward the third object. Everybody has to make a living, or to live off someone else who has done so. Everybody wants wealth, and, broadly speaking, everybody wants the community in which he lives to be prosperous.

"That there is so little agreement as to the best methods by which this third object may be attained arises largely from the fact that everybody is so deeply and immediately interested, and everybody's interest in community wealth is necessarily twisted and contorted by his own private desires for personal fortunes.

"The fourth object, which may be summarized as the community opportunities for the cultivation of the amenities of life, is most complex of all. It has to do with the use to which each individual may put that leisure time which is, for most of us, increasing rapidly or, at any rate, which is becoming more widely distributed. For centuries the community supported a few of its fortunately placed ones in almost complete leisure. It now endeavors to find some leisure for all. For a long time the employment of leisure was looked upon as the most private and personal thing imaginable, but now the community has found that here again it must step in to do as a group the individual things which individuals cannot do for themselves.

Assembling the Group

"Government provides parks and playing fields. Corporations provide amusement places. Voluntary societies without number, from golf clubs to settlement houses, try to blend play with health, play with education, play with play for play's own sake.

"Government, voluntary societies, and corporations support art galleries, symphony orchestras, and the opera, in order that the community may offer opportunity for cultural development to its citizens.

"The church has done its share for the other three objects, contributing notably to mental hygiene in a field which it has had, almost unwittingly, mostly for its own; taking the chief burden for ethical and religious education; and giving supernatural sanctions to accepted standards of trade and industry stabilizing the delicate balance of the machinery for wealth. In this fourth field, it has its greatest work—offering the opportunity for spiritual development. Citizens who themselves spurn the church and ignore religion openly or covertly, support it as an absolutely necessary community institution. The church itself, despite its primary occupation with the individual, tends more and more to recognize its community obligations. Union of the denominations of the churches is as far away as ever, perhaps, but in countless communities we have seen Christian and Jew, Catholic and Protestant, unite for common aims when the opportunities for common spiritual development of the community may be advanced.

"So we see here that government, public utility corporations, voluntary societies of citizens (which in this country includes the church) all have a varying share in the effort to advance the community toward the attainment of its four objects. And we see also that the functional divisions of the municipal governmental machinery are divided according to functions, administrative or traditional, and not according to objects, aims or purposes."

That statement in essence became the first part of a speech I was frequently to deliver. I gave it first to the International City Managers' Association convention in Asheville, North Carolina, in the autumn of 1928. I repeated it by request the next year when the City Managers' Association, meeting in Fort Worth, Texas, held its banquet session in the neighboring city of Dallas. And I am compelled to confess that I used it in speeches over and over again to many audiences under many circumstances.

But, of course, I knew all the time that it was unfinished.

[247]

I tried to set out the differentiation between the goals of government and the functional departmentalization set up to achieve them. This compelled me always to finish the speech by pointing out that many, in fact practically all, of the functional administrative establishments in government found a vast part of their work in dealing not with advancement toward these ultimate goals but with the results of the failures to achieve them.

Just as the several functional organizations set up to consider the health of the people were also compelled to deal with the problems of those in ill-health, so the organizations set up to achieve education were forced to deal with the failures of that program and with the disabilities, handicaps, and difficulties of the uneducated and the untrained. The municipal housekeeping establishments set up for facilitating the business of making a living were always faced with the troubles of the persons who had not been able to achieve economic satisfactions. And, of course, in the progress toward this particular object, the local governments had but a relatively small part to play in what, after all, was largely under the control of national or world events. As to the fourth object, all the functional establishments set up to support advance had also to deal with failures.

As I developed these thoughts, I became more and more acutely aware of the particular problems, constantly arising in public administration, of bringing the various functional, administrative, and departmental establishments into some sort of general relationship that would enable them to work together for ultimate aims without subjecting them to the handicaps inherent in absolute domination by superior hierarchical determination. Thus was formed in my mind a plan of action which had two purposes: one was, by persuasion only, to induce public administrators to recognize that their particular specialties could make a contribution in a much wider field of endeavor. The other was to induce the practitioner of each specialty to take counsel of what his colleagues in the same specialty were doing to improve their techniques and methodologies.

Having rejected my definition of one great over-all organization for the accomplishment of these purposes, I began to plan for a general scheme in which organized persuasion would be accomplished without organizational compulsion.

CHAPTER XXIII

CREATION OF PACH

It was one thing for Beardsley Ruml and me to sit on the terrace of the Beau Rivage Hotel in Geneva and decide to go ahead with the establishment of our center for organizations of officials in the field of public administration, but it was quite another thing to translate that determination into realization.

Mr. Ruml and Professor Merriam, shortly after my rendezvous with Ruml in Geneva, met in England and retreated to Cambridge for a week's work on the problem. Dr. Merriam easily agreed with the Geneva decision and began to address himself to the immediate problem of how to go about establishing the center. The result of the Cambridge convocation was a program which, early in the autumn of 1930, was submitted to the trustees of the Spelman Fund, where it found approval.

Guy Moffett, who was Mr. Ruml's assistant as executive of the Spelman Fund, had been at work on the general problem for nearly two years, and it was he, in concert with Mr. Ruml, who drew up a chart outlining the general purpose of the Spelman Fund's decision.

That chart consisted essentially of a circle in the middle of a page labeled, "Central Clearing of Information." From it radiated lines which led to circles at the top of the page labeled with the names of organizations such as the Assembly of Civil Service Commissions, the City Managers' Association, the Governor's Conference, the Legislators' Association, and one other labeled "other organizations of public officials." Under these was the note: "Secretariats of the above organizations to be located as far as possible at the same place as the central clearing house of information." At the right of the center circle, one line ran to a circle labeled "Coordination of Publication Activities." On the lower part of the page the lines ran from the center to circles designating existing research organizations such as the National Institute of Public Administration, Brookings Institution, private consulting organizations, universities, and other technical groups. Underneath these was a note: "Activities correlated to some extent to Social Science Research Council." This chart had been in circulation within the offices of the Spelman Fund for perhaps six months before Ruml and Merriam met in Cambridge.

In the meantime, in the autumn of 1929, the Public Administration Committee of the Social Science Research Council, then under the chairmanship of Leonard D. White of the University of Chicago, had employed Professor John Gaus of the University of Wisconsin to make a survey of research in public administration. His report, a brilliant exposition of the amount and kinds of research being done by a heterogeneous group of governmental agencies, organized public officials, functional groups, semipublic organizations, and universities, pointed toward the conclusion that a central clearing organization could be of great usefulness in establishing contact between these groups and in keeping track of their efforts and their output.

Both Mr. Ruml and Dr. Merriam were members of the Social Science Research Council, which, indeed, had been founded on the initiative of Dr. Merriam. In October, 1930, Luther Gulick, Director of the Institute of Public Administration, succeeded Dr. White as chairman of the council's public administration committee. Dr. Gulick joined Merriam and Ruml in asking me to write a memorandum outlining my ideas of the kind of program which the proposed center could usefully carry out.

The next item in strategy was to secure a sponsor and widespread support for the new organization in the particular field of its interest. Gulick presented the project to the Public Administration Committee at its meeting of November 3 and 4, 1930, and it agreed to act as the sponsor for the proposed exchange. Then he moved on to the National Conference on Improving Government held in Cleveland in November and there, using the memorandum which I had written to explain the proposal, secured the indorsement of representatives of the American Municipal Association, the American Legislators' Association, and the City Managers' Association.

The memorandum read as follows:

Creation of PACH

I. *Purpose*

To contribute toward a more complete and rapid interchange of knowledge and experience in the field of public administration; toward the elimination of needless duplication in research; and toward a closer and more effective cooperation between operating officials, research units and technical experts in public administration; with a view of reducing the gap between theory and practice and making available to those who are charged with responsibility of final decisions a better factual basis for action.

II. *Scope*

1. Contact with existing sources of information in the field of public administration with special emphasis on the state and local fields.
2. Cooperation with organized bodies of public administrators.
3. Cooperation with existing research agencies.
4. Cooperation with technical experts and consultants.
5. Cooperation with the Social Science Research Council and the learned societies.

III. *Method*

1. Act as a central clearing house for exchange of information and results of research.
2. Establish and maintain continuing personal contact with cooperating agencies in the field.
3. Encourage closer relations among organized bodies of administrators in order to improve the service rendered by each organization to its members, and constituents, by placing combined resources of information and experience at the disposal of each organization, thus enabling the organizations to prevent overlapping of program and duplication of effort.

IV. *Organization*

An incorporated board of directors composed of outstanding national characters with a definite knowledge of public administration.

Such representation is to be predicated on general interest in the several fields and not by virtue of direct nomination by organized groups in these fields. Direct representation from organizations in the present uncoordinated condition would produce a board unwieldy in members and of unbalanced constituencies and would result in endless delays.

V. *Limitations*

1. The Clearing House will advocate no particular form of governmental organization nor support specific political plans proposed for the remedy of administrative ills, being concerned solely with making available to those engaged in the operation and study of government such information and results of experience as will assist them most intelligently to decide upon a course of action.

[251]

2. The Clearing House will not undertake to render technical advisory service to public officials or citizen groups or to make administrative surveys.
3. In the prosecution of its activities, the Clearing House will guard against invasion of the fields of other existing organizations, or the duplication of existing facilities, its province being that of coordination and cooperation in the common interest and for the common advantage.
4. In order to protect and strengthen the special organizations of officials, of legislators, of administrators, or researchers, and of similar groups, the Clearing House will not normally deal with their members or potential members without the request of, or notice to, the appropriate secretaries.

That I would be the director of the clearing center was generally and publicly understood. Most of the persons concerned knew that I had been interested for years in just such a project.

The Spelman Fund had demonstrated its concern with the field by its grants to several of the organizations which then existed.

In conversation with Mr. Ruml and Dr. Gulick I had frequently stressed what I thought was one of the most important problems in setting up the new institution—that of the choice of a board of trustees under whose direction its affairs would be administered. From the first, we were in agreement that the chairman should be former Governor Frank O. Lowden of Illinois, if he could be persuaded to accept the post. Governor Lowden had become interested two or three years earlier in the Spelman Fund's work on the improvement of public administration generally in the country. As governor of Illinois in 1917, he had been a leader in the movement for the reorganization of state governments in this country and had demonstrated its utility by his own revamping of the Illinois state government in the interest of economy, efficiency, and greater responsiveness to the needs of the state as expressed by its citizens. Much of the work in state government reorganization had been done under the auspices of the National Institute of Public Administration, of which Gulick was the director. Quite naturally, then, we turned toward the leaders of Gulick's institution for names of men especially fitted to serve as trustees for the new institution. This was all the more important in our thinking because Gulick's institute was primarily a research organization, doing much of its work in surveys of state and local government—indeed, it had had its origin in the Bureau of Municipal Research, established in 1906 for research in the affairs of the government of New York City. Governor Lowden was one of the directors of the institute. When Dr. Gulick wrote to him, outlining the purposes of the new organization and asking him to serve as chairman, he replied: "Though I have been saying for some time that I could not interest myself in new organizations, I regard the proposed governmental information exchange as so vitally needed that I am willing to serve upon its board on the conditions you name."

Then, among the members of the directors of the Institute of Public Administration, we also approached several other men. I was particularly eager that Newton D. Baker, former secretary of war and former mayor and city attorney of Cleveland, be asked to serve. My acquaintance with Mr. Baker began in 1910 when he was city attorney, was continued through his service as mayor, and had been greatly strengthened by our intimate relationship during his service as secretary of war during World War I. Another choice was that of Harry F. Byrd, then the governor of Virginia, a state which had but recently effected a thoroughgoing reorganization of its administration.

Still another was Richard S. Childs, president of the National Municipal League. He had been the initiator and leader in two important governmental reforms. He had organized, with the backing of Woodrow Wilson, then president of Princeton University, the "Short-Ballot Association," which had created a general interest in almost all parts of the country in the effort to concentrate responsibility for the conduct of public affairs by taking many local offices out of the hurly-burly of electoral contests and placing them under the direct guidance of a smaller number of responsible elected officials.

Mr. Childs also was the originator of the council-manager plan. I had known him first through his work and had come to regard him as the pre-eminent leader in fighting for the cause of better municipal administration. I had been in close contact with him for more than a decade. Also, he was a member of Dr. Gulick's board and had been consulted by the Spelman Fund concerning the establishment of the new organization.

Then, in order to get wider geographic distribution, and also to bring into the group a representative of journalism, we decided to ask Chester H. Rowell, the editor of the *San Francisco Chronicle,* who had devoted much of his time to municipal affairs.

A highly satisfactory board of directors assured, it was time to conclude the final arrangements with the Spelman Fund for financing the organization. On November 26, 1930, Gulick wrote to Ruml suggesting that a definite commitment from the fund would be necessary before calling the prospective trustees together. Early in December, Mr. Ruml replied that the fund was prepared to appropriate $500,000, covering a ten-year period, to the "central exchange unit in public administration" provided the necessary legal incorporation was arranged. The board tentatively selected, he indicated, was entirely satisfactory. His letter continued, "We should, of course, in making any appropriation, wish to leave the entire management in the hands of the Board of Trustees, and would wish the individuals accepting the membership on the Board to have this thought in mind."

In the course of the conversations with the Spelman Fund and Dr. Gulick, it had come to be accepted that the new organization would be located in Chicago, and all the prospective trustees had been so advised. Earlier, there had been a good deal of discussion of whether it would be better to set up the new establishment in Chicago or in Washington, where an association with the Library of Congress might be worked out.

However, I strongly opposed Washington. I said that in my opinion it would be impossible for the staff of such an organization in Washington to think in terms of state and local government, that whatever was the original purpose, the overshadowing presence of the federal government would almost compel the staff to think federally.

It came to be generally agreed that the new institution would be asked to establish close relations with the University of Chicago, especially with the political science faculty and the other faculties of its Social Science Division, which then was being greatly strengthened.

It was also becoming understood that Beardsley Ruml himself would soon resign as executive of the Spelman Fund and go to the University of Chicago as the new dean of its Social Science Division.

At last there remained only the final step of christening and incorporating the new organization, which had been called by so many different names. Finally, Gulick and I decided on the name and filed the application for a charter in the office of the secretary of state of Illinois on December 18, 1930. We received a certificate for the organization of the "Public Administration Clearing House" as a corporation not for pecuniary profit under the laws of the state of Illinois; thus PACH came into legal existence. The incorporators named in the certificate were Louis Brownlow, Richard S. Childs, and Luther Gulick. The incorporators then called for a meeting of those who had accepted the invitation to become trustees.

That meeting was held in the office of Newton D. Baker in Cleveland, Ohio, on December 31, 1930. At that time, Governor Lowden was selected as chairman of the board, and I was formally named director of the Public Administration Clearing House. Bylaws were adopted, a tentative budget approved, and the organization was launched.

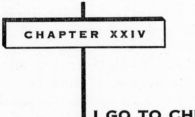

CHAPTER XXIV

I GO TO CHICAGO

After the first board meeting I took the train for Chicago. With me was Governor Lowden. It was the first chance I had had to talk with him alone. He greatly impressed me with his zeal for the improvement of the administrative processes of government, and he believed with me that in local and state government, at the very least, there was a difference between politics and administration; that skill in one of these branches of government did not necessarily mean skill in the other; that a good politician was not necessarily a good administrator; and, on the contrary, that the abilities of a good administrator did not necessarily equip him to be a good politician.

This New Year's Day trip to Chicago was different from my previous visits there. I had come to spy out the land. I had come as the director of a new establishment in the field of public administration which as yet, for all our outlines and our planning, was an amorphous thing. It had neither physical headquarters nor staff. Its purpose had been announced only in quite general terms, and I realized that it was up to me to convert these general ideas into specific work programs.

The depression was having more and more effect. It seems easy to say now that the Great Depression began in the autumn of 1929 with the collapse of the stock market and the break in that great speculative fever that had characterized the late twenties and, generally speaking, the whole Coolidge era. As a matter of fact, however, while it didn't plumb its depths for a considerable length of time, there was a continuing faith, renewed almost every month, that the bottom had been reached and that prosperity was, as Mr. Hoover said, "just around the corner."

In Chicago there was an institution called the American School. It was the second largest correspondence school in the country and occupied a handsome, large, three-story, red-brick, ivy-covered building very near the university. Established in 1887, its standards and its reputation were high, but the depression had begun to cut into its income. I found that it would be glad to get additional income from renting some rooms. I arranged for space for the new organization at 850 East Fifty-eighth Street, where State Senator Henry W. Toll of Colorado had already set up the American Legislators' Association with some Spelman Fund support. Thus, with PACH second in order, began the cluster of organizations in the field of public administration soon to become known collectively as "850."

The deepening depression notwithstanding, I found Chicago in my first contacts to be a friendly place. I found the university to have a warm atmosphere, and when, a few days later, I took the train to go back to New York to make arrangements for quitting my job with the City Housing Corporation and, with my wife, to leave Radburn for a new home, I was filled with confidence.

But my wife and I were hardly started on the long journey back to Chicago by automobile when I began to have a troubled mind. I had done all that I possibly could to bring about the organization of the Clearing House. I had set out as clearly as I could my concept of its purposes and methods. The project also had been clearly outlined by Mr. Moffett and Mr. Ruml of the Spelman Fund. The whole thing had been thoroughly discussed and approved at the first meeting of the board of trustees in Cleveland.

However, as we started for Chicago, the realization overwhelmed me that, while the project had been defined, the detailed program of what to do first and just how to do it had not been elaborated. In a few days I would find myself in Chicago directly up against the problem of beginning the work.

When we drove through the steel city of Gary and other western Indiana industrial towns, few indeed of the many smokestacks were wearing their great plumes of smoke and steam. The steel industry was very sick. But I had almost no eyes or ears for that. My own troubles were too great. Frankly, I was frightened.

When the road signs indicated that we had reached the Indiana boundary and were about to enter Chicago itself, I turned the car over to Bess. She drove along the lakeside roads and then, as we neared our destination, into Jackson Park. Suddenly she stopped the car. I had no idea what was the matter.

"Look at that," she said.

She pointed to a statue of a woman in Grecian costume wearing across her breast a plaque inscribed with two words: "I Will."

It was the symbolic statue of Chicago, and it carried the motto epitomizing the Chicago spirit of pioneering enterprise and determination. She had seen it first, when she was nine years old, at the great Columbian Exposition of 1893. To her it was indeed Chicago. It was our welcome.

Then and there I realized that it was up to me to adopt the Chicago motto in beginning the actual work. I still was firm in my conviction that the new institution should not have any hierarchical relationship with any particular organizations of public administration. That had been determined as a matter of policy. The members of the board of trustees had been chosen from the general field of government, and the idea of representation, direct or indirect, of the different organizations in the field had been rejected.

I still was sure that particular groups of public administrators and governmental officials could be brought together in a cluster of agencies. At the same time, I was firmly convinced that a group of such organizations would prosper only if it was voluntary in character and only if each organization remained utterly autonomous in its own field. I was sure that none would permit any authoritarian direction or dictation. Their reluctance not only to admit authority but even to envisage interdependence was a fact which I deemed to be not only unchangeable but one that ought not to be changed. Their voluntary participation in the group would be a reflection of the essential status of American local and state government and a natural outgrowth of American federalism.

At that time my thoughts were concentrated on local government, with some attention to state governments, perhaps, but with almost none to the federal government, except as some of its agencies could be of value as sources of information. At the same time I was thinking more and more not only of the organizations that might be grouped around the Chicago center but also of the much more numerous ones all over the country which had a part in public administration.

The advantages of propinquity as the basis for more intimate relationships had been demonstrated to me among the health and welfare agencies in New York and the educational agencies in Washington, each of them voluntary, each of them independent, but each of them profiting greatly from rubbing shoulders in elevators and holding conversations in corridors. At the same time my plan was to bring about a greater exchange of information among all such organizations everywhere. The Public Administration Clearing House was to have a roving commission. It was to keep in touch not only with organizations of governmental practitioners but also with universities, research institutions, and other groups which might prove to be sources of information which could be distributed for the general benefit.

As head of the new Clearing House, I was actually to be what years later, on the occasion of my retirement, was termed by Robert Maynard Hutchins, then president of the University of Chicago, "ambassador-at-large, minister without portfolio, professor without chair."

With a great flash of insight as I stopped and looked at the statue "I Will," I determined that I as a person would not be subsumed by the institution, that I would be free for all possible contacts everywhere that could help us gather and distribute information, not only through documents, publications, and speeches but by every other possible means of inducing curiosity and exciting interest.

I was free to do the things that I had so long hoped to be able to do. No set of circumstances could have made me happier. Yet, when I came to face the fact, I was not happy. My trouble was that I was too free. Nobody above me had laid down any hierarchical system that required conformance. Nobody superior to me had set any rules for my conduct. Nobody was in a position to tell me what to do. I was on my own.

When I was a child, I was set apart from the boys of my age because of my invalidism. I did not compete, and I was permitted to evade any responsibility for failure in competition because of the fact that I was sickly. When I went in the summertime with the other boys to the old swimming hole in Greasy Creek back of the Hendrickson place, I waded in timidly, but I never learned to swim. I never even tried. Furthermore, I was not thrown shivering, screeching, trembling into the deep water to swim out on my own, which was the standard Spartan pedagogical method of swimming teachers in our neck of the woods. The other boys let me alone. It wasn't so much, I think, that they recognized my timidity and my essential physical cowardice as that they were afraid I was too delicate to profit by their ministrations. In other words, they might have said of me some decades later, "He couldn't take it."

Thereafter, for years and years, decades and decades, I was tortured in my dreams by those older boys picking me up, throwing me into the deepest part of the old swimming hole, and expecting me to swim out, but in these terrible dreams I never swam.

A deep impression was made upon me by Daniel Webster's "Supposed Speech of John Adams" in the Continental Congress on the adoption of the Declaration of Independence. That speech I said over and over again in my dreams when Frank Morrow or Dean Stanley or Bob Furth threw me in the deep water:

"Sink or swim! Live or die!"

And in my dreams there was only the desperate effort to remember the next three words. I always awakened as I drowned, before I could finish the quotation with, "Survive or perish."

Always I had relied upon help from above, either from those who laid down rules to which I would conform or from those who laid down rules to which I refused to conform but who forgave me and saved me from condign punishment because of the special dispensation due me as a person already doomed to die, and doomed to die soon.

But now here in Chicago in February, 1931, it was up to me to start a new institution, one which I had outlined, one which represented my fondest hopes and dreams. Then and there I discovered that I was deprived of a prime element of surety on which I had always relied.

Now, in old age, as I look back over the years, I think it probably fortunate that I did take counsel of my fears as well as of my determination. I determined to begin with a survey of all the organizations in the field to which I was now devoted both by my own will and by my commitments to others. At the same time, I was prompted to take counsel of my fears, and thus I reached my first methodological decision. It was, "Go slow."

Go slow I did. Then, as the weeks passed by and grew into months and the months stretched into quarters and, somewhat astonished by my temerity, I began to submit detailed quarterly reports to my somewhat astonished board of trustees (most of whom had expected only annual summaries), I found to the great comfort of my soul that I had not been expected to move too rapidly. While the economic crisis was deepening, there was yet no common apprehension of universal danger, no general notion that the peace of 1918 would not go on, that the difficulties in the monetary and trade problems of the world would not be solved, and that such admittedly imperfect institutions as the League of Nations would not in time be brought to perfection, so that the world might confidently face an era of undisturbed peace, of restored prosperity, and of the gradual disappearance of hatred, fear, and war.

It also was a time when men in all countries whose lives were fixed and whose interests were determined by the techniques of administration were disdainful of the political world; they no longer looked forward to any immediate acceptance of any particular scheme of government. They were more and more tolerant of variations in constitutional differences, but at the same time they were beginning to think more of the usefulness of an interchange of information on methods pursued in the administrative branches of all governments.

Certainly in the United States those of us who were active in this movement were much obsessed by our custom of differentiation. We tended to separate local government in the United States from state government and to set a sharp distinction between those two realms and that of the federal government. In a certain way this habit was common to all countries, except that in those not federal there were but two levels: the national and the local. Indeed, in many that were denominated "federal," there still was no such sharp division into three layers.

However, under the skilful guidance of Senator Émile Vinck of Brussels, the secretary-general of the International Union of Local Authorities, at least one common concern was defined. There had been some difficulty about the very name of that organization. When we Americans first learned of it, it was known in English as the International Union of Cities. That was an adequate title in American English, but it was utterly confusing to the Englishman. So in deference to English English, its English name became the International Union of Local Authorities.

The Clearing House encouraged several organizations to attend the meeting of this international body to be held in London in 1932. The City Managers' Association had been directly affiliated with it for some years, and other municipal groups were greatly interested in its work.

When the International Union was set up before World War I, it had been established as the custom that its triennial congresses each should center upon a report from the many local governmental authorities on two particular questions, one major, the other minor. The major question was to be concerned with the essential definition and character of the different concepts of local government, the minor one with some particular technical aspect of administration. For the great London conference in 1932 the major question was: In your country, what is the difference between the constitutional and legal institutions for local government and the way in which they actually are conducted?

The local governments in more than forty countries responded to this question. In all of them without, I think, one exception, the reply was that there is very little correspondence between what is laid down in the laws and the actual working procedures of the local governments. All the European and Asiatic countries which did reply—there was no response from Russia—seemed to be delighted to point out the differences between the theoretical constitutions of local governments and the way in which they actually were operated.

From what we knew then about the United States, we could point out that there might be a generalized notion here about the position of local government; but, as a matter of fact, there were forty-eight different types set up in conformity with forty-eight different state constitutions. In many of the states further variations depended upon tradition, historical differentiation, and the extent to which home rule had been granted by the state governments. The federal government had recognized the existence of the municipal establishments neither in its Constitution nor, to any great extent, in its administration or in its statutory enactments.

Each of us Americans who set sail for London on the British steamship "Majestic" was eagerly looking for something, and, for the most part, each of us was looking for something quite different. But Moffett and I were in general looking out for the same quarry. We both indulged the notion that administrative techniques were transferable from one language to another, from one country to another, and from one form of political organization to another. We already had proceeded pretty far along the path that led us to the conclusion that in this comparability we would not find the thing we were seeking in the realm of constitutional law, not in social organization, and not in formalized political science, but rather in administrative techniques. In this hope we had, I suspect, relied too much on the easy day-to-day business of transferring to American experience the results of British establishments, the ease being vaguely indicated by what seemed to be a common language. We were just beginning to discover that it was sometimes much more difficult to translate English English into American English than it was to translate either German or French or Italian into our American vernacular.

In this international convocation of municipalities at London, however, it soon was evident that the British and American peoples had some common characteristics that were alien to the other countries of the world. One was in the mere matter of organization. In this International Union of Local Authorities and in other international conventions, so far as France or Germany or the Netherlands or Belgium or Italy was concerned, the membership and participation were matters that had to be passed upon by a central governmental organization or a national ministry dealing with municipal affairs. In all but the United States and the United Kingdom, membership in, contribution to, and financial support of the international municipal organization was something that had required and had received the blessing of the national government.

That was not true in the United Kingdom, although it did have a central administrative ministry, the Ministry of Health, which controlled, in essence, the municipal establishments in the United Kingdom. Particular branches of local government not under the Ministry of Health were controlled by the Home Office. In the United States there was nothing of that kind at all. Participation in international organizations was something left entirely to voluntary action by the cities themselves or by organizations of municipal officials, such as I was at that time representing. In England there could be no question of outsiders' participating in any one of the comparable organizations of municipal officials. The membership was by custom and, indeed, by law confined to actual municipal officials responsibly elected by councils or appointed in due course by the elected officials.

In the United States most of the organizations of municipal officials had been established by lay citizens. The municipal research movement activated by these citizens had spread until interested citizens participated in the organization of local government officials, and this in turn had led to the participation and, indeed, to the financial support of these institutions by foundations which had no other part in the business of government. Such indeed was the Public Administration Clearing House. Such indeed was a pattern which had been found to be for the most part quite acceptable in American practice. The British had not that experience and found it difficult to understand. For the rest of Europe it was a method of organization utterly unthinkable.

Then there was another difference. The very reason that we couldn't use the word "city" or "cities" in this international organization was that the English connotation of "city"—an urban community that was graced by the presence of a cathedral—was for decades something of a problem for the ordinary American to understand. The City of London is an entirely different establishment from the administrative county of London. The county of London contains two cities and many boroughs. Outside the county of London in England there are municipal establishments which Americans would call "cities" or "municipalities"; these are known variously as county councils, "borough councils," "urban district councils," "rural district councils," and the like.

Within these areas there is another essentially linguistic difficulty. In England the corporation is the council. In the United States the corporation is all the people inhabiting a certain limited geographical area, the voting members of which have the opportunity to select a governing body called the council. Among the other difficulties at the meeting of the International Union was that we in America had not recognized the transition that took place when a few urban people about the time of the Jacksonian democratic revolution had, by the simple act of transferring the electoral franchise from those with basic property qualifications to all men, changed the character of our urban establishments without at all changing what we thought were the essential forms. It is true that in a few cities after the American Revolution the municipal corporations were self-renewing by co-optation; but in most of them the popular franchise, even if limited by property qualifications, had been acquired much earlier, as in New England, by the ultrademocratic process of the town meeting. We Americans who attended that meeting in London were a little bit astonished that the English organizations roughly comparable to our own were then engaged in the preparation of a volume on local government which was to be published in 1935 and was to mark the centenary of the establishment of local government in England. We in our innocence had thought that England had had "local governments" for centuries.

We were apt to put our awareness of these differences in terms of techniques. What we were doing at the meeting, as a matter of fact, was a basic study of the different methods pursued in the different countries under varying conditions of urban housekeeping problems. There was everywhere the great problem of health, of water supply, of sewage and refuse disposal, of hospital organization, and of the control of contagious diseases. There was everywhere the problem of the education of the young, not so much committed to governmental institutions in the other countries as in the United States, but still recognized as a responsibility of the democratic process. There was the common concern for transport and transit, and of course there were the over-all questions of the control of crime and punishment and of the amelioration of the ravages of poverty.

The essential difference between England and the United States was that in the United Kingdom the central organizations dealing with these problems were official in character. They were made up essentially of public officials or of the public corporations. They were organized with the assent and under the more or less rigid supervision of a central governmental agency. On the other hand, some of them were strictly trade unions, such as the National Association of Local Governmental Officials, and the like. Nowhere was any outsider admitted to their meetings, unless he was a visitor from another country or, rarely, a university professor, and in no event was it thinkable that aside from the labor unions such an organization could spring up without the assent of the central government.

Because we in the United States had kept the same words and phrases that had been used to describe a different order in Great Britain, we had not recognized the sharp point of change. The British knew that their present form of local government, which went back to the commoners in the electorate, had not existed prior to the reforms of the 1830's.

The Reform Bill, the essential democratic revolution in the 1830's in Britain, had been brought about without the aid or participation of such voluntary associations as De Tocqueville had discovered on his visit to America in the early 1830's. We had based our American notions on some aspect of voluntary association, ranging from a political party to an organization of blacksmiths or harness-makers endeavoring to stem the rising tide of automobilism under the name of the American Association for the Protection of the Horse.

This gradual recognition at the meeting threw us more and more back to the matter of techniques and more and more to a consideration of the reliability of processes as a means of intercommunication among the nations. And all that threw us more and more back on the notion of functional organizations, which had been at the root of the movement that had set up the Public Administration Clearing House.

I came back from Europe to pick up the business of the organization of the Public Administration Clearing House, and, so far as possible, without any hint of direction or domination, to reach into the things that were going on in the various organizations that then had been brought into the cluster. The generalizations that I had arrived at in Europe, the long conversations I had had with Mr. Moffett, the projections into the future of programs based on our notions of functional organizations had to be adjourned for the moment, because back in Chicago I was up against the gun.

Before I left I had not only attempted to bring in several organizations, some of which were older, some of which were younger, but I had tried to organize a staff. To my associate director, Charles S. Ascher, I had intrusted many chores, one of them the establishment of a library, and another that of continuing to improve contacts between public administrators, such as those that we were bringing together, and the faculties in political science, law, and, indeed, all the social sciences in the University of Chicago. Mr. Ascher was a lawyer, he was precise, he was meticulous, and he was eager. Not only would he always carry out an instruction, but it also was the habit of his mind and his basic motivation to do just a little bit more than he had been told to do.

I had given Robert M. Paige the task of discovering the organizations of public administration in this country and in Canada and had instructed him to set up a directory. Actually, of course, none of us knew at that time the corpus of public administration in North America. We didn't know how many such organizations there were. We didn't know what they did.

The directory was ready in proof sheets when I got back from Europe. It was actually published in October, 1932. I was greatly astonished at the score which was measured up for the first time in *Organizations in the Field of Public Administration: A Directory*. We had a good deal of difficulty with definitions. We distinguished among those organizations that included local groups of citizens, the local agencies that confined their activities to a single urban locality, and those that were primarily devoted to the promotion of a particular professional, commercial, religious, or other specialized interest.

The application of the general definitions assumed had resulted in a listing of no less than 1,744 organizations. I had predicted that there might be at least 50 such national organizations. There were 466. I had predicted that we might find as many as 300 state organizations. Even after drastic combing and screening, there were 1,131. Regional government or regional public administration I had thought of as confined to a very, very few groups, such as the Regional Plan Association of Chicago and the Regional Plan Association of New York. Of these, we found 65. And in Canada, where we were even more rigorous in our exclusion of local groups, we found not less than 82.

The publication of that directory was the first extensive activity of the Clearing House. But important as it was, it really was not nearly so effective or so influential as an intensive experiment which I had launched and which I delegated to Mr. Ascher before taking that European voyage: the organization by the Public Administration Clearing House of a library. Mr. Ascher, seeking to gain the adherence of the other groups of public administrators that had already been brought into the cluster, gave it a new name, one which I would not have approved and which certainly never would have been admitted had I been in the country. He called it a "Joint Reference Library." This gave to some of the organizations already in the group the idea that the library would be jointly administered, an idea which appealed particularly to the assistant directors and the office managers of the other organizations. Mr. Ascher highly approved of this. The minute I got back to Chicago I knew that I could not change the name, but I also knew that the library thus administered would never amount to anything, because I was persuaded then to a view to which I have clung all my life, that nothing can be adequately administered by a committee or a board. It was a good deal of trouble to me to take over the Joint Reference Library because it did depend to a limited extent upon contributions from the other agencies. Each of them was persuaded to use the library; each of them was persuaded to send to the library as much of its printed, published, or even mimeographed material as possible; and from each was asked a token payment for its support. Within a very short time nearly all the organizations, each of which had begun to carry its own library responsibilities, discovered that it was cheaper and more convenient to send its material to the joint library.

Mr. Ascher may have made, as I think he did, some errors in the setup of this organization, but at the same time he builded much better than he knew, and much better than I would have approved, a congenial atmosphere of collaboration. There was a little hair-pulling and a good many slight fracases, but during the existence of the joint committee the habit of using the library was set up, and the internecine warfare and the fraternal fights ceased when I took positive action and abolished the administrative committee.

The library was established at 850 East Fifty-eighth Street in the summer of 1932, under the extremely able administration of two marvelously fortunate choices, Mrs. Lucile L. Keck, as librarian, and Mrs. Grace B. Weiner, as assistant. They had found by the time I got back from Europe no less than 350 periodicals in the field. At the time of my retirement as director of the Clearing House in 1945, the library received regularly no less than 800 periodicals devoted to public administration and regularly published in the United States, Canada, and in more than fifty other nations of the world.

While I had been immersed in my own problems, and my central interest was in my own project of setting up a center for the exchange of information in the field of public administration, it was impossible that I could be insensitive to the effect of politics upon public administration or that I should, in my intimate and daily concern with the processes of government, ever for one moment forget that the policies of government are determined by politics.

During the late winter of 1930 at a farm in northern New Jersey, thirteen of us who were interested in housing and planning held a meeting. We sat down and organized the Regional Planning Association of the United States of America. In order to encourage more discussion and public interest in the field we set up at the University of Virginia in Charlottesville in July of 1931 a conference on regional planning. I also had been insistent that we in the United States had not yet been able to discover any meaningful differentiation of the words "regional" and "sectional." I ventured the notion that what we really needed was discussion of regional planning in the sense of common characteristics of land or of peoples and resources and not sectional planning in the sense of sections set off by such political considerations as growth westward, the differentiation between the coastal and Mississippi Valley plains, the mountains and the Pacific area, or, certainly, that sectional division that arose over the issue of slavery and brought on the Civil War.

To this end I suggested that we invite representatives of the sectional views to speak to the conference at Charlottesville. There was a handy compendium of one such view in a recent volume by twelve neo-Confederates called *I'll Take My Stand*. That was agreed to. Then also it was agreed that these sectionalists should be overwhelmed or at least controverted by our friends Clarence S. Stein and Henry Wright, who had been looking at the regional planning in New York and had reported to Governor Smith. There was no money for expenses for the conference. I suggested to Clarence Stein that it was extremely important that the commissioner of conservation of the state of New York, Henry Morgenthau, Jr., be invited to the conference. Because I had known his father when he was treasurer of the National Democratic Committee, I seriously doubted whether Mr. Morgenthau, although a wealthy man, would care to pay his own expenses. So I suggested to Clarence Stein that the thing to do was to go to Albany and invite the governor, Franklin D. Roosevelt, to the meeting. I was quite sure the governor would decline but that as a substitute he would send his commissioner of conservation, Mr. Morgenthau.

All of us were bowled over when Franklin D. Roosevelt accepted. It already was quite apparent that he was a candidate for the Democratic nomination for President of the United States and would endeavor to capture the Democratic National Convention twelve months later. Governor Roosevelt had not been seen in public outside of New York on many occasions since his paralysis, and I had not seen him since his attack.

I was the chairman of the series of round tables in Charlottesville. Governor Roosevelt consented to write a speech on state and local governmental relationships. He also consented to appear before a round table in Cabell Hall on the general subject of regional planning.

He adjusted his braces and stood up. Mr. Morgenthau was on the platform. Mrs. Roosevelt and Mrs. Morgenthau were down in front along with Roosevelt's old chief, Josephus Daniels, his old boating companion at Campobello, Governor Harry Byrd of Virginia, and numerous other old friends. Mr. Roosevelt spoke for about thirty minutes and then asked for questions.

Mrs. Roosevelt became much agitated because her husband was standing too long. She sent a note up to Morgenthau, who handed it to me and asked would I please pull the governor's coattail and ask him to sit down. I said I couldn't do that but told Morgenthau to do it. Morgenthau didn't dare. The governor stood for more than an hour, and later I discovered that that was the longest time he had ever stood up with his braces. He answered numerous questions from the floor and the gallery.

Then and there we heard Franklin D. Roosevelt, governor of New York, give that little lecture which he so frequently used when he was trying to convert an opponent, sometimes when he did not desire to hear what some visitor was eager to say—his little lecture on the Hudson Valley and its subsidiary valleys of Dutchess County. He told us all about his notion of river development; he gave us a complete blueprint of the yet-to-come Tennessee Valley Authority and the Columbia Valley development; but not one of the entire audience seemed to sense the significance of what he was saying.

In early 1932 the candidacy of Mr. Roosevelt for the presidential nomination became more and more pronounced. He had asked me at Charlottesville if I would not come to Albany to see him. I was eager to go, I will admit, but I had put my foot in the path of the non-partisan, non-political adventure of the Public Administration Clearing House. I did not accept the invitation.

However, by the spring of 1932, I began to doubt my adherence to his cause. He said some things about the tariff that I did not like. He seemed to be cool to the League of Nations, to which in Wilson's name I had been devoted. In other words, he seemed to me to be appeasing, too much and too often, too many groups. I began to write letters to my friends Daniel C. Roper and Robert W. Woolley in which I said that I was afraid we had banked too much on "F. D. R.," that he was turning too much toward the Republicans, even though it was only toward the Progressive Republicanism of his cousin Theodore Roosevelt. I was beginning to think that the Democrats ought not to compromise in 1932 when it seemed to me so certain, in view of the Great Depression, that they would win. I suggested that we all switch to Newton D. Baker.

Baker's only chance, of course, was as a dark horse and a sleeper. The contest was between Al Smith and Roosevelt. Greatly as I had admired Smith in his work in New York, I had thought that his defeat in 1928 made him impossible as a candidate. While I was in Europe the convention was held; the most fortunate trades were made, and Franklin D. Roosevelt's apparent appeasement brought together the more forward-looking groups in the Democratic party, some of which I was bound to admit were more forward-looking than those that had lately clustered around Newton D. Baker.

When I came home from Europe, nobody asked me to intervene in politics; nobody tempted me away from my path of non-partisanship. To be sure, some university professors during this campaign tried their best and sometimes succeeded in leading me a bit astray from my dedicated path. I had some slight acquaintance with some of the members of Roosevelt's Brain Trust. During the campaign there was a meeting in the University of Chicago Social Science Building's Common Room; it included Robert M. Hutchins, Beardsley Ruml, Charles E. Merriam, Professor Duddy of the School of Business Administration (a specialist in the field of agriculture), and Professor Simeon E. Leland of the Department of Economics. Also, at the instance of Mr. Ruml, M. L. Wilson, president of the University of Montana, had been invited. The purpose was to write a speech on agriculture which candidate Roosevelt might be persuaded to make. It was, with a little help from me, bootlegged to the Roosevelt Brain Trust and delivered in substance at Wichita, Kansas.

And then came what I thought was a terrible speech, an advance copy of which was shown me in Washington by Daniel C. Roper, who was soon to be secretary of commerce, and Robert W. Woolley, who had been my colleague through many political campaigns. It was a speech which seemed to be founded on the notion that all that had to be done to restore prosperity and cure the depression was to cut governmental expenditures: the Pittsburgh speech. I urged Roper and Woolley to attempt to veto it. I sent two telegrams addressed to members of the Brain Trust asking them for heaven's sake to see that the speech was not made. I don't know whether either of the telegrams ever reached the candidate's train. The speech was given and proved a source of embarrassment to Roosevelt for years to come.

In June, 1932, under very great pressure and with the greatest reluctance, President Hoover had signed a congressional measure authorizing the Reconstruction Finance Corporation to lend money to the states for relief, with the proviso that every such loan was to be subtracted from the next year's appropriations for grants-in-aid for public highways.

Frank Bane, director of the American Public Welfare Association in the Chicago group, was then thrown into the very midst of the greatest of activities. Fred Croxton of Ohio was appointed by the RFC to administer these grants. However, in most states there was no organization either to receive them or, much less, to administer and control their expenditure. Relief in most of the urban communities had been a matter for private social agencies. Public relief had been very largely confined to the terminal extremities of the poorhouses and the support of paupers. Bane was setting up, at the request, often at the insistence, of the governors all over the country, schemes for improvement of such welfare organizations as existed, and in many states he was establishing *de novo* public welfare departments. It was a creaky machinery, for the most part unorganized. The privately organized charities were reluctant, alarmed, and in many cases utterly unprepared administratively to handle the burden.

Unemployment became greater and greater. The distress and suffering represented by unemployment statistics was being translated into actually hungry persons. The individually owned grocery stores and meat markets, which had been such vital parts of community life and which for years had operated on a credit basis, had continued to extend credit to friends and neighbors who had been their customers for years and who were of course but "temporarily" out of a job. Once these unemployed breadwinners did find a little job, they often did not pay the back bills but went to a chain store and bought for cash. The little grocery stores and the little meat markets collapsed into the abyss of bankruptcy, into which then began to fall not only the little community banks but the bigger and bigger banks. Things were worsening. The outlook was grim.

But it was immediately evident that Governor Roosevelt, who had done more in New York than had been done in any other state to deal with the problem of relief of the unemployed, would project into his administration when he took office as President some of the experimental activities chosen from among the several and sometimes contradictory proposals that he had advocated in his campaign speeches.

The Spelman Fund had arranged, among other things, for the Public Administration Clearing House to finance and manage *ad hoc* conferences at which various unrelated organizations and persons might be brought together to deal with new or rapidly emerging problems in administrative requirements. Working with Miss Edith Abbott and Miss Sophonisba Breckinridge, of the School of Social Service Administration of the University of Chicago, and with Frank Bane, director of the American Public Welfare Association, I assembled a conference in Chicago on November 18, 1932—as soon as possible after the results of the election had been determined—to consider what to do administratively about unemployment relief on a national scale. To this conference were invited representatives of practically all the nationally organized bodies having to do with either public or private welfare and relief. Most of them, of course, were from private agencies. There were also as many as we could assemble of the representatives of state and local welfare agencies. In all, the group of seventy-eight or eighty persons was a cross-section of the welfare administrators—private and public—of the nation.

It gave me an opportunity to do something a little different from the usual programing of a conference. There was no program, no set speeches; there were only the general topics that had been announced. There was utter freedom of discussion. There were sharp differences of opinion. There were those who for many years had asserted that the ultimate responsibility for welfare work was governmental and those who during long years of work in private welfare administration had held to the belief that government was unfitted to carry out relief and, in fact, that governments, being political and being managed by politicians, never could hope to rise to meet the rigorous standards demanded in this field.

Mr. Bane reviewed what actually was happening in government, and then the conference was thrown open. There was plenty of criticism of how the $200 million which was authorized to be loaned by the Reconstruction Finance Corporation under the act of June, 1932, had been administered. It was now November, and of that $200 million only $67 million actually had been transmitted to the states. The administrative problem had proved too great. Much was said which today seems as dead as a parliamentary discussion on the Elizabethan Poor Laws. The result of this conference was the adoption of a set of principles, or, it is perhaps not too much to say, a set of rules, which has determined the federal, state, and local administration of public welfare, as far as relief is concerned, since that time.

All this was done by the end of three days of intense discussion by deeply interested and fully dedicated persons addressing themselves directly to the main problem of relief of the unemployed and otherwise handicapped and displaced persons in the country. It took the form of a set of five resolutions:

1. The major responsibility for the relief of destitution rests with government. This responsibility can only be met adequately by the active participation of the federal, state, and local governments. All participating agencies should establish effective means for the development and maintenance of efficient standards of administration.

2. An effective state administrative unit should be established for the direction and supervision of the expenditure of all state and federal. funds appropriated or borrowed for relief purposes.

Federal and state funds should be made available to local units upon a basis of need rather than population or wealth, and should be so administered as to stimulate adequate and effective welfare programs.

Local units should be of such area and population as to lend themselves to effective administration. In most of the states [and there was considerable discussion on this point] the county is the smallest practical unit for public welfare administration. Unification of public welfare services in both state and county is necessary to secure efficient and economical administration.

3. Public funds should be administered only by regularly established public agencies.

4. In any appropriation for relief a definite allocation of funds for administrative purposes should be included in order to insure proper standards of administration.

5. Public welfare administration is a technical function of government and includes types of services which require properly prepared, qualified personnel. Personnel standards are a primary concern to all state and local welfare systems, and can best be attained by stressing education and experience rather than residence.

Thus ended what was then regarded with horror as the "dole." Thus ended the aversion to governmental aid to "the idle." Thus, all unnoticed and unnoted, began in the United States of America the then dreaded but now embraced "Welfare State."

CHAPTER XXV

EVENTS OF 1933

The interim between Franklin D. Roosevelt's winning the presidential election in November, 1932, and his taking office on March 4, 1933, was a time of doubt and anxiety. My own work was largely centered on giving as much help as I and my staff could to Frank Bane and the American Public Welfare Association in recruiting and helping to establish welfare machinery in the states; in doing what I possibly could to assist Carl Chatters and the Municipal Finance Officers' Association in their struggle with the fiscal difficulties of municipal governments, and generally in discovering the ways in which the Clearing House could help the newly created and struggling organizations of officials to meet the deluge of problems the deepening depression cascaded upon them.

Nineteen hundred and thirty-three came in the midst of gloom. During January municipalities were defaulting on their interest obligations. Cities were retrenching and dismissing employees, thus adding to the lengthening lists of unemployed and the mounting demands for relief. The Public Administration Clearing House removed its deposit of some twenty-odd thousand dollars from the neighborhood bank, which had been selected in the first place on account of its proximity, to the much stronger First National Bank of Chicago only four days before the local bank closed its doors.

I sat at luncheon nearly every day with colleagues from the organizations grouped around the Clearing House and with those on the social science faculty of the University of Chicago at the round table of the social sciences at the Quadrangle Club. The city council of Kenosha, Wisconsin, had been in session for more than forty-eight hours while the city hall was surrounded by hoards of the unemployed and hungry, demanding relief. During the week something of the

[275]

same sort happened at Gary, Indiana. We had a serious discussion of how those of us at the table, all of whom had automobiles, could possibly escape with our families from Chicago in the event of a general strike—something acutely feared—if the railroads were stopped and the unemployed decided in desperation to barricade the principal motor routes. So deep was the despair that many of us around the table reached the conclusion that there was no way out.

I had not been well, and, after a few days in bed in February, I decided to follow my physician's advice and take a rest. Aware of a banking and monetary situation infinitely worse than that which had stranded me in Oklahoma City in the Panic of 1907, I drew out $800 in cash and with my wife went to Jacksonville, Florida, where we stayed with my brother for ten days or so.

It was in my brother's living room on March 4, 1933, that I listened over the radio to the inaugural address of Franklin D. Roosevelt and heard that electrifying sentence which restored hope in me just as it did in the minds of millions and millions of Americans: "We have nothing to fear but fear itself."

Perhaps it is too much to credit my recovery from my deep-seated malaise, my sore throat, and my running nose to "F.D.R.'s" inaugural address. Perhaps it might be better to say that the Florida sunshine on Jacksonville Beach had brought about that miracle of recovery, and, of course, there is the possibility that resting for a week or ten days might have had something to do with it. At any rate, it was borne in on me from every direction that there had been a great change. The roads no longer ran, so far as I was concerned, to city halls or to state capitols. No longer was I afraid that there might be too much centralization of government in Washington. No matter what influence any of these philosophical considerations, these political ideologies, these varying and contradictory economic currents had had on me, I yielded immediately to the same impulse that seemed to activate thousands and thousands of others. We realized that all roads led to Washington. I put my foot in that path.

It may be that I touched base in Chicago—I am not quite sure—but certainly mid-March found me ensconced in the Willard Hotel in Washington. Here I was the messenger—informal, it was true, and without credentials—of a half-dozen organizations of public officials. I was supposed to listen and to learn. By definition I was to communicate to the then growing group of organizations in Chicago whatever I could tell them about what was to be done in Washington. That was hard to do because nobody in Washington in those first few weeks knew. What was much more important was that I was to attend to what was going on among the groups in Chicago and then to endeavor to find, if possible, the appropriate ear in Washington into which to pour their several tales of woe and to present their various schemes and plans. Then I was to communicate the results to each of them while leaving them entirely uncommitted; each group could do what it pleased with what I had found out.

In those first few weeks of the Roosevelt administration in Washington I found myself with a tangled skein out of which I was expected to weave a seamless web. Days usually began at half-past six or seven in the morning. There were breakfast meetings; there were forenoon dates; there were long-distance telephone conversations; there were luncheon appointments; there were efforts to see in the afternoon many among the great who were, for the most part on account of reasonable and necessary duties of their own, quite unseeable. Meetings around sundown, despite the fact that prohibition was not yet legally extinguished, were sometimes hardly to be differentiated from their later successors, the cocktail parties. There were quick dinners, and then there were meetings that went on until midnight. My experience was not unique. Thousands of persons were similarly engaged. Hundreds were in the nation's capital intent upon trying to help the new administration lift itself out of the Slough of Despond. Many job-seekers interpreted the change of administration in a purely partisan political fashion as the occasion upon which, if not to shake the plum tree, if not to divide the pie, at the very least to pass the apple dumplings.

Here I met with a personal problem. My old friend Daniel C. Roper was Roosevelt's secretary of commerce. He urged me to become an assistant secretary of commerce. Some years earlier this prospect might have greatly intrigued me. But there were a good many reasons why I was not tempted now. One was—although I must admit it was a minor consideration—that I had so earnestly urged Mr. Roper himself not to approve Governor Roosevelt's Pittsburgh speech, the one that said that everything, all the economic ills of the country, would be cured by balancing the budget and that that balance could be achieved merely by cutting the appropriations for federal departments. Later,

Mr. Roosevelt, in one of his early press conferences, animadverted on what he seemed to consider the gross expansion of the services of the Department of Commerce. Under Mr. Herbert Hoover's regime it had been housed in a new building, which was, up to that time (with the single exception of the United States Capitol itself), the largest office building in Washington. Mr. Roosevelt told the reporters that he had succeeded in circumnavigating the "Department of Commerce Building." I didn't like that, and I was afraid that Mr. Roper had tended to agree with the President's aspersions on the growth of that department. I was entirely prepared to sympathize, in a way, with Mr. Roosevelt's irritation with his predecessor, Herbert Hoover, who had made the Department of Commerce into a great institution. In fact I somewhat shared the new President's irritation with the old President. While I was still District commissioner, I had come to the conclusion, because of the services that the government of the District of Columbia obtained from the various federal departments, that some sort of informational service ought to be set up in Washington to give the local governments all over the country the same opportunity that I had had in the District government. Later, as city manager of Petersburg, Virginia, and Knoxville, Tennessee, I had exploited these services by obtaining aid and advice from such agencies as the Bureau of Standards and the Bureau of the Census.

Indeed, while Mr. Wilson was still President and W. C. Redfield was secretary of commerce, I had gone with Harold C. Buttenheim, the editor of the *American City,* to see the secretary of commerce. We had urged him to set up in Washington something that Buttenheim, with his great skill in public relations, had labeled "U. S. Post Office Box Number One," through which any local government might apply for information from whatever federal department or agency might be helpful in improving local standards. Mr. Redfield was sympathetic, but World War I was on. Nothing was done. Later, Mr. Buttenheim and I had gone to see Joshua Alexander, who had succeeded Redfield as secretary of commerce in the closing years of the Wilson administration. Mr. Alexander had been sympathetic and had even made some gestures toward helping us out; but by that time the Republicans had won the House of Representatives and he had met a chilly reception in the House Appropriations Committee.

I had known Herbert Hoover when he was federal food administrator during World War I. Later, when he had become secretary of commerce, I, still in the company of Mr. Buttenheim, besought his aid in establishing an organization within the Department of Commerce to give technical aid and assistance to municipalities and other local government agencies in the same way that Mr. Hoover was so earnestly endeavoring, with such great success, to aid business enterprise. Mr. Hoover was quite cordial. He turned us over to his appropriate administrative aides. I don't think that anything ever got up to the President during the Harding administration, but later, when Mr. Coolidge was President and the appropriate staff work had been done, we heard (although not directly from Mr. Hoover himself) that the secretary of commerce had presented the matter to President Coolidge. President Coolidge, a former governor, had taken a negative attitude because in his opinion local governments were merely creatures of state governments, and he deprecated any direct communication between the federal government and the local governments except through the channels ordained by the several states. So Mr. Hoover lost.

Then, when Mr. Hoover became President, Mr. Buttenheim and I went to see the secretary of commerce, Mr. Chapin. By this time we were absolutely confident that we would succeed in our quest. Mr. Chapin turned us over to his aide, Mr. John M. Gries, who had been in touch with the problem for many years. He heartily agreed with us. The secretary of commerce thereupon took the proposal to the President. President Hoover promptly turned thumbs down on the very same proposition that Secretary Hoover had approved.

Perhaps by mid-March, 1933, I still was influenced by this long and unsuccessful campaign I had carried on, in collaboration with other persons interested in municipal government, to create a direct line of communication between the federal government in Washington and local governments. However, there were other considerations. On the side of accepting the post of assistant secretary there were these: an opportunity to be a part of the new administration and to help it achieve recovery in a particularly important branch of the government; the professional kudos it would give me to become a member of the sub-Cabinet group, something that perhaps had more appeal to me because of my long residence in Washington than it would to others; and the opportunity for helping in the publicity field, which was a particular part of Secretary Roper's insistence on my coming into his organization.

On the other side, one consideration against accepting the post was something else that I was beginning to find important. I was beginning to sense that one's positive influence in persuading persons and institutions to work together seemed to be in direct proportion to one's keeping his name out of the newspapers and his personality in the background. And then there was my conviction that from my position in the Public Administration Clearing House I was better able to persuade persons and institutions to co-operate more closely in government work and public service than I would be from any particular position within the governmental structure. In other words, I did not desire to become a specialist if, by dint of work and by continuation of my organizational advantages, I could be a generalist.

Guy Moffett of the Spelman Fund and I had agreed that he, rather than I, should be the first to approach the President in the White House. In his long years of work in the federal government, particularly on the staff of the Civil Service Commission, he had come to be closely acquainted with Louis Howe, who had been secretary to Mr. Roosevelt when the latter had been assistant secretary of the Navy in the Wilson administration and who had continued his close relationship. Mr. Moffett took to Mr. Howe a proposal from Public Administration Clearing House which suggested the President might possibly decide to make certain specific studies and inquiries for which no existing appropriation was available and that, in such event, upon the written request of a member of the Cabinet, the Clearing House would make available, within limits, a sufficient amount of money to finance these studies. The Clearing House also undertook not merely to advance the necessary cash but to leave to the Cabinet member concerned the question of whether or not the Clearing House would have anything to say about the study, the personnel employed, or the result achieved; indeed, it would let responsible governmental officials determine whether or not the Clearing House would even be permitted to know what the result was.

President Roosevelt accepted this proposal, and the several heads of departments constituting the Cabinet were notified accordingly. Immediately requests began to come in. One from the secretary of war, Mr. Dern, was for a study of the relations between the Panama Canal and the Panama Railroad Company; another from Mr. Roper, secretary of commerce, was for a study of currency. The Clearing House did not participate in this study but financed the report that eventually resulted in the devaluation of the dollar and the abandonment of the gold standard by the United States.

Mr. Roper also asked PACH to finance a study in the field of scientific research and development. The $10,000 that I made available for this particular project to Professor Karl T. Compton and his young assistant, Carroll Wilson, resulted in the establishment of the whole series of agencies for research and development not only in science and industry but in the military service. These led eventually to the establishment of the organization to which, after consulting Dr. Einstein, President Roosevelt intrusted the experiments which resulted in the successful splitting of the atom and the development of atomic energy. A good many such requests from a good many of the Cabinet officers continued over a considerable period of years—indeed the last one was received from Mr. Ickes, the secretary of the interior, during the administration of President Truman and had to do with a study of taxation in the territory of Alaska. Transactions such as these concerned me only in an institutional fashion. They did not require my active participation. But other requests did engage my own participation, and these came thick and fast.

With the President's blessing, measures were introduced in the Congress designed to effect the restoration of the national economy. One of these led eventually to the enactment of the National Industrial Recovery Act of 1933, the NIRA. The President selected General Hugh Johnson, "Old Iron Pants," to head the endeavor. Johnson himself plunged into the organization of the industrial half of the problem but delegated the public works portion to Colonel George R. Spalding of the Corps of Engineers. Under Colonel Spalding's leadership, the American Society of Civil Engineers was requested to assemble in Washington a group of leading engineers of the country to plan the public works program. Among those who came were Colonel Henry M. Waite, a former city manager of Dayton, Ohio, and John P. Hogan, a consulting engineer of New York. These two decided that there must be an immediate contact with all the organizations in the field of state and local government. They demanded that I come to Washington. We used the quarters assigned to Colonel Spalding in the Commerce

Building for our daytime work. In the early morning, later afternoon, and night our headquarters were in the Willard Hotel. The work actually went on around the clock. Just as I had been trying to help Mr. Bane of the American Public Welfare Association to establish welfare organizations in all the states, so Waite, Hogan, and I, and others associated with us, began at once to recruit engineering personnel for state public works organizations which were designed to be regional branches of the central public works agency. By the time NIRA was enacted we had succeeded in establishing in each of the forty-eight states a tentative organization complete with a cadre of qualified engineers.

The summer came hot and early that year. It was in the pre-air-conditioning era. The work was terrific, and the results were slow. Colonel Waite, particularly, met delays and frustrations every day owing to his inability to get clearances and interim approvals from Colonel Spalding or General Johnson. Practically every afternoon at five o'clock Mr. Hogan and I met in Colonel Waite's room at the Willard. What we did there was a combination of soothing talk, persuasive argument, and physical intervention. We found Colonel Waite nearly every afternoon packing his bags to take the train for Cincinnati. Hogan and I unpacked his bags, quieted him down, and kept him in town. Then there was something to eat and the beginning of another long, long night session.

Of course I had my job in Chicago to do. I couldn't stay all the time in Washington. Thus it happened that, just after the bill was passed, I went to Chicago. One day there came utterly unexpected news. At the end of a few days' cruise that the President and the members of the Cabinet had taken together on the U.S.S. "Indianapolis," when the ship had put in at Annapolis, the startling news was announced. President Roosevelt had decided to put the two titles of NIRA in different organizations. A Cabinet committee under the chairmanship of Secretary of Commerce Daniel C. Roper, was set up to supervise General Johnson in the industrial title. Another cabinet committee under the chairmanship of Secretary of Interior Harold Ickes was set up to supervise the public works title. I read this news in the paper early one morning and spent the rest of the forenoon on the long-distance telephone. At noon while I was eating at the Quadrangle Club with Merriam a long-distance telephone call came in for him. He left the table to answer it. In a few minutes he came back and said, "That was Ickes. He wants to know whom he can get to operate the public works organization under him. I told him that you had been working already on a tentative organization. He wants to talk to you."

I went to the telephone. Mr. Ickes said, "Merriam tells me that you already have picked somebody to run the public works. Who is he?"

"Colonel Henry M. Waite," I said.

"Who is Waite?"

"Waite is a distinguished engineer, as straight as a string. He was city engineer of Cincinnati under the reform administration of Mayor Harry T. Hunt; he was the first city manager of Dayton, Ohio, one of the leading city managers of the country, a distinguished railroad engineer with a remarkably successful record in France in the World War, and I think the man for the job."

"Well, if he is the man for the job, how will he get people all over the country to help him?"

"Well, Mr. Secretary," I responded, "as a matter of fact, I have been working with Colonel Waite and others, and there already is a tentative organization of competent, trustworthy engineers in every state in the Union."

"Huh! I will look up Waite. Can you get here in the morning?"

Later that afternoon there was a call from Dan Roper. It amounted to the same thing, "Can you get here in the morning?"

To both of them I responded in the affirmative and found myself, as in those days I so often found myself late in the afternoon, one of the few passengers aboard a Pullman car, on the Capitol Limited train of the Baltimore and Ohio traveling from Chicago to Washington through the silent, smokeless, closed-down industrial plants that lined the railways.

The next morning I went first to Mr. Ickes' office. The Cabinet committee was in session. I arranged to come back. Then I dashed down to the Commerce Department. That committee was in session. I waited awhile in Mr. Roper's office, that magnificent room which had been built in accordance with the plans and personal desires of a former secretary of commerce, Herbert Hoover. The Cabinet committee had been meeting in another room. I hadn't waited long before Mr. Roper came in. He was dejected. General Johnson, who after all had been chosen by the President, had all but summarily dismissed the committee. He had been gruff, and it was gruffly, not graciously, that he agreed to give the committee reports of what he was doing. He made it extremely clear that, if Mr. Roper and his colleagues undertook actively to supervise his work, he would quit. That Cabinet committee never was active.

Then back to the Interior Department. Mr. Ickes was full of fuss, fury, and determination. He told me that the committee after a great deal of discussion had left the job of administrative organization to him as chairman but that the committee would meet daily. "I have not yet broached the proposition about Waite. I want to know more about him. Where can I find out more about him? To whom shall I talk about him?"

All these questions were shot at me with machine-gun rapidity. I attempted to answer. And then, "The transcript of the Cabinet meeting proceedings will be ready in the morning. You be here at a quarter to nine when the transcript is promised. I want you to read it before the committee meets at nine-thirty."

That went on for a week or ten days. Every morning I showed up in Ickes' office. The transcript was put before me. I read it most hurriedly, of necessity, and then had a chance to talk for two, three, or sometimes as many as four minutes with Mr. Ickes before he disappeared to take the chair in the committee.

The principal difficulty with public works encountered by the committee was one that I and many of my colleagues had long anticipated: "What public works? and where?"

Miss Frances Perkins, the secretary of labor, had asked all the municipal organizations then in Chicago—the American Municipal Association, the International City Managers' Association—as well as others elsewhere, "What public works?" There had been floods and floods of letters and telegrams. Every state, every county, every city, every village needed a bridge, a school, or this, that, or the other. But of planned public works on which a firm estimate of cost could be based, which could be begun in any reasonable time, and which could put men to work—of those there was little tangible evidence.

The Cabinet committee one day discussed at great length the necessity for better planning. That morning I had only about two minutes to talk to the secretary, "Why don't you," I said, "set up a planning committee?"

"Where can I get anybody that we can trust for a planning committee?"

"Well," I said, "you can get Mr. Delano, the President's uncle with whom you used to work when he was the head of the Chicago Regional Planning Association, and you can get Dr. Charles E. Merriam, whose campaign you managed when he was running for mayor of Chicago in 1911, and you can get Wesley C. Mitchell."

"Who in the heck is Wesley Mitchell?"

I told him that he was a distinguished economist of Columbia University and that he had been associated closely with Dr. Merriam.

"Will Merriam vouch for him?"

I said, "Unquestionably and undoubtedly."

I did not tell him that Dr. Merriam and Mr. Mitchell, as members of President Hoover's commissions on recent social and economic trends, had joined in a recommendation that a national planning board be established, nor that they had gathered the impression from conversations with Mr. Hoover that he had approved the recommendation. But I did have the notion in my mind that the work under Hoover might usefully be continued under Roosevelt.

He disappeared into the Cabinet committee. That morning the National Planning Committee, composed of Frederic A. Delano, chairman, Charles E. Merriam, and Wesley C. Mitchell, was appointed. Out of it grew the National Planning Board, later the National Resources Planning Board, and later, although after many adventures and many ups and downs, such organizations in both the economic and physical planning fields as now exist in the national government.

Mr. Ickes did appoint Henry M. Waite deputy administrator of public works. The Public Works Administration was set up. The organization that Waite, Hogan, I, and others had planned was adopted with relatively few changes. Colonel Philip Fleming of the Corps of Engineers was brought in, but all this was done after a period of a month or six weeks during which the task had been nominally devolved upon Colonel Donald H. Sawyer. He and Mr. Ickes failed to see eye to eye. Mr. Ickes took over. He soon "mislaid" his Cabinet committee, but he was thereafter not only in name but in very fact the sole and only administrator of the public works program. Colonel Fleming and Colonel Waite helped him, but it was to be strictly an Ickes show.

A Passion for Anonymity

The blue eagle flag of the National Recovery Administration was unfurled over many, many reopened industrial plants; the Public Works Administration was furiously at work examining applications for grants and loans and, indeed, making contracts. The Federal Emergency Relief Administration under the direction of Harry Hopkins was rapidly extending its relief programs through state agencies throughout the country.

But in spite of all this, the lists of unemployed grew and the rolls of the relief-seekers and the lists of the hungry continued rapidly to increase.

Among the persons chosen by Mr. Bane as field agents for the American Public Welfare Association in 1932 was Aubrey Williams, a social worker from Wisconsin. He, working for Mr. Bane, was active in setting up new emergency relief agencies in state after state. Williams was brought into the FERA by Hopkins as his principal assistant and in that job continued his task of traveling through the states, looking into the administration of the unemployment relief programs, and generally appraising the situation.

One day in mid-October, Aubrey Williams came to Chicago. He had asked Frank Bane and me to meet him at the railroad station. He was extremely worried. He told us that the situation was worsening at a catastrophic rate and that, with cold weather coming on, he was extremely worried about what could be done to feed the hungry and succor the suffering people. Industrial recovery had not advanced sufficiently; the payrolls were lagging behind the needs; the number of unemployed in many sections was increasing rather than diminishing, and, above all, the relief expected from the public works program was delayed and was not yet reaching the people. This was on a Thursday. He told us that his superior, Harry Hopkins, intended to get to Chicago on Saturday for a conversation with President Hutchins of the University of Chicago, while he, Mr. Williams, was scheduled to go on to New Orleans to make a speech on behalf of the Community Chest Fund of that city. He urged Bane and me to see Hopkins, to tell Hopkins the gist of what he had found in the states of the Midwest, the Great Lakes area, and farther south. He asked us to urge Hopkins to go to President Roosevelt at once and use every means to induce the President to set up some emergency scheme that would have the effect of getting more of the unemployed immediately on the pay-

[286]

roll, and indeed, so far as the relief was concerned, to abandon the means test for the time being.

Bane and I met Hopkins on Saturday morning, October 28. We had a long talk with him. We found that he also was becoming greatly alarmed, although Harry Hopkins would never on any occasion display as much emotional enthusiasm for any program as Aubrey Williams was wont to do. Bane and I took Hopkins to luncheon at the Quadrangle Club, where we were joined by President Hutchins. The conversation at the table was confined to speculation about how best to meet what we generally agreed was a rapidly onrushing catastrophe of proportions never before experienced or contemplated in the United States.

Mr. Hopkins had said that he believed it would be at least two or three weeks before it would be possible to set up a plan and get it approved by the President. Where the money was to come from was not discussed in detail, but it was generally agreed that in some way it would have to be withdrawn from the general appropriation for the NIRA and in all probability from the Public Works Administration funds. That would mean, as we all recognized, a struggle with Mr. Ickes. But there seemed to be no other way at that time except to persuade the President to take summary action. On Wednesday, Mr. Hopkins telephoned me that he had decided to go to the President with the general idea even before setting up an outline for the new scheme.

On Friday afternoon, Mr. Hopkins telephoned me that he had just come from lunch with the President and that, instead of taking two or three weeks of persuasion, the President had acceded at once and had told Hopkins to get the new organization going next week. Hopkins asked me, and, as it later developed, he also telephoned Bane to come immediately to Washington. He brought in Aubrey Williams and some of his other FERA people from the field and held a group meeting at the Powhatan Hotel, now the Roger Smith Hotel, on Saturday night.

Preliminary plans were sketched that night for a decentralized program which would give employment to four million persons, without a means test and without red tape. In this program any person who applied for work would be hired to do whatever job could be rapidly devised, and everyone would be paid cash wages.

The next day, Sunday, the whole group, with other aides and assistants, spent the entire day and much of the night in the unheated office of Mr. Hopkins' temporary headquarters in the Walker-Johnston Building at Eighteenth Street and New York Avenue.

There was much to do. One thing that seemed to be important was what name to give the program. Jacob Baker, one of Hopkins' assistants, suggested, "Civil Works Administration." The baptismal rites were soon over and it was so named. One of the major questions was how to induce local governments, local administrators, and others to waive their customary habits of caution and to hire applicants as they came, paying cash wages instead of grocery tickets. But an even more knotty problem was how to pay out the cash.

The principal purpose was to get money in circulation and put it in the pockets of those who needed it for bread and milk and clothing. The adults often had been hungry so long that they were not physically fit to do hard work, and the greatest tragedy of all was the hunger of the little children. Donald C. Stone, director of the Public Administration Service, was among those present. He suggested that probably the only way to get the money out promptly was to use the decentralized regional offices of the Veterans Administration, with its check-writing machinery, to meet the payrolls. As each suggestion came up, there was discussion free and open, and then, usually by consensus and sometimes, where there was a deep division, by edict, Harry Hopkins made the decision and assigned the tasks and delegated the work to one of the men in the room. That was on Sunday. Eight days afterward, on a Monday, the machinery was moving, and by the following Saturday paychecks were distributed to thousands.

The results were immediate. For example, in one city, Columbus, Ohio, the shelves of the shoestores were swept bare by midnight, for the stores were forced to keep open. That had an immediate effect two weeks later at the annual shoe fair in St. Louis, where buyers for the shoestores placed orders with the manufacturers in a volume that had not been at all anticipated and was larger than the manufacturers had experienced in at least three years.

Busy as I was in Washington in 1933, especially after the Roosevelt administration came in, there was no lack of goings-on in Chicago. New agencies were being brought into the cluster around "850." Beardsley Ruml was dean of the Social Science Division of the university. Dr. Merriam was at the height of his activity as the head of the

Political Science Department. I was in constant contact with many of the university leaders, particularly in the fields of politics, economics, history and in the professional schools of education and social service administration. The Common Room on the second floor of the Social Science Building was the scene every afternoon of a tea. Here members of the faculty met and mingled with the graduate students. There was a samovar. One went in, put down a nickel, picked up a cup of tea and a cookie, and plunged into the maelstrom of conversation. And in 1933 the conversation was almost always about immediate crises. There was little concern then with what later became one of the preoccupations at such gatherings, the philosophy of St. Thomas Aquinas. There were a few students who were much more interested in Karl Marx, communism, and advanced socialism; there were some ardent devotees of the new religion of technocracy. Nearly everybody knew somebody who was hungry. Many of these hungry people were members of the students' families, and many of the students were scrambling to find some kind of part-time employment in order that they too might have enough to eat. There was intense preoccupation among some of them with pacifism and with the Oxford oath, and some of the same pacifists from time to time would embark on extremely violent excursions into the coal fields of southern Illinois. There was certainly ferment. Harold Lasswell was attempting to apply the then relatively new Freudian psychological notions to the process of politics. He was one of the group that Merriam had directed in a particular path—as he did Harold Gosnell into mathematics and politics, V. O. Key into history and politics, John Vieg and Albert Lepawsky into law and politics—while attempting to keep them pure and unspotted from any dealings with the Law School.

There were Charles H. Judd and Floyd W. Reeves in the School of Education who, together with Merriam and, indeed, Beardsley Ruml, had outlined and charted the so-called New Plan so that it would be ready when the university got a new president, as they had in 1929, when the young dean of the Yale Law School, Robert M. Hutchins, came to Chicago as its president. All this was less than two years old. It all was centered in the new Social Science Building, which Beardsley Ruml had succeeded in financing as a part of his theory that related activities in education or management should be assembled in a common physical facility. It was extremely exciting to me, who up to that time had had no contact with universities. I was not only puzzled but completely obfuscated and dismayed by some of the things I heard for the first time out of the philosophers, and at the same time I found a warm and instant relationship with one of the philosophers, Thomas Vernor Smith. In history there were my friends William E. Dodd and Bernadotte Schmitt, both of whom I had known earlier. There were the economists Jacob Viner, Simeon E. Leland, Louis Wirth, and Frank Knight, and a host of other social scientists. So that, with the afternoon tea in the Common Room, with the social science round table at the Quadrangle Club for lunch, and with my regular afternoon sessions with Ruml and Merriam, I found a new world of intense interest.

Of course Ruml and Merriam were sharing, with me and with Guy Moffett, who had succeeded Ruml as executive of the Spelman Fund, on his frequent trips to Chicago and my frequent trips to New York, in the expansion and to a certain extent the program of completion of our planned agglomeration of organizations of administrative officials.

In this work there was a division of labor. Mr. Ruml, Mr. Merriam, and I canvassed the situation carefully; Mr. Moffett of the Spelman Fund made the most meticulous examinations. In most cases the task of selecting a competent executive director was turned over to me. That I did usually, however, after consultation with Mr. Moffett and frequently with his advice.

Indeed, during this period one of my principal tasks was the selection of competent organizational personnel. It was of course good to have the advice of professional personnel men such as Mr. Ruml and Mr. Moffett, but it also was a responsibility laid upon my shoulders that I took quite as seriously as I did the assembly of my own staff in the Public Administration Clearing House.

In most of these cases I still congratulate myself that my choices were good, as has been demonstrated by their successful careers, both when serving these organizations and later. It was on the whole a remarkable group of administrators. They worked together well in such bodies as the Board of Directors of the Public Administration Service. They worked together well in smaller groups when matters came up of common interest. But I always was careful, extremely careful, not to attempt to bind them together in any way as a corporate body, and I was meticulous in observing their utter independence.

Sometimes this was a notion that was not fully shared by some of my own subordinates in the Clearing House. I remember that one of my assistant directors once earnestly urged me to establish uniform rules for holidays that would be observed by everybody in the cluster. That I declined to do. Then my whole staff besieged me. They said that the mimeograph room managed by the Clearing House and used by all the others ought to establish its own rules for holidays which would conform to those I observed in my own office, and they couldn't see why in the world anybody would object to circulating a notice about these holidays. Reluctantly, most reluctantly, after weeks of pressure and against my better judgment, I finally consented. A mimeographed sheet was sent out to all the organizations saying, in effect, "For your information the Mimeograph Room of Public Administration Clearing House will observe the following holidays: January 1, New Year's Day; May 30, Memorial Day; July 4, Independence Day; the last Thursday in November, Thanksgiving Day; December 25, Christmas Day."

That was all. Now it was perfectly evident that these five holidays would be observed by every one of the organizations, but just as I expected a revolution broke out. Director after director descended upon me in fury. It was not the business of the Clearing House, it was not your business, they said to me, to try to dictate to us in our organizations what holidays we will observe. There was nothing to do but formally to withdraw the circular. My only solace was that I had won a battle with my own subordinates and quelled an internal revolution among my associates.

After that nobody, in my own organization at any rate, resisted me or tried to refute me when I asserted that every one of the organizations at 850 East Fifty-eighth Street or later at 1313 East Sixtieth Street was autonomous, independent, and utterly on its own.

CHAPTER XXVI

ADMINISTRATION AND THE SOCIAL SCIENCE RE-SEARCH COUNCIL

The Social Science Research Council was set up mainly on the initiative of Charles E. Merriam. He had encountered many difficulties in attempting in his own university to bring together the resources of scholars in the ever increasing number of divisions in the social sciences. The council was a remedy suggested by him. Comprised of representatives from the American Anthropological Association, the American Historical Association, the American Economics Association, the American Political Science Association, the American Psychological Association, the American Sociological Society, and the American Statistical Association, governed by representatives freely elected by these autonomous associations, it obtained early some important support from the great foundations and after not too long a time found itself being consulted by the foundations about other research grants. For a number of years there had been occasional discussions of how to set up some scheme which would accomplish in America the type of research activities carried on in England by the royal commissions of inquiry. That particular project had been very much in the minds of some leaders in the council, particularly Beardsley Ruml and Dr. Merriam.

In January, 1933, the report of President Hoover's Committee on Recent Social Trends had recommended extended inquiries into several different fields. At last it was decided to try the commission-of-inquiry technique, not under government auspices, but in an experimental form that might be financed by foundations. The Social Science Research Council then adopted an outline for three such commissions of inquiry: one on the subject of international trade; one on population problems; and one on public service personnel.

The last one was financed by the Spelman Fund. Its chairman was Lotus D. Coffman, president of the University of Minnesota, and its other members were Ralph Budd, president of the Chicago, Burlington and Quincy Railroad; Arthur L. Day, vice-president of the Corning Glass Works, a scientist for many years connected with the Coast and Geodetic Survey; Charles E. Merriam; and I. Luther Gulick, director of the Institute of Public Administration and at that time a professor of public administration at Columbia University, was selected as secretary and director of research.

What we had in mind was to discover what could be done not only to improve the quality of public service but to attract into its ranks men and women of greater ability, what could be done to increase the prestige of public employment, and what to do to get more effective personnel for governments—federal, state, and local.

Some of these tasks we assigned to members of our research staff. In 1935 our final report, together with a thick volume of minutes of evidence taken by those who testified before us, was published along with several other monographs. One was a bibliography of civil service and personnel administration; one was a compendium of monographs by competent scholars on the British, Canadian, French, and German civil services; another was a volume on the methods used for training public employees in Great Britain; another, a collection of monographs on the problems encountered in the United States; and then another, on the general subject of government by merit in which there was an analysis of the problem of government personnel.

Useful as were the staff studies not only to members of the commission but to scholars and organizations of citizens interested in the problem, actually the commission itself for its own report depended to a much greater extent upon what it learned in the public hearings it held in various cities in all sections of the United States and in England.

In the London hearings we learned a great deal about the British Civil Service in its upper reaches and a great deal about governmental employees at the lower levels, especially in local government. Here also we had an opportunity to talk to important British public administration leaders about the problems of the higher administrative class, for which there is practically no American analogue. So, too, did some of the members of the staff in other countries. But most of all, from our hearings here we got a sense of the developing feeling in the United States of the need for better personnel in government.

In Washington the federal service was principally discussed. In New

York, Chicago, Minneapolis, St. Paul, Seattle, San Francisco, Berkeley, Los Angeles, and Richmond the emphasis was on state and local governments. Witnesses were also called in from Milwaukee, Columbus, Cleveland, Albany, Madison, Duluth, Sacramento, Takoma, Walla Walla, Spokane, Portland, Pasadena, Baltimore, Atlanta, Raleigh, and Knoxville, as well as from Ottawa in Canada—we heard competent responsible persons representing both the employing groups and the employed discuss at length the problems of state and local government personnel practices. In Palo Alto we spent several hours with former President Hoover taking his testimony on federal employees.

In some of these hearings we heard a great deal about the techniques employed by the United States Civil Service Commission and other civil service bodies in states and cities, only to be faced with a variety of opinions on testing and rating practices. There were continuing disputations concerning the evaluation placed upon these techniques by the men who gave them, the men who were supposed to use them, and the persons tested and rated.

These opinions represented a wide range of experience. Former President Hoover, for instance, believed that the testing methods employed by the various civil service commissions were excellent in determining who were the most efficient persons for routine and repetitive tasks, but he did not believe that these methods could be effective so far as the supervisory and, more especially, the higher administrative positions were concerned. Others, including such men as Professor Leonard D. White, soon to become a member of the United States Civil Service Commission, and principal employees of that commission, were confident that personnel machinery could and should be used for public employees in all but the highest policy-determining positions—the positions in which the opinions and decisions taken in the democratic processes of elections should be implemented.

Within the particular services, we found in some cities the opinion that the civil service machinery was applicable perhaps to the police and fire and health departments but would not be effective in other positions. There also were the inevitable differences of opinion between those who put a high value on the practice of open examination and those who (especially among the educational people and some others) preferred the system of professional certification as established in the public schools in most parts of the country. There were at that time only eight state civil service commissions—only eight states in which the employment at the state level was differentiated in any way by any formal scheme from partisan or factional political patronage. Many, many cities had introduced some formal personnel practices, but in most of them it applied only to certain departments, and in many of them the whole system was practically defeated by the device of exempting temporary employees, whose "temporary" character sometimes ran along year after year. Then also we discovered among some of the better-administered cities the growing belief that all the employees should be subject to a centralized personnel practice by a specially created personnel body. Then too we found support for such an all-inclusive system from representatives in large industries. However, on the other side, there always was kept before us the difficulty, in full coverage of all employees, of establishing some orderly personnel system for getting rid of deadwood. This was particularly stressed from the employers' side when the problem of dealing with organizations of employees and unions came up.

Once in a while we got something very interesting. For instance, at a hearing in Washington I asked a representative of a postal-clerks' union a leading question. He was a tall, red-faced, white-haired person of obviously Irish extraction complete with brogue. My question was, "If some selective epidemic were to strike the country tonight and all the first- and second-class postmasters in the United States [then considered to have only political patronage posts] were to die, how long would the delivery of the mail be delayed tomorrow morning?"

"Well," he replied, stroking his jaw and chin and with great deliberation, "it would all depend on how many of the boys were told off to act as pall-bearers."

We discovered also the differences of individual opinions in regional attitudes. For instance, in Chicago there was little if any reliance placed upon the effectiveness of the civil service system partly because of the local experience with evasions. In a city like Richmond, in the discussion of the problems of the state government and also of many of the local governments, we discovered little doubt of the feasibility of a merit system but some question of whether a formal personnel system was needed, since the Virginia tradition for generations had been to employ the best of its more highly educated persons to maintain prestige and to grant life tenure in office regardless of elections; in fact, many positions there were considered to be hereditary.

In our long train trips across the country and in our frequent conferences held after the close of particular hearings, the commission gradually came to the unanimous opinion that what was needed most of all was a radical change in the attitude not only of the citizens but of the administrators of the personnel systems. No longer would it suffice to advocate merely civil service reform to fight the spoils system. No longer would it suffice, in the task of meeting the demands of the thoughtful citizenry for economy and efficiency in government in the face of the government's increasing costly obligations, merely to take the negative side and fight the corrupt politicians. So at the end of 1934 a generalized draft report of the type on which we had agreed was submitted to us by the secretary, Luther Gulick.

We six men sat down at the table in a hotel in Richmond. The draft was taken up sentence by sentence. When it was finished (after a session of twenty-two hours with only a few short rests for food), practically every sentence had been gone over, criticized, and rewritten in accordance with the consensus. It was a *unanimous* report.

Its impact was virtually immediate. State after state began the installation of personnel machinery. But the most important effect, one that was to last for decades, was its influence upon the words and phrases used in American speech about this particular governmental problem. In essence, we dealt first with the fallacies in American thinking about public employment, among which we detailed several errors: the false notion that to the victor belongs the spoils; the mistaken idea that the duties of government are simple; the false idea that charity begins on the public payroll; the erroneous assumption that patronage is the price of democracy; the monstrous notion that the best public servant is the worst one because (as we had heard a thoroughly first-rate man in business testify) the able public servant is corrosive and eats holes in our liberties—the better he is and the longer he stays, the greater is the danger; the erroneous thought that tenure is the cure of spoils; the superficial idea that the way to eradicate spoils and favoritism is to begin at the bottom with clerks and stenographers and policemen and firemen and work up; the wrong-headed belief in hometown jobs for hometown boys; the notion that the public service is always less capable and less efficient than private enterprise; and the erroneous idea that the spoils system, the eleemosynary system and other corrosive influences can be driven out of the public service through the prohibition by law of specific abuses. We went on to say that time and time again the commission had been told that laws have not cured the trouble. What was clearly required, we declared, was not negative laws but positive and militant handling of the problem of personnel with the active backing of the public, the press, and all organized bodies of the citizenry.

The detailing of these fallacies was followed by consideration of the necessity of the adjustment of government to the changing social order. All this was followed by our statement:

The establishment of a career service is in the judgment of this Commission the required next step in the history of American government. In the federal government, in the state governments, in the local governments, what we now need is the transformation of the public service to a career basis. . . .

By career is meant a life work. It is an honorable occupation which one normally takes up in youth with the expectation of advancement and pursues until retirement.

The commission then divided the distinguishable kinds of governmental work into five classes: (1) administrative work; (2) professional work; (3) clerical work; (4) skilled and trade work; and (5) unskilled work. And we recommended that all five be included in the career service by orderly recruitment, by the use of modern and advanced educational methods in training before entry, in post-entry training, and in the general application of the merit system not only to appointment but to promotion and to compensation.

The result was that the report of the commission marked, even if it did not cause, a change in the nomenclature with which the problem was discussed. We began to hear more and more about the career service, the merit system, and the need for better organization for personnel administration and less about the spoils system and even less about the civil service system as a means of fighting it.

The report and all its accompanying documents were published by the McGraw-Hill Company. Within less than a year it was out of print. The report itself was republished in a paperback edition selling for twenty-five cents, and in that form the League of Women Voters, chambers of commerce, and citizens' associations soon exhausted the supply.

The report was completed and signed on January 7, 1935. Twenty years later it was extremely difficult to discover a copy anywhere except in the larger and better-guarded libraries. Nothing yet has been done in this country to follow up in any general way this experiment with the type of testing and sampling of public opinion that is done in England, in Canada, and in the other states of the British Commonwealth by the royal commissions on inquiry. Mr. Ruml's and Dr. Merriam's dream has not yet come true.

Several years earlier, in 1928, the Social Science Research Council, recognizing the increasing importance of studies in the field of public administration, created a committee of scholars to consider what might be done. Leonard D. White was made chairman. After two years, he was succeeded by Luther Gulick of the Institute of Public Administration. During his chairmanship Mr. Gulick took the lead in the organization and incorporation of the Public Administration Clearing House. In 1934 he resigned. One problem that had been stressed by both Dr. White and Mr. Gulick was the difficulty of testing the opinions of those who worked in the ivory towers of the universities against the experiences of those who worked in the day-to-day activities of government.

It was decided that my desk as director of the Public Administration Clearing House was a crossroads where communications among many groups of public officials and many groups of academicians would meet. My name was submitted and I was chosen (in my absence) to be chairman of the Public Administration Committee. Both White and Gulick told me not to accept the position unless I was assured of the assistance of a paid, full-time staff and in addition of a sufficient fund to operate properly a positive program of action. The president of the council, Dr. Robert T. Crane, did not approve, as a general proposition, of providing staff aid for the committees of the council. I presented to him the conditions on which I would accept the position. For a long time I heard nothing. Then Dr. Ezra E. Day, the head of the social science division of the Rockefeller Foundation, took a hand. He said that the foundation would be willing to make quite liberal grants to the council for this committee's work if the conditions that I had made were accepted. Dr. Crane, still with great reluctance, agreed to make an application to the foundation for a fund to support the committee's staff, its conferences, its publications, and other activities under my chairmanship.

Administration and the Social Science Research Council

I chose my associate director, Charles S. Ascher, to be secretary of the committee. The committee in a meeting at Princeton with my approval chose Joseph P. Harris, then a professor at the University of Washington, to be director of research.

Almost every member of the committee, almost every organization in the Chicago cluster, many similar groups elsewhere, and practically every professor of public administration in the United States immediately developed plans for researches and publications. Mr. Ascher and Dr. Harris had all that they could do, and there was enough left over for me.

During those four years my committee initiated many studies in many fields. Among them were several in city management as represented by the council-manager form of government. Another group of studies was made of grants-in-aid, such as the administration of grants to the states from the federal government of the United States, from the federal government of Canada to the provinces, and from the central government in England to the local governments in that country. There were special studies of the National Recovery Administration codes and of the administration of Federal Work Relief, both administrative centers intensely interesting at that time but now belonging more or less to ancient history. There were also studies in such new fields as federal administration of Social Security and its related Public Assistance and Employment Services.

In the meantime, as the year 1935 wore on, I, as chairman of the Public Administration Committee, became even more intricately involved in the work of the National Resources Committee in its current studies in the field of administration.

I became convinced, as did my colleagues on the committee, the members of my staff, the members and staff of the National Resources Committee, that what we had been doing in the field of public administration about functional organizations for improvement of the techniques of administration in all governments and at the levels of departments, divisions, and jurisdictions was not sufficient. We became more and more convinced as the months wore on and the work piled up that there should be a greater and more intense effort to study the problems in the realm of top management and devise solutions for them. That led us straight to the White House.

In this respect I had not only the support of the members of the Pub-

[299]

lic Administration Committee but also the enthusiastic and hearty approval of the chairman of the Board of Directors of the Public Administration Clearing House, Frank O. Lowden, who during his governorship of Illinois had been one of the first state administrators to invite close examination of the work of a state and to approve recommendations for a thorough reorganization of the state government, a project which he carried through to a successful conclusion in 1917. It was a pioneer work. It was the most important forward step taken up to that time in top management in the governmental field. Governor Lowden, in 1935 living in retirement on Sinnissippi Farm near Oregon, Illinois, followed every step I made and counseled with me frequently, in person when he came to Chicago and every few days over the telephone. Thus I had at this time the hearty support not only of my staff but of the board of the Clearing House and the members of the Public Administration Committee, and I was working in the closest possible harmony with the National Resources Committee and the officials of the Spelman Fund, the Rockefeller Foundation, and the Carnegie Corporation.

So far as I was concerned there was hard work and lots of it, but also there was continual encouragement and valiant support from leaders not only in public administration but in political science and in the social sciences in general.

As the interest in a careful study of the top management of the administration of the federal government grew and developed, I had several conversations with the members of the National Resources Committee about the problem. Its chairman, Frederic A. Delano, told us that he had tentatively discussed the matter with the President himself and that the President had agreed that under the proper auspices some such exploration should be made.

That fact I reported to a meeting of the Public Administration Committee held in New York in September, 1935. There was unanimous agreement among those present that such a study should be undertaken, that it would be entirely feasible to obtain the necessary financial support, and that there was an encouraging possibility of rendering a valuable public service. However, one member of the committee, Lindsay Rogers, professor of public law at Columbia University, raised a question. In view of the fact that the presidential election would be held in the following year, 1936, he doubted whether the committee ought to undertake any major effort in that field unless and until the President himself had requested or at least specifically approved the undertaking. Professor Rogers' good sense in making that comment was unanimously accepted. The result was that I reported to Mr. Delano that the Public Administration Committee would be willing to undertake a major study of the problem of the over-all organization of the federal government, but only if requested to do so by the President of the United States. There the matter lay.

CHAPTER XXVII

EUROPE IN 1934

While there was much to do in Washington, some of us, including particularly Mr. Moffett and Dr. Merriam, were deeply interested in events in Europe. We were still holding to the theory that administrative methods and practices were transferable despite radical differences in political controls and that what had proved successful and workable as an administrative device in one country could be imported and adapted for use in another.

Then, too, we were puzzled by circumstances which apparently differentiated the methodology of research in administration in the United States from that pursued in practically all other countries. Here in the United States the problem of administrative research had been tackled in an orderly and scientific fashion at the municipal level. In 1906 the New York Bureau of Municipal Research was established as a citizens' organization, privately financed but designed to work in closest harmony with the city government. In its first year the movement was not particularly welcome at the City Hall, but very shortly thereafter, under the mayoralty of John Purroy Mitchel, the bureau and the City Hall worked together, and great advances were made. About the same time similar movements were undertaken at the state level, notably by the Ohio Institute in Columbus and the University of Wisconsin in Madison.

In the federal government there had been attempts at improving departmental methods of work as early as the appointment, in Grover Cleveland's second administration, of Senator Francis Marion Cockrell, of Missouri, and Representative Alexander M. Dockery, also of Missouri, as a committee which with congressional blessing made a joint attempt at early administrative improvement in the Cockrell-Dockery report. That, however, had not had a very great impact except in some phases of the postal administration.

Theodore Roosevelt, when he was President, intrusted to a committee in the Treasury Department under the chairmanship of Charles Hallam Keep, assistant secretary of the treasury, the first of the orderly examinations into administrative problems. He thus initiated a movement in which followed other interim commissions appointed by himself and the great Commission on Economy and Efficiency established by President Taft. This in turn led to activities during the Wilson administration which led to the enactment at the very beginning of Harding's administration of the Budget and Accounting Act—a great milestone in the history of public administration in this country. It introduced in the federal government the principle of the executive budget, which already had been demonstrated in several cities and in such states as Illinois under Governor Frank O. Lowden and New York under Governor Al Smith.

In the meantime, bureaus of municipal research had sprung up in many cities. Nearly all were privately financed and usually headed by committees which were, if not hostile, at least coldly suspicious of the persons actually charged with the responsibility for local government. This attitude had resulted, in many agencies, in a fixed habit of hostility to government, a habit which induced the publication of reports in a form that practically said to the city hall "We dare you!" And sometimes some of these bureaus were apparently secretly delighted when the city hall did not take up the dare. It was "outside" research.

Nevertheless, more and more cities did take up the dare. More and more cities did use these surveys and actually brought in as consultants within the governmental machinery the very persons who but a few years before had been the all but declared enemies of the city hall. More important, the movement had the effect in the federal government, in some state governments, and in many city governments of setting up within the governmental structure research units, often only temporary, to deal with some particular phase of government such as accounting, or a better traffic control practice, or a better fire alarm system. In 1934 this movement was tending toward generalized permanent research activity into the over-all problems of administration. In our search among foreign countries, especially those of western Europe, for administrative practices that might be transferable, we had been, as I now recall, a little taken aback by the fact that the private research agency was almost unknown, and, if it had been even so much as contemplated, it had been met with implacable hostility on the part of the more orderly and more long-established governmental organizations of the European municipalities and national states. For instance, in England, where we had learned so much from the British Institute of Public Administration, we were not a little astonished to discover that it was made up entirely of the higher administrative class in the national government working together with men in the higher brackets of local governments.

There was little in either to fit into our American practice. Here was what we then thought was a gap that if bridged would be of great reciprocal benefit.

For more than a year Merriam, Ruml, Moffett, and I had been attempting to assemble somewhere in Europe a general conference on research in government. The place finally selected was Paris. In the organization of this conference the Public Administration Clearing House was given a liberal grant of money to pay the expenses of the delegates invited. The list was carefully chosen and meticulously checked with some of our European colleagues who already were persuaded that something should be done to improve the quality and to increase the quantity of administrative research in European countries. To this conference in Paris, then, I invited ten representatives of national governments, ten representatives of local governments, and ten representatives of universities and academic institutions. This and other engagements in Europe made it absolutely imperative that I get across the Atlantic as early as possible in the summer of 1934. I had also undertaken a quick tour of consultation with the International Labor Office in Geneva and wanted to visit again some of my friends in Berlin.

The 1934 conference of the International Union of Local Authorities at Lyons was largely at the technical level. It considered in detail a long report on advanced methods for refuse disposal. With the American delegation was Donald C. Stone, executive director of Public Administration Service, who contributed from his experiences in similar work in the United States, as did the delegates from many other countries. This seemed to Moffett and the rest of us a clear demonstration of the utility of the exchange of information in the Western world of experiments, experiences, and advances. Similarly, it seemed to us that since the responsibility for particular technical services among different countries varied considerably (ranging from federal-state and independent local establishments in the United States to centralized control in France), it would be necessary to effect the exchange as much as possible by international organizations which could bring local governments and national governments closer together.

Lyons, an industrial city, an ancient seat of power, was famous for its annual trade fair which all Europe was accustomed to attend. It had a certain international, industrial, commercial, and civic character. On the other hand, it had had in modern times little or no international political significance. It had been less disturbed than most French cities by the French Revolution. It had gone on weaving its silks and satins, its brocades, and its velvets.

Our host was the mayor of the city, M. Edouard Herriot. He was a great orator, a great musician, and a great historian of music. He already was elderly; his body was tortured by arthritis. He gave us a breakfast in the Hôtel de Ville, a beautiful early eighteenth-century building containing what reputedly was the only wine cellar that had suffered no injury, damage, or even diminution during the French Revolution. The "breakfast" began at noon and lasted until after five o'clock. Each of us was given a tiny glass—a half-thimbleful—of a Madeira that had been laid down in the reign of Louis XV. At every place at the table there was a huge carafe containing new champagne. And then there were at least a dozen glasses of appropriate size and shape for a dozen other samplings of the treasures of that cellar. It was a noble example of the best that the French can do with wines and with cuisine, an example of what Lyons and perhaps only Lyons could do.

There were of course a good many speeches in a good many languages by representatives of many of the forty nations present. And there was one great oration. I did not understand the French but I understood that when M. Herriot was speaking he was full of his subject and that it was a great occasion. Later in translation we discovered it showed not only great oratory but also profound scholarship in the history of the development and the growth of civic institutions and urban civilizations throughout European civilization.

The mayor also gave us an evening reception in the spacious, perfectly tended gardens of his home. It was a night of music—great singers and great songs—a program arranged by the mayor himself, who, hobbling from table to table on his cane, evidently in great pain, sat and visited with every delegate of the international convention. One could not escape the conclusion that in his country he was a great historian of the arts, a great democratic administrator, and, above all, a great personal politician. It would have been difficult then to believe that he would survive yet another world war; that he would defy Hitler, despise and reject Pétain, become president of the National Assembly of the Fourth Republic, and live until 1957.

From Lyons some of us Americans proceeded to Paris, while others scattered to various cities and capitals in Europe, all convinced of the utility and great value of the International Institute of Administrative Sciences.

The principal interest of the Clearing House was the conference in Paris. Senator Émile Vinck and M. Edmond Lesoir, the directors, respectively, of the International Union of Local Authorities and of the International Institute of Administrative Sciences, had made the local arrangements for the meeting.

The meetings were held in a conference room in the building erected for the Institute of Low Cost Housing of the Department of the Seine, a building then famous for being the only one in Paris with American up-and-down sash windows. M. Seillier, the head of the institute, had long sought to improve the communications on low-cost housing between nations to the east and west of France and had been an active leader in the International Union.

While we saw him every day, he was always behind in his work and rarely had a chance to attend meetings. The only regular French delegate in attendance was Professor Oualid of the School of Urbanism of the University of Paris. Some of us had known him when he was a visiting professor at the University of Chicago. He was a master of the English tongue. As it turned out, everybody present could speak either English or German with one exception—a member of the Supreme Court of Poland. He insisted that translations be made into French. It was not until the conference was over that we discovered that he didn't understand French either. Since French was the acknowledged international diplomatic language, he had demanded it as a matter of protocol.

The conference went on for a week, meeting in the morning, at noon, in the afternoon, and sometimes at night. Many of the delegates were puzzled at our combining university men with local government officials and local government officials with representatives of national governments in a meeting not devoted to subjects of exclusive interest to any one group. One delegate who was a master of all three languages, William E. Rappard, of the Institute of Higher Learning of Geneva, was not only bored by the constant repetition of the interpretation but confessed himself to be unable to understand why such diverse elements could possibly have common interests that were not available in published works of law and history.

Then, too, over the meeting hung a grave shadow. There was present Baron von Leyden, who two years earlier at a meeting of the International Union of Cities in London had made one of the greatest contributions to the discussion. At that time he was the Prussian minister of the interior and, as such, had intimate and direct knowledge of the municipal experiences of the major state in the German Empire. We had asked him to come because we had seen that he was sensitive even in a centralized government to the necessity of encouraging local government initiative. But also there was Kurt Jeserich, the new head of the German organization of municipal government created by the new German chancellor, Adolf Hitler.

Baron von Leyden's English was perfect, but Kurt Jeserich, who also spoke good English, had been instructed to speak only in German. He was the shadow of the Führer. Von Leyden was distraught. There at the table sat that surety agent. Jeserich also was unhappy. He had not yet been admitted to membership in the Nazi party. When his turn came to speak, he talked a long time, beginning every paragraph with: "In Deutschland wir. . . ." He instructed us precisely how to carry on not only local government but national governments built strictly in accordance with the *Führerprinzip*. And through the speech, sometimes overtly, sometimes implicitly, he denigrated the utility or the prognosis of the longevity of any democratic procedure whatsoever. Baron von Leyden left for Berlin after the first day. After the second day, Mr. Jeserich was also summoned back to Berlin.

The conference came to a unanimous agreement that there should be set up in Brussels a common center in which the International Institute and the International Union could be brought together with a common library and complete interchange of publications and information under the auspices of a Joint Committee on Planning and Cooperation. I was made president of that committee. That action necessitated a return visit to Brussels. The joint committee, on which there were representatives of several countries, was assembled there. We began to negotiate with the Spelman Fund for a grant-in-aid, to establish an immediate protocol of exchange between the two offices, and to adopt a plan for a new establishment in which the two organizations, each preserving its autonomy, would work together in very much the same pattern that had been established by the Public Administration Clearing House in Chicago in its relations with the cluster of autonomous organizations surrounding it. My Belgian confreres immediately adopted the name of International Clearing House.

The problem was to staff it. I undertook to find in the United States some person with experience in government, in organizational work, and in university work, who could spend two or three years, if necessary, in the Brussels establishment. It also was decided to take precisely the same first step I had taken in the Clearing House in Chicago, namely, to compile and publish a directory of international organizations in the field of public administration.

After I came back to the United States, I selected Rowland Egger for this task. He was then a professor of public administration at the University of Virginia. He was the son of a university professor who had been on duty in France immediately after World War I. His father had superintended his education. He sent his son to secondary schools in France where, of course, he had gained command of that language. I deemed him to be a man who would be able to understand not only the diverse languages but also the diverse institutions. Actually he spent about a year and a half in Brussels. He brought the two organizations together in one common building. The two libraries were brought together into that building but were not consolidated. The library of the International Union had been indexed under the American Dewey decimal system; the library of the International Institute was catalogued under a French system, and, while the amalgamation was programed, it never was effected. Senator Vinck and the International Union in some of its office arrangements and in the library were further along in the adaptations of the principles and recommendations advocated by the scientific management group than were many American offices—in

[308]

fact, further along in some aspects of office management than was any one of the organizations in the Chicago cluster.

Egger not only established common headquarters but compiled and edited the *Directory of International Organizations in the Field of Public Administration,* which was published in May, 1936, just prior to meetings of the Union of Local Authorities in Berlin and the International Institute in Warsaw.

But all this was to anticipate events unappreciated or perhaps even unknown to any of us at the conference in the summer of 1934. However, that conference did foreshadow our changing opinions and our ripening decisions about the utility of continued international exchanges concerning administrative actions in both local and national government. It also foreshadowed a shift in our notions of the methodology to be employed. We still were convinced that the techniques of administration were transferable. But we were shifting to the point of view that these exchanges would have to be made and the necessary contacts established to effect them through the use of more or less centralized organizations in each of the countries included in the programs. As far as possible, these organizations, diverse as they might be, of necessity must be persuaded to deal more and more with the problems of top management, with less emphasis on documentary detail, if the results of the flow of information were to achieve any practical objective.

In the summer of 1934, after these meetings, my wife and I went to the Hotel Bristol on Unter den Linden in Berlin. It was a shockingly altered Berlin that we found. We arrived a scant week after the famous "blood purge" in which Hitler himself had shot and killed one of his principal lieutenants, Röhm, and in which many other Nazi party leaders and their principal military adherents had been put to death. The streets of Berlin were deserted. There was an ominous quiet everywhere. Mrs. Brownlow and I quite naturally went to see the American ambassador, our friend whom we had known for many, many years, William E. Dodd, who had lived in Chicago only a block away from us. Mrs. Dodd and the other members of his family, his daughter and his son, were away. He had that very morning encountered some difficulty with the German Foreign Office in helping the American journalist Dorothy Thompson to get safely out of Germany. He had done a good many things during the events of the previous week to help some of the more distinguished German leaders escape the Hitlerian wrath. He believed, indeed, that he had saved Franz von Papen from "liquidation." He was tremendously upset and was more pessimistic in his assessment of the lengths to which the Nazi fanatics would go than was almost anybody else I had seen in Europe and, for that matter, much more gloomy than anybody I saw in the United States upon my return.

I did, however, stick to protocol and make my call on the offices of the German Municipal Union (the Deutscher Stadtestag) to see Kurt Jeserich, who was the new man in charge. I had known some of his predecessors: Dr. Elsass, who at one time had been the Oberbürgermeister of Berlin, and Dr. Hans Luther, who a little later was sent by the Hitler regime to be ambassador to Washington. I inquired in vain for some of my friends who had been active in municipal governmental studies in the University of Berlin. It was a disheartening experience.

But the Nazi government recognized that something would have to be done to restore the tone of the town. Free excursion tickets were distributed among the Hitlerian Brown Shirts in the small towns and villages of the country, entitling each recipient to free travel, hotel accommodations, and entertainment in Berlin. The trains poured out the Brown Shirts, their wives, and their children by the thousands. The streets soon were filled. The restaurants that had been deserted were crowded again. The city regained, at least for a short time, its old appearance of bustle and activity by day and by night.

The free tickets served a double purpose. Not only was Berlin active again but, since Hitler had decided to disarm his Brown Shirts, these free excursions made their military demotion much more palatable to them. Bess and I sat together one night in the great Kempinsky restaurant and saw these rural Brown Shirts come in for their free dinners, their free beer, and their free night club shows. We could recognize these people by their bearing. Their attitudes had the outward manifestations that we instantly associated with the members of the Ku Klux Klan of Alabama or Indiana—attitudes characteristic of the believing dupes of demagogic leaders fired by their ignorance of the world and their superstitious faith in nationalistic exclusiveness.

After that Berlin visit, we were glad, indeed, again to stop in Paris and Brussels and London on our way home and particularly happy when we landed in New York.

PART III

WASHINGTON AGAIN

CHAPTER XXVIII

THE PRESIDENT'S COMMITTEE ON
ADMINISTRATIVE MANAGEMENT

The President's Committee on Administrative Management was set up by Franklin Roosevelt in March, 1936. It made its report to the President, who promptly sent it to the Congress with his blessing in January, 1937. The measures designed to effectuate the committee's recommendations, after a long struggle, were defeated in 1938. But the next year the Congress passed the Reorganization Act of 1939, based on the report of my committee. Under its authority the Executive Office of the President was established. Also under its authority a good many other changes were made in the structure of the top management of the federal government by means of inter- and intradepartmental transfers of functions and bureaus.

But the most revolutionary result was the establishment of the Executive Office of the President. Still later, working on the same pattern, the Reorganization Act of 1945 was passed. And still later the essential features of the report having to do with top management in the federal government were indorsed and re-emphasized by the two commissions headed by former President Hoover; other supplementary reorganization acts were passed by the Congress; and its essential and central themes were elaborated by many so-called Little Hoover Commissions in the states.

It would be transparent folly even to try to search out the suggestions made by hundreds of students of government and public administration, hundreds of writers and editors, and literally thousands of public servants, who in the past had sensed the need of such improvement and had already made positive suggestions of how it might be brought about.

Rather, I shall confine myself to the particular incidents that, piled one on top of the other, amounted to this particular result. That there were separate and even parallel sequences of events influencing the course taken by those of us who collaborated in this work, I have not the slightest doubt. But these, if they seem important, must be recorded by those who know about them.

The stream of events which I shall try to describe had its prime source in a series of conversations held in the hot summer of 1933 in the Hay-Adams House in Washington. The talkers were Charles E. Merriam, Beardsley Ruml, Guy Moffett, and I. That is, we were the principal talkers. There were from time to time many others, singly and in groups, who came in or were brought in to the discussion.

On the fourth of the previous March, Mr. Hoover had left the White House and Mr. Roosevelt had come in. The divisions of opinion that later were to result in open conflict were not yet discernible beneath the surface of the great co-operative effort that seemingly engaged the hearty interest of everybody in the country.

The talks that went on in that summer and autumn of 1933 at the meetings of the National Planning Board, which were held sometimes in the Department of Interior and often at the Cosmos Club and at which I was frequently present, were concerned in large part with the question of how to improve the co-ordination of the several programs being carried on to increase employment and to relieve the victims of unemployment.

The first definite action looking toward an attempted solution of the top management problem that I can discover in my diary is under the date of November 30, 1933. It is as follows:

"I had a talk at luncheon today with Dr. Merriam who told me that the Public Works Administration had approved an appropriation of $35,000 for the National Planning Board to enable it to undertake to draft a 'plan for a plan.'

"Mr. Delano and the Secretary of the Board, Mr. Eliot, will be primarily responsible for the actual physical public works plan; Mr. Wesley C. Mitchell, the economist on the Board, will give primary consideration to a scheme for economic planning; and Dr. Merriam, the other member of the Board, will take primary responsibility for developing a scheme for a governmental and political plan.

"We discussed the part that might be played in assisting him (Merriam) in this work by Leonard D. White, Lewis Meriam, Luther Gulick, Arnold Bennett Hall and his colleagues at Brookings, Charles

S. Ascher, and others. We made no attempt to reach any decision—indeed, I have no part in the decision—but we agreed to talk it all over after the next Sunday's meeting on metropolitan regional research problems."

That there was then need for a "plan for a plan" of the governmental structure was becoming evident not only to members of the Planning Board but, plainly, to the general public (although the public might not have used the word "plan") and also, painfully, to "that man" in the White House.

In the very beginning of his presidency, Mr. Roosevelt made it manifest that he intended to make a supreme effort to restore the broken economy of the nation and that he was willing to listen to suggestions from almost any source. He also made it clear that he was not committed to a single method of approach. On the contrary, he was willing to pursue, as actually he did pursue, varied, different, and even conflicting and contradictory courses of action.

It is possible by dint of exaggerated oversimplification to divide the thousands and thousands of advisers then concentrating on the White House into two general classes: the Savers and the Spenders. By the same sort of oversimplification, it is possible to divide all those advisers into two other groups, one of which would save the country by Private Enterprise and the other by Government Enterprise. And so one might go on with a long series of dichotomies. It was from this seething sea of opposing opinions that the President had to draw out the leviathan of recovery with the hook of the New Deal.

On the side of the Savers, he backed Lewis Douglas, the director of the budget, in an attempt at a 25 per cent cut in government expenditures. That reduction was carried successfully through the Congress and not only affected the ordinary operations of many governmental establishments but actually reduced the benefits being received by veterans. Also on the side of the Savers, he put tightfisted, economy-minded men in places of control, some of whom went so far, in my opinion, as to do permanent damage to necessary governmental institutions, as, for instance, the National Bureau of Standards and the Bureau of the Census.

On the side of the Spenders, he recognized that the relief needs of the country could not be met by private charity or by local or state government and were not being met with any degree of adequacy by the federal aid begun under the Reconstruction Finance Corporation in the summer of 1932, in Mr. Hoover's administration. And to meet that relief need, he was willing to go part of the way with those who wanted the job done by direct relief (some called it a "dole"), and part of the way with those who wanted to try something new, such as the Civilian Conservation Corps. For all these, in that same summer of 1933, he did succeed in getting what up to that time was the greatest appropriation ever made by Congress to be spent largely at the discretion of a President—$3.3 billion—for the national industrial recovery program.

On the side of Private Enterprise, he was willing to take—and did take—the recommendations of the United States Chamber of Commerce and of other leading industrial, financial, and business groups in the country to set up the National Recovery Administration, which was to solve all our problems by a system of codes devised by industry itself for the self-regulation of the national economy. The banner of the blue eagle was broken out over every factory in the land. Washington burst at the seams with representatives of business devising some five hundred codes, and more, for some five hundred or more industries.

These categories do not include, by any means, all the advisers who were concentrating on the White House. There were those who believed in loans. They might be called the Lenders; and while practically every Lender was enrolled in the ranks of either the Savers or the Spenders, his was a special interest which manifested itself in "floors." There had been ropes around the necks of judges in Iowa when holders of farm mortgages threatened to foreclose, and all over the land the mortgage was looked upon no longer as an aid to the establishment of a family estate but as a devouring monster about to dispossess and destroy the household. So a floor had to be put under the mortgages, and to that end the Farm Credit Administration and the Home Owners' Loan Corporation set about their work of salvage. Furthermore, in these beginning days it was thought that new houses were needed, and new houses would need new mortgages, and to get such mortgages there must be government insurance. And so came about the Federal Housing Administration and its scheme of guaranteed amortizable loans for homes. There had to be floors under dropping prices, too, and so not only the blue eagle codes for the townfolks, but the Agricultural Adjustment Administration for the folks on the farm were busy building new floors. At that time but few ceilings seem to have been indicated.

All this was very confusing. Much of it was contradictory. And all was moving ahead at a pace far too swift for administration by the regularly established departments of the government, far too swift for the traditional procedures of congressional committees. So, while the Congress may not have been a rubber stamp, it certainly was passing out blank checks. And the chief contest on the Hill was whether or not Bert Snell, the Republican leader, could beat Joe Byrns, the Democratic floor leader, to the draw with the biggest and blankest of checks.

But along in July and August things got to such a pass that something had to be done. No longer could a group of Cabinet officers, each severally in touch with bunches of brain trusters, industrialists, labor leaders, social workers, and what not, continue merely to generate schemes, even if those schemes were given the instant approval of the Congress.

The thing had to be administered—that is to say, *all* these things had to be administered. And many and varied were the ways in which the work was started.

Louis Howe was setting up the Civilian Conservation Corps from the White House itself. Harry Hopkins and Harold Ickes were fighting over who should spend what and where for relief and for works. Harry was trying to give away more in grants and lend less on loans; Harold was trying to put more in loans and less in grants; and Lew Douglas was trying to stop both grants and loans, or, if he could not do that, at least to raise the interest rate on the loans. The Agriculture Department was leery of the Agricultural Adjustment Administration. The Department of Labor was leery of all these new things in its field. The Department of Commerce was reeling beneath the combined blows of budget cuts and Hugh Johnson's hoity-toity disregard.

Even within the departments and the new emergency agencies there were conflicting notions about how actually to do the work now that the new administration was under way. Cordell Hull was most emphatically not seeing eye to eye with Ray Moley, who was scuttling the International Economic Conference in England. And there were plenty of other places where similar quarrels over direction and administration were going on, even if they were not always so spectacularly publicized.

There was but one man who could settle any of the issues, and he was fairly busy starting still newer things.

The man at the center was not as blind to all these goings-on as some people thought. Practically everybody prayed that he would be completely blind to everybody else but himself, but he had a wide-ranging eye and a capacious memory. He was a continuous fountain of both encouragement and discouragement to the people under him. Nearly every one of them was a specialist on a particular method of carrying out a particular project. Mr. President could hear the objectors to that project as well as its advocates. And, above all, he was the one person who had the ultimate responsibility for the entire government, the whole economy of the nation, and the welfare of all its people.

Very early he began his attempts at co-ordinating the work of his lieutenants, seemingly so intent upon taking divergent paths.

Thus when the National Industrial Recovery Act was being drafted and when it was finding its way through the House of Representatives and the Senate, it was the general opinion that the President would put it all under one administrator. Instead, he divided it into two parts, appointed a separate administrator for each, and superimposed upon each administrator an advisory board composed of Cabinet officers and other high officials.

These two committees were, of course, only interdepartmental committees. The utmost that could have been expected of them was to bring together the consideration of the administrative problems of such particular programs as concerned the executive departments and the new emergency agencies.

At the very same time, the President gave public manifestation to what seems to have been his growing anxiety for some general co-ordination of the already far-flung and the constantly growing number of administrative agencies. On June 11, 1933, he created what he called a Temporary Executive Council.

This council, established by Executive Order under the authority of the relief and recovery acts, consisted of the President himself, the ten heads of the regular executive departments, the director of the budget, and the heads of nine emergency organizations, of which two or three had been created under President Hoover and the rest after Roosevelt's inauguration. These nine men were the administrators of National Recovery, Agricultural Adjustment, and the Federal Emergency Relief; the co-ordinator of transportation, the governor of the Farm Credit Administration; the chairmen of the Reconstruction Finance Corporation, the Home Owners' Loan Corporation, and the Tennessee Valley Authority; and the director of Emergency Conservation Work. Two other members of the council were the secretary to the President and the assistant secretary of the treasury, L. W. Robert, under whose jurisdiction at that time was the Office of the Supervising Architect and the Procurement Division, with its two branches of Safety and Public Buildings.

Then to that aggregation of twenty-three persons there was added the executive secretary of the council itself. To that position, also established by Executive Order, the President appointed Frank C. Walker under circumstances that clearly indicated that he expected Mr. Walker to be the actual co-ordinator of the whole outfit, reporting directly and confidentially to the President.

Thus, Frank Walker became, under the administration of Franklin D. Roosevelt, the first of a long line of so-called assistant presidents. Mr. Walker and most of his successors in this particular position, which often changed so far as its technical establishment was concerned, rendered valuable service to the President and to the country by their efforts to set up and maintain orderly channels of communication to and from the one responsible head of the government—the President himself.

In this brief review, I have by no means exhausted the lists of co-ordinating efforts that were set up under interdepartmental committees and by other devices. But it is perhaps useful here to refer only to those that were undertaken at the center and were designed to comprehend practically the whole of the government.

Of these organizations designed to assist in the huge task of co-ordination, the Executive Council took a prime place. For many years it had been the custom for the Cabinet to meet with the President on Tuesdays and Fridays. In July, 1933, the Tuesday meeting was expanded to take in the whole Executive Council, of which every member of the Cabinet was a member. These meetings, so President Roosevelt told me long afterward, were exceedingly useful in keeping him informed of what was going on, especially in the emergency agencies. Each member of the council at each meeting made a brief report of progress and of immediate plans and urgent current problems.

On the other hand, the utility of such a large body, great as it was in bringing information to the President and in keeping each member informed of what the others were up to, was questionable when the President desired to use it to give directions or to undertake the management of the program, even though it had an able executive secretary.

Furthermore, the Executive Council began to proliferate its own subordinates. It set up an economic adviser. It began to establish subcommittees, some formal and some informal, but each with a secretariat of its own. And it had almost no money.

These and similar considerations led in November, 1933, to the creation of the National Emergency Council, which, at first, was conceived to be a working secretariat for the Executive Council. It was provided with funds from an emergency appropriation and was designated the central agency for keeping the records of the Executive Council and for carrying on a systematic exchange of information about the progress of the recovery measures. Furthermore, the new agency was charged with the duty of keeping the public informed about what was going on in the emergency agencies. This National Emergency Council was composed of ten persons. Four were members of the Cabinet: the secretary of the interior, who also was administrator of public works, and the secretaries of agriculture, of commerce, and of labor. The six others were the agricultural adjustment administrator, the federal emergency relief administrator, the industrial recovery administrator, the chairman of the Home Owners' Loan Corporation, the governor of the Farm Credit Administration, and a representative of the Consumers' Council. Frank C. Walker was made executive director. A month later the attorney general, the director of the budget, and the chairman of the Federal Trade Commission were added.

At the very first meeting of the National Emergency Council an utterly new step was taken in the effort at co-ordination. It was decided to appoint directors of the National Emergency Council in each state, each of whom would have responsibility for supervision and co-ordination in a general way of the field representatives of all the emergency agencies.

Not only was the National Emergency Council becoming institutionalized by the necessity of riding herd on its forty-eight state directors, which led to the creation of the Division of Field Operations, but it spawned still other subordinate divisions such as the United States

Information Service, the Consumers' Division, and the Better Housing Division.

The National Emergency Council and the Executive Council held meetings with the President on alternate weeks until June, 1934. Then, the distinction between the two bodies becoming increasingly difficult, both met together until October, 1934, when the two councils were consolidated under the name of the National Emergency Council.

At about the same time, the President made the National Emergency Council a secretariat for all interdepartmental and interagency committees regardless of whether or not the agencies represented on the committee had membership on the council.

In July, 1934, Mr. Walker, who had been serving as executive secretary and executive director without compensation, asked the President to be relieved. He was succeeded by Donald R. Richberg. Mr. Walker came back as executive in April, 1935, when events had taken an entirely new turn.

In talking with me much later about the National Emergency Council, its predecessor, the Executive Council, and its whole cluster of subordinate, auxiliary, and ancillary agencies, President Roosevelt said in substance:

"The whole NEC was a wonderful essay in democracy. It was exactly like a New England town meeting. It gave everybody a chance to blow off. I learned many things there—many things that those who were reporting never suspected that I learned and some that they wouldn't have liked me to know anything about. They also learned a lot about each other. At the beginning it was a wonderful device for keeping up the morale of the whole team, as long as instant relief and recovery were the sole goals.

"But like a New England town meeting, it was too big to do much actual work. It had to be split up into committees and subcommittees until in the end I couldn't take it any more because I found myself making stump speeches to the council instead of listening to its members. The time came when I could get most out of it by just talking to Frank Walker alone, especially after the organization of the whole relief setup in the spring of '35."

What President Roosevelt was experiencing at that time was very similar to what nearly always happens to a general manager who attempts to co-ordinate a great number of diverse activities and who separates operations by means of a representative committee. In order to make it work he has to break it up into working subcommittees whose programs either have something in common or are in such conflict that the operating chiefs recognize the need for accommodation and definition of their respective fields. All such multiple-member separate co-ordinating bodies tend almost from the beginning to institutionalize themselves, almost always to proliferate new operating divisions, nearly always to enter into activities actually in competition with those of the agencies that they were set up to correlate, and always to wind up by presenting the general manager with a new problem—how to co-ordinate the co-ordinators with those who were to have been co-ordinated. In plain words, the multiple-member co-ordinating body nearly always transfers its identification of interest from that of the general manager who appointed it to its own interest as a separate and distinct institution.

What seems to be the inherent tendency of multiple-member co-ordinating agencies to spawn operating divisions cannot, however, always be charged to the desire of such a committee or council for power over the existing agencies or to a desire to supplant them. What frequently happens is that the co-ordinating committee discovers gaps in the structure for which no agency is responsible, and therefore it sets up *ad hoc* divisions to fill in these gaps. Frequently divisions established to fill in these lacunae survive the co-ordinating committee, which nearly always dies when it reaches the point where it no longer serves its original purpose.

Again in 1935 the Congress decided to make its appropriations for recovery and relief in a huge lump sum to be apportioned by the President. Again this imposed upon the President a greater immediate task of direct management than theretofore had fallen upon the shoulders of a President.

Mr. Roosevelt was far from unwilling. He believed, and he was able to convince the Congress, that the necessary speed and flexibility could be attained in no other way. The Executive Council and the National Emergency Council by now were consolidated. But there was still plenty of work to be done. It may have been hard enough to co-ordinate the Rural Electrification Administration and the Bureau of Reclamation with the work of the Soil Conservation Service and the Forest Service—and it was hard. But that was nothing at all when compared to the task of attempting to co-ordinate Harold Ickes and Harry Hopkins.

In 1933 the Congress had voted $3.3 billion to the President. In 1935 it voted him $4.8 billion, a billion and a half more than before. There had been outcries, wails, and gnashing of teeth about the spending and the waste, the leaf-raking and the boondoggling. But, nevertheless, the program was expanded, not diminished.

The big question then was: How would the President divide up the money, and who would direct and control its expenditure?

One day early in May the President did something that, I believe, shocked every student of public administration to the marrow of his bones. He set up a perfectly impossible plan which a good many of us at once dubbed the "five-ring-circus." The weird piece of machinery for administering the new Emergency Relief Appropriation Act was made up of several elements.

First, a new unit was established in the National Emergency Council called the Division of Applications and Information, under the supervision of Frank Walker, who had been recalled to his old job as executive director for that very purpose. All applications for projects were to come to Frank Walker and be examined and reviewed by him with the aid and assistance of all governmental departments and agencies. Then Walker was to transmit the application to another new outfit.

Second, the Advisory Committee on Allotments was set up to receive the applications after they had been processed by Walker. This committeee had Harold Ickes, secretary of the interior and public works administrator, as its chairman. It had twenty-three members, including Franklin D. Roosevelt. There were two other members of the Cabinet besides Ickes: Henry Wallace of agriculture and Frances Perkins of labor. The others were the executive director of the National Emergency Council, Frank Walker; the administrator of the Works Progress Administration, which up to that time had not existed but was created in the same Executive Order, and which turned out to be Harry Hopkins; the director of the budget; the director of procurement *in propria persona;* the chief of engineers of the Army; the commissioner of reclamation; the director of soil conservation; the chief of the Forest Service; the director of emergency conservation work (CCC); the chief of the Public Roads Bureau; the resettlement administrator; the rural electrification administrator; the emergency relief administrator, which put Harry Hopkins in twice for good luck; the director of the Housing Division of the National Emergency Council; the vice-chairman of the National Resources Board; and five non-governmental members representing the Business Advisory Council of the Department of Commerce, organized labor, farm organizations, the American Bankers Association, and the United States Conference of Mayors.

This Advisory Committee on Allotments was supposed to make recommendations to the President on the allotment of funds for the projects passed on to the committee by Frank Walker and the Division of Applications.

Third, he set up the Works Progress Administration, which was to be responsible for the co-ordinated execution of the work relief program as a whole and was to move as many persons as possible from the relief rolls to work projects or private employment in the shortest possible time. The federal emergency relief administrator, under the terms of the order, was to serve as head of the Works Progress Administration. This meant Harry Hopkins.

Fourth, the secretary of the treasury was required to set up disbursing and accounting facilities and maintain a system of accounts which would enable the President to exercise direct executive control over the funds and to provide current accounting information for all the agencies concerned.

Fifth, the control of the allotment of funds for administrative expenses of all of the agencies was turned over to the director of the budget.

This was the five-ring circus. This was what shocked the experts. The applications were to go to Frank Walker. If he approved them, a huge committee presided over by Ickes would pass them to the President. When the President personally approved them, they would go to Harry Hopkins to be executed, with Morgenthau keeping the accounts and with Danny Bell doling out a nickel here and a dime there for administrative expenses. It confused nearly everybody and particularly the practitioners of orderly administration. But the confusion the experts then suffered was greatly to be compounded later on.

The thing worked!

It is true that it was not long until Harry Hopkins emerged from the mass carrying the ball. It is true that the Ickes-Hopkins feud was not entirely settled, but it is also true that the Public Works Administration continued to carry on, as did many of the other agencies engaged in the battle against unemployment, even if Hopkins and the Works Progress Administration did run away with most of it. It is also true that the accounting system then set up, which gave the President on the third day of the month a complete and accurate accounting review of all that had been done during the prior month, was the swiftest and most complete financial reporting of a project of such size ever known before or since.

Perhaps this weird scheme would not have worked for any other man but Franklin D. Roosevelt. In fact, in my opinion, it could not have worked for any other person, and it would not have served his needs had he not personally undertaken the tremendous burden of the actual task of co-ordination. Ickes has confessed that he felt embarrassed presiding over that Committee on Allotments in the White House with the President sitting there as a member of the committee. He has also indicated that the presence of the President in all probability was persuasive in holding down fights and preventing the creation of cliques. Once Ickes and Morris Cooke voted "no" against all the others, but most of the time the committee was unanimous.

About this time the President began to listen more and more to those of his advisers who thought that the emergency agencies should be subsumed as rapidly as possible into the regular establishment of the government and that the departments and agencies should begin to prepare their estimates for regular budgetary appropriations. He was getting tired of having to do it all himself.

From President Roosevelt himself, in many conversations in 1936 and after while I was chairman of the President's Committee on Administrative Management, I learned that in his mind the series of experiences with the Executive Council, the National Emergency Council and its divisions, and the five-ring circus brought him to the conclusion that something ought to be done to give the President more effective control over the general management of the government.

However, the same problem was under almost constant discussion in places less concerned and much less important than the White House. In some of these conversations I had a part. The general notion of how to improve management in government—local, state, and federal—was the warp and the woof of my daily work in the Public Administration

[325]

Clearing House. In its more particular manifestations the subject, of necessity, was given greater emphasis in three particular groups with which I was continually in contact.

One was the Commission of Inquiry on Public Service Personnel, and another was the Public Administration Committee of the Social Science Research Council. The third was the National Resources Board, nee Planning Board, of which I was not a member but the meetings of which I usually attended; also, I was in constant touch with many of its members and staff. Here, again, especially when the discussion of the co-ordination of varying phases of resources planning would arise, there would be the inevitable questions: How are these things to be run? Who is to run them? What machinery will he require to run them well? Again it was apparent, at least so far as the federal government was concerned, that the final responsibility for running the show would be on the President of the United States.

The problem was how to give him authority over the establishment commensurate with his responsibility for its end product. Members of the National Resources Board (which became the National Resources Committee) began to discuss this central problem with President Roosevelt at several meetings in the spring and summer of 1935. The vice-chairman of the National Resources Board sat on the Advisory Committee on Allotments, which was the Ickes ring of the circus set up within the White House with the President at the table.

At one of these White House conferences with the members of the National Resources Committee, the President asked Dr. Merriam particularly to submit a memorandum on the subject. At the time the phrase we usually employed to denominate this subject was "over-all management." Sometimes we used the word "supervision" rather than "management," and sometimes the preceding adjective was "top" or "general." And then many of us developed a habit of using two adjectives and speaking of "over-all administrative management."

In October, 1935, Dr. Merriam prepared the memorandum on a "plan for a plan," which President Roosevelt had requested. Since it was the first recorded official document in the series which led up to the creation of the President's Committee on Administrative Management, and since I had an active part in its preparation, revision, and final draft, I shall set it out in full as it was approved by the advisory committee and as it was later submitted to President Roosevelt:

The President's Committee on Administrative Management

One of the greatest assets of America is that of executive skills, sometimes developed in industry, sometimes in education and engineering, sometimes in the domain of government. The city manager, the large scale industrial executive, the national executive officer, are examples of leadership which have justly attracted attention everywhere.

From the point of view of national planning of natural and human resources, it is evident that management is of fundamental importance. Management and administration are national resources of incalculable importance, highly developed in various sections of our national activities. Our resources have meaning and effect in proportion to the skill with which they are managed by those responsible for their administration. In particular it is clear that it is important to canvass with the greatest care the arrangements by and through which the planning function and agency can best fit into and be more effective in our national organization. The National Resources Committee is conceived as a general staff to the Executive and in order to be most useful must be adjusted with the greatest pains to the other technical functions and agencies of the going concern known as administration.

The organization, development, and position of the American Executive is one of the great contributions of American genius; and the continuance and development of this agency is one of the brightest prospects of modern democracy. It is important, however, that the Executive office be developed on the side of management and administrative supervision as well as on the political side if its full possibilities are to be realized in our national affairs.

The political relations of the Executive are organized in the political parties and its officials, in the party caucus in the Congress and the various congressional leaders, and in the Cabinet, reflecting representative political leadership. These relations seem likely to go forward with relatively little change, and in any case require special and separate consideration.

The technical services, however, present a different problem in view of the rapid increase of functions, the development of specialized ability, the increasing number of industrial and scientific contacts, the necessity for continuity in administration, and a form of over-all administrative supervision or management. Steps have already been taken on the personnel side in the establishment of the merit system and the civil service commission; on the fiscal side through the establishment of the budget director and the comptroller general; and in the coordination of long-time planning policies through the National Resources Committee.

It would be possible to make a thorough study of this whole problem as it develops in American public life—a study directed toward the institutional arrangements, general understandings and practices which would most effectively aid the Executive in the double task of management plus political leadership and direction.

Should the National Resources Committee request the Public Administration Committee of the Social Science Research Council to make a study of management in Federal Administration? (Reporting December, 1936?)

[327]

Such a study might involve, roughly an examination of the trends, emerging problems and possible rearrangement of such national services as are directed primarily toward what may be called management in the larger sense of the term. The research would go back some distance—perhaps to the Civil War period when the work of government began to expand rapidly—reviewing the development of functions and mechanisms and the problems arising in their growth and interrelationship.

The Committee suggested above is already engaged in the task of contemporary observation of the Works Progress Administration on its administrative side, and in a series of research studies in the field of public administration, and it might be persuaded to broaden the scope of its inquiry, if requested to do so by the National Resources Committee—with the understanding that the report was to be made in November or December of 1936, in order that it might have a non-political setting and effect.

This Committee has as its chairman Louis Brownlow, who has had long experience in Washington (D.C. Commissioner under Wilson); has had wide journalistic experience and is now director of the Public Administration Clearing House. The services of technicians such as Lewis Meriam, Arthur Macmahon, Lindsay Rogers, Leonard White, Colonel Henry M. Waite, and others with wide knowledge and experience would undoubtedly be available for such a study. In addition the judgment of a number of men with wide experience in management, political and industrial, might be solicited and utilized in such a manner as to give great public weight to the finds and recommendations of the Committee.

At that time the National Resources Committee consisted of a Cabinet committee under the chairmanship of Secretary Ickes, although its active work was carried on by an advisory committee whose members were Mr. Delano, chairman, Dr. Merriam, vice-chairman, and Dr. Wesley C. Mitchell.

Mr. Delano sent the Merriam memorandum on to Mr. Ickes on October 30, 1935, accompanied by the following memorandum:

I attach herewith a memorandum which was written by Dr. Charles E. Merriam and which he handed to me to consider. It refers to a study of important problems of city, state, and national government by a group of experts which has been set up in Chicago. You know the men connected with it and have, I am sure, as I have, a high opinion of their accomplishments.

Dr. Merriam thinks it would be very desirable to have the study, which he has indicated here made, and it will cost at least $100,000, and perhaps $150,000 or $200,000. The National Resources Committee has no funds to have this study made, and I dare say that it would be advisable that it should be made entirely outside of our framework. On the other hand, you or the President might think it was a mistake to encourage the Brownlow group to make this study. I personally am in favor of it, with only one condition—

that the results of this study be made public *after* the November election of 1936.

Will you kindly think over the problem and let me hear from you?

Mr. Delano and Dr. Merriam also discussed the matter directly with the President. My diary, under date of November 13, 1935, contains the following entry:

"Dr. Merriam told me that Mr. Delano, chairman of the National Resources Committee, had taken the matter up with the President and that the President expressed himself as being very much interested. The President also said that he was interested in having a study made of the possibilities of reorganization of the several departments, commissions, and agencies of the Federal Government; that this ought to be undertaken by some non-governmental agency, and that he might possibly ask the Public Administration Committee of the Social Science Research Council to undertake that task also with the understanding, of course, in the case of both studies, that no report would be expected until after the election, so as not to involve the thing in the politics of the forthcoming campaign. The President said that he could think of no better body than our Committee to undertake the work.

"I told Dr. Merriam that he might tell Mr. Delano to say to the President that my Committee already had passed in principle upon the first study, and that we would be glad indeed to receive his request to proceed with it; that with respect to the second study, Mr. Delano could say that the Committee had not yet considered it, but that I would place it before the Committee at its meeting in Atlanta in the last week of December with the recommendation that it be favorably acted upon. I am quite sure that it would be possible to finance the first study, that of the reorganization of the White House staff and its relation to the problem of over-all management administration. I hope that it will be possible to finance and staff the study into the operations of the offices of the Comptroller General and the Bureau of the Budget.

"I am not at all clear as to how it would be possible in such a short time either to finance or to staff the big study in the reorganization of the entire Federal Governmental structure."

Thus, for the first time, so far as I was concerned, the subject of reorganization of the departments and agencies of the executive branch was introduced into the discussion. Up to that time the project I had talked about with the persons in the several groups with which I was associated, formally or informally, was concerned exclusively with the problem of over-all co-ordination in top management or what we had gradually come to call "administrative management." We had not contemplated a detailed study of departmental and agency reorganization, nor, indeed, had we thought of the chief problem as one of reorganization at all, except insofar as some reorganization might be required the better to equip the President with the staff agencies necessary for him to run the huge and intricate governmental machinery for which, under the Constitution and the laws, he was responsible. It will have been noted that my first reaction was to shy away from the detailed departmental reorganization task, perhaps partly on account of money, partly on account of the size of the task. As far back as 1933, those of us in what may be called the specialized public administration group were giving great emphasis to the need for the establishment of better central management machinery, and some of us had some doubts about the practical utility of detailed studies of departmental and agency organization. In fact, I, at any rate, was inclined to the belief that such detailed reorganization studies ought to be made by some central staff agency directly under the President as a continual and continuing process. To illustrate what was in the minds of some of us, it is interesting to read a memorandum prepared by Mr. Lewis Meriam of the Brookings Institution for Dr. Charles E. Merriam in October, 1935. In fact, I doubt that our group opinion concerning the two types of studies proposed was ever better expressed than in the concluding paragraph of the Lewis Meriam memorandum:

> To some observers of public administration in the United States such a study seems infinitely more promising than any new study of the reorganization of the administrative departments because reorganization is static whereas Presidential control of the administrative departments must be dynamic.

While this general problem was the subject of some further conversations by the President with Mr. Ickes and Mr. Delano, no further action was taken until December.

In mid-December, I attended a meeting of the advisory committee of the National Resources Committee in Chicago, called by Mr. Delano. The other members present were Mr. Delano and Dr. Merriam, Wesley C. Mitchell having resigned early in December (eventually to be succeeded by Beardsley Ruml and Henry S. Dennison). I was accompanied to this meeting by Mr. Joseph P. Harris and Mr. Charles S. Ascher, director of research and secretary, respectively, of the Public Administration Committee (of which I was chairman) of the Social Science Research Council.

In my diary of that date (December 15, 1935) I wrote: "Mr. Delano said that he had had some further discussion with President Roosevelt with respect to the study of a general staff for the White House, and the President had again indicated that he was much interested."

At that Chicago meeting, I presented to the National Resources Committee a suggested letter from that committee to the President. It stated that, if the President would indicate his interest and his desire for this study to go forward through the Public Administration Committee, I would again take the matter up with that committee at its meeting in Atlanta on December 29. This letter was approved by the advisory committee and, signed by Mr. Ickes, transmitted to the President on December 20, 1935.

Some of us had fallen into what turned out to be a very bad habit of using the phrase "general staff for the White House" instead of "staff agency for the President," a circumstance that caused a great flutteration in the dovecot in the West Wing of the White House.

Mr. Delano afterward told me that one of the President's secretaries, Mr. Marvin H. McIntyre, was considerably agitated. He took the notion that "Uncle Fred" was moving in entirely too close to the center. He seemed to suspect the venerable Mr. Delano of a design for planning a "New Deal" among the President's personal secretaries.

Some time later Mr. McIntyre confirmed this impression of Mr. Delano to me, and I was at some pains to soothe his ruffled feathers and to tell him that ours was a bigger and somewhat more comprehensive plan.

The Public Administration Committee met in Atlanta during the week between Christmas and New Year's on the occasion of the annual meeting of the American Political Science Association. The committee meeting had plenty of work to do, and it was considerably helped in sticking to its knitting by the fact that nobody could leave the hotel on account of the worst blizzard and ice storm in Atlanta's history. But I, other members as well, and the committee staff all were on tenterhooks because there was no word from the White House. We could not find out whether or not we were to get the green light from the President. I attempted to telephone Mr. Delano, but the ice storm had interfered with telephone service, and it was a long time before I was able to get through to him.

At last I got a telegram from Mr. Delano saying that the President had made no decision.

Some of us had been so sure—too sure, as the event proved—that the committee would be asked to make the study that we had gone ahead with tentative plans. Indeed, in Washington on December 16 I held what was called "A Conference on a Study of Over-all Management in the Federal Government." The others present were Mr. Harris, the research director; Mr. Ascher, the secretary; and Mr. Lewis Meriam, the vice-chairman of the committee. We decided that this over-all management study should be delegated to a special committee with me as chairman, Lewis Meriam as vice-chairman, and Luther Gulick, Harold W. Dodds, and Lindsay Rogers. It was to be supported by an advisory committee composed of Clarence Dykstra, Arthur Holcombe, Winfield Riefler, Walter Sharpe, James Hart, John Gaus, John Fairlie, and Edwin Cottrell.

The conference agreed with my statement that the study should be concerned with the central problems of devising means to enable "the President to exercise executive supervision, and should not go into internal administration . . . but might concern the broad question of the functions of the departments and their relations with the President."

This special committee was to be provided with an executive director, and two names were suggested for the position: Clarence A. Dykstra and Luther Gulick.

This forehandedness may not have been altogether lost motion, as things turned out, but the Public Administration Committee of the Social Science Research Council never got the presidential nod.

In Washington on January 2, 1936, Mr. Delano, Dr. Merriam, and I went to see Secretary Ickes. Mr. Ickes said that the President had been so busy that he had not had time to determine his plan of action, and, as Mr. Ickes was about to set out for Puerto Rico, he asked Mr. Delano to follow up with his distinguished nephew.

I found myself in Washington on January 18 and 19 to attend a meeting of the National Resources Committee. For the first time as formally appointed members Beardsley Ruml, of R. H. Macy and

Company, and Henry Dennison, of the Dennison Manufacturing Company, met with Dr. Charles E. Merriam, Chairman Frederic A. Delano, and me. We again were told by Mr. Ickes that the President had not made up his mind.

Then, in Washington on January 31, Mr. Ickes said that he had again talked with the President and that the President still desired the Public Administration Committee to go through with the project, but that he did not want it started until a little later and, therefore, would not send the letter of authorization and direction until March 15.

On February 8 Mr. Ickes wrote to the President to tell him what I had said about the difficulty of delay, especially as we had not yet the funds in hand to do the work. On February 20 Secretary Ickes, Mr. Delano, and Dr. Merriam saw the President. With them was the Executive Director of the National Resources Committee, Charles W. Eliot II. That afternoon Mr. Eliot, as was his custom, dictated a confidential memorandum concerning the conference. The pertinent paragraphs follow:

When we entered, the President asked if this was the shakedown to get some more money. Mr. Delano explained he had hoped to present Mr. Dennison and Mr. Ruml, but that in their absence we wished to proceed with the further discussion of the Government Management Study. The President reiterated his belief that politically the name of Rockefeller in connection with such a study would have a bad effect on the Hill. As an example, he made some reference to the recent reports of the Brookings Institution. Upon Dr. Merriam's suggestion that the Spelman Fund had been asked to assist municipalities, the President remarked that the city problem was much more universal and therefore possible to handle as a single problem in all parts of the country, whereas State problems differed widely in different sections, and that in the Federal field he was afraid of theoretical suggestions.

In connection with theoretical suggestions, he referred to Secretary Wallace's proposed "Elder Statesmen." The President then commented on the English Cabinet's experience—the growth during the War to thirty-three departments, later cut down to about twenty-two, and the development within the Cabinet of the executive committee. He remarked that he would not wish Mr. Brownlow's committee to recommend adoption of that procedure for this country, because he might have another idea. As a second example he discussed the current proposal for four or five assistants to the President, or Assistant Presidents, through whom the President might channel his requests and reports for various Federal activities. Again he repeated that if Brownlow's organization favored such a set-up and he had a better idea, the public effect of a disagreement would make impossible any action because of the difference in the recommendations. . . .

Dr. Merriam pointed out that through an outside agency some things could be said much more effectively than if they came from the President, as, for instance, comments on the arrogation of policy powers by the Comptroller General and the proper use of Executive orders and the delegation of Congressional powers. If the President himself discussed these matters, it would almost inevitably be interpreted as a reach for more power for himself. . . .

Dr. Merriam suggested that Brownlow be asked to prepare a precis on certain subjects which might be included in the report. . . .

The President restated his intention to submit to the Congress a message near the end of the session in which no action would be requested, an informative message, as he described it,—in which procedure for a study of Government reorganization or management would be explained to the Congress. Mr. Eliot restated the original suggestion of a request to the National Resources Committee for such a study with the understanding that the Resources Committee would in turn ask Mr. Brownlow's committee or other experts to prepare parts of the material. The President requested the submission to him of a draft for his message, with variations, and in simple language, from which he could compile a form of expression suitable to his purposes. He discussed the possibility of naming a committee to include the advisory group of the National Resources Committee, plus Brownlow, and plus one or two others—this total group to be set up as a special board but financed by the National Resources Committee.

Dr. Merriam and Mr. Eliot wrote to me in Florida where I was taking a vacation. No secretarial or stenographic services were available to me there, and I knew, of course, of the President's notion—one that he had got from Woodrow Wilson—that no memorandum for him ought to be longer than one page. So I wrote the précis, as it had been called, in pencil on hotel stationery one day toward the end of February and sent the original to Merriam in Washington.

Some persons who have read it have commented on the fact that this document, which was entitled "Rough Notes on Kind of Study Needed," bears a strong family resemblance to the final report of the President's Committee on Administrative Management. And for that reason I set it out here in full. Actually, when it was typed in single space (with narrow margins), it was but one page long.

What is needed is a careful study of the managerial and administrative relationships of the President to *all* the far flung and complicated agencies of the Federal government. After all the President is responsible in fact if not always in law for all of them and cannot escape that responsibility. The recognition of this central fact makes it impossible to devolve his prerogative.

In its exercise he must work with and through staff agencies for the control and direction of fiscal, personnel, planning, legal(?) [*sic*] aspects of *all* agencies (including those charged with performing staff functions). This relationship may differ in its mechanics as among (1) staff, (2) operating, (3) regulatory agencies; and again as the administration of each is (1) centralized, (2) regionalized, (3) decentralized with or to the states or other selective and non-national agencies.

Over-all management requires coordination of all these relationships to make effective the President's responsible control but without depriving him of coordinated information and recommendations and without adding to his burdens and by diminishing the number of agencies reporting directly to him.

Always (almost) in our country when in local, state, or federal government a new activity is set up we also set up a new agency. At first there is the advantage of enthusiasm and devotion which later disappears under the disadvantages of *competition* for attention and the other bitter fruits of failure to coordinate with other related (although sometimes but obscurely related) activities.

Some of the problems are tending to center in the expression by the President of the executive direction under authority of Congress in Executive Orders. The process of preparation and publication of these, leaving initiation where it is in the interested agency, but with the effect on all other agencies considered, is a major problem.

The budget-expenditures and revenues
The accounting and auditing problem
The planning problem
The personnel problem
The legal problem

In retrospect, I am particularly proud of one thing in this document: in its second paragraph when I described the staff agencies as having to do with "fiscal, personnel, planning, legal(?) aspects of *all* agencies," I had sufficient foresight to put an interrogation point in parentheses after the word "legal."

All this detail that I have set out about the origins of the study of administrative management in the federal government may seem to be but the dry bones of a skeleton, without flesh and blood or brain; it may seem to be nothing but a piling-up of mechanistic trivia; it may seem to have little or nothing to do with the problems of people in their daily lives, but to some of us that was not so. Dr. Merriam and I, especially, were deeply concerned about the increasing threats to the survival of the democratic political system, not only in Europe, but in the world. Few seemed to share our apprehension, but during the summers I spent with him in Europe in 1930, 1932, and 1934, we had seen, or thought we saw, a new challenge to the whole democratic system. We also thought that the individuals and the groups who were denying the validity of the essential concepts of democracy were at the same time succeeding to a large extent in persuading the democrats in all the democratic countries to accept not their own basic definitions of democracy but new definitions invented by the enemies of democracy. And furthermore, in our own country as in other democratic countries, we were seeing democracy defined as an endless debating society, as a form of organization that was futile and futilitarian and that inevitably selected governments which would not, could not, act. It was our belief that the presidency of the United States was the institution around and behind which democrats might rally to repel the enemy. And, to that end, it was not only desirable but absolutely necessary that the President be better equipped for his tremendous task.

On February 29, I got a telegram from Senator Harry F. Byrd of Virginia. Senator Byrd told me that he had been appointed chairman of a Senate committee on reorganization of the executive agencies and that he would like to talk with me about the committee's program as soon as possible.

I got to Washington on March 3 and talked that day with Dr. Harris, Mr. Ascher, Mr. Eliot, and others concerning the special committee, which the President had talked about on February 20, to take over the study now that he had come to the conclusion that it would not be politically expedient to use private funds for the purpose. This study, as we understood it, was to deal with over-all management. I also talked to them about the proposed Senate committee which, we assumed, would deal with the problems of departmental and agency reorganization.

The next day (March 4) I went to see Senator Byrd. He told me that the Senate was about to set up a special committee of five, of which he was to be chairman, to make a study of the reorganization of the federal government with special reference to overlapping and conflicting functions and the simplification of the governmental structure. I then told him about the conversations that had been going on with the President since the previous October about a study of the problem of general over-all management. He thought there would be no conflict between the two projects.

He asked me to serve as chairman of an advisory committee to his committee along with Luther Gulick, Harold W. Dodds, president of Princeton University, Tudor Gardiner, former governor of Maine, and perhaps two or three other members; and he asked me to suggest other names to him not later than the following week.

Senator Byrd discussed with me also the problem of staffing his committee. I told him that in view of the fact that both Gulick and I would be fully occupied with the task of the proposed President's committee, I believed it would be better for him to make arrangements with the Brookings Institution, which had both the staff and the experience to qualify for an intensive study of departmental organization. This he said he would attempt to do and upon my request authorized me to so inform the President.

After leaving Senator Byrd, I went back to talk with Mr. Delano. While I was there the White House telephoned to say the President would like to see me.

My diary for that day says:

"At 2 o'clock I went to the White House, saw the President immediately, and was with him for an hour and fifteen minutes. I told him of my conversation with Senator Byrd. He seemed to be very much pleased and said he was very glad that I had told Senator Byrd as much as I had about his plans and he only regretted that he hadn't been able to see me before I went to see Senator Byrd, because if he had he would have authorized me to have shown Senator Byrd all of the documents. We discussed in considerable detail the problem of over-all management in the Government, the relation of the President to the staff agencies, the line agencies, and the regulatory bodies, and found ourselves in quite close agreement as to the nature of the problem.

"Essentially the problem is how to implement the President with simple but effective machinery which will enable him to exercise managerial direction and control appropriate to the burden of responsibility imposed upon him by the Constitution.

"We agreed, however, that the spring board was to say that the time had come to consider the new agencies created during the emergency, and, to the extent that they were to be made permanent, how to fit them into the regular establishment; that to do this adequately would require a study of the regular establishment itself and the relationships and lines of responsibility from the several agencies up to the President.

"I said that it might be possible for his committee to work on the main problems of management and relationships and devolve upon the Senate committee to do the more detailed examinations into the overlappings and conflicts.

"I suggested at one time that perhaps it might be wise to get Byrd's committee to make a special study of the Comptroller General's office. He said that would be all right but that he doubted if there was anybody at Brookings who could do that, but if Byrd would not confine himself to Brookings we could get Gulick to let him have Eugene Buck, that Buck was the man to do that and he was sorry that John Edy, assistant director of the budget, had left to become city manager of Toledo because he thought Edy would be of great help to Buck in that particular problem.

"He said, without suggestion from me, that the Bureau of the Budget had never exercised its functions with respect to continuing examinations of the organization because it had been led astray by General Dawes' decision that the Budget Bureau should keep a small staff and thereby be an example of economy to other bureaus; that this precedent established by Dawes had been followed by all of the other budget directors, and that the Bureau of the Budget never had been adequately staffed to enable it to do the work it does undertake, much less to undertake the other job. At the end, the President said that if he took no action until the Senate Committee came to see him that two things would happen, that it might appear that the Senate Committee had forced his hand, although as a matter of fact, he had been considering this problem for months, and that it would leave the House of Representatives out. Therefore, he asked me what I thought of his writing a letter to the Vice-President and the Speaker of the House saying to both of them that he had been working on this problem since October and intended to appoint a committee to make the study from the point of view of the Executive Branch; saying to the Vice-President that the Senate already has appointed such a committee, and invite through that committee the cooperation of the Senate, and saying to the Speaker that he invite the House of Representatives to appoint a similar special committee through which the House of Representatives could collaborate with him and his committee in the study.

"He asked me to draft letters to the Vice-President and the Speaker of the House and to discuss the matter with Mr. Delano and Dr. Merriam. Later in the afternoon, I did draft the letters, discussed them with Mr. Delano in person and with Dr. Merriam who was in Chicago, over the telephone. Mr. Delano is to take the letters to the President Friday morning.

"With the letters I sent a short memorandum in which I made bold to suggest that this device of writing the letters to the presiding officers of the two Houses of Congress instead of sending the formal message to Congress, which he had been considering, would undoubtedly enable him to capture the leadership of the movement so far as present publicity was concerned, but that I thought he ought still to consider whether or not it would not involve him too much with the two separate houses of Congress during the time the study was to be made, and I was bold enough further to suggest that before determining this question he talk the matter over with Mr. Garner (the Vice-President) and Mr. Byrns (now the Speaker of the House of Representatives).

"During the conversation the President said to me that he had decided on the composition of the Committee, that he thought it ought to be very small, and that the Committee would consist of Mr. Delano, Dr. Merriam, and me.

"I had not been sufficiently informed with respect to the previous conversations to hazard any counter suggestion, but I told him I would discuss it with the other two men.

"I did so discuss it. Mr. Delano said that he thought the President was wrong and that he personally should not be a member of the committee, that he would work with it, but that he ought not to be on the committee on account of his relationship. Dr. Merriam said that the committee was too small and that it ought to be enlarged to at least five, and that he thought the committee would be very much stronger if it included such men as former Governor Frank O. Lowden, Ralph Budd, Owen D. Young, Harold Dodds, and Luther Gulick. Mr. Delano undertook to carry back to the President our impressions with respect to the composition of the committee.

"It was clear that the President wanted to use the thought and experience of the membership of the Advisory Committee of the National Resources Committee. It was equally clear that he did not want to use the National Resources Committee itself because that would include certain members of the Cabinet and not others, and that the Cabinet members of the National Resources Committee would think it invidious if he selected the entire Advisory Committee, and for that reason he had determined to exclude Mr. Ruml and Mr. Dennison.

"It will be necessary for me to have further conversations and at a later time to dictate another memorandum which will be concerned with the actual administrative problems which the President discussed."

A meeting of the advisory committee of the National Resources Committee was scheduled for March 14, and, in view of the fact that the whole management study project had originated in that committee, I had deemed it necessary to get as far forward as possible with the plans for the work of the President's committee and the proposed division of labor between the President's committee on the one hand, dealing with over-all management, and the Senate and House committees, dealing with departmental and agency organization. To that end, I went to Chicago, talked the problem over with Dr. Merriam, and by telephone made engagements with Senator Byrd, Joseph W. Byrns, speaker of the House of Representatives, and the President. My diary on March 13 tells that part of the story:

"The newspapers this morning carried a story concerning the preliminary meeting of Senator Byrd's Committee and a statement by Senator Byrd that it intended to set up an Advisory Committee, which would include such persons as Luther Gulick, of the Institute of Public Administration, Harold W. Dodds, President of Princeton University, and myself.

"I went to the White House at noon and met Senator Byrd, who was just leaving after having seen the President. He said that he had had a satisfactory interview and that he was confident that the President's Committee and his Committee could work in harmony and that the President would try to get the House of Representatives to set up a special Committee, similar to the Senate Committee and it probably would name either the same Advisory Committee or at least make arrangements for overlapping membership. He said that the President had approved his Committee's choice of the Brookings Institution to carry on the research for it.

"I then saw President Roosevelt for a few minutes and he told me about his conversation with Senator Byrd and that he intended to send drafts of letters to the Vice-President and the Speaker of the House to

The President's Committee on Administrative Management

Senator Byrd for revision and suggestions. He said these letters would get to Byrd on Monday and that Byrd and I could go over them together. He hoped that the plan would result in my becoming Chairman of each of the three Advisory Committees and that with me in this position we ought to be able to work out a division of labor so as to avoid unnecessary duplication of effort and competitive attitudes.

"In the afternoon I went to Senator Byrd's office and met there Mr. Harold G. Moulton of the Brookings Institution with Mr. Fred Powell of his staff. Senator O'Mahoney and Dr. Clark of the University of Nebraska also came in. Senator Byrd told us that his Committee had agreed on the personnel of the Advisory Committee which is to be composed of me as chairman, Mr. Gulick, Mr. Dodds, William Tudor Gardiner, former governor of Maine, and Professor Clark of the University of Nebraska, formerly of the University of Wyoming. Senator Byrd asked the Brookings Institution to undertake the research task for his Committee. In the discussion, I suggested that the President's Advisory Committee would be more particularly concerned with the management feature and that the Senatorial Committee, with the House Committee if it is set up, might consider more particularly the detailed work of the several agencies of the Government in conformity to the approach outlined in the Senate resolution. Mr. Powell said that there were distinct problems and he thought that it would be possible to work out a division of labor on these general lines, provided the staffs maintained close contact."

On the next day, I reported to the advisory committee of the National Resources Committee. Those present were Mr. Delano, chairman, Dr. Merriam, Beardsley Ruml, Henry S. Dennison, and Charles W. Eliot II. My report, which was later given the title of "Management Study," was approved.

The story is continued in my diary of Monday, March 16:

"I accompanied the members of the Advisory Committee of the National Resources Committee to the White House. In the course of the conversation with the President he asked me for suggestions of two other names to serve on his Committee with Dr. Merriam, Mr. Gulick, and me. He was particularly anxious to get Governor Lowden to serve and asked me to communicate with the Governor. He gave me the drafts of the proposed letters to the Vice-President and the Speaker of the House and asked me to get Senator Byrd's suggestions.

"Later I went over with the members of the National Resources Committee the possible names for our Committee and we agreed to include Governor Lowden if he would serve, but to reserve action with respect to any other names until later, as the time is so short before the President leaves for Florida Thursday that it is difficult to carry on any negotiations with persons who might be acceptable."

On Tuesday, March 17, the diary reads:

"I saw Senator Byrd early this morning and obtained from him some suggestions that he had to make with respect to the letters to the Vice-President and the Speaker of the House and also other suggestions that had been drafted by Senator O'Mahoney. I took these suggestions to the White House and talked them over with Mr. McIntyre and later drafted the letters and sent them over for the President's consideration.

"While I was at the White House I saw Vice-President Garner and Senator Robinson (of Arkansas, majority leader of the Senate) and talked with them very briefly about the proposed set-up for the Committees of the two houses and the President's own Committee.

"A few minutes later I saw Speaker Byrns, who told me the President had been in conversation with him and that he was quite sure that he could get the House to authorize him to appoint a Committee that would work with us. He said that he would select the best possible men he could get to serve and those who would be satisfactory to the President, and that he would like to talk that problem over with me. He said he was sure he could get a House Committee that would not hold hearings until the beginning of the next Congress and that would be willing to appoint an Advisory Committee either identical with, or with overlapping membership, of the Senate Committee, and which would include me."

Both Mr. Delano and I talked over the telephone with Governor Lowden, who was in Chandler, Arizona, recuperating from an illness. We told him what the President had said about how much he valued Governor Lowden's advice in matters of administration and that the President very much hoped he could serve. The next day (March 19) I gave Mr. McIntyre the following memorandum for the President:

Governor Lowden told Mr. Delano and me that his health would not permit him to serve on the Committee. He is ill in Arizona and is going to Baden Baden as soon as he is able.

Mr. Delano and I thought it might be better to name only the three members agreed upon at this moment and then add others that you might select when there was time enough to get their acceptances. Mr. Delano will talk with you further about this.

Speaker Byrns told me that as soon as the House passes the resolution setting up a House Committee he will talk to me about its membership as well as the personnel of its Advisory Committee.

For two or three days I was extremely busy with all sorts of conversations and conferences, in an endeavor to get the President's committee set up and to work out a division of labor with the Byrd committee and the proposed House committee. With Daniel W. Bell, director of the budget, and F. J. Bailey of his staff, it was decided that the committee would be an adjunct of the National Emergency Council, which was authorized by law to study the emergency agencies and how to fit them into the regular establishment. I also had further conversations with members of the staff of the Brookings Institution and asked them for suggestions for a director and members of the staff of the President's committee.

In addition, I had long talks with Speaker Byrns and Representative Bert Snell, Republican leader of the House, about the proposed House committee. Both of them at that time were proceeding on the theory that the House committee when set up would name an advisory committee of which I would be chairman. Thus it was believed at the time that the work of the three committees would be co-ordinated through me as chairman of the President's committee and as chairman of the advisory committees of both the Senate and House committees, but later my name was dropped from consideration by reason of the objection of Mr. Buchanan of Texas, chairman of the House Appropriations Committee, who desired to use his own staff and did not feel an advisory committee was necessary.

On Friday, March 20, the President wrote to me establishing the committee and sent similar letters to Dr. Merriam and Mr. Gulick. The form of this letter is somewhat odd, since it was determined not by the President but by somebody on the staff of Mr. McCarl, the comptroller general, in conference with Mr. Bailey of the Bureau of the Budget, and was deemed by Mr. Bailey and Mr. Bell to be satisfactory to Mr. McCarl.

The President said to me, in discussing it, that he did not like its tone, he did not like its English, and he was not particularly enthusiastic about being compelled, as President of the United States, to submit his letters in advance to the comptroller general. The letter follows:

By this letter of appointment, I am drafting you to serve as Chairman of a Committee, as an adjunct of the National Emergency Council, that would be composed of yourself, Charles E. Merriam, and Luther Gulick, to make a study of the relation of the existing regular organizations of the Executive Branch of the Government, of the many new agencies which have been created during the emergency. Some of these agencies doubtless will be dropped or greatly curtailed, while others may have to be fitted into the permanent organization of the Executive Branch. To accomplish the purpose of such a study and determine the best way of fitting new agencies into the regular organization will require, I think, that your study cover the regular as well as the emergency agencies.

It would be my intention that you should present your report to me in time for submission to the 75th Congress of such recommendations as may be based on the report.

On March 22 the White House announced in a release to the press the appointment of the committee, and, at the same time, released the text of the President's letters to Vice-President Garner and Speaker Byrns.

There was nothing for me to do but to get busy. My diary on March 22 says:

"Luther Gulick came down from New York to talk with me about the work in the field of reorganization of the Executive Branch of the Federal Government. Dr. Merriam was in St. Augustine so that we could not have a full meeting of the President's Committee. Indeed, although I had been advised that the letters of appointment had been signed by the President, neither Gulick nor I had yet received the letters.

"It took considerable time for me to bring Gulick up to date on all that happened, only the high lights of which have been recorded in this diary, and then we addressed ourselves to the problem of what to do. Perhaps the three leading institutions in the country in the field of public administration are the Institute of Public Administration of New York, of which Gulick is Director, the Institution of Government Research in Brookings Institution, both of which are research organizations, and Public Administration Clearing House, which endeavors to work with organizations of administrative officials. That Gulick and I have been called in by the President, by the Senate, and probably will be also by the House, brings these three institutions into a peculiarly close relationship.

"The demand made upon the three institutions by both the Executive and Legislative branches of the Federal government constitutes a major challenge. I am sure that both Gulick and I appreciate the difficulties inherent in the situation.

"Gulick agreed that our Committee would have to work in close cooperation with the Brookings Institution. He also agreed, and I was very glad of this, that the division of labor between the two investigating staffs that I have suggested was practical and realistic, provided there was sufficient liaison between the investigating staffs. This means that the President's Committee will take that part of the field which is concerned with administrative management, and the Brookings Institution will take that part of the field which is concerned with actual operations, especially with respect to consolidations, the elimination of overlapping and duplicating functions, etc.

"Both of us realize that much would depend upon the selection of Chief of Staff for our Committee. Of course, we will have to talk the whole thing over with Dr. Merriam, who may have better suggestions than we were able to develop. At the end, we decided that, if possible, we ought to get Dykstra to take the job with the Chicago group and then throw him into this picture as Chief of staff of the President's Committee; that Dykstra be flanked by Floyd W. Reeves of the University of Chicago, who is now working with Gulick in New York, and who was formerly with the Tennessee Valley Authority; and that Eugene Buck of Gulick's staff be brought in on the fiscal control side of the work, and that he be flanked by Charles McKinley of Reed College, in order to assure that the planning concept be not forgotten in consideration of budgetary problems; that the major staff members ought to be selected as soon as possible in order to have them sit with the Committee in preparing the general plans for the study; that we go ahead with the idea that was originated when it was thought that the Public Administration Committee would handle the job and get Lindsay Rogers of Columbia to bring up to date his studies of the central administrative controls in the English and French governments; and that an effort be made to work with the Brookings Institution in its preliminary planning so as to keep out of each other's way and effectuate the division of labor to which we already have agreed in principle."

The somewhat cryptic reference to Mr. Dykstra pertains to the fact that at that time I was negotiating with him to come to Chicago to be associate director of the Public Administration Clearing House, my principal assistant and presumably my successor.

My diary goes on to say:

"The newspapers carried an announcement of the appointment of the President's Committee this morning and I am already getting applications for jobs on the staff. However, I think that the newspaper attitude generally will be that this is 'just another one of those things' and that we will not be bothered much by publicity. That, of course, will give us an opportunity to do some work and give this whole thing a little better chance for some measure of success."

Then in conversation with all persons concerned we set out in detail what I, at the time, thought was a manageable division of labor. The President's committee was to proceed with the study of the top management by the President of the executive branch of the federal government; the Brookings Institution for Senator Byrd's committee was to proceed from the particular to the general, from the parts to the whole.

It was now the end of March. The work of the President's committee and the Senate committee, as well as that of the House committee not yet established, had to be completed during the nine remaining months of the year, and that of the President's committee, particularly, in time to be presented to the President to form the basis of his message to the Seventy-fifth Congress. Who would be elected President in November no one could say, but if it were a new President, he would come into office on January 20, and Mr. Roosevelt's committee's work had to be done before that time.

Merriam and I were inextricably engaged in enterprises that would require us to spend most of the summer in Europe. Gulick was overwhelmed with the educational inquiry he was conducting in Albany for New York State. There was no time for dillydally or delay. So, I called the first meeting for April 1 in Chicago. My diary says:

"Dr. Merriam, Mr. Gulick, and I met today for the first informal session of the President's Committee on Administrative Management."

Then and there, in quite informal fashion and, I must confess, without consulting the President, we gave the committee a name. The first time that the phrase "administrative management" was used, so far as I can discover, was in the draft of the letter that I prepared for the National Resources Committee already quoted, and it, in turn, was based upon Dr. Merriam's use of the adjective "administrative" as one of a series of adjectives modifying the word "management" set out in his memorandum, also already quoted, in October, 1935. His sentence was: "The technical services, however, present a different problem in view of the rapid increase of functions, the development of specialized ability, the increasing number of industrial and scientific contacts, the necessity for continuity in administration, and a form of over-all administrative supervision or management."

I find that I used the name "President's Committee on Administrative Management" again on April 7, in conversations with Governor Lowden in Chicago, with a good many persons in conversations in Washington and New York on April 9, in the minutes of the second meeting on April 11, in New York and Princeton on April 15 and 16, and, indeed, so frequently that I fear that I had all but forgotten that as yet it had no sanction.

On April 28, I saw the President. My diary says:

"I had about half an hour with President Roosevelt this afternoon discussing in general terms the work of the President's Committee on Administrative Management. Incidentally, he approved that particular title for the Committee. This Committee was set up for technical reasons as an adjunct to the National Emergency Council, but it had not been named. Dr. Merriam, Mr. Gulick, and I had got in the habit of calling it the President's Committee on Administrative Management and I was not a little relieved when I found that the President thought that it was a good title and authorized us to use it officially and formally."

As a matter of fact, that is a very cool record of what actually happened. When I told the President we had already given his baby a name and asked him to bless the christening ex post facto, he threw back his head and said, "Maybe we had better think a little about that." After a moment's pause he called in his secretary, Marvin McIntyre, and said in effect: "Mac, about this committee. You've been griping around here about 'reorganization,' and you don't like it, and there ought not to be any attempt at reorganization. Louis has got a name for it that does not use the word 'reorganization.'"

Mac said, "There ought not to be any committee, but certainly it ought not have any 'reorganization' in the name."

The President said, "Louis calls it the Committee on Administrative Management."

"That's something!" said Mac. "That's getting away from stirring up everybody about whether they are going to be shifted from one place to another."

Then the President asked Stephen Early to come in. He asked Steve what he thought would be the reaction of the press, the public, and the general congeries of things that fall under the vinculum of public relations to this new name for the committee.

Steve, who took a low and dim view of the entire enterprise, finally said that it would be better under that name perhaps than under some other name, but, while he did not say it out loud, his manner showed that he thought nothing ought to be done about it at all.

There had been a memorandum in the correspondence with Mr. Delano saying that one of the things that needed treatment was the White House itself, and so, naturally, skeptical views were taken by these gentlemen who were in the White House. The President did not seem to bother so much about that.

As a matter of fact, this was not merely an exercise in variegated nomenclature. It was a serious business that went to the very heart of the problem. When the matter first came up in the Public Administration Committee of the Social Science Research Council in 1935, the general opinion was that there was no point in such a committee undertaking a task of reorganization, that it was not interested in the shifting of bureaus hither and yon, that it did not deem itself the proper body to sit in judgment on overlappings and duplications, and that under no circumstances would it consider substituting its judgment for that of the President and the Congress in order to give voice to an opinion that this, that, or the other function of government should be abandoned or abolished.

Indeed, when the Public Administration Committee met in Atlanta in December, there already were signs in the Congress, in the press, and elsewhere of a coming demand for reorganization. Taking cognizance of these signs, the committee decided that even if the President were to ask it to undertake a study of the executive branch of the federal government, it would respectfully decline if the purpose of the inquiry were to be reorganization *qua* reorganization.

The committee was unanimous in the opinion that what was needed was an exploration of the ways and means to equip the President the better to carry out the task of the executive top management of the government and a discovery, if possible, of practical ways in which the presidential authority might be made more nearly commensurate with its responsibility.

Later, in his conversations with members of the National Resources Committee and with me in February and March, it was quite clear that what President Roosevelt wanted was the study in the field of top management.

Thus, when Senator Byrd made his proposal and the special Senate committee was set up for the specific purpose of making recommendations on reorganization, I did not hesitate to accept the position of chairman of Senator Byrd's advisory committee. Similarly, the President had no hesitation in agreeing to what we thought at the time was a sharp and clear division of labor. The President's committee was to deal with the over-all machinery of government, with the problems of administrative management, in fact; and the Senate committee was to deal with reorganization, with duplication, overlappings, and the like.

In my conversation with Senator Byrd, I endeavored to make it clear that neither of the committees could go beyond the decisions of the government then in force with respect to what were the proper functions of the government and that neither had a mandate to say that this, that, or the other thing now being done by the federal government should be stopped or turned over to the states or dismissed to voluntary private agencies. The senator expressed his hearty agreement with my views on that point.

Mr. Gulick had been closely associated with Senator Byrd when the latter was governor of Virginia and Mr. Gulick, as head of the Institute of Public Administration, had made a study for the reorganization of the government of Virginia. That study, under the leadership of Governor Byrd, had improved the management of the Virginia government, had resulted in marked economies, and had been regarded by informed and interested persons as one of the more successful efforts ever made to improve the machinery of a state government. Senator

Byrd had been a member of the Board of Trustees of the Institute of Public Administration and also of the Public Administration Clearing House. The senator desired the institute, which had done the work for him in Virginia, to undertake the task for the Senate committee, but Mr. Gulick felt as I had predicted, that his staff was so fully occupied with a survey of the educational system in New York State and that his own time and thought would be so much engaged by his membership on the President's committee that he could not undertake the task. He heartily agreed with me that the Brookings Institution was better qualified to do the work.

Speaker Byrns was very favorable to this whole enterprise, partly because, I think, of his personal relations with me. I had come to know him when he was the speaker of the House of Representatives of the Tennessee legislature and I was the cigar clerk in the Maxwell House, which was the political headquarters in Nashville. Two years later, when, as a reporter for the *Nashville Banner,* I had a seat on the floor of the Tennessee State Senate, Mr. Byrns was there as a senator. And in the following year I was an adviser and press agent for Mr. Byrns in his unsuccessful candidacy for attorney general of Davidson County (a position analogous to that of prosecuting attorney or district attorney in other states). It was Mr. Byrns's defeat in this race that put him in line for his successful candidacy for Congress. During all the intervening thirty-five years, I had kept up my friendship with him.

But the speaker had a tough customer to deal with in the person of Mr. Buchanan, the chairman of the Appropriations Committee, and action by the House was delayed.

To go back to the first of April when the President's committee held its first meeting, it then seemed perfectly clear that its course would be to deal with the problems of the presidency and the task of over-all management and to undertake only such studies of departmental and agency organization as would necessarily be involved in the consideration of how better to equip the President for his administrative responsibilities.

The committee asked Mr. Clarence A. Dykstra, the city manager of Cincinnati, to head up its staff work, but he said that his local situation would keep him from undertaking the task until June. We then asked Dr. Joseph P. Harris, director of research of the Public Administration Committee, to undertake the initial work of organization. It turned out that Mr. Dykstra never came and that what was a temporary assignment to Dr. Harris, already extremely busy with the supervision of a great number of research projects, became permanent. He attacked the task with vigor and carried it to its conclusion with signal success.

As I have said, the President's committee was set up as an adjunct of the National Emergency Council. Early in April Mr. Lyle T. Alverson, then the acting executive director of the council, and his assistant, Mr. Eugene S. Leggett, got from the President an allocation of $40,000 for the work of the President's committee, and arrangements were made to set up its offices in the Commercial National Bank Building at Fourteenth and G streets, which was occupied by the National Emergency Council and in which rooms and office equipment, as well as stenographic, clerical, and mimeograph services were available. Mr. Leggett told me on April 12, so my diary records, that the President's request to the comptroller general for permission to allocate this amount was on Mr. McCarl's desk and was expected to be signed that day or the next.

Upon this assurance, although we had no money, we proceeded to organize a staff. Dr. Merriam, Mr. Gulick, and I had several meetings, talked with Dr. Harris, and at last arranged a meeting to be held in New York on May 9 and 10, of the persons we intended to ask to work on the study.

On May 6, I had lunch with Dr. Harris in the Occidental Restaurant. As we were leaving, Mr. James L. Baity, who was seated at a table with a group of four or five other men, all high officers of the staff of the comptroller general, called out to me, "Louis, Mr. McCarl is going to act on that paper about your committee this afternoon."

"Thank you, Jim," I said. And I was goose enough to think that our financial troubles were over.

But on the next day the bomb exploded. The comptroller general, Mr. McCarl, decided to refuse the allocation, although the President's letter in which he requested it had been drafted in Mr. McCarl's office.

Mr. Leggett, in the meantime, had told a representative of the comptroller general that we had called a preliminary staff conference to meet in New York on May 9, and the comptroller general was gracious enough to say that it would be all right to spend the money for the travel expenses of the persons invited to that meeting. But we could not spend any money on the study itself. In other words, I presume, it would have been quite all right for us to have held $40,000 worth of meetings provided only that we did not do anything.

I went to see the President. He told me that we should not worry too much but should go ahead and do the best we could on a diet of air, water, and travel expenses until he could persuade the Congress to grant the necessary authority for him to use his emergency funds for the committee's work. That that could not be done either easily or quickly he seemed then not to suspect.

In New York on Saturday and Sunday, May 9 and 10, in the offices of the Social Science Research Council, the President's committee met with Dr. Harris and twelve or fifteen political scientists and government officials who had been tentatively invited to serve on the staff. And here again we found some confusion arising out of the varying connotations placed upon words.

All who were there who had sat in on the meetings of the Public Administration Committee were quite clear that the task set was adequately described by the phrase "administrative management," or, if that phrase were insufficient, the subject could be clarified by such additional phrases as "over-all management," "top management," and the like. A good many of the others, who had not sat in on the earlier meetings, were thinking in terms of departmental reorganization, of the shifting and regrouping of bureaus and divisions in the departments and agencies, and many of them could not at first accept the idea of the division of labor between our committee, on the one hand, and the Senate committee and the Brookings Institution, on the other.

I, as chairman, supported by both Dr. Merriam and Mr. Gulick, made it clear that we constituted the President's committee in fact as well as in name, that we were to make our report to the President after the election in November, and that the President would be free to do with it what he pleased. We attempted to make it very clear that this would not have been the case had the study been made by the Public Administration Committee of the Social Science Research Council, as had been formerly contemplated, because in that event the committee and the council would have been free to publish the report, which might have been made without consultation with the President and which would have represented the opinions of the Public Administration Committee itself.

Now, however, under the new arrangement, the committee was

named by the President to advise him and was to be supported by funds made available by the Congress to the President, and, therefore, it was to be understood that neither the committee itself nor any member of the staff would have any proprietary interest in any of the documents, reports, memorandums, or other material that might be developed. We wanted to make it very plain to those present that if they accepted positions on the staff they would be subject to these terms.

We did know, of course, that it would be impossible to get presidential funds for any studies abroad. Therefore, I had set aside Public Administration Clearing House funds to enable Professor Lindsay Rogers to go to Europe to make a study of the central administrative machinery of the governments of Great Britain and France, with the understanding that the resulting document would be his own property but would be made available to our committee. Dr. Rogers was present at the New York meeting, but it was understood that he was not to serve on the staff.

A few of those present said that they did not like these terms and conditions and that, therefore, they would not be interested in joining the staff. Of those present who did accept positions on the staff and others who later were added, only two violated the terms. One distinguished professor either did not understand or affected not to understand. He made a beeline to the White House to see the President; but he did it only once. It certainly did no harm, although I doubt if he ever quite forgave Dr. Merriam and Mr. Gulick or me for the castigations he received at the President's hands. One young woman took the document that she had prepared for the committee, submitted it as a doctoral dissertation, and later published it as a book. The committee had already rejected it, so that did very little harm.

In view of the fact that we were dealing with a very touchy subject with our academic brethren—that of their personal ownership of their own studies—it seems to me now that we came out very well indeed.

Of course, the important thing was that we had promised the President that we would not see him or communicate with him about the subject matter of the study until after the election. In early May, 1936, it was accepted as a fact that President Roosevelt would be renominated, but what candidate the Republicans would name, or what would be the result of the election in November, no man knew.

And as for me, on the morning of May 13, I sailed for Europe.

However, the fact that I was compelled by my engagements to leave the country had no effect on the activities of the committee. Dr. Harris proceeded with the organization of the staff to make the particular studies that had been agreed upon. Dr. Merriam and Mr. Gulick held formal meetings of the committee, and things went on.

But there was no money. Since Dr. Merriam was in Chicago nearly all the time and Mr. Gulick was in Albany, the full burden of the negotiations for funds fell upon Dr. Harris. He was in constant touch with me by cable and with the other two members by telephone. Harris kept a diary in which he meticulously recorded all the happenings every day, and I heard from him with every new mail in London, or Paris, or Berlin, or Warsaw, or wherever I could get the news.

The House of Representatives finally decided to set up a committee under the chairmanship of Mr. Buchanan of Texas, who was also chairman of the Appropriations Committee. Mr. Buchanan was unwilling to set up an advisory committee, which certainly did not disturb me in the least. But what was much worse than that was that he heartily disapproved of the plan to have the President's committee study over-all management. What he wanted was a study which would recommend that certain functions and positions in the government be abolished. Thousands of miles away I trembled at the temerity of Dr. Harris, who, in one of his conversations, suggested to Mr. Buchanan that the Agricultural Adjustment Administration might be abolished. But Mr. Buchanan said no, that was not the kind of thing he meant.

Both the President and Senator Byrd talked with Mr. Buchanan, but he was adamant. The result was that nothing was done until the deficiency appropriation bill was about to be reported to the House. Then, in a last-minute switch, the National Emergency Council was eliminated and the President was authorized to allocate directly to the President's Committee on Administrative Management $100,000, and a clause was added requiring the committee to "ascertain whether the activities of any such agency overlap with the activities of any other such agency and whether in the interest of simplification, efficiency, and economy any of such agencies should be coordinated with other agencies or abolished or the personnel thereof reduced and make recommendations with respect thereto. Copies of the report or reports of such studies and recommendations shall be transmitted to the President and to Congress."

Mr. Buchanan stood his ground and had his way, and the deficiency bill passed both houses on June 18. Then Mr. Buchanan began another series of negotiations with Mr. Harris. The President's committee had had in the beginning an appropriation of $20,000 from its funds, when, as, and if there were any, for the use of the Senate committee. Then, according to the agreement, the President's committee was to apportion another $20,000 from its funds to the House committee. This presumably would have left $60,000 for the use of the President's committee. Mr. Buchanan now proposed that if our committee would grant another $10,000 to the Senate committee for the support of the Brookings Institution study, he would regard that action as fulfilment of the new obligation laid upon the committee by the language of the deficiency appropriation bill. He also attached a proviso that all three members of the President's committee agree to this arrangement. That we did with alacrity—Gulick by telephone from Albany, Merriam, who in the meantime had joined me in Europe, and I by cable. Actually the bill was signed on June 22, and the President then, with full congressional authority, directed the secretary of the treasury to allocate $100,000 from the President's relief and rehabilitation fund to our committee.

Not a few members of the staff already had gone to work knowing quite well that they might never be paid. In fact, Dr. Harris' formal manual of instructions to the staff was issued on June 11. It seemed to us all that we were ready to go. However, there was yet another hurdle. The President's letter of allotment to the committee was signed by the President, but the comptroller general announced that he would consider it in a week or two. Finally, however, Mr. McCarl did acknowledge by his signature the validity of an act of Congress passed unanimously by both Houses and signed by the President. So by the end of June the money was available; the staff continued at work; the Brookings staff went on our committee's payroll, and, meanwhile, Merriam and I, Leonard D. White, Lindsay Rogers, and others pursued our researches in the general field of administrative management in Europe.

CHAPTER XXIX

EUROPEAN INTERLUDE, 1936

During the summer of 1936 we remained in Europe. Both Merriam and I did some chores for the President's committee. Not only was Lindsay Rogers working on his study of the central administrative machinery of the British and French governments, but both Merriam and I were keeping our eyes open to discover anything that would be of value to us in our business of recommending top-management changes in the executive branch of the United States government.

Shortly after the end of World War I the Committee on Imperial Defense set up inside the British Cabinet was converted into a Cabinet secretariat with Maurice Hankey in charge. Much had been said in the United States about the possibility of our following the British example by giving the President a Cabinet secretariat, a proposition that implied, of course, an essential change in the institutional character and responsibility of the Cabinet itself.

This proposition was reinforced by the curious notion, especially widespread among political scientists, that the American government would be better if the presidential system were abandoned and the parliamentary system adopted or at least if every step short of the utter subversion of the constitutional separation of powers were taken that would bring us nearer and nearer to the better British model. While neither Merriam nor I shared this oddly persistent notion, we were impressed, and I think rightly so, by what we had heard of the improvement in top-management practices that had followed the establishment of the Cabinet secretariat in Whitehall.

As a newspaper correspondent, I had been in England during the two hotly contested parliamentary elections of 1910—elections which centered on a radical budget measure introduced by David Lloyd

George, then chancellor of the exchequer in the Asquith government. They had resulted in the House of Lords being moved from an equal body to a subordinate position in the British legislature, with only a suspensive veto over measures passed by the House of Commons. During those campaigns, I had met a then quite young Welshman who was one of the secretaries to Mr. Lloyd George. His name was Tom Jones.

Twenty-five years later, in the summer of 1936, I found him in his office where he presided over the Pilgrims' Trust, the British analogue of the American Carnegie Corporation. In the meantime, he had been private secretary to three prime ministers: David Lloyd George, Ramsay MacDonald, and Stanley Baldwin.

I told Mr. Jones what I was up to, and he gave me a glowing account of the successes of both the Committee on Imperial Defense and the Cabinet secretariat. But, being both a Welshman and a veteran of many parliamentary and ministerial battles, he was inclined to put the emphasis on the man rather than on the institution and, therefore, talked more about Sir Maurice Hankey than he did about the Cabinet secretariat. Then he asked me if I would take a message to President Roosevelt for him, a mission which I gladly undertook. The message was this:

"Tell the President that the way to solve his problem is to find that one man who would turn out to be another Maurice Hankey, a man possessed of high competence, great physical vigor, and a passion for anonymity."

Later, when we rejected the one-man idea and proposed, among other new aids recommended for the President, six administrative assistants, we used Tom Jones's language to describe their qualifications.

Merriam and I began to suspect that some of the credit for the excellent things to be observed in top management in the British government was due not only to Sir Maurice Hankey but also to the fact that the prime minister was frequently a more powerful figure as an individual than he was in constitutional theory. In theory he was merely the first minister to the king, one who presided over a Cabinet composed of himself and other ministers having equally distributed and collective responsibility to the Parliament.

Some weeks later, Merriam and I were on the platform of a railway station in Paris about to board a train for Warsaw. A bookseller's cart came by. On it was displayed a new book by Léon Blum, then the premier of France. Merriam bought it and later that day gave me a free rendering of the French text. The book turned out to be a translation into the French of a series of articles that Léon Blum had written in English in 1919 for publication in the English magazine *Nineteenth Century and After.* These articles on administrative reform in government had appeared anonymously, but, now that M. Blum was prime minister of France, he had translated them back into his native language and had publicly avowed them by permitting them to be printed over his signature.

Merriam and I were much inclined to agree with M. Blum that some of the top management and not a little of the middle-level management in the British government was the result of what the French statesman called "a long and happy series of usurpations" by the British Treasury.

The principal commitments that Merriam and I had made, which compelled us to go to Europe that summer to attend meetings of international organizations in which we were interested, were two: the meeting of the International Union of Local Authorities in Berlin and Munich and the meeting of the International Institute of Administrative Sciences in Warsaw.

A large delegation of Americans was present at both conferences. As the chairman of the Common Services of both organizations at their headquarters in Brussels, I had been represented for more than a year in Europe by Dr. Rowland Egger. His *Directory of International Organizations in the Field of Public Administration* was ready for publication.

The International Union of Local Authorities, the organization of municipal governments and officials, had been holding its plenary conferences every three years. The last had been held in London in 1932, at which a resolution was taken to hold the next one in Berlin. In 1935, however, the governing board of the union was loath to call a conference to meet in Hitlerian Germany. Nonetheless, the German members insisted that the Berlin conference should be held and met the objections, both voiced and unvoiced, by a solemn undertaking that the meeting, to be held for the first few days in Berlin and the latter few days in Munich, would not be interfered with in any way by the officials of the Nazi party or of Hitler's government. Late in 1935 this assurance had been accepted, and the conference was called to meet in the two German cities in the early summer of 1936. A delegation of some twenty Americans was chosen and accredited to the conference by appointment of the United States Department of State. I myself had left a little early, but not until after I had had a conversation in the German Embassy in Washington with the ambassador, Dr. Hans Luther, with whom I had become acquainted several years earlier when he was the executive director of the German Union of Cities. He again assured me that the delegates would find a hearty welcome from the German municipal officials and that there would be no untoward incidents.

Mrs. Brownlow and her sister Mrs. William L. Beale, Sr., of Washington, went to Germany with me. After our visit to London, we went to Brussels, where we were joined by Dr. Merriam, Mr. Ruml, Mr. Egger, Senator Vinck, and his assistant, Mr. René Didisheim, and thence to Berlin. The atmosphere in Berlin was distinctly calmer than on my last visit, in 1934, and the observable tension was almost nil. At the same time, there was no possibility of escaping the all-pervasive Nazi domination. Upon entering a room, every person, even the maid at the hotel, raised his right hand with the salutation, "Heil Hitler." Indeed, "Heil Hitler" had taken the place of every form of polite salutation marking the passing of the time of day.

The convention itself was held in the Kroll Oper, which, after the destruction of the Reichstag building, had been the seat of the German parliament. I, as the accredited head of the American delegation, was given a particular seat. When I assumed it I could not help noticing that the hundreds of German municipal officials, all in uniform, applauded me. It was not until the next day that I discovered the signal honor that had been conferred upon me. I had been given the seat reserved for der Führer, Adolf Hitler, himself.

Actually, the meetings progressed according to program with the single exception that the applause from the overwhelming number of German officials seemed to be concerted and directed, as if led by a cheerleader at an American college football game. One of the speakers representing Germany was Dr. Jeserich, now head of the German Union of Cities. He spoke on the subject of municipal science. Certainly Merriam, Leonard White, Beardsley Ruml, and I, all of the University of Chicago, were greatly amused when this representative of the Nazi centralized power over all municipal government in Germany proclaimed that the one and only genuine municipal scientist in the world was Dr. Louis Wirth of the University of Chicago. Kurt Jeserich had no notion that Louis Wirth was a Jew.

Then it was announced that the chancellor would receive a delegation from the conference consisting of two delegates each from France, the United Kingdom, and the United States and one each from all the other countries represented. This was in violation of the protocol. The convention had not agreed to send a delegation to see Hitler, and, in fact, it had relied upon the assurance that there would be no such contact. Yet, it seemed to be impossible to turn down the invitation. The secretary general, Émile Vinck, suddenly found that it was necessary for him to fly to Brussels for at least a day.

From the United States the two delegates were John G. Stutz, of the Kansas Municipal League, and I. The president of the conference, G. Montagu Harris of England, led the delegation. We were shown into the chancellor's headquarters—not the one later built in which Hitler perished when Berlin fell to Russian arms, but the older chancellor's office in Frederichstrasse.

It, too, was a long rectangular room with a desk in one corner. We went in. Somebody arranged us standing in a semicircle. Then Hitler, who was sitting at the desk in the corner, arose and walked over to greet us. I was standing immediately behind Montagu Harris. Mr. Harris made a formal address, speaking in German, to which Hitler replied in, of course, the same language. It was nothing more than the formal exchange of meaningless pleasantries. But it did take a little time. Almost every person in the delegation stood stiffly at attention, perhaps in either conscious or unconscious imitation of the Germans there who had accompanied the delegation and who were, in fact, in the majority. Mr. Harris was visibly embarrassed by having to go through this routine and he constantly clasped and unclasped his hands, which he held behind him.

But Hitler, as he walked over to greet the group clad in his corporal's uniform, kept his right hand in his trousers pocket and assumed a careless and most unmilitary posture. I touched the elbow of Henri Puget, the Frenchman standing next to me. Neither of us had assumed a rigid aspect. I plunged my hand into my right trousers pocket and so did Puget. Whereupon Hitler put his left hand in his left trousers pocket. Puget and I followed his example. And then as he shifted his weight from one foot to the other, Puget and I followed him in imitation. There is no doubt that he caught the gestures, even if not their significance. There is no doubt that he identified Puget and me as two of the persons who were not totally overwhelmed by the honor he was according us. He made other changes in posture; we imitated; and his blue eyes responded in a twinkle of humor. He was then so much the absolute master of Germany, so certain of his march to the mastery of the world, that he indulged in a little amusement with this byplay with the French and American delegates.

The closing sessions of the conference were held in Munich. It was there that we were entertained in a rich and easy atmosphere, so far as our delegates and our hosts were concerned, with typical Bavarian hospitality in the beer halls, in the theater, in the Royal Palace, and in the tours through the magnificent museums.

The Oberbürgermeister, Herr Feiling, sent a limousine with a chauffeur to be at my command. Dr. Merriam, Leonard D. White, Mrs. Brownlow, her sister, and I decided to stay in Munich a day or two after the conference adjourned. The car was still at our disposal. Its chauffeur, the Oberbürgermeister told me, was none other than the chauffeur of Adolf Hitler himself. The car was the car Hitler used when he came to Munich, and I was constrained to admit in one way or another (at least to the driver and the hotel porter) the high honor thus bestowed upon me.

At the last day of the conference the governing board had a meeting to arrange for the next conference, to ratify the arrangements that were being made in Brussels for the Common Services for the union and the institute. This meeting seemed to be going very well when, all of a sudden, the Germans threw another bombshell. Dr. Jeserich proposed that he be appointed executive vice-president of the union and assume the management and direction of the international headquarters in Brussels. This resulted in no little confusion. Despite the fact that the Germans were our hosts and had showered us with entertainment and civilities, it found no support and was promptly voted down. Thus the conference came to an end in an atmosphere of strain and even of suspicion.

After Munich, Merriam and Leonard White went by rail through Milan with Mrs. Beale, Mrs. Brownlow, and me, and on to Cannes on the French Riviera for a delightful three-weeks' holiday before proceeding to Warsaw. We returned via Paris. There my wife became ill, and, while she soon recovered, the physicians refused to permit her to go to Warsaw. So, leaving Bess in Paris with her sister, Merriam and I went on to the meeting in the Polish capital of the International Institute of Administrative Sciences.

In Warsaw we were joined by a large delegation of Americans headed by Professor Leonard D. White of the University of Chicago, all appointed by Secretary of State Cordell Hull as the official representatives of the United States.

During our three weeks in Cannes we had had a chance to see the great "stay-in" strike, as the French called it—a phrase later translated as "sit-down" strike in the United States—which stopped the railroads, closed the stores and shops, and reduced hotel service, on which we, of course, existed, to a black-market "upstairs" minimum. We also had an opportunity to attend political meetings of the Social Democrats, the Radical Socialists, and the Communists.

What we found in Warsaw was the gulf, wide and deep, between the democratic and the authoritarian modes of thought, a division of power not only in professed theory but in daily practice.

We found the democrats in the center, professing in one way or another, and with varying emphases, the doctrine that governments derive their just powers from the consent of the governed. We found the authoritarians to the right and to the left professing the doctrine that governments require an all-powerful man to tell them and their people what to do and to govern them without obtaining the assent or tolerating the dissent of popular electoral processes.

The Nazis and the Fascists were at the peak of their power, and they had no doubt that their system would prevail; the Communists seemed then, so far as the West was concerned, a minor group, but they were undoubtedly absolute in Russia. In retrospect, Dr. Merriam and I and some of the others who were there often talked about what we saw— the portent of the debacle that was but three short years away. But we did not suspect, of course, any more than did the Germans or the Poles, that within a decade Berlin would be a ruin, Warsaw a shambles, and the threat to the democratic system shifted from the West to the East, from the right to the left. Because I saw then but darkly and since, in retrospect, I might be too greatly tempted to commit the sin of presentism, I shall set down here the story of the "Battle of Warsaw," as we called it, as I recorded it then in my diary:

"The International Institute met at Warsaw on July 9, and lasted until the 16th. There were nineteen countries represented.

"The greater number of the Americans attended Section III, which was devoted to the subject of the staff auxiliary of the chief executive of the national government. This was a subject which was of very great interest to a good many of the Americans, especially to Dr. Merriam and me who are members of the President's Committee on Administrative Management. Reports on the organization of such staff auxiliaries had been sent to the Institute during the last two years from some twenty-odd countries and a general report incorporating the results was presented by Professor Zoltan Magyary of the University of Budapest. At the first session of this section Dr. Magyary read an English summary of his report. At the next session Lindsay Rogers (of Columbia University) led the discussion, and while giving unstinted praise to Magyary for his industry and in large part for the results of his work, ventured to point out some omissions and some varying interpretations. This displeased Mr. Magyary very much, especially as other people then followed in a general discussion. It was not until later that we discovered that it was not the intention to have any frank discussion of this particular paper, and at the next session, Mr. Magyary brought in a resolution which, in English, read as follows:

RESOLUTION

The Sixth International Congress of Administrative Sciences gathered in Warsaw from July 9–16, 1936,

having considered the general report submitted by Zoltan Magyary, Professor of the University of Budapest, Hungary, concerning 'The Chief Executive and his Auxiliary Agencies:' after discussion and on the proposal of the third section

DECLARES

1. the governmental systems of most of the countries exist since times previous to the technical revolution in force since the middle of the 19th century;

2. the evolution of the State apparatus during the last fifty years has involved a definite preponderance of the executive power;

3. in consequence the administrative function of government has developed in such a manner that its importance has equaled in importance its political function;

4. the Chief Executive requires to fulfill his administrative tasks: (a) powers increased by the concentration in his hands of the general administration; (b) a highly specialized auxiliary agency, i.e., civil general staff;

5. that according to the experience and practice of several governments in different fields of public activity, the chiefs of that auxiliary agency should rank immediately next to the Chief Executive 'A VERITABLE EXTENSION OF THE PERSONALITY OF THE CHIEF EXECUTIVE.'

MOVES

I. that the general report presented to the Congress on this subject may be given as wide publicity as possible;

II. that the International Institute of Administrative Sciences may present its report to the governments concerned;

III. that the next Congress should put on its Agenda the question: 'THE STATE AND ECONOMIC LIFE FROM THE POINT OF VIEW OF THE CHIEF EXECUTIVE':

IV. that the International Institute of Administrative Sciences may take the initiative of coordinating and furthering the research concerning this question, which appears to have become one of the key problems of the future.

"The French text, of which the English was a very imperfect translation, was much stronger in that it stated that the evolution of the state during the last fifty years had resulted in a decisive preponderance of the executive power over the legislative and judicial. Immediately after this resolution was presented the section adjourned to meet again later in the afternoon.

"During the interim the American delegation held a caucus and decided that it could not support a resolution which in the first place was not based on the report; which entered into the field of grand politics instead of sticking to the administrative side of government; and third, was a distinct recognition and approval of the totalitarian and authoritarian state. We decided that when the section met again in the afternoon, Dr. Merriam would undertake to state the objections from the point of view of democratic systems in a general way and that Dr. Fairlie (John Fairlie of the University of Illinois) who had been a member of the Institute since its inception and was informed about its history should point out the danger the Institute as an organization was incurring in making an expression of opinion that departed from questions of administration and got into the field of politics.

"When the section met again I took the names of Dr. Merriam and Dr. Fairlie up to the chairman, a Pole, who told me that one other

[364]

speaker already was on the program. When we met he called Professor Mohammed Abdullah al-Araby, professor of administrative law in the University of Egypt at Cairo. As I said later when I was teasing Merriam and Fairlie, the Egyptian started off by making Merriam's speech and then he made Fairlie's speech, and then he led the embattled democratic nations into a head-on attack on the Fascist fortress. When he got through, Merriam got up and said his piece, Fairlie said his, to be followed by the Czech, the Swiss, the Belgian, the French, and the Dutch. There was only one Italian in attendance at Warsaw and he was in another roundtable. The German delegates and the other Hungarian delegates sat silent. Everybody followed the line taken by our Egyptian friend with the exception of the two Poles.

"Suddenly the chairman in French and without giving the interpreter an opportunity to translate his statement into English announced that since no other person had asked for an opportunity to speak to the motion, the resolution was carried and the meeting was adjourned *sine die*. This was on Saturday afternoon, and the printed program had called for more meetings of this section, two meetings on Monday and one on Tuesday. Some of us Americans couldn't understand what the Chairman had said, but fortunately Dr. Merriam, Dr. White, Dr. Rogers, and Dr. Fairlie understood French and arose en masse in protest. The chairman stuck to his decision that there had been discussion, that the resolution was passed because nobody had proposed a definite change, and since nobody else had asked for the floor before adjournment the meeting was over.

"The democrats, led by the Americans and with the support from the other democratic countries, wouldn't take this lying down, and with a barrage of every type of motion known to Jefferson's Manual or Robert's Rules of Order, charge after charge was made until the ruling was reversed. The victors announced that there would be a meeting after all and endeavored to get the chair to put a motion for the appointment of a committee to revise the resolution. The chair's only reply to that was that anybody who wanted to could revise the resolutions and I constituted myself chairman of the committee on revision. On Sunday we had a meeting of this committee and blocked out a revision and then we invited Dr. Magyary to the meeting and he assented. The resolution as revised follows:

A Passion for Anonymity

The Sixth International Congress of Administrative Sciences gathered in Warsaw from July 9–16, 1936,

having considered the general report submitted by Dr. Zoltan Magyary, Professor of the University of Budapest, Hungary, concerning THE CHIEF EXECUTIVE AND HIS AUXILIARY AGENCIES, after discussion of this question, with restrictions against incursions into the constitutional system of the states represented, and on the proposal of the third section,

DECLARES

1. that the functions and administrative apparatus have developed both in depth and scope during the last fifty years, and at a greatly quickened tempo since 1914;

2. that whatever the constitutional system may be, the need for coordination has made itself felt at the same time as the need for efficient organization of the administrative structure;

3. that experience shows that every large-scale organization requires an auxiliary agency to assist the chief executive in conducting general administrative activities;

4. that these auxiliary administrative agencies are, or should be, responsible to the Chief Executive and should act for him. Nevertheless, in designing and applying such a system, it is indispensable not only to insure professional competence, but also to be certain that the principles of stability and permanence are maintained;

MOVES

1. that the general report of the Congress on this subject be given the widest possible publicity;

2. that the International Institute of Administrative Sciences, in particular, should submit it to the governments of its member states;

3. that the next Congress place on its agenda consideration of the 'Technical and Administrative Problems of the Relations between the State and Economic Life from the Viewpoint of the Chief Executive';

4. that the International Institute of Administrative Sciences take the initiative of coordinating and furthering scientific research on this question which appears to be one of the key problems of the future.

"The resolutions which were adopted by the other sections of the Congress were appended. They were adopted without the explosion which attended the session relating to the Chief Executive and his Auxiliary Agencies.

"A non-participating observer at these sessions would have found it very interesting, I think, to witness this head-on collision between the authoritarian and the democratic governments and especially in the end to witness the discomfiture of the authoritarians who, true to the *Führerprinzip,* announced a conclusion and presented the convention with a *fait accompli* only to discover that there was still some life in the old democratic war horse, especially when some democratic practitioners were goaded into delivering some delayed, but effective parliamentary punches."

The bare record of the "Battle of Warsaw" set down at the time is, I dare say, but partly true. What I did not confide in my diary then was the fact that a feeling of fear permeated the very atmosphere; that there was a sense of impending great change that, for some, was the elation of dominance soon to be realized, of power, and irresponsible power, soon to be theirs, and for others, a sense of impending doom, of deepening darkness.

Dr. Zoltan Magyary was furious when delegates from the democratic countries dared to question his report that put the executive power in supreme authority over the legislative and the judicial and that recognized the staff agents of the executive only as veritable extensions of his personality. He had worked for two years on his thesis. He had been in Rome. He had been in many parts of Italy. He had two years earlier spent some months in the United States, in England, and in France.

Democracies were decadent, thought Dr. Magyary. Their parliaments and congresses were mere debating societies. Their prime ministers and presidents were prisoners of quarreling politicians. Their social institutions were crumbling away, and their economies were bankrupt. Witness the Great Depression in the United States, the thousands of idle on the dole in England, the "stay-in" strike in France, the weakening of the armies and the navies of the Western powers. On the other hand, witness the trains running on time in Italy and the draining of the Pontine Marshes; witness the rigorous discipline of the German people. A scholar who had looked at his world and had made a report on its politics and had come to have full faith in authority could brook no questioning. For him, dissent was insult and debate intolerable.

So, when the session ended and his report had not been adopted, Dr. Magyary came up to Professor White, the chairman of the American delegation, to protest. I happened to be standing there.

"I demand that the American delegation disavow the unfortunate intervention of Professor Lindsay Rogers!" screamed Magyary. "I demand an apology from the United States."

I fear that both White and I were so astonished that for a moment neither of us could say a word. Then White replied, "Every member of the American delegation is privileged to say what he desires to say. Furthermore, I happen to agree with Lindsay Rogers."

"I do, too," I put in.

And then we were joined by three or four other Americans attracted by the loud talk and quarrelsome tones.

Later, when the Egyptian professor, schooled by British civil servants in the Sudan and in Egypt, a master of the theory and a veteran of the practice of democratic institutions even under the restrictions of colonial administration and the dubious constitutional basis of the English rule in Egypt, made the defense for all the democrats, we were thrilled and excited just as the totalitarians seemed to be outraged. And when that session was over, the American delegation repaired to the courtyard of the hotel to have their photographs taken, with their Egyptian champion in the place of honor in the center.

But Magyary's fury was not the only reaction to what he called Professor Lindsay Rogers' "unfortunate intervention."

There were two Germans in attendance, Dr. Kurt Jeserich and Dr. Harry Goetz, the director and the assistant director of the German Union of Cities. They had been our hosts at the meeting of the International Union of Cities in Berlin a month earlier, and on this day they had invited the members of the American delegation, as well as those from England, France, and the other countries, to a luncheon at the German Embassy. When the Magyary report was not instantly adopted and debate was demanded, these two gentlemen had a conversation on the telephone with Berlin. Whether they initiated the telephone call or whether it came to them from Berlin I do not know. But Berlin did decree that they could not stay in a meeting where the authoritarian principle was even being debated. So they wrote us notes recalling the invitation to lunch and took the train for Berlin. But they reckoned without their host. The German ambassador at once communicated with us and said that the invitation had come from him, that Jeserich and Goetz had no right to withdraw it, and he urged us to do him the honor to come to the embassy for lunch. Most of us went.

The German ambassador was General von Moltke, the grandson of the great Field Marshal von Moltke. It so happened that Dr. Merriam and I were among the earlier guests at the embassy and, as we stood talking to the ambassador, it turned out that he and Dr. Merriam had been students in the University of Berlin at the same time. This put the conversation on an easy and pleasant basis.

I looked up on the wall and saw a portrait of the great field marshal, and, to make talk, I said, "Your Excellency, that is a portrait of Field Marshal von Moltke I never saw. The one that always stays in my mind is the one of him in a cap looking out of a round window down the Rue de Rivoli."

"Oh," he said, "I like that best, too, and so did he. It now hangs in my wife's boudoir. She is out of the city, and I am sure that we can get away for a moment to see it."

So he led the way, and Dr. Merriam and I followed him upstairs, where we looked at the portrait.

Nothing was said that was not about that picture—nothing touching upon politics either of the Bismarkian–von Moltke era or of the Hitlerian. But the ambassador did say to Dr. Merriam in a tone of regret, speaking English out of courtesy to me, "Oh, how times have changed since our student days!"

That afternoon Merriam and I agreed between ourselves that the ambassador had showed us this courtesy merely to indicate to us that he was no Nazi.

Magyary did not survive the war. When the Russian soldiers came into Budapest, he shot and killed his wife and then killed himself.

Nor did von Moltke. On the night of July 22, 1944, when the plot to kill Hitler failed—a plot that, as we now know, was concocted at a meeting in von Moltke's Silesian country house—on that night von Moltke, the ambassador to Madrid, died, so his subordinates at the embassy reported, of a heart attack.

All in all, Merriam, White, and I and all the others thought that we learned a good deal during those ten days in Warsaw, much of which, as far as Warsaw itself and Poland are concerned, I have set down elsewhere, but a good deal of which later was to appear in the report of the President's Committee on Administrative Management, as witness this paragraph:

A Passion for Anonymity

As an instrument for carrying out the judgment and will of the people of a nation, the American Executive occupies an enviable position among the executives of the states of the world, combining as it does the elements of popular control and the means for vigorous action and leadership—uniting stability and flexibility. The American Executive as an institution stands across the path of those who mistakenly assert that democracy must fail because it can neither decide promptly nor act vigorously.

The question had been posed in Warsaw: Was the chief executive of a modern nation to be absolute or was he to be the freely chosen, democratically controlled, popularly responsible leader of a nation of free men?

CHAPTER XXX

WE REPORT TO THE PRESIDENT

Early in August I landed back in New York and at once began looking toward the preparation of the report which was to be delivered as soon after the November election as possible to the man elected to the presidency—either Franklin D. Roosevelt or Alfred M. Landon.

Not one of us harbored a single doubt that our task amid the gathering world storm was so to strengthen the presidency that the President of the United States might be the better equipped not only to manage the affairs of the government but to defend the freedom of the American people.

The full committee, Dr. Merriam, Mr. Gulick, and I, met usually every alternate week for three or four days, having sessions morning, noon, and night, at which we reviewed in detail with each staff member his or her work.

In addition to these sessions, Merriam, Gulick, and I had many long talks with all but one of the principal men in the federal government. We did not see the President, nor did we communicate with him directly or indirectly. It is true that Dr. Merriam saw him occasionally in his capacity as a member of the National Resources Committee, but care was exercised that on these occasions no word concerning the work of our committee was uttered. We were sticking literally to our engagement not to communicate with the President until after the November election. During that whole summer I myself heard from the President but once, and that was a message through Daniel W. Bell, acting director of the budget, asking me to make suggestions of names for a committee on the fiscal affairs of the District of Columbia, which Congress had authorized and the members of which the President was to appoint. But, while we did not see the President, we saw many members of his official family.

I remember particularly a Sunday when we had in three of the top-ranking career administrators in the federal government: William H. McReynolds of the Treasury; E. K. Burlew of the Department of the Interior; and William A. Jump of the Department of Agriculture. That talk began about ten in the morning, went through midday dinner, lasted all afternoon, through supper, and continued late into the night. I, and I am sure my colleagues also, learned more in that one day about the actual management of the executive branch of the federal government than we could have found out in a whole month in any other fashion.

These three men we had selected, not because of their position in the particular departments they served, but because we had found out that they were generally recognized as perhaps the ablest career administrators in the government and that they were intensely interested in our work and were willing to give us the benefit of their knowledge and experience quite objectively. Mr. McReynolds was working with us, with Dr. Harris, and with other members of our staff almost daily. The other two we could call upon at any minute. There was, during that hot summer in Washington, no truce in the long war that had been waged for five decades between the Department of the Interior and the Department of Agriculture. Yet, here, we had the advice and counsel of the two top administrators of those two feuding agencies, and, aside from an occasional joke or two, not once was the departmental jealousy apparent.

All these men were loyal to their department heads, but in discussing the problems of governmental management with us they rose above the departmental level and gave us most valuable assistance in our task, which was, of course, to look to the top management of the whole executive establishment.

We saw most of the members of the Cabinet, many of them more than once, sometimes in their own offices and frequently in our May-flower Hotel retreat. Most of them—indeed, I think all of them—quite naturally took the departmental rather than the general approach. As a rule, each Cabinet member thought that the ideal reorganization plan would leave his department intact but bring into it, and thus under his control, a bunch of bureaus now unfortunately misplaced and badly managed under the direction of other members of the Cabinet.

Mr. Henry Morgenthau took a dim view of anything being taken away from the Treasury. He was especially fearful that the Bureau of the Budget might go. He thought the Public Health Service should stay. He was a little nervous lest the Secret Service be disturbed.

Mr. Harold L. Ickes had definite views about the Department of the Interior. It should keep what it had, but, of course, it ought to take the Forest Service away from Agriculture. And if pressed, he was willing also to take over the fisheries, the wildlife, and all the other things that might properly be placed in a department of conservation. He had no objection to the changing of the name of his department—a change which we later recommended. If Mr. Ickes made any effort to conceal his views on any topic, it was not apparent.

Mr. Henry A. Wallace defended the integrity of the Department of Agriculture but was quite willing to take over the control of the grazing lands from the Department of Interior. The deep sincerity of his belief that the Department of Agriculture should maintain a quasi-independent status within the executive branch was evident. His grandfather had been the principal leader of the movement which resulted in the establishment of the Department of Agriculture. His father had been secretary of agriculture. He was secretary of agriculture. To him, it was not only the field of his chosen life work, but it was a patrimony, the foundation of family pride, and, in very truth, a dynastic privilege.

Miss Frances Perkins, of all the members of the Cabinet with whom we had long talks, made, in my opinion, the most logical and objective arguments for her position, which was that anything and everything that had to do with labor should be put in the Labor Department. Less emotional than either Mr. Ickes or Mr. Wallace, she elaborated her thesis that the welfare and health activities, and especially the social security program, ought to be in the Department of Labor. Yet, it was manifest that she thought of labor only as industrial labor and thus was willing to divide the world of workers with the Department of Agriculture. Her political loyalty to President Roosevelt was always in evidence, but it was also plain to see that she did not think that budgetary, personnel, or planning procedures should be organized on any government-wide basis. She thought the departments, or at least the Labor Department, should roll its own.

So it was generally with other Cabinet members, although none of the others displayed either the intellectual conviction or the emotional interest to such a high degree as did Mr. Ickes, Mr. Wallace, and Miss Perkins.

Besides the members of the Cabinet and career administrators, we talked to many other key persons in the executive branch, sometimes with all three members of the committee present, sometimes in interviews with only one member representing the committee. And to some of these we turned again and again for advice and counsel.

Through Mr. McReynolds, we had not only his own help but the invaluable aid of Clinton A. Hestor, counsel for the Treasury, and F. J. Bailey, of the legislative reference section of the Bureau of the Budget, more especially in the latter stages when we began to discuss how our recommendations might be translated into legislative form. From the beginning, we had also the help of Herbert Emmerich, then executive officer and deputy governor of the Farm Credit Administration, help that proved to be so valuable that we borrowed him from the government, and he became one of the principal members of the staff of the committee, devoting his full time to the project.

As a matter of course, the staff, the members of which had been assigned particular topics for study, interviewed scores of people in the government, read hundreds of books, and employed as reference material literally thousands of governmental reports. Simultaneously, the Senate committee under the chairmanship of Senator Byrd and the House committee under the chairmanship of Mr. Buchanan were pursuing their own investigations.

The Senate committee, operating through the Brookings Institution, sent carefully prepared questionnaires to all the departments, agencies, bureaus, and divisions in the executive branch. The Buchanan committee employed Colonel C. C. Wren as its investigator, and he, too, sent questionnaires broadcast throughout the government. Dr. Harris and the members of his staff used the questionnaire method but rarely, depending rather upon the techniques of documentary research and personal interviews. This choice of a different methodology at the time reflected nothing more than what our committee regarded as a logical distinction, corollary to the division of labor between our staff and the Brookings Institution. Our primary purpose was to deal with the top management of the executive branch, and, therefore, we were concerned with the lines of responsibility running from each unit in the executive establishment upward through channels to the White House. The Brookings Institution, operating for the Senate committee, on the other hand, was to concern itself principally with departmental reorganization—the regrouping of units, the identification of duplication and overlapping activities, and so on.

At the beginning of the work, the most cordial relations existed between Dr. Harris and our staff and the staff of the Brookings Institution, which was headed by Dr. Fred Powell. Indeed, the staff of our committee expected in the beginning to rely largely upon the material assembled by the Brookings Institution and, from the answers obtained to its questionnaires, to get factual material upon which we might base our appraisal of the management problems involved.

The primary division of labor was originally agreed upon between the President and Senator Byrd. It apparently was expected by both of them to work more smoothly because I was chairman of the President's committee and at the same time chairman of Senator Byrd's advisory committee.

Toward the end of June, Dr. Harris had cabled me that he had had a conference with Senator Byrd, Mr. Buchanan, and the Brookings Institution in which it was agreed that our committee would make a contribution of $20,000 to the Byrd committee work, contingent upon my approval. I at once approved the transfer.

However, what then seemed to be bright prospects for amicable cooperation among the three committees soon were dimmed and in the end were obliterated in conflict and controversy arising from a basic disagreement over the separation of powers between the legislative and executive branches.

Hot as the weather was in Washington, the temperature there did not so exacerbate men's nerves as did the even hotter presidential election campaign. Roosevelt and Garner were running against Landon and Knox. The opposition to Roosevelt and the New Deal was not only forthright but vociferous. Most of the newspapers were for Landon. The *Literary Digest* poll predicted Roosevelt's defeat. Never at any time during the whole summer and fall was the outcome generally considered to be a foregone conclusion.

The election came on November 2. Roosevelt carried every state in the Union but two—Vermont and Maine. The Democratic party carried both houses of Congress, and, for the first time in the history of the Republic since the formation of political parties, one political party had more than a two-thirds majority in both the House and the Senate. The Republican opposition was stunned.

All during the month of October the committee had been reading, reviewing, and revising the reports of its staff and drafting and redrafting proposed sections of its report. Now we knew that there would not be a change in the White House come January and it was time to get at least an outline of the report in shape to discuss with the President.

On November 5 I wrote a memorandum to the committee which was designed to raise the crucial questions concerning the content and order of the proposed report. This memorandum was approved by my colleagues and was adopted as the skeletal framework for the report. Indeed, allowing for the changes inherent in the process of elaboration and detailed presentation, it might well serve as a summary of the final report, except for the change from the White House secretariat suggested in my memorandum to the broader concept of the Executive Office of the President, a change which resulted in part from our later conversations with President Roosevelt, in part from our conversations with Frank O. Lowden, former governor of Illinois (who, at that time, was chairman of the board of the Public Administration Clearing House), and in part from the committee's own deliberations.

My memorandum follows:

The report should declare:

That managerial direction and control of all departments and agencies of the Executive Branch of the Government should be centered in the President;

That while he now has popular responsibility for this direction and control he is not equipped with adequate legal authority or administrative machinery to enable him to exercise it; and

That certain changes in law and administrative practice are required to restore the Executive to that position of power balanced with compensating responsibility which is the clear purpose and intent of our Constitutional system.

The report should recommend:

That the staff or institutional agencies be made directly responsible to the President; that the President establish a White House secretariat which will include not only such functions as have been exercised in the past, but which under an executive secretary will establish the direct lines of communication with all the staff agencies except the Budget (which should report directly to the President);

That through the development of such a White House executive secretariat the President coordinate the work of the line and operating agencies with respect to information and recommendations;

That to facilitate coordinated over-all management and to improve internal agency administration a single responsible administrator be placed at the head of all administrative agencies, staff and line, which are now headed by boards or commissions;

That while no recommendation may be made at this time for the segregation of administrative duties from the quasi-judicial duties of the regulatory agencies now in existence, the danger of the development of an irresponsible Fourth branch of the government be recognized and that consideration be given in all future regulatory legislation to the devolution of such work upon the regular departments of Government as already often has been done;

That the President be given continuing power, subject to a Congressional veto of the type provided in the Economy Act of 1933 to regroup, rearrange, consolidate, and reorganize the departments, agencies, and bureaus; and that to facilitate his work in this respect there be developed in the Bureau of the Budget the research function already provided for by law.

That in the presence of an emergency the temporary creation of emergency agencies to handle new types of activities is not only justified but necessary; that as the emergency situation lessens the new activities be fitted into the permanent establishment by order of the President (subject to the same type of Congressional veto suggested above);

That to effectuate these recommendations which are to be elaborated in detail, it is necessary to establish direct lines of relationship which will enable the President to control effectively the fiscal machinery of the government, to extend the merit system to all branches of the Executive excluding only policy making positions, to command the research and intellectual resources of an adequately equipped planning agency; to require the coordination of statistical and reporting services and to establish a coordinated scheme for the clearance of legislative recommendations or reports proper to the sphere of the Executive as well as to provide clearance and control for the issue of Executive Orders and administrative rules and regulations which require presidential authority or approval;

That effective Congressional control of the Executive cannot be exercised by detailed and uncoordinated legislative action whether by general law or limitations attached to particular budgetary items of appropriation bills or by the type of control exercised by the Comptroller General who is the agent of Congress but who in fact is irresponsible to either the Executive or Legislative branch; but that Congressional control of the Executive will be advantaged by a concentration of administrative responsibility upon the President in accordance with the Constitution, and will be made fully effective only by the creation by Congress of its own agent to review and audit the conduct of the Executive Branch and to report to Congress through committees especially set up by the two Houses of Congress to receive and digest the results of such a review and audit.

A Passion for Anonymity

Our committee held what was perhaps its most significant and determinative session in New York on November 6, 7, and 8, when we elaborated the memorandum in outline form. This outline, when typed, covered fewer than half-a-dozen pages. It was turned over to the staff as the guide for the preparation of drafts for the several sections of the report, and the committee determined that it would thereafter make no major changes in its matter or scope.

This outline also was to serve as the basis for our talk with President Roosevelt. The President fixed Saturday, November 14, as the date for the meeting to be held in his study in the White House proper. Unfortunately, Dr. Merriam could not make that engagement because his daughter was being married in Chicago that afternoon.

So it was that Luther Gulick and I went unaccompanied to see the President. Perhaps the best way to tell the story of what happened at that meeting is to set out here, with the permission of Luther Gulick, the notes that he wrote out later that afternoon and which I read and approved that night; with the omission of references to a few conversations about the late election and other things that had nothing whatever to do with our committee, the Gulick memorandum reads:

. . . we were taken down the hall to the President's study. It is in the center of the White House, facing south toward the Washington Monument. . . .

"How are you getting on?" was his way of turning to our business. Louis Brownlow handed him our first one-page summary on Administrative Management. He read it through word for word, and slowly, "One hundred per cent," banging his fist on the table with each word. He went over the points out loud, touching only the key words, like "the Budget" and "Long-term planning," commented particularly on the continuous research task of the Bureau of the Budget, and said "Splendid. It's all there but one thing—but that's a hot one." When we asked him what it was he said "Independent regulatory agencies, the fourth branch of the Government." We said, "That's covered in part under the General Accounting Office recommendations and in part in the second memo." He turned to it immediately and read the one-page summary. He started to discuss this, however, before finishing it. His first comment was: "Under No. 1 (The President's power to reorganize) there will be political difficulty. It will probably be necessary to limit the power to one or two years." We agreed, but said that as a matter of principle we would recommend it. This he approved.

On No. 3 (reduction of agencies with departmental tie-in) which he read out loud very slowly, he said: "Every single one, under a department."

No. 4 (abolition of administrative boards) started a discussion, the President saying that the boards give him prestigeful posts for big business men and regenerate bankers who cannot be brought in as "assistants" nor on any

$7,000 level. As an illustration, he mentioned "old man Merriam" and Mitchell, both of the Federal Reserve Board. "Eccles needs them," he said, "but how could we get them as subordinates?" When Louis Brownlow asked him if advisory boards wouldn't serve, he said he thought they might, but that there would have to be some with salaries.

On No. 5 (regulatory commissions) he showed some disappointment with the question, "Is that all you can say?" After some defense on our part of the strategy, he indicated a readiness to go forward now to tie in also the existing regulatory commissions as to all of their functions "with the single exception of the issuance of orders of a United States District Court." He went on to say that "quasi-judicial" is a pretty but loose phrase and includes, as a matter of fact, a great deal of investigation, prosecution, enforcement, and management which are not at all judicial.

As a tie-in for Interstate Commerce Commission, Inland Waterways Corporation, Maritime Commission, etc., he suggested a new Transportation Division in the Department of Commerce "with the biggest building in town, but doing what?" He suggested that the Federal Trade Commission should also go to Commerce.

Coming to our *Tentative Proposals,* he exploded with agreement over the two new departments of Public Welfare and Public Works. "Not an hour ago, this morning, I said just that!"

He read the other points out loud, very slowly, approving as he went. He stopped at No. 4 and again said, "Yes, sir, every one."

The next page, already covered in the summary, he skipped over hastily and landed on "undersecretary" under No. 3. He said that undersecretaries could not be career men as they have to represent the Departments in the absence of the Secretary at Cabinet meetings, etc. We explained that the undersecretary was the top permanent post and not a political deputy, which was another job. He caught our plan immediately, agreed that each department should have such a single career manager, and accepted Louis Brownlow's suggestion that we call our man the "principal officer." He said he had read in some Landon speech the statement that all but eight or ten posts in Washington would be under civil service—but that this was utterly impossible, civil service should be carried up to the top, but that there would be a great many more than ten posts needed for policy control.

The President paused quite a while over C (granting the department head the right to reorganize his department), but came back with emphatic approval—"Put it up to them. The Budget Bureau can work on it and the secretaries can carry it out." He even went on to show just how it would work out with a change of secretaries. "When an old Secretary goes out and a new one comes in, the Budget Bureau and the permanent Secretary could bring out a plan all prepared to take the department out of the rut. This is just a horseback opinion, of course, but I think it's very good." He agreed with Louis Brownlow that this would be more acceptable to Congress than a similar grant to the President.

When the "Department of Conservation" was reached on page 5, Mr.

Roosevelt suggested that we call it "Public Lands." This brought on a discussion in which we said that "lands" would not do for the Civilian Conservation Corps and Education, or for water resources. He was surprised that Education was not going to Welfare. Louis Brownlow said Education could not be put in with relief and prisons, that as a matter of "grand expediency" you can't combine relief or welfare with the failures with education and development for the normal and have it work. The President said that he had puzzled a great deal over the proper dividing line between Agriculture and Interior which he said "is an irrational zig-zag now," and that Henry Wallace had suggested that organic and inorganic chemistry be the basis of allotment. This amused him greatly. He said he had thought it out on the basis of giving to Interior the management of all the lands of the United States Government, including all matters primarily connected with this public estate. Louis Brownlow then developed still further our conception of the department as dealing with conservation and development of natural and human resources. After more discussion, FDR assented, "I'm wrong, you fellows are right. Go ahead." And so we went on to the next point. I said that we knew that there was difficulty with Agriculture, but that a thoroughly logical nomenclature was not possible. I quoted Charles E. Merriam's words that the three great new drives of the Government are public works, public welfare, and conservation, and said that the recognition of this in department nomenclature was sensible. He liked this and stated that the forestry service clearly belonged in Conservation and not in Agriculture.

The President looked over the functional assignments under Point 5. He approved each one as he went, stopping a while to discuss the Social Security Board. He thought it should go to Public Welfare, but that the employment offices should be under Labor with an interdepartmental tie-in of some kind. In the course of the discussion he turned to Louis Brownlow and said, "You know, last spring when we talked about this I told you to find a new name for 'Welfare.' If you would just find that, we'd be all right." He approved all of the other assignments until he reached the lending agencies on the last page. Here he suggested that the Federal Deposit Insurance Corporation Board be retained as Trustees of the fund, like the Postal Savings Board, and the other functions be taken to the Federal Reserve Board along with the national bank audit of the Controller of the Currency. He said that he had this suggestion from Eccles. About the rest, he said, "I want to keep them around, even if we cut them down to one man and tie them in. I want to have them around in case something blows up."

We discussed the Resettlement Administration, the President accepting Louis Brownlow's suggestion that it should go to Agriculture unless Housing is set up under Public Works, in which case the Suburban section should go there. The President told us of his visit the previous day to Greenbelt, Maryland. He said that the manager there told him that the central procurement of brick, cement, etc. had worked very badly because the procurement division had never bought such quantities before. Louis Brownlow turned this to support our recommendation that the public works branch of the procurement division was to be separated from the office supplies and put into Public Works. After some thought and discussion, FDR heartily endorsed the plan.

Louis Brownlow took the discussion back to the Executive Secretary, turning the President's copy to the proper page. He read only the first paragraph and started to outline what he thought he needed. . . . "Executive Assistant to the President" was the title he suggested for each of the members of the "Secretariat." He went on to outline their duties in these terms: "There would be one for foreign affairs. He would go out in the morning and see Hull, and then go to the Treasury, to Agriculture, to Commerce, to the Federal Reserve, and find out what was up, touching foreign relations wherever it was. And he would come back and tell me. Another executive assistant would cover the business relations. A third would deal with financial affairs, and the fourth would handle welfare and conservation. "You can't have just one Executive Secretary. The damn columnists would never let him alone. They are always looking for the 'white haired boy.' Just now they are writing up Corcoran. Way back, it was Raymond Moley, and there was no truth in that either." This was, I thought, a shot at me. He said that the papers would not get onto the four men in the same way. Louis Brownlow came in with, "That's all right, but you left one out."

"What's that," said the President and Brownie said,

"Planning and personnel." And then as the President approved, Louis Brownlow went on with the thought that there would be some confusion and lack of coordination and much waste time for four men reporting directly to the President, and that he could get just what he was after by adding a man for liaison with planning and personnel who would be tacitly placed by the President as "primus inter pares." FDR was enthusiastic and added, "Yes, that's the fellow who never goes out." We called his attention to the fact that career men might well be brought into the Secretariat from the various departments. He agreed and said that they could be tried out and sent back if necessary.

We took him into the next paragraph, where the duties of the White House secretariat were spelled out. He got as far as "high competence, great physical vigor, and a passion for anonymity" when he burst out chuckling and laughing, and read the phrase out loud a second time. I made Brownie tell him how the phrase had come from Tom Jones. FDR relished it highly and said, "But tell your British friend that he doesn't know his American press." FDR observed, "I thought the White House office was all set for twenty-five years, but already it is too small. But I can move the files and machinery over to State, War, and Navy, and build a tunnel." We suggested that this would have other anonymity values as well.

Louis Brownlow said that we had considered building the White House secretariat about the Bureau of the Budget, but that we had given up the idea. FDR said the idea wouldn't work at all, and "anyway, he'll have plenty to do under this." . . .

Our civil service plan came in for discussion. I thought he had skipped over it a little hastily the first time over, but found that he had a perfectly clear notion of what we were up to when we turned back to the separate memorandum on the merit system. He said he was "thoroughly satisfied" with the plan, but expected that there would be some reluctance from the civil servants. He said that the great trouble is dead wood, and added, "there must be more power to let a man retire." He told how he had been responsible for the abolition of the plucking board in the Navy and for the introduction of the plan now used under which a man eligible for promotion but passed over three times was automatically retired. "There must be a promotion flow, with the elimination of those who cannot go up." He said that the plan might have to be modified, but that power to move in this direction must be secured. We suggested that the President already had the power under the law, which put him back on his heels a bit, but that he was powerless to act for lack of effective machinery, which we were providing both in the departments and in the over-all structure. With a wave of the hand he told us what he thought of the existing set-up, and agreed that the Commission was hopeless, and that if he asked them a question right in his study, they "would have to go out into the hall to caucus." In connection with our proposed Civil Service Board, he observed, "That idea may help us elsewhere too." . . .

Louis Brownlow said that he had recently seen O'Mahoney and had told him a little of the situation as O'Mahoney is on Byrd's committee, and suggested that the President telephone him and Robinson to pass on the message regarding the stopping of the open hearings. The President made a pencil note, and said he would.

At one point he said, "We have to get over the notion that the purpose of reorganization is economy. I had that out with Al Smith in New York. I pleaded with him not to go before the people with the pledge of economy. But he did, and his first budget after reorganization was way up over the previous budget, though there was some saving in administrative salaries. The reason for reorganization is good management."

As we were getting up to leave, Louis Brownlow asked if we were headed right and what FDR wanted next. He came back with an enthusiastic approval of the plans submitted and said we should go on to finish our report and have it ready by December 17, when he would be back from Buenos Aires, and would want to see us to work out his message to the Congress. Louis Brownlow said that our report would deal primarily with administrative management, and only secondarily with the general principles and over-all plan of reorganization, and that we would not go into details of assignment of activities in the report itself. He said, "That's just right. We can talk about those other things." Louis Brownlow said that we would adhere to our policy of complete public silence. The President approved heartily.

However, in the weeks following our first talk with "F. D. R." on November 14, our committee was in practically continuous session, since it was now necessary for us to have a completed draft of the report ready for the President upon his return from his trip to Brazil and the Argentine.

CHAPTER XXXI

THE PRESIDENT AND CONGRESS

Actually the principal parts of the report were written before Gulick and I saw the President. What remained to be done was the editing of some of the supporting documents.

At this task the three members of the committee sat continuously, relying directly on the aid of Dr. Joseph P. Harris, chief of the research staff, on his assistant, John Miller, and, for meticulous editorial scrutiny, on Miss Laverne Burchfield, whom we had borrowed from the editorial staff of the Tennessee Valley Authority. Yet, there was a deadline to be met. We had promised the President to give him the report at the beginning of the new year and, as is usually the case, many things remained to be done. On the very last night, Dr. Harris was at home ill and was endeavoring to talk to Miss Burchfield between seizures of laryngitis. Merriam, Gulick, and I had our heads together going over every sentence and every revision suggested by the staff. About three o'clock in the morning we were startled by an outburst of laughter in the next room. It came from the mild-mannered John Miller, who never raised his voice unless something tickled him tremendously and then his laughter could be heard for blocks. At that time Miller was very much in love and was engaged to be married. He wrote to his fiancée every day. The day before had been strenuous, but he had finally gotten his letter written and addressed. He looked at the envelope and exploded. All three of us rushed in to see what was the matter. He had addressed the letter to his sweetheart, "Miss Management."

We decided to call it a day, or a night, or a morning, or something, and told Miss Burchfield to put the whole bunch of documents in an envelope and see that they got to the printer early the next morning. There were no more revisions.

The page proofs reached us on Saturday, January 2. On Sunday morning I took the page proofs of the principal sections of the report to the White House. The President went over them carefully in a session which lasted for more than three hours, interrupted only by a telephone conversation with our ambassador in Paris, William Bullitt, a conversation which Mr. Roosevelt cut off very shortly by telling Mr. Bullitt that he was too busy with an important matter to discuss whatever it was. By the end of that session the President had thoroughly mastered the document and was able in his discussions to quote whole sentences, and sometimes three or four sentences together, verbatim.

Mr. Roosevelt was very proud of his memory—some persons thought, inordinately proud. Once when I was in his office he talked with me about the task of the presidency and especially about the things he could not delegate if he hoped to retain effective control over the vast machinery of the government. On that occasion he told me that he had checked with Rudolph Forster, who had been in the White House since the time of Grover Cleveland, and asked him to make a careful calculation of the relative number of things that came to his desk for decision as compared with the desks of former presidents, especially Calvin Coolidge. The report came back that he handled at least thirty-five decisions to one made by Mr. Coolidge.

"You know, Louis," the President said, "there is only one way I can do it. My memory. They can't fool me. I have a long memory, an accurate memory, and when they talk to me or write to me and try to obfuscate the past events, I simply know better."

His pride in his memory was demonstrated over and over again during that first week in January. The bound volumes of the report, excluding the supplementary documents, were ready the first of the week, and on Tuesday, the fifth, I took perhaps twelve or twenty copies to the President. It was then, of course, a confidential document. There was no doubt whatever that his secretaries, Stephen Early and Marvin H. McIntyre, had taken from the beginning a dim view of the whole procedure. The President let them read it but told Steve that he would handle the press himself.

On Friday, the eighth, he outlined the report to the Cabinet, not having it before him but relying entirely on his memory. This fact I did not know at the time but heard later from Vice-President Garner.

The President and Congress

The President fixed Sunday afternoon as the time for discussing the report with the Democratic leaders of the Congress.

It was in some respects a historic occasion. For the first time since the development of political parties in the administration of General Washington, one political party had won in an election not only the presidency but more than two-thirds of both houses of the Congress. It hasn't happened since. Fresh from the election, a Democratic President was meeting an overwhelmingly Democratic Congress, which was convening the first week in January after being elected in November, a circumstance in itself unprecedented, the result of the ratification of the Twentieth Amendment.

Also, it was the first time that any President ever had essayed to take directly to the Congress a general proposal to vest in the President the power to manage the executive branch of the government through an organization determined directly by him. The departmental organization, and the establishment of bureaus, divisions, sections, and so on, from the first had been controlled directly by congressional action. It is true that for some time a great many members of the Congress had realized and had said publicly that the only way actually to manage the tremendous establishment of the executive was to vest greater powers in the President. During the administration of Woodrow Wilson, as a war measure, the Congress had passed the Overman Act, which under certain circumstances gave the President as a part of his war powers the authority to shift bureaus and divisions and to make certain limited reorganizational changes. During the administration of Herbert Hoover, the Congress had passed a law permitting the President to make certain organizational changes by Executive Order, to be effective, unless disapproved by one house of the Congress, within sixty days. All the Hoover executive orders issued under this authority were promptly vetoed by a Democratic house in the last half of the Hoover administration. At the beginning of the administration of Franklin D. Roosevelt a similar act was passed by the Congress, and under it the President actually did make some minor reorganizational changes which were not vetoed and actually did go into effect. Under one of these a case had reached the Supreme Court of the United States, and the validity of the Executive Order was sustained, so far as the constitutionality of the procedure was concerned.

But the President now was asking for almost complete authority over the disposition and organization of the executive branch. In summary, the President was about to ask the Congress for the authority to issue executive orders which would become effective unless disapproved by both houses of Congress within sixty days. Through these orders he would:

1. Consolidate all boards, commissions, corporations, and agencies of the federal government under twelve major departments, the two new ones being Social Welfare and Public Works, and change the name of the Interior Department to "Department of Conservation."

2. Place the whole governmental administrative service on a career and merit basis by including in the civil service all non-policy determining positions under the President.

3. Change the existing comptroller general into an "auditor general" responsible solely to the Congress for the post-audit of federal fiscal activities; and transfer the existing pre-audit function to the Treasury and the quasi-judicial function to the attorney general.

4. Strengthen the Budget Bureau and consolidate in a national resources board the responsibility for national planning and constant research to improve governmental efficiency, directly under the President.

5. Give the President a few administrative assistants to take much work off his shoulders and serve him in a strictly confidential capacity.

The work of the President's committee had been carried on without publicity. With one or two exceptions, no person in the executive branch knew what the recommendations were to be. No member of the Congress knew. The general impression was that it would be, as one newspaperman said, "just another one of those things."

That Sunday afternoon, in addition to the congressional leaders, the President asked Merriam, Gulick, and me, and a few members of our staff to see him in his study on the second floor of the White House at two o'clock. The group assembled in the Green Room, and some of them began to discuss the probable nature of the report. Speaker Bankhead of the House and Chairman Doughton of the Ways and Means Committee talked about the number of unsuccessful attempts that had been made to reorganize the Executive Department by congressional action, and both, together with Vice-President Garner, said that they doubted that the Congress through its regular legislative procedure ever would be able to accomplish very much along this line. They felt that the effective reorganization would have to be done by executive action and that the legislation would not possibly succeed if the changes to be made were written out in detail in advance.

Those present were Vice-President John Nance Garner; William B. Bankhead, the speaker of the House of Representatives who had succeeded my old friend Joseph W. Byrns, who had died the preceding June; Robert Lee Doughton, chairman of the House Ways and Means Committee; James Paul Buchanan, chairman of the House Appropriations Committee; Joseph Robinson of Arkansas, the majority leader of the Senate; Patrick Harrison of Mississippi, chairman of the Senate Finance Committee; the President's son, James Roosevelt; and, from our committee, Merriam, Gulick, and I, Dr. Harris, Mr. McReynolds, Mr. Hester, and Mr. Emmerich.

During the entire conference the President was seated on a leather couch facing the rest of the group. The committee of three sat on the side of the room; the senators and representatives in the center in front of the President; and the members of the staff and James Roosevelt in the back row. It was raining hard outside, and the room was rather cool, in fact unpleasantly so to many of the persons present. The fragrance of Havana tobacco emanated from an enormous inlaid-wood humidor on a table in the middle of the room to which the congressional members made frequent trips. The President wore a light-gray suit, soft collar, and smoked cigarettes in a long paper holder. He successfully hid his physical disability—it was only evident once in a while when he crossed his legs, which he very quickly did by lifting them with his hands. His detailed presentation of the committee's recommendation was a huge undertaking for one sitting. At every point its forthright suggestions of radical changes necessarily shocked congressional habit patterns. The President presented the entire program himself, relying upon Gulick, Merriam, and me only occasionally for questions.

The President knew the report in general and in detail as well as did either Merriam, Gulick, or I. The few questions he asked of us were only to bring out emphases rather than to make up for his lack of knowledge. He had done his homework superbly. He had not only the text but the implications of the recommendations at his tongue's end.

On the previous Sunday afternoon, after the President went up and down, across and around the report and convinced me, which was an incident, and convinced himself, which was important, that he knew all of it, he felt a lack of something. As I rose to leave he said, "Louis, two things I would like you to do to help me out before I meet the congressional leaders. I would like you to get somebody, a skilled legislative draftsman, to write a bill which will incorporate these recommendations. You know, of course, that what you and Merriam and Gulick have done is not in legislative language.

I replied that of course we knew it was not, that none of us was a legislative draftsman, but that I thought we had a man who could do it: Clinton M. Hester, a lawyer in the Treasury Department whose services had been made available to us by McReynolds.

"Fine," said the President. "Get up the bill, have it mimeographed, and let me have several copies. I may or I may not hand them around when the congressional boys come in here next Sunday.

"Also I would like you—and I wish you would do this personally— to draft a message that I can send to the Congress along with the report. I intend to tell the boys Sunday that I will send it up next week with a message."

I did not believe that I was sufficiently acquainted with Mr. Roosevelt's vocabulary, diction, syntax, or the peculiar properties of his rhetorical arrangement to draft the message. That job I delegated to Luther Gulick. Luther was rocked back on his heels. He said he didn't believe anybody could imitate "F. D. R." I told him, and I was backed up by Merriam, that he had been in Albany often during Roosevelt's period of service in the state legislature and as governor and that he himself was a priceless imitator. Luther didn't like that much. He didn't seem to think that it was a compliment, as, indeed, both Merriam and I had intended it.

Nevertheless, one morning after a sleepless night, he got up at four o'clock and in pen and ink on slick yellow sheets wrote a message from the President of the United States to the Congress. Merriam and I thought it was good. Merriam was more dubious than I about its imitative nature. Gulick went away, and that night I went with Dr. Merriam and two or three others to dinner with the President's uncle, Mr. Delano, at 2400 Sixteenth Street. I told the group that this was the message the President intended to send to the Congress. When I had finished reading it aloud, Mr. Delano said, "The President wrote that himself. Those are his very words."

As a matter of fact it was pure Gulick.

When the President read the draft, he made no comment. I could not detect from his poker face whether he was pleased or displeased. The next time I saw it, it was in print from the Government Printing Office. The President had changed only one word, and Luther Gulick never again objected when I called him a priceless imitator. The word he changed was this: Gulick had written, "It is a state document of permanent importance." The President had stricken out the word "state" and substituted the word "great."

That Sunday afternoon, when the congressional leaders came, the President was careful not to intimate that he had already prepared his message. He told them that on the next Tuesday he would send the report up with a message. He was a bit careful about showing any of them copies of the report. He did have a few copies of the proposed bill scattered around, and that caused him trouble. He had flirted with the idea, as he told me later, that this might be a good time to fool around with a notion of sending up a prepared bill. He told me it was very dangerous, and he was alarmed when he found out that our staff had mimeographed not a half-dozen but more than five hundred copies of the proposed bill. The great bulk of these copies he impounded in the office of the White House. Members of his own staff read them and were alarmed. They had communicated that alarm to him sometime before our meeting.

He was wary, and yet, as I afterward came to think, he thought he would lead with the worst he had to say in order to be able from time to time to make tactical retreats without sacrificing his strategical position. He gave them the bill first.

While they were attempting to glance through it, he launched free-hand into the body of the report. As I have said before, he had done his homework. He didn't take it up in order. He said little or nothing about the emphasis in the introduction on the importance of the presidential office as the high symbol of the executive in the field of American government and American leadership in the world.

He took up first with the congressional leaders the things he thought might appeal to all of them or to as many of them as possible, but sometimes he addressed only one of them. There was no doubt, as he ran through the summary, that these leaders of the Congress, as the newspapers were to say over and over again in the next week, were stunned. They could hardly believe their ears. Yet, here was the leader of their party speaking to them immediately after the greatest political victory at the polls in the whole history of the American Republic.

He began by saying that he had had nothing to do with the committee's work, that he had set it up in March, that he had ordered it not to communicate with him until after the election, that it was a presidential committee and its duty was to report to whoever was elected president in November, and that he had had no notion whatever of what it contained until November 14.

Then he launched into a little homily about the report. "In effect, what I like about it most is the word 'management,' as management is a most admirable American trait. Everybody in the United States loves a good manager. A good wife is described as a good manager of the household. A good storekeeper is called a good manager. A successful banker is called a good manager. In fact, I believe that one of the highest encomiums that one American can give to another with respect to the work he is doing or has done is to say 'He is a good manager.' The whole business of this report is to emphasize management."

None of the committee or its staff took any notes, naturally, but with my own memory, refreshed by a memorandum written that night by Herbert Emmerich, I believe I have a reasonably accurate recollection of what went on. The congressional leaders, I must say, did not respond heartily to his homily upon the business of management. Each of them as a member of his own house, each of them as a member of a powerful committee, had been long convinced of the utility and, indeed, the immutability of the President's traditional right, as head of the executive branch, to recommend what to do about the management of the business of the government. But each thought it was the business of the Congress—which often meant a committee of the Congress, more often a subcommittee of the Congress, and even more often a single member of a subcommittee in concert with the head of a division or a bureau of the government—to make the final arrangements for actual management, actual administration.

But the President sensed that every single congressional representative there, jealous of his own prerogative, was also doubtful of the exercise of a similar prerogative by any other member of either the House or the Senate. So he led with his ace, and that was Economy and Efficiency. There were too many bureaus, too many divisions; nobody could find out exactly what was going on in each, and, as he went on with that denunciation of the frustrating fractionalization of bureau organization, he found heads nodding in agreement. He took a pot shot on the liberation of government corporations. With that, for the first time, he elicited a warm response. Mr. Roosevelt—and I am sure he knew what he was doing—seized upon Mr. Buchanan's enmity to the proliferation of government corporations. Indeed, the committee had shared that feeling. There were too many of them. Many of them were corporations chartered under the state of Delaware. They had not worked well. Their operations were not sufficiently under the executive surveillance, and in an obscure corner of our report, which we ourselves had not emphasized, the President had caught that one thing. Thereafter for a half-hour nearly everything he said began with "Buch and I"—"Buch and I know this," "Buch and I know," "This is the kind of thing that Buch and I have been fighting."

Then somebody, I am quite sure it was not the President, came around to the question of the over-all recommendation that the scores and scores of the various bureaus and divisions—all, without exception —should be placed under the control of twelve executive departments. Sam Rayburn, chairman of the House Committee on Interstate Commerce, had, as had all his predecessors and successors in that position, a special predilection for the Interstate Commerce Commission, which was the first independent regulatory commission ever set up in the government. Sam, but lately become the majority leader of the House, interjected in modest but firm tones the question, "Does this apply to all the regulatory agencies? Is not the Interstate Commerce Commission, which is so popular and so successful, an exception?"

The President came back at Sam with the only possible way to come back at Sam Rayburn. He said, "There will be no exceptions, not one."

That sally from the President was greeted with shocked silence. The President was quiet. He waited. Nobody said a word. At last the President said, "Of course, you know nothing in this applies to anything except the administrative and executive duties of these regulatory agencies. In their judicial duties of hearing and determining the cases before them they will be just as independent as any United States district court, just as independent, as you well know, as the Tax Court now attached to the Treasury Department.

As Mr. Emmerich wrote in his diary that night, "The President in presenting the report jumped around like a cat, three steps ahead of everyone. Among the numerous branches of this complicated tree, he barely touched the branches which seemed to give slightly under his weight and rested securely on those which seemed to support him."

Mr. Roosevelt in a press conference shortly after the election in 1936 had said that the Republicans never did hit on the chief weakness of the "New Deal" and that he could have made a better attack on himself than did Alf Landon and his backers. A reporter asked him, "What was your chief weakness?"

"Administration," responded the President.

Here, that Sunday afternoon in the White House, for the first time in the history of the great American Republic, a President of the United States, deeming himself in fact as well as in name the head of the executive branch of the government, had come to close grips with the leaders of the legislative branch, who from the beginning of the government had considered themselves responsible for the control, confinement, bridling, and ultimate determination of the organization of all branches of the government.

Mr. Winston Churchill, in his recent *History of the English-speaking People,* put his finger on this great difference between the several branches of the English-speaking democratic peoples. It is the question of whether the final responsibility for determination of policy, expenditure, and action should be intrusted to the executive—which always has been distrusted by democrats—or to the legislature, which always has been distrusted because of its mercurial disposition; or whether there should be a final appeal to an umpire, the judicial branch.

In England at various times, but particularly during the Glorious Revolution of 1688 when the Divine Right of kings was subordinated to the divine right of a majority of the members of Parliament, there were attempts to find a way to put the government of law above the government of men. It was not done in England—the English found no umpire. It was done, although unwittingly, by the inventors of the Constitution of the United States. They, however, had an advantage which their English ancestors had not. They had a mandate to draft a written constitution. No doubt none of the members of the convention that originated that constitution and probably few if any of the members of state legislatures which ratified it in convention had any notion that in the third branch of the government—the judiciary—they were setting up an all-powerful umpire. There is also some question of whether the persons appointed to be members of the Supreme Court of the United States would have had the courage to substitute the government of law for the Divine Right of kings, which had adhered in the executive branch, or whether there would have been the revolutionary participation of the representatives of the people in the parliamentary branch had not there been one single mind who against all obstacles asserted the rule of law. Interestingly enough, popularly, both children and grownups still think of United Staes history in terms of the names of the persons at the head of the executive branch, the names of the Presidents of the United States from George Washington on down. It seems to be in a second state in our acceptance of the history of our own country that we think in terms of and refer to the names of legislative leaders. And only later do we ordinarily ascribe important historical events to the names of those justices of the Supreme Court of the United States who have set the bounds to our governmental sanctions. This they have done in every instance except in the crisis of the Civil War, decided by what the orators in those days fondly referred to as the "arbitrament of the sword."

Perhaps this tripartite popular evolution of the Constitution of the United States has reflected in practice the philosophical assumptions which controlled the Constitutional Convention in setting up the three co-ordinate branches of the government.

However, on that particular Sunday afternoon in the White House, as far as I can recall, not one word was said about the Supreme Court or, indeed, except in a very slanting reference, about the Constitution of the United States. More importantly, not one word was said about the perennial conflict between the jurisdiction of the federal government and the state governments; in this conflict the assertion of sovereignty on the part of the forty-eight constituent states supervened not only in theory but in practice the control of the federal government over the ordinary lives of the people of the states. There was little said that afternoon, except by the President himself, about the relation of the United States of America to the other countries of the world and much less, indeed, about whether some of those countries were parliamentary democracies, federal democracies, or totalitarian states controlled by monarchs vested with Divine Right or by party leaders enthroned upon the universal acceptance of one and only one political premise.

One thing, however, stands out clearly in my memory. That was that the President was extremely careful not to offend the concept of the legislative supremacy and, also, not to transgress the personal prejudices of any member of the congressional hierarchy, the members of which had been chosen by his own party for their high positions and had been intrusted by his own party with legislative leadership.

He was canny; he was crafty. He searched out carefully the prejudicial views even when they were not shared by many of his hearers. He invited and indeed sought contradictory ideas and notions, but, as it seemed to me in retrospect, only in the fields in which there was a possibility of a difference of definition. He readily admitted, of course, that the legislative power controlled the purse. He was strictly constitutional.

At the same time, he said in one way or another, over and over again, "The executive branch should have the authority to conduct its affairs commensurate with the responsibility imposed upon it by the Constitution, by the laws, by the voters, by public opinion."

It was a head-on collision, probably the first and, so far as I know, the very last in the whole history of the United States between a vocal President and the leaders of his political party in the Congress, and certainly and statistically the last between a President of the United States having at his command as leader of his party more than a two-thirds majority of both houses of the Congress.

The discussions that came up were mostly on detail. Neither the President himself nor any of his congressional party associates were able, that afternoon at any rate, to put into words the real and realistic difficulties. For instance, the President wanted to reform the Civil Service. He said that in accordance with the report of the committee he would like to abolish the bipartisan Civil Service Commission. What he wanted was a single Civil Service administrator; at the same time— and I think their silence generally reflected the deepest shock at this— he said that the merit system should be extended to all employees of the government, upward, outward, and downward, except to those who were responsible for policy and therefore directly related to the mandate of the electorate.

Many of those congressional leaders winced at that, but none, at least on that afternoon, brought up the subject. The reaction was similar when the President said that, in order to have authority commensurate with his responsibility, he would like to have all the administrative divisions of the United States collected into twelve departments—what he actually said was, "within twelve separate and determinable tents, each of which will be within my range of vision." They may have winced, but they didn't say much. Each was quite conscious of his own position in the multiple-facet legislative organization. Each was necessarily quite conscious of his own position in his own state; each always remembered that his political life was not geared, as was that of the President, to the entire constituency of all the voters of the United States.

Not perhaps in the terms of the issue of the drama in the last act, not perhaps in terms of head-on collisions, not perhaps in either political or personal opposition, it was a Sunday afternoon in which—and I believe with the best will in the world—a representative of the executive branch, who can only be the President of the United States, and representatives of the legislative branch, who can only be leaders of the majority party in the two houses of Congress, and the representatives of the students of political science and public administration met together to thresh things out.

In retrospect I cannot recall one single reference to the Supreme Court or to any of its decisions, except those which had been formally, informally, and intellectually, as well as politically, accepted by all the people as the current authoritative restatement of the constitutional law of the Republic; and certainly not one word was said that afternoon concerning what would happen to the proposals then under discussion at the collateral but not yet envisioned head-on collision between the President and the Supreme Court. Yet it was that problem which, within the next year, determined the fate of the proposals set forward in the report of the President's Committee on Administrative Management.

The meeting that had begun at two o'clock broke up at six. The congressional leaders were first to retire. And then, when they had left in respectful and troubled silence, all these great men, the vice-president, who under the Constitution is president of the Senate, the speaker of the House of Representatives, and the other legislative leaders filed out. I am quite sure that they saw and properly interpreted the gesture of the President's right hand which, in effect, ordered the members of the committee and its staff to stay behind. Certainly no one of them, each being a practical politician, could escape the fact that the President intended to give a little postlude lecture to us. It was brief. After the leaders had gone, I introduced to the President the members of our staff and he introduced each of us, with some frivolous or joking reference, to his son James and also to his younger son Franklin D., Jr., who had come into the room.

And then as we stood up to take our leave, the President turned to me and said, "You see, Louis, what I am up against. This was quite a little package to give them this afternoon. Every time they recovered from a blow, I socked them under the jaw with another. I will see you at four o'clock Monday afternoon at the press conference."

On Monday, January 11, the President convoked a press conference. He elected himself professor and termed the meeting a seminar. Sitting behind the President were all the members of his Cabinet, his own three secretaries, the three members of the President's committee, plus two or three members of its staff.

When all the correspondents had been admitted and were seated, the President assumed a severe, stern mien, rapped on his desk, and said, "How many of you have done your homework?" None had done any because up to that time none had had an opportunity to see the report or to know what was in it. The President took a copy from his desk, indicated that a sufficient number of copies were in the outer room to give every person there as many copies as he liked, and then began to explain the report. He used a different method from that which he had used with the legislative leaders. This time he took up the report from the first page and went through it section by section and, indeed, in some of its parts, paragraph by paragraph. He placed particular emphasis on the introduction discussing the place of the executive in the governmental hierarchy and the constitutional scheme of the United States, and he also emphasized the responsibility of the President as the general manager of the executive branch.

He paid particular attention to the proposals for the extension and improvement of the White House staff. And here he hit upon that unfortunate phrase that I had gotten from Tom Jones specifying the qualifications of his immediate assistants, that "they should be pos-

The President and Congress

sessed of high competence, great physical vigor, and a passion for anonymity."

"Sharpen your pencils," said the President, "and take this down. This is a purple patch, one you will never forget."

The President got a laugh, as he had expected, but he also got a chorus of various clearly audible expressions of cynical disbelief. In fact one man spoke up and said, "There ain't no such animal."

This apparently took Mr. Roosevelt aback just a little. He turned and said, "Gentlemen, have you ever met Rudolph Forster, who is here in the room?"

Now Mr. Forster had been in the Executive Office since the days of Grover Cleveland. He was known to every Washington correspondent, every White House reporter, and yet none had ever got from him a story, none had ever so much as accused him of a leak, and everyone knew that indeed he did have a "passion for anonymity." But that wasn't enough. The purple patch which the President had so much enjoyed was utterly unconvincing to those cynical correspondents, for most of the persons they met were of the other variety of human beings—the ones who shrank from anonymity and whose primal desire was publicity, publicity, and more publicity.

The President went on to emphasize the recommendations for the three great agencies that in his opinion were required: agencies in fiscal management, personnel management, and planning management. He strongly emphasized the proposal to extend the merit system upward, outward, and downward, to include all employees of the government except those charged with top policy decisions. He laid great stress on the proposal to bring the more than one hundred bureaus and divisions of the executive branch under the twelve departments outlined in the report, to which he gave the name "twelve big tents." He also gave strong support to the recommendations that we had made to change radically the duties of the comptroller general.

As the lecture went on, the President again evidenced his complete familiarity with everything in the report. Somebody asked why, if the proposed auditor general was to be accountable to the special Joint Committee of the two houses of Congress, he should be appointed by the President. The President turned to me and repeated the question. I said that the attorney general had advised us that there was no constitutional means by which the Congress could make the appointment.

Mr. Homer Cummings, the attorney general, spoke up and said that it was true, that he had so advised the committee.

No other question was asked of a member of the committee. No other word was uttered by a member of the Cabinet. The President did it all himself—answered all the queries by the correspondents, engaged in little acidulous spats with some of them, made jokes with some of them, and had them laughing and sometimes gasping by the audacity of his repeated assertions that the President should have authority commensurate with his responsibility as the chief of the executive branch.

The next day the papers of the country were full of the story. The headlines and the leads, with but few exceptions, played up the impact of the President's recommendations on the Congress. The message which he had told the correspondents would accompany the report when he sent it to Congress on the next day but one was not then available, but the President quoted from it so frequently and with such verbal accuracy that, when it was released two days later, no correspondent who was there so much as suspected that it was not written word for word by Mr. Roosevelt himself. It was still Luther Gulick's text, which the President had completely and absolutely adopted save for one single word.

Nearly all the newspapers of the country supported the proposals. But of course that did not mean that the realistic Washington correspondents had any notion whatever that the report and its recommendations would be readily or easily adopted. As Turner Catledge of the *New York Times* said in his summary article, "It will mean a fight every step of the way in Congress."

Arthur Krock, in his column of the *Times* on the same page in which the *Times* editorially had praised the report, led the chorus of sneers concerning the "Self-less Six."

The part of the report that most alarmed the politicians was the recommendation for the extension of the merit system to comprise all the government employees except those charged with high responsibilities for policies. What most alarmed the government employees was the recommendation for putting all of the bureaus and divisions under the direct control of twelve departments. What most alarmed the regulatory agencies and the businesses and industries regulated by them was the proposal to put those agencies also under departmental supervision for all their activities except those quasi-judicial in character.

In fact, nearly every person in the government was alarmed. The words "stunned," "shocked," "alarmed," and "amazed" were often used to describe the consternation that the President's revelation of the report had occasioned.

Then on January 12, eleven days after the President had first read the full text of the report, he transmitted it to the Congress with the formal message strongly supporting its recommendations. The hundreds of published copies of the report that had been circulated already had been exhausted, and the Government Printing Office issued a new and much larger edition in which was included the four pages of the presidential message dated at the White House on January 12, 1937.

The fight was on!

Despite the predictions of the opposition, at the beginning paths seemed to be relatively smooth. There were, of course, parliamentary entanglements. Although there was a special committee in the Senate headed by Senator Byrd of Virginia and another in the House of Representatives headed by Mr. Buchanan, chairman of the House Appropriations Committee, early in February both houses created a Joint Committee on Government Reorganization to consider the message of the President and the report of our committee.

Membership in the joint committee overlapped in certain respects the membership of the two select committees. The cochairmen of the joint committee were Joseph T. Robinson, senator from Arkansas, majority leader of the Senate, and John J. Cochran, representative from Missouri, chairman of the House Committee on Government Operations.

The committee borrowed from the Bureau of the Budget the services of Frederick J. Lawton, who was to act as its consultant and adviser. Death interrupted the service of the committee. Both of the cochairmen, Senator Robinson and Representative Cochran, died suddenly during the progress of the hearings. They were succeeded by Senator Byrnes of South Carolina and Representative Lindsay C. Warren of North Carolina. Also during the course of the hearings the chairman of the House select committee, Representative Buchanan, died, and that committee practically ceased its activities.

The hearings before the joint committee were begun on February 18.

I opened with a preliminary statement and submitted copies of the suggested draft of the bill which we had prepared. And then the questions began.

The clash of opinions between the President's committee and the Brookings Institution, especially over the matter of fiscal controls, took up a great deal of the committee's time. But as yet there was little evidence of serious opposition to the main recommendation of our committee, with the normal exception of the political opposition voiced by the Republican members and the little-more-than-normal congressional doubt about intrusting more power to the President.

The joint committee decided to leave to the representatives of each house the task of drafting the legislative measures to be voted upon. As a result a tremendous triumph for the proposal came when the House of Representatives, on August 12, 1937, passed the bill by a vote of 283 to 75, a majority of more than two-thirds, which was far greater than had been anticipated by anybody. It was evident however, that the bill then to go to the Senate could not be acted upon in that session of the Congress and would have to go over to the next session.

In the meantime, another fight came on. This one was a tornado. The President made his recommendation to the Congress for an increase in the number of members of the Supreme Court of the United States. It was, according to the President, a reform. It was, according to his opponents, a court-packing measure. Despite the nominal control of both houses of Congress by a more than two-thirds majority of Democrats, the ensuing fight erased party lines and brought about a head-on collision between the legislative and the executive branches, and the judiciary did not stand aside.

But in all this ruckus and in all these hassles and quarrels, I was but little concerned personally.

On May 30, 1937, Memorial Day, my wife and I greatly enjoyed a visit from Guy and Carol Moffett, two of our very good friends, and we were glad to have a holiday from more than a little incidental conversation about the state of the Union and the progress of the report of the President's committee.

But early the next morning I was awakened by an intense pain in my chest. For a little while I was not greatly disturbed. I thought it was indigestion, took some soda and aspirin, and went back to bed. But there was no relief. Within an hour it occurred to me that this was a heart attack. Without mentioning that, I asked Mrs. Brownlow to send for a doctor. The house physician came. He immediately gave me an injection of morphine and said he would be back in an hour and that he had to go to get some more ammunition.

I said to him, "Doctor, this is the first time I ever have had a heart attack."

He said, "Well, that is good. At least you know what is the matter. I shall send a heart specialist in the morning. Do you have any preference?"

I said that I would prefer to see Dr. Thomas S. Lee, who had treated several members of my family for various heart ailments. After an hour or two the doctor came back and gave me another injection of morphine. The pain subsided, and he left. He told my wife to be sure to see that I stayed in bed and kept exertion to a minimum.

In the morning Dr. Lee came, and with him was his assistant, young Dr. White. They brought with them an electrocardiograph machine. When Dr. Lee sat down with me, I said, "Doctor, this is a coronary thrombosis."

He looked a little startled and said, "Well, now that you have actually used the words, I may as well tell you what I already have told Mrs. Brownlow. I shall give you a careful examination, but I think it will be necessary for you to have complete rest for six weeks—no business of any kind for at least six weeks."

That was that!

During the first two weeks, I saw nobody at all except my wife, our maid, the doctors, and the three nurses. At the end of two weeks Dr. Merriam came to see me, but there was little conversation about the progress of the legislation. I was obeying orders. I saw no newspaper and did not know what was going on. Occasionally my wife would read to me something amusing but never anything that even so much as touched on public affairs. I was really isolated, packed away in insulation that kept me from knowing anything. However, one morning, after consultation with the doctor, Bess came and told me that there was some bad news. She told me that Senator Robinson had been found dead alone in his apartment, where he evidently had suffered a heart attack and had been unable to summon assistance.

It got terrifically hot in Washington that June. Our apartment had a large living room, a bedroom with twin beds, a bathroom, a dining

room, and a kitchen. An air-conditioning unit was installed in the bedroom, but it was impossible to furnish one for the other parts of the
apartment. My poor wife suffered greatly during that long season by
being forced to come in and out of the heat—the heat where she necessarily spent a large part of the days and the cool of the room in which
we slept at night. It wasn't very long until the night nurse was dispensed with, but the two others watched me and took care of me.

Whether or not the pace at which I had been going was the direct
cause of the heart attack, I do not know for certain, but surely the physicians, my wife, and, as soon as I began to see them, my close friends
told me that I would have to slow down; that I could not go on working at the fourteen-hour-a-day schedule which I had been pursuing for
so many years.

There were difficulties indeed. The new building at 1313 East Sixtieth Street in Chicago was under construction, and the question of dis-
posing of the space in that building to the various organizations clustered at 850 East Fifty-eighth Street was a difficult one.

I selected Herbert Emmerich, who had worked with us on the President's committee, and persuaded him to leave his position with the
Farm Credit Administration in Washington to go to Chicago and become my associate director. Then, despite the gloomy predictions that I
would not and could not do it, I delegated to him the great task of getting the new building ready, assigning the space, and agreeing upon
the terms of the rental, so that actually Emmerich did practically all
the work preceding the moving into the building in the spring of 1938.
While the building was not to be finished until the next spring, all the
necessary agreements had to be made, and even after my recovery when
I was back in Chicago, I left such matters almost entirely in the hands
of Mr. Emmerich and my business manager, Miss Doras Brown.

Actually, at the next session of the Congress, I did not appear before
a committee. I went only once or twice to see Senator Byrnes, the
chairman of the joint committee whose task it was to pilot the measure
through the Senate.

What happened was that the chorus of denunciation against the bill
grew and grew and grew. It was called a "dictator bill." It was denounced far and wide as a part of Roosevelt's plan to seize entire control of the government, just as he was subverting the Supreme Court.
This bill, it was charged, was intended to abolish the Congress and in-

trust total dictatorial power to one autocrat, Franklin D. Roosevelt, in the White House.

At last Senator Byrnes, through a terrific struggle and his great parliamentary skill, succeeded in getting the bill passed by the Senate by a majority of one vote. Then he was deprived of the fruits of his victory by a parliamentary maneuver in which his attention was distracted and somebody else made the usual motion to substitute the House bill for the Senate bill in order that the measure might go directly to a conference between the two houses. And that motion was laid on the table. There was to be no conference. Then, a little later, amid all the heat of the battle over the Supreme Court and about the "dictator bill," the House killed the whole Senate measure; the same House that had passed a similar measure by more than a two-thirds' majority, with an affirmative vote of more than half the Democrats as well as more than half the Republicans, killed the bill.

On account of my illness, during all these struggles in the Senate and later in the House, I had little contact with events. Dr. Merriam and Luther Gulick were always available when their presence was required before committees. Dr. Harris was in frequent requisition and had almost daily contacts with Mr. Lawton and with Senator Byrnes. The fight was over. The President had lost. The report of the President's committee apparently was dead. That it was to be revived and a very large part of the recommendations of the committee adopted in the Reorganization Act of 1939 was an event then impossible to predict.

I had other things to do: to get well; to reorganize my working life; to learn to leave more and more matters to my subordinates; to preside over the changing environment and atmosphere at the cluster of organizations of administrative and public officials in Chicago; and to resume my contacts in international public administration. In short, I changed my way of living for the better. I learned to relax, to take it easy. I absolutely cut off some chores, such as the daily dictation of my detailed diary, that seemed to me not absolutely necessary. In spite of this change in my working habits, I did not diminish the content of my activities. Indeed, if there was any change, I took a greater interest in a wider range of problems in the administrative field than I had earlier when I had been so overwhelmed with details.

CHAPTER XXXII

INTERLUDES IN BELGIUM AND LATIN AMERICA

It had been decided that the Clearing House would call a conference of representatives of the principal European nations to meet sometime in the autumn of 1937 to review the various aspects of the art and science of governmental planning machinery in several countries, in an effort to determine whether any consensus of international thought could be discovered. The Clearing House had engaged the services of a distinguished British civil servant, Sir Henry N. Bunbury, K.C.B., who, after serving in several capacities in the higher echelons of the British administrative service, had retired at the conclusion of his work as comptroller general of the British Post Office. It was during this tour of duty that Sir Henry had modernized the telephone system of Great Britain, had been the principal creator of a governmental corporation to take charge of the new business of radio transmission, which became the British Broadcasting Corporation, and had been one of the principal architects of the Royal Institute of Public Administration. He had visited nearly all the countries of Europe. He had been in close correspondence with his colleagues and opposite numbers in the field of transportation and communications represented by the Post Office, and he had been a frequent visitor to the United States. I had engaged his services and had made it possible for him to visit most of the European countries as well as to take a fresh look at the work of the National Resources Board, several state planning agencies, and similar organizations here in the United States, as well as in Canada.

The meeting was set for September in Belgium at the Château d'Ardennes, an old royal domain converted into a national park. Operated under a concession as a resort hotel, the palace was located in the midst of a charming park in the center of an ancient royal forest,

a part of the Forest of Ardennes which had been the scene of cumulative fighting by the American Army toward the end of World War I
and which was destined again to be overrun in World War II. Indeed,
the Ardennes was a part of the classic cockpit of Europe.

It was a rough and tempestuous voyage. One evening after dinner
at the captain's table we were assembled for coffee and cognac in the
great hall at the head of a double spiral stairway on a gallery also
occupied by the orchestra. The ship had been rolling. It began to pitch.
The bass drum broke loose from its moorings, escaped the drummer,
and rattled down the spiral stairway. The grand piano broke loose
from its anchorage and was all but catapulted over the railing, being
recaptured with difficulty by a half-dozen musicians.

And here was I, with not only my wife but with Merriam and Moffett, all four of us pretty sure that this would be the end of me with my
bad heart. After a while the captain of the ship with another officer
came to me, supported me, helped me, took me to an elevator, held
me up while we waited for an interval when the elevator could operate,
and finally escorted me in the grandest of style to my stateroom. There
I went to bed and there for two days I stayed, watching the pendulum
action of my topcoat which hung on a hook in front of a closet at the
foot of my bed. Fortunately the pitching somewhat subsided, but that
ship continued to roll.

Nothing the worse for it, I finally disembarked. We found ourselves
in a railway carriage on the way to the Château d'Ardennes. Unfortunately, there had to be a change, and that change was in an obscure
station in Belgium where there were no attendants to take care of the
bags. Moffett and Merriam shoved their bags out through the windows,
but there was nobody to pick them up. My wife was hardly able to
move ours, and I was forbidden to do so. Merriam and Moffett caught
the bags as we shoved them out. The train started to move. It was with
the greatest difficulty that the conductor was persuaded to blow his
whistle to stop the train before we were swept on into Germany.

We found our quarters at the Château d'Ardennes ideally situated,
since my wife and I were given a beautiful suite on the ground floor
where I would not have to encounter stairsteps, still forbidden for me
if there were more than three at a time. It turned out, however, that
the meeting room was in an adjoining building, and it could not be
reached except by climbing twelve steps. I took three, rested, took three

[405]

again, rested, and so on until I finally reached the room. There I was to preside. There was a long table covered with the green baize which was the very symbol of committees, boards, and conferences.

Not all the persons that we had invited were able to come. There was, as so often happened, "a crisis of the franc" in France, and the two French delegates we had invited could not come. From Germany there was the president of the German Chamber of Commerce, a distinguished industrialist and businessman who occupied a very special position in the then existing state of German affairs and politics. It had been he who had bailed Adolf Hitler out of prison at the time of the abortive *Putsch* in Munich in 1923. He was reputed to be the only man in Germany who was permitted to address the Führer with the familiar "du." He was a Pomeranian of ancient noble lineage. He also was well versed in the English language, and he operated an industrial concern in Tonawanda, New York.

Italy, another totalitarian country, was represented by a charming gentleman whose understanding of English was quick and accurate and who, after a few days, readily learned to trust his speaking of it. From England there were Sir Henry Bunbury and two or three others. From Czechoslovakia, the head of the planning division of the Masaryk Institute, Frank Munk; from Belgium, not only our old friend Senator Émile Vinck and his assistant, René Didisheim, but a brilliant young economist who had spent a very large part of his youth in Harvard University as a refugee from World War I and who already had become a principal adviser of economic planning to the Belgian government. From Sweden there was a handsome Senator Ohlin; and there were others from Norway, Switzerland, and the International Labor Office.

My American colleagues later confided to me that at the first meeting my voice was weak; my attitude and general appearance was that of a tottering old man, and, worse than that, I apparently was not able to collect my thoughts. I am not quite persuaded that it was as bad as they thought. I was attempting, as I have so often done when called upon to be a chairman of a group of persons unknown to each other and representing entirely different patterns of thought, to idle along until I could get some leads and some help from some members of the group. This help was forthcoming almost immediately from a Dutchman, Dr. Kaag, a personable, quick-witted, kindly man who was not only a professor of economics but the personal instructor in the field of economics and politics of the Princess Juliana. He had at once set up a rapport with Beardsley Ruml, who was his opposite number in good fellowship, in discriminating taste for food and wines, and pound for pound and inch for inch, in weight and girth. Also, the young Belgian with the Harvard background was willing to help me out, as was the young Czech professor, Frank Munk. With their help, the dismay, which had fallen not only upon my American colleagues but on my British and European familiars, Bunbury, Vinck, and Didisheim, passed, and we began to thresh things out as we entered upon the week's adventure. At the end of five days we had come to some concert of opinion, and I had recovered my self-confidence. We were sorry that the French were not there. We were even more regretful that the Russians had not responded to the invitation. And we greatly regretted the absence of the Turkish delegate whom we had invited. The entirely different political backgrounds of delegates were mutually appreciated and did not utterly obscure a developing general opinion that organization within the government, whatever its form, was necessary. Some general planning machinery was needed to encompass the fields of economics, of industry, of public and private construction, and, above all, of political guidance not only for fiscal and program control but for the search for popular consent. All this later was ably reviewed by Sir Henry Bunbury in a report that was published by Public Administration Service and soon achieved worldwide circulation and repute.

Nevertheless, there was tension in the atmosphere and the inescapable feeling that the Europe about which we were vainly talking, the America which we were attempting to relate to world affairs, and the very world itself were in grave danger.

Our hotel was operated under a concession to a Spanish chain-hotel corporation. This particular corporation was made up of Spaniards who were devoted to the Republic and intensely hostile to the Franco regime. The political and social atmosphere of the time pervaded the entire establishment. We discovered after the first few meals that the waiters made a point of carefully neglecting the German and the Italian delegates. It became necessary to take measures. I had Mrs. Brownlow seated next to the venerable German delegate to see to it that, when others were served, he was served. And René Didisheim performed the same service for the Italian.

The excellent cuisine and the vintage wine were wonderful; the only shadow that hung over our communal meals was that of politics. It was easy to see that the young Frank Munk, the Czech, was secretly pleased by the rough treatment shown the representatives of Nazi Germany and Fascist Italy. If Franco Spain had been invited, which it was not, and had sent representatives, which it did not, I fear there would have been a general outrage. Even as it was, when we dispersed Professor Munk was in considerable difficulty. He had been scheduled on several planes, each of which made a stop in Germany. That was a risk he would not run; he waited and waited until at last he could arrange a non-stop flight from Brussels to Prague, difficult in those days to do.

The atmosphere in the autumn of 1937 was not propitious for personal contacts among representatives of different nations, but that very fact did incline every delegate to be meticulous in his conduct around the conference table, and in the end we reached not a formal agreement but a concert of ideas and an acceptance of a series of standards for governmental machinery for planning. It might have been of very great importance had not the world of that day been all but destroyed a few years later in the fury of World War II.

Then came a Latin-American interlude which greatly interested me, occupied a great deal of my time and thought, and incidentally involved the expenditure of a good deal of money by the Public Administration Clearing House.

The International Conference of American States, the precursor of what is now the Organization of American States, adopted a resolution at its meeting in 1928 in Havana looking toward an inter-American municipal organization modeled along the general lines of the International Union of Local Authorities at Brussels. It took a decade to get the project under way. The inspiration for this movement had come from Señor Ruy de Lugo-Viña, president of the city council of Havana, who had attended meetings of the IULA in Europe. He started out to make a tour of the American republics in 1937 in an effort to create interest in the project, but unfortunately on that trip he was killed in an airplane accident. Then the work was taken up vigorously by the municipal government of Havana, which, toward the end of 1937, called an organizational meeting for the spring of 1938. This call was sent only to the American Municipal Association in the United States. Clifford W. Ham, then director of that association during my absence in Europe, had consulted with other organizations in the Chicago group and with Mr. Moffett of the Spelman Fund. The direct result of that consultation was that early in 1938 Mr. Moffett, accompanied by Mr. Ham and Mr. Rowland Egger, who had been the Public Administration Clearing House's representative in the Brussels center, went to Havana. They interviewed the organizing committee. They were struck with what they considered to be the inadequate preparations for the conference and succeeded in persuading the Cuban committee to postpone the meeting until autumn.

Although Cuba is a Spanish-speaking country, Havana has an English-language newspaper. The visit of Mr. Moffett of the Spelman Fund to Havana was entirely obscured in its headlines, which were devoted to the team of Ham and Egger. The pun was perfectly understandable to the Spanish-speaking people also, and a great deal of publicity medicine was made for the new show. The organizing committee was expanded. The mayor of Havana, Dr. Antonio Beruff Mendieta, assumed its chairmanship, and the American groups of officials were invited to assist in the preparation for the conference.

To that end, in April, 1938, I went to Havana and began to do what I could to help with the organization. At least two members of the organizing committee were heartily in sympathy with the expanded and more practical program suggested. One of them was Dr. Carlos M. Moran, corporation counsel of the city of Havana, and the other was Dr. Gustavo Gutiérrez, a former minister of justice who had a great interest in municipal and administrative law. With some financial help from the Clearing House, the committee greatly expanded the scope of its work, and my name was added to its membership.

Very soon I saw that it would be impossible for me and my colleagues in the United States to do our full part toward launching this new organization if my communications were limited to the mails. I decided that I would have to have somebody resident in Havana during the summer to keep me in constant touch with the progress of affairs.

Whereupon I wrote to six professors of political science and public administration, friends of mine, in six different universities in the

United States. I asked each of them whether he had a graduate student whose services I could employ during the months from June to October, the primary qualification being that the student be able fluently to speak, read, and write Spanish. Three of my professorial friends turned up with a man. One wrote a letter; one sent a telegram; but Lindsay Rogers of Columbia University used the long-distance telephone. He said he had the ideal candidatae provided I had no insuperable prejudice against personal pulchritude. I had none. So I employed Rogers' graduate student, John J. Kennedy, to go to Havana and act as my liaison secretary with the organizing committee for the first Pan-American Congress of Municipalities. It was not just a four-month job for him; it turned out to be a four-year job. It increased his knowledge of Latin American, but it also delayed his taking his Ph.D. for a good many years. Nevertheless, during that four years and before he went into the Navy, he visited nineteen of the twenty Latin-American republics and in each of them made contact with the central government, with some of the municipal governments, and with the universities, and in a half-dozen or more was the inspiration for the organization of national leagues of municipalities.

The show that was put on at the organizing conference in Havana in October was a big one. The city of Havana and the republic of Cuba were generous in their contributions. Delegates came from all but one or two of the Latin-American republics. Technical and general articles, including a Spanish translation of a report on municipal government by the National Resources Board under the title "Our Cities," were prepared and issued in both languages and circulated weeks in advance.

The American delegation was made up of representatives from all the organizations in the Chicago cluster. Then also there was Harold L. Ickes, secretary of the interior. I was especially urged by some of the Latin Americans to have him attend because he, as director of the Public Works Administration, had demonstrated, so my South American friends told me, that large sums could be expended in public works without even the hint of graft or corruption. Then also there was a Latin who was the mayor of the greatest city in the Western world, Fiorello H. LaGuardia. Then there was particularly wanted some representation from the socialists, which the United States provided in the person of Daniel W. Hoan, at that time in his twenty-fifth year as a Socialist mayor of the city of Milwaukee. There were dozens of others from the United States who were met by large delegations from all the more important Latin-American states with the exception of Brazil, which was represented only by its resident ambassador in Havana.

Many of the American delegates, including me, were accompanied by their wives, and so were many of the Latin Americans. It was a most successful conference. Its meetings were well attended. Its discussions were at a high level and the new organization showed every prospect of success.

Some of my American colleagues agreed with me that one of the difficulties of maintaining the vitality of such an organization in Latin America was the habit of limiting activities to annual or biennial conferences, without maintaining any permanent secretariats for the continuation of services. That was something also that in former years had characterized most United States organizations in the field of government administration, but here we had, we thought, learned better and had begun to think that the lifeblood of an organization really was its permanent secretariat and its continuing services, which in turn greatly helped the general conferences and conventions that were held.

So I sought and obtained from the Spelman Fund a special grant to enable me to call a meeting of the Board of Directors that was established to consider the problem of organization. This meeting I assembled in Chicago late in November, 1939. Attended by delegates from a dozen countries, it was held in the conference room of the sparklingly new building at 1313 East Sixtieth Street. Its resources for the Spanish-speaking people astonished me. We discovered in the building no less than seven stenographers who could take and transcribe correspondence in Spanish. This circumstance made the greatest impression upon the Latin-American visitors that could be imagined. Then also I attempted to return the hospitality that we had received in Havana. Each delegate had a car and a driver at his disposal. There were luncheons, and there was one great banquet graced by the presence of Edward J. Kelly, the mayor of Chicago. This left no doubt whatever in the minds of the visitors that the Americans professionally and technically interested in municipal government were sincere in their desire to help out such an organization.

It was decided there to make the organization permanent, to set up a permanent secretariat in Havana to be presided over by Dr. Carlos M.

Moran, and so the Inter-American Municipal Organization was formally launched.

It had its troubles during the war. It held a conference in Chile in 1941, when I was too busy to attend it. Since that time it has grown, and at its Sixth Biennial Congress held in Panama in 1956 it proved its continuing and ever increasing value as one of the important parts of the general movement toward the unity of municipalities of the Western world. It is unique in one particular. Its sessions are attended not only by the representatives of the twenty-one American republics but also by those of Canada, so that it comprises all the municipal organizations of the Western hemisphere.

CHAPTER XXXIII

THE REORGANIZATION
ACT OF 1939

The death of the proposed reorganizations recommended in 1937 by the President's Committee on Administrative Management turned out to be not so final as a great many persons thought. They were resurrected from the grave after the Democrats won the congressional elections in 1938. The President did not call in the members of his reorganization committee. Instead he consulted his party leaders in the Congress and urged them to meet the situation in every way possible.

The result was that without very much fuss or fury, with but a modicum of denunciation of the "dictator bill," there emerged from Congress the Reorganization Act of 1939, and the President signed it on April 3, 1939. This measure was based on the report of the Brownlow Committee, and it went some distance toward carrying out the recommendations the President had submitted in January, 1937. But the opposition of some of the federal agencies and of some of the congressional committees required a compromise.

Furthermore, somewhere on Capitol Hill, I think it was in the office of the legislative counsel (perhaps the handiwork of Middleton Beaman), a great improvement was made in the legislation over what we had recommended as a matter of procedure. In the other acts giving the President power to reorganize the executive branch, the device had been to empower him to issue executive orders which would come into effect if they had not been disapproved by the Congress within a period of sixty days. The new measure, however, employed a device which went a long way toward easing the classic conflict between the Congress and the chief executive. It simply made the President an agent of the legislature. Then, with no executive orders, no flaunting of the presidential power, the President was to submit reorganization plans to the Congress and, if these plans were not vetoed by the legislature, they would come into full force and effect as public laws and be published as statutes; they were therefore subject to change only by the joint action of the President and of both houses of Congress.

Certainly neither Merriam, Gulick, nor I knew anything about the proposed change. It was a device invented by the congressional staff to meet congressional purposes, placing upon a legislative agent who merely happened to be the President of the United States the duty of preparing plans to be considered by the Congress.

President Roosevelt lost no time in seeing to it that the provisions of the law were put into effect. He telephoned me and asked me to see to it that Merriam, Gulick, and I came to town. This time there was no fanfare or publicity. We merely gathered in my suite in the Hay-Adams House and began work.

Earlier that spring Henry Morgenthau, Jr., the secretary of the treasury, and Daniel W. Bell, acting director of the budget, had called me in for a consultation on the problem of whom to recommend to the President for appointment as director of the budget. I met the two gentlemen in the Treasury, in a room on the basement floor. Their office staffs knew nothing about our meeting. Mr. Morgenthau asked me to recommend somebody of a general city-manager type who had experience and had proved his skill in administrative work, especially of a budgetary character, but who had not been an active partisan politician.

I told them that I had two men in mind who might meet their qualifications, and in addition each had been at the head of a state budget office. One was A. E. Stockburger, formerly city manager of Ventura, California, and the other was Harold D. Smith, at that time director of the budget of the state of Michigan, who had had wide municipal experience as the secretary of the Michigan Municipal League. I attempted to give them my estimate of the abilities of the two gentlemen in question.

Smith was offered the position, and he accepted. He came to Washington and took over the quarters of the director of the Bureau of the Budget in the Treasury Building.

The Reorganization Act was passed. The President's committee, without staff except that furnished by Smith in the Budget Office and by the attorney general of the United States, began again to function. Within a week or so we had prepared Plan I and Plan II.

There was no change in the Rooseveltian pace. Three days after we submitted the plans to the President, Smith and I had lunch with him and spent three hours discussing Plan II and the possibilities of a Plan III. On May 3 we had lunch with the President and put in two hours discussing the form of the plans, both those already prepared and those in the works. During all these conferences the President behaved himself as if he actually were a legislator and not the President, as if he actually were a member of a committee, not the authority to which a committee would report. Even at the first session he greeted us, "Fellow members of the Reorganization Committee, we have got a big job of work to do. Let's get at it."

Actually, Plan I was sent up on April 25. It caused quite a little splash in the legislative pool. Perhaps that is the reason Senator Byrnes and Representative Warren were called in before the President sent up Plan II, which was submitted on May 9, three days after that White House conference in which the congressional representatives participated.

But then a different sort of trouble arose. The plans, which had far-reaching effects on the executive branch, would come into effect sixty days after submission and approximately two weeks apart. The timing was not geared to the fiscal year. That could have caused an awful lot of trouble. Whereupon the Congress, by unanimous action of both houses, adopted a joint resolution declaring that the provisions of Plan I and Plan II should take effect on July 1, 1939, notwithstanding the provisions of the Reorganization Act.

That settled it. Plan I and Plan II became the law of the land, and, so far as I know, the first laws on the statute books of the United States which had passed Congress twice. There were still people in some of the affected departments, agencies, bureaus, and divisions who believed, or at least pretended to believe, that the plan procedure had been irregular. The joint resolution and the second enactment of the new laws settled that.

By the time the first two reorganization plans were finished and sent to the Congress, the President was completely familiar with every consideration and, with his customary rapid pace, he had afforded the new director of the budget, Harold Smith, a speedy and thorough introduction into the business of the government of the United States and the intimate relationship of the director of the budget to the chief executive. Smith, with his characteristic adaptability and great ability, then became, in fact as well as in theory, the captain of the team, so far as organization of the executive branch was concerned. He kept in close touch, as time went on, with Merriam, Gulick, and me, not particularly because we had once been members of the President's Committee on Administrative Management, but because he had been keeping in close touch with us for a good many years, just as he had with other persons in all parts of the country who were interested in administrative management. He gave us no greater consideration than he did dozens of others upon whose knowledge he thought he could rely or whose brains he thought he could pick.

Plan I was a revolutionary document. In the message accompanying it the President took exception to the fact that the Congress had exempted twenty-one independent agencies and bureaus from the provisions of the act. He reviewed the attempts that had been made for a rational reorganization of the executive branch of the government over a period of decades and then set up the arguments for the plan, which fell into four parts:

Part I created the Executive Office of the President. It was then apparent, and subsequent events have proved, that that was the major revolutionary feature of the whole business. A great many students of administration have expressed the opinion that the establishment of the Executive Office, the effective co-ordination of the tremendously widespread federal machinery, enabled the United States to win World War II and meet the consequent problems with which the nation had to deal.

The Executive Office as it was conceived and organized under Plan I in the summer of 1939 was indeed a little thing compared to its present size. It expanded under President Roosevelt during the war years; it continued to expand and was further regularized by statute, by appropriation acts, and by more reorganization plans under President Truman. Under President Eisenhower it has had a tremendous expansion not only in the number of its personnel but in the scope of its organization.

The President of the United States did all his work in the White House itself until the administration of Theodore Roosevelt, when a small office wing was built on the west end of the White House. That sufficed until the administration of President Hoover, when the wing was greatly enlarged. During World War II another office structure was erected at the East Wing of the White House.

In the summer of 1939, however, the Bureau of the Budget, which had been transferred from the Treasury Department to the new Executive Office of the President, was physically moved from the Treasury Building into quarters in the old State, War, and Navy Building. That building, one of the more regrettable architectural features of the Washington scene, was built during and after the Civil War and in my time—when I first came to Washington as a Washington correspondent in the time of Theodore Roosevelt—actually contained the entire State Department, War Department, and Navy Department. Now, in 1957, it houses nothing but the Executive Office of the President. It isn't big enough. The President and the Congress are now awaiting the report of the special commission created for the purpose of devising larger and better quarters for the Executive Office of the President. I am quite sure that Franklin D. Roosevelt, when he sent up Plan I, had not in his wildest dreams conceived of such an expansion.

Part 2 of Plan I set up a Federal Security Agency. This was to take the place of the department of social welfare that had been a feature of our original recommendations. Forbidden to create a department, "F. D. R." created an agency. Forbidden to call its head a "secretary," he called him an "administrator." Forbidden to give a salary of $10,000 a year, equal to that of members of the Cabinet and incidentally to that of members of the two houses of Congress, he provided for the administrator a salary of $9,000 a year. Actually, the Federal Security Agency became in everything but words a major department of the government, although it was not until the early days of the Eisenhower administration that it was set up as the Department of Health, Education, and Welfare and its administrator blessed with the title of "secretary."

The Federal Security Agency was named "security" instead of "welfare" because the vice-president, John Nance Garner, told the President that there was a great objection to the terms "welfare," "social welfare," "public welfare," etc., in Congress, that its use could only lead to a continuation of the welfare activities of the government, which should be stopped as soon as possible, but that there was no objection to the word "security" because it looked as if the Social Security Board might be a pretty good thing.

A Public Works Agency was also set up, and this, in similar fashion, was in lieu of the Public Works Department which we had originally recommended.

Then there was also established the Federal Loan Agency. That, neither the President's committee nor the President had recommended in 1937. It had been the President's original plan to consolidate the federal loan agencies in the Department of Commerce. Suggestions had been made to put them in the Treasury Department, but the President had said to us, "That won't work. If they put them in the Treasury, not one of them will ever make a loan to anybody for any purpose. There are too darned many glass-eyed bankers in the Treasury."

But Jesse Jones, the head of the Reconstruction Finance Corporation, the biggest of the loan agencies, was dead against being transferred along with the other loan agencies into the Department of Commerce. And with him stood many others who similarly objected. So it happened that Mr. Jones, together with Vice-President Garner and Speaker Rayburn, all three Texans, all three party leaders, told the President where to get off. The result was the Federal Loan Agency.

There is an interesting tale of why the Federal Loan Agency was so short-lived. During the war the President, through his counsel, Sam Rosenman, decided to send up a plan for the establishment of a National Housing Administration. I was ill in the Hay-Adams House at the time. I hadn't seen the President in a long time, but Sam came over to see me and said the President would like to see my initials on the housing plan. I said, "Sam, I'll make a trade. If he will send up another plan to throw the Federal Loan Agency back into the Department of Commerce where it belongs, I will initial this."

"But how in the world can we do that?"

"It is very easy now," I said. "Jesse Jones is now the secretary of commerce."

It was done.

These, then, are the four principal features of Plan I as it was submitted to the Congress. Into the Executive Office were placed the Bureau of the Budget, transferred from the Treasury, and the Central Statistical Board, on which many departments were represented; the Central Statistical Committee was abolished; the National Resources

Committee was renamed the National Resources Planning Board and transferred to the Executive Office; the Federal Employment and Stabilization Office was abolished and the transfer of funds and personnel appropriately arranged.

Into the Federal Security Agency were transferred the Social Security Board, the United States Employment Service, the Office of Education, the Public Health Service, the National Youth Administration, and the Civilian Conservation Corps. The secretary of the treasury was never quite able to forgive me or Harold Smith, my nominee, for taking the Bureau of the Budget out from under his wing. Although, as a matter of law, it had been legally responsible only to the President from the time of the enactment of the Accounting and Budget Act of 1921, its physical situation in the Treasury Department and the necessarily intimate relationships between the Treasury and Budget had enabled each succeeding secretary to consider the bureau one of his own, despite the vigorous opposition to any such subjection to the secretary of the treasury made by General Charles G. Dawes, the first director of the Bureau of the Budget.

However, there was one amusing circumstance. In one of our meetings the President, in going over plans, said, "Now this committee has been remarkable in keeping its mouth shut. These new plans are going to cause a tremendous flutter in the dovecotes, but there is one particularly sensitive spot that I think you, Merriam, ought to look after. I know that you have been very close to Ickes for many years, that Ickes was the manager of your campaign when you ran for mayor in 1911, and that you as a member of the National Resources Committee have had your outfit set up under the Department of the Interior. I think it would be a good idea in this one case for you to 'leak.' "

Then turning to Smith he said, "You know, if I may address Dishonest Harold, Honest Harold has a peculiar trait. He is as honest as he is reputed to be, but he is like an honest cop patrolling a city market. He won't let anybody steal a peanut, but every once in a while he will reward himself with an apple here or a banana there as a tribute to his own honesty. Thus it is with Harold Ickes. He won't let anyone else take a bureau away from him, but he will be glad to pick up one or two if convenient in order to maintain his strict honesty. Merriam, I think you had better talk to Honest Harold and tell him we are actually taking the Office of Education away from him and putting it in the new agency."

Merriam and I discussed the problem. He was loath to act. I invited Ickes to come to lunch in my suite at the Hay-Adams. There was nobody there but Merriam and me. Ickes was nervous. He knew these plans were being drawn up. He was all prickles and thorns, fearful of what was going to happen to him. I waited for Merriam to speak. Merriam never said a word. The lunch was over and Ickes was about to leave, and so I made bold to speak.

"Mr. Secretary, the plans are going up and one bureau is being taken away from the Department of Interior."

Oh, how he bristled! "What's that? What's that?"

I said, "The Office of Education."

"Thank God. I never wanted the so-and-so anyhow. You and Merriam put him over on me and I am glad to get rid of him."

There was no trouble there. And in another plan several bureaus were transferred to Mr. Ickes' department, but we didn't "leak" that information.

In the message accompanying Plan I, the President took occasion to make a slap at Congress for exempting the Civil Service Commission from the provisions of the Reorganization Act. He was perfectly aware that the proposal for a single Civil Service administrator in the proposed act of 1937 was most unpopular on the Hill, and he also knew, of course, as did anyone who read the papers or heard the talk, that the members of the legislature were not particularly enthusiastic about his proposal to extend the merit system upward, outward, and downward to take in all but the top policy forming positions. Also, he had another reason. He was opposed to boards in general as administrative agents. He was for single administrators. Once he said to me, "The difficulty is that the Civil Service Commission, in law and theory, is actually an appendage of the presidency. It isn't a regulatory body. It operates under rules which, in accordance with constitutional principles, are promulgated by the President. In theory, at least, any President at any time could abolish the whole works simply by exempting from the application of the rules in the law every employee of the government. Yet, the statute requires that I appoint three persons to its board, and not more than two of them can be members of the same political party. Of course, I know it is set up to keep bipartisan control over the civil service, but the way it works, the President is handicapped in trying to find out what the commission wants. If they come into this office and I ask them a question, all three of them have to go out in the corridor or some other place, hold a caucus, and come back and answer me. If anything comes up that doesn't admit of a two-to-one vote of 'yes' or 'no,' then they listen, and sometimes weeks later they may give me some sort of an answer. I would like to deal with one man alone."

When he sent up his first reorganization plan, he said, among other things, "Because of an exemption in the act, it is impossible to transfer to the Executive Office the administration of the third managerial function of the government, that of personnel. However, I desire to inform the Congress that it is my purpose to name one of the administrative assistants to the President, authorized in the Reorganization Act of 1939, to serve as a liaison agent of the White House on personnel management.

"In this manner, the President will be given for the first time direct access to the three principal necessary management agencies of the government. None of the three belongs in any existing department. With their assistance and this reorganization, it will be possible for the President to continue the task of making investigations of the organization of the government in order to control expenditures, increase efficiency, and eliminate overlapping."

When the plan went into effect, the President named William H. McReynolds as one of his administrative assistants and made him liaison man with the Civil Service Commission. It worked well. The three Civil Service commissioners saw Mr. McReynolds once or twice a week at regularly appointed times. Mr. McReynolds then reported to the President what was in the minds of the commission and was able at the next meeting to tell the commission what was in the mind of the President with respect to the administration of the entire personnel of the federal government.

This system worked well until the beginning of World War II, when Mr. McReynolds' time began to be taken up with his liaison duties with the revived Council of National Defense.

After Mr. Eisenhower became President, while the Civil Service Commission was still composed of three persons, its chairman was moved into the White House and made the direct liaison agent between the President and personnel.

[421]

The Reorganization Act of 1939 expired by limitation on January 27, 1941. Before it expired, the war in Europe was on, and the President was given authority to transfer divisions and bureaus under two acts of Congress—War Powers Act I and War Powers Act II. A great many transfers, consolidations, and abolitions were accomplished under these two acts. But the difficulty was that they were temporary. That led President Truman to ask for another reorganization act providing for continuing authority, which was given him under the Reorganization Act of 1945. That act also revived the procedure of the President submitting plans to the Congress, the plans to be effective unless they were vetoed. That act also expired by limitation and was succeeded under the administration of President Truman by the Reorganization Act of 1949, which introduced another change, in that all exemptions were dropped and both houses of Congress were required to concur in the veto. That act, I believe, is still in effect, or, if it is not, its terminal date has been extended.

Thus it came about that the radical and revolutionary proposal of giving the President of the United States managerial control over the executive branch at last was accepted. Otherwise it is doubtful if any of the recommendations of the Hoover Commission I or the Hoover Commission II ever would have come into effect.

CHAPTER XXXIV

PREPARATION FOR WAR

During his presidency it was frequently said that Franklin Delano Roosevelt's greatest excellence was that of a magician, that he could pull a rabbit out of the hat at will. Whatever history may finally determine were his most salient qualifications as a statesman, there is one thing sure about his qualifications as a magician. The reason he was always able to pull the rabbit out of the hat at the right moment was that several months before he had always carefully installed it there. Certainly this was true of the events of the two or three years before the attack on Pearl Harbor catapulted the United States into the maelstrom of World War II.

Mr. Roosevelt had carefully laid the ground for subsequent action at a time when action was legislatively and politically impossible by his 1937 speech at the dedication of the Chicago bridge, in which he talked about a quarantine against war. During 1938 and 1939 he had pushed forward as much as he could by doing a little here and a little there, persuading one group after another by every means at his disposal, and trying to instil in the country a consciousness of the danger arising from the advent of fascism in Europe, a danger constantly in his mind.

Of course, he was not by any means the only person interested. Even after the end of World War I there had been a group of persons, some civilian, some military, some in and some out of the government, who had insisted upon current planning for the eventuality of a war, so that this country would not be at such a disadvantage in the mobilization of men, material, and money as that experienced in 1916 and 1917.

These stirrings had resulted in the creation in the late twenties of the Army and Navy Munitions Board. Proceeding almost, if not quite, independently of the executive or of the Congress, it prepared successive revisions of an industrial mobilization plan. The first was issued in 1931, and subsequent revisions were published in 1933, 1936, and 1939.

In the summer of 1939 it seemed more and more certain that Hitler would launch a European war and, to many minds, that that war would ultimately involve the United States. Assistant Secretary of War Louis Johnson was talking to the President from time to time about the industrial mobilization plans. The upshot was the appointment by the President early in August, 1939, of a body known as the War Resources Board.

One day I was invited to lunch at the White House with the President. He asked me if I had read the published industrial mobilization plans. I had not. He asked me to read them, to let him know what I thought about the administrative aspects of the recommendations, what I thought could be done about obtaining from Congress special legislation for special organizational plans for preparedness, and what I thought could be found in the statute books that would enable him to proceed without new legislation.

During this conversation a good deal was said about President Wilson's difficulties with administrative organization. More especially we talked about how Wilson had found it necessary not only to go to the Congress for every new agency that the situation required but to return to the Congress to get that agency abolished or changed. This conversation was along the same line as many we had had over the report of the President's Committee on Administrative Management. It was also in line with my earnest recommendation that the executive of the United States be given far greater flexibility in the administration and in the management of the work of the government.

A few days later I saw the President, again at his request. I told him then that in my opinion it would be almost impossible to get greater powers from the Congress than already were obtained in the Reorganization Act of 1939, which, falling short of what he had requested in 1937, would not suffice to meet the problem of industrial mobilization. I told him I had not had time fully to study the reports on industrial mobilization. He asked me to be sure to read them and then to come back. I was a bit more careful about doing my homework. I was invited to come to the White House to lunch on Tuesday, August 29, 1939.

"What is your report?" he asked after a rather longish discursive talk over the luncheon at his desk. I had tried several times during the meal to begin my report, but, with his consummate skill, he had prevented my saying anything until he was ready to ask the question.

"Well, Mr. President," I replied, "I have two or three reports."

"But certainly you ought to have. The last time you hadn't done your homework. Have you done it?

"Yes."

"What do you think of it?"

"Well, it seems to me that any President who accepts the recommendations of these mobilization plans would do a little bit better to resign."

"In other words, you think resignation is more dignified than abdication."

I said, "Certainly."

Of course I know that he had consulted dozens of others. I am quite sure that he also had reached the same bald, basic decision in his conversation with others. He went on:

"Yes, indeed. If I were to set up a scheme such as recommended by this report, turning over the sole administration of the economy of the country, even the public relations of the White House, to a single war administrator—even though he were appointed by me—I would simply be abdicating the presidency to some other person. I might choose that person, but I would be expected to select him from a small group of big businessmen whose names were submitted to me by a committee, most of the members of which would desire above everything else in the world that some person other than 'F. D. R.' were President of the United States."

"Next question," said the President. "How will I go about it?"

"Mr. President," I said, "I believe that the only way to proceed is to use the act of August 26, 1916, setting up the National Defense Council. Re-create it, name it 'advisory committee,' and then set it up in the Executive Office of the President. The power to do this has been granted to you in the Reorganization Act of April 3, this year."

"Several people have told me that the act of August 29, 1916, was probably my only recourse, but I had not thought before of utilizing the Executive Office."

"That, I think, Mr. President, will give you the necessary power to control the operation of the council and enable you to grant or to withhold power, to create or dissolve subsidiary agencies and committees, and to retain control over them all."

"That's an idea. The council, of course, is composed of six members of the Cabinet, but the law authorized an advisory committee. I could reconstitute the council, tell the Cabinet officers to get lost, and run the thing through the advisory committee as part of my own office."

"That, I think, is your way out."

Then he drew a pad before him and began to draw a chart. He said, "Louis, I know that you don't like charts, and in some respects I share your antipathy, but if it is still fresh, I can understand my own shorthand."

Then, as I waited across the desk, he gave me the two sheets. I was astounded. Immediately I said, "Mr. President, you've got the wrong sow by the ear. I am not your man for that job. I don't think I am qualified, and I am sure that you can get somebody else who can handle the whole thing for you much more quickly and much better than I."

Then he said some very nice things about me to the general effect that I had been a great help, as chairman of the committee, in drawing up plans for the administrative organization of the executive branch. I interposed the state of my health. I told him that during the struggle with the proposed reorganization act of 1937, I had suffered, as he knew, a coronary occlusion and that I was quite confident that I did not have the physical strength to undertake the job, even if I thought, as I did not, that I was otherwise qualified.

"Don't talk physical difficulties to me," he said. It was the only time in my many conversations with him that he ever referred directly or indirectly to his physical infirmity.

I persisted. He then said, "Who, then, can I get?"

I said, "Mr. President, you ought to get somebody who is not a Big Shot, who will not try to become assistant president, but who is skilled in the administrative work of government and who really has a passion for anonymity."

"As for instance," he came back.

"Bill McReynolds," I answered.

"Maybe, maybe, maybe."

"But," he said, "tomorrow I am going to talk to the Stettinius board.

It will have a recommendation for me. I don't know just how I will handle it. I don't know whether I will handle it at all at this time. I am going to sleep on it tonight, but on the whole I am inclined to think that you are right and that the thing to do is to revive the old Council of National Defense and pull it right straight into my own office. If we are really headed for trouble, I will at least be my own boss and will not be compelled to turn over the presidency of the United States to some other man, a man who, I am sure, would never be nominated by a Democratic convention and never be elected by the people."

It was hot that day. The luncheon had been served at one o'clock. It was after five when I left the President's room. Everybody had gone home except Stephen Early and Marvin H. McIntyre, one his secretary for the press, one his secretary for appointments. The two frequently did not see eye to eye, but both were determined to protect the President from any person urging precipitate decisions upon him.

Steve said, "Louis, what is going on?"

I handed the two charts to them. They almost expired.

This, they immediately saw, would put me in a superior position, with direct contact with the President, and would give me what they had long suspected was my ambition—a chance not only to reorganize the presidency but to take over their jobs.

Before either had recovered sufficiently to speak, I said, "Don't worry. I have turned it down. I have turned it down flat."

Until this day I do not know whether the President offered me that high position in order to test me or because he really wanted me to take it. Until this day I do not know whether, if I had said "yes," he would have persisted in the offer or would have immediately ditched the plan. He knew, I am sure much better than I, the danger lurking in the creation of such a position for an administrative assistant—the same danger he had recognized lying behind the beautiful charts and the persuasive phraseology of the various reports on industrial mobilization—that is, the effort to cut the President out of any direct and continuing control of the industrial mobilization of the country.

That was the day the rabbit was put in the hat. It was not pulled out until months later—until May of the following year.

But there was another little rabbit stowed in the hat at the same time. The other little rabbit never was destined to grow to be so big, but it had a very important part to play.

The day after I had that lunch with the President, he met the War Resources Board, headed by Edward R. Stettinius, Jr. Mr. Roosevelt told the members of the board to go ahead and file their report, that it would be given careful study, but at the same time he intimated that he might have some different ideas. Two days later Hitler sent the German hordes across the Polish border. World War II was on. That was September 1, 1939.

Again I had a call from the White House. The President was very busy that day. I had perhaps three or four minutes with him. He said he already had talked with Harold Smith, the director of the budget, and had told Smith that he would like to have me draw up an Executive Order activating the Executive Office of the President and its several divisions.

The next two or three days, along with Harold Smith, Donald C. Stone, head of the administrative management division of the budget, and Judge Townsend of the Department of Justice, I was very busy. I myself wrote the final draft of the Executive Order. Mr. Smith took it to the White House, and it was given to the President just before he was leaving by train to go to Hyde Park for the week end.

In it I set up the several divisions of the Executive Office of the President according to the general plan that the Bureau of the Budget had worked out, which had been approved generally by the President and had been talked over by him with me. However, I put in one new thing. In addition to the Bureau of the Budget, the National Resources Planning Board, the Office for Government Reports, the Liaison Office for Personnel Management, and the immediate White House Office itself—the things that had been theretofore agreed upon—I added, "There should be in that Office in the event of a national emergency or threat of a national emergency such an office for emergency management as the President shall determine."

The presidential statement (which I also wrote) accompanying the Executive Order noted that in periods of emergency it has "always been found necessary to establish administrative machinery in addition to that required by the normal work of the government. Set up in a time of stress these special facilities sometimes had worked at cross purposes sometimes within themselves and with the regular departments and agencies. In order that the Nation may not be again caught unaware, adequate resources for management should be provided in advance of such periods of emergency."

This proviso of the Executive Order was eventually to serve as one of the legal bases for the erection of the major part of the governmental machinery used for defense in war. It was a novel and unprecedented feature in that it permitted the government to act immediately in time of an emergency.

I also spelled out in my draft of the Executive Order a special relationship between governmental functions and the several administrative assistants whose appointment had been authorized by the Congress.

I next saw the draft of the order when it was issued on September 8, 1939. Not one word had been changed, except that the two paragraphs specifiying special relations between administrative assistants and functional departments of the government had been entirely eliminated.

Thus the little rabbit that went in on August 29 came out ten days later on September 8, but was so disguised in small print, with no capital letters, that it occasioned no remark in the press or in the general discussions that then raged furiously throughout the country and the world about whether or not the United States would become involved in the war that Hitler had started in Poland. That little rabbit went right back in the hat.

The war went on. But after the first fury in Poland it seemed to die down. The period of the "phony war," as we called it, the "Sitzkrieg," as the Germans called it, ensued. The world was amazed by the apparent moderation of the Nazi high command; the war was not being accompanied by the frightfulness that accompanied the Kaiser's war in 1914. There was a lull.

But the next May, in 1940, with the occupation of Denmark and the invasion of the Low Countries, the lull came abruptly to an end. It was then that the magician pulled the rabbits out of the hat for keeps. On May 25 he issued an Executive Order setting up in the Executive Office of the President an Office of Emergency Management with William H. McReynolds at its head as liaison officer. On May 28 he reactivated the Defense Council, under the authority of the act of August 29, 1916. On May 29 he notified the Cabinet that one meeting of the National Defense Council would be quite sufficient, that thereafter the Advisory Commission would report directly to him or through his administrative assistant, McReynolds. And then to that Advisory Commission he appointed William S. Knudsen, an immigrant from Denmark who rose from the job of mechanic to the presidency of General Motors Corporation, as adviser on industrial production; Edward R. Stettinius, Jr., of the United States Steel Corporation, as adviser on industrial materials; Sidney Hillman, a Lithuanian immigrant tailor who had climbed to the position of president of the Amalgamated Clothing Workers of America, as adviser on employment; Leon Henderson, who had been a member of the Securities and Exchange Commission, as adviser on prices; Chester C. Davis, former administrator of the Agricultural Adjustment Administration and sometime governor of the Federal Reserve Board, as adviser on farm products; Ralph Budd, president of the Chicago, Burlington and Quincy Railroad and also president of the Association of American Railroads, as adviser on transportation; and Harriet Elliott, a political scientist at the University of North Carolina and a leading figure in women's activities, as adviser on consumers' interests.

This Advisory Commission met for the first time in the President's office on the morning of Memorial Day, May 30, while the British Army was being evacuated from Dunkirk. The President, the vice-president, members of the Cabinet, the speaker of the House, the Army chief of staff, the chief of naval operations, the President's secretary, his military aide, and William H. McReynolds were also present.

Once or twice in the interim he had discussed with me the names of persons for these various advisory positions. Mr. Stettinius was always on the list. He had mentioned once or twice Daniel W. Hoan, the Socialist mayor of Milwaukee, to head the consumers' division; he had also mentioned Dr. Martha Eliot of the Children's Bureau for that place. As the list came out, there was no name on it that he had not discussed with me except those of Chester C. Davis for farm products and Miss Harriet Elliott for the consumers' division. I have always suspected that there was some administrative slip-up that changed the name of Martha Eliot to Harriet Elliott. The reason that either was considered was, as the President told me, that "Frances and the two Eleanors are after me to be sure to put a woman on the board." "Frances," of course, was Miss Perkins, secretary of labor, and the two Eleanors were "Eleanor"—Mrs. Roosevelt, and "Elinor"—Mrs. Henry Morgenthau, Jr. The names of William S. Knudsen and Sidney Hillman, which had not been on the chart of August 29, 1939, he had discussed with me several times before the actual appointment.

During the time of the dormancy of his scheme, between August, 1939, and May, 1940, the President once asked me to take his plan to Chicago to discuss it in strict confidence with some leading businessmen. I undertook the task with some misgiving. I went first to the chairman of the board of the Public Administration Clearing House, Ralph Budd. Despite its informality, Mr. Budd, somewhat surprisingly to me, approved the plan.

I asked his advice about someone else to go to. He called Edward Eagle Brown, president of the First National Bank, and made an appointment for me. Mr. Brown was a man of ample girth and a matching amplitude of understanding. He also was understandably proud of the fact that in isolationist Chicago he was an all but isolated Democrat. He listened. The next day he called me on the telephone. "It is unorthodox, but maybe what we need is a good big dose of unorthodoxy."

I reported Mr. Budd's and Mr. Brown's reactions to President Roosevelt. He said nothing. Both these men occasionally asked me later, in effect, "What did he say?"

My only reply was, "He didn't say a word."

From the point of view of the report of the War Resources Board of 1939, of the various editions of the industrial mobilization plan, and, I believe, of the great majority of professional administrators in business and government, the new organization was a monstrosity. It had no head but the President, which was a very difficult thing for anybody in the Executive Department to understand. It had no chairman except the President himself, something very difficult for people in business to understand, since he was presumably busy with several other matters. Mr. Knudsen, at the first meeting held with the President in the White House on May 30, with his inimitable Danish accent, said he had one question that he would like to ask the President.

"What is that?"

"Who is the boss?"

"I am," said "F. D. R."

The scheme didn't please anybody particularly, except one man. He seemed to like it, and he was in a position to determine what scheme was to be used. Under it, despite all the lets and hindrances, the gripes and the groans, the war was fought and won, and this fact has never been satisfactorily explained to those who had different ideas of administrative hierarchy and efficient organization. The best way I can explain it is to tell a story about Bill Knudsen, one not directly connected with these events but one that does go far in my mind to explain them.

Long after the President had again violated all the principles laid down in the textbooks on administration by making Knudsen and Hillman cochairmen of the Office of Production Management, something was being considered by the Appropriations Committee of the Senate. Among those who had appeared there were Herbert Emmerich, then secretary of the War Production Board, Nelson Rockefeller, and one or two others. There was considerable difficulty. The chairman of the committee, Senator Kenneth D. McKellar of Tennessee, was obviously not impressed by the arguments being made for a certain appropriation. Mr. Emmerich persuaded Mr. Knudsen to go with him before the committee. When Mr. Knudsen came in, the chairman and the members of the committee rose to receive them. When they had resumed their seats, Mr. McKellar said, "Mr. Knudsen, this is what we think ought to be substituted for what has been submitted," and then proceeded to read the amendment.

"What do you think of that?"

"It von't vork."

"Why won't it work, Mr. Knudsen?"

"I have been paid all this money all these years by the General Motors Company to say 'it vill vork,' and 'it von't vork,' I never have been paid to say vy it von't vork or vy it vill vork."

The amendment went into the ash can.

On the way out, Mr. Knudsen nudged Emmerich on the elbow and whispered, "Herbert, vy von't it vork?"

Mr. Roosevelt had made up his mind what to do on August 29, 1939. But the crisis he expected then was delayed, and he knew he couldn't get what he wanted until there was a most unmistakable and a most alarming crisis. He bided his time.

The magician was magnificent—but also he had been forehanded.

CHAPTER XXXV

STIMSON AND KNOX

My talks with President Roosevelt were nearly always about administration. Rarely was a word said about politics, either the politics of parties or of persons. Occasionally there was a passing remark, but nearly all the time we stuck strictly to our knitting. This, of course, is not to say that either of us thought that administration can be carried on in a vacuum from which all political atmosphere has been exhausted, but, at least for the time being, both of us were concerned with the administrative aspects of governmental operation.

Once, and once only, did I bring up a political topic. Having been brought up, it recurred again and again in subsequent talks, until it had its final issue in the appointment of two eminent Republicans to places in the Cabinet. The appointment of Henry L. Stimson as secretary of war and Frank Knox as secretary of the Navy in June, 1940, just as France surrendered to the Hitler hordes and just before the opening of the Republican National Convention which nominated Wendell Willkie for President, was not the result of a sudden decision growing out of the crisis of the hour. The problem of how to include outstanding Republicans in the administration in the event of a dangerous crisis had long been under consideration by the President. I am sure that he talked with many persons about it, and I am equally sure that the part I played in it was not determining. It just so happens that this particular problem was the only political topic about which I ever talked with President Roosevelt on my own initiative.

My part came about in this way. At about the time of the Munich negotiations, I had luncheon one day with Mr. Frederic A. Delano and Dr. Charles E. Merriam of the National Resources Planning Board. In discussing the incident about which the whole world's tongue was wagging that day, we three found ourselves in entire agreement. We were sure that Mr. Chamberlain was wrong, that Mr. Daladier was deceived, and that there would not be "peace in our time." We were sure that Hitler would have the war he wanted. We were naturally not sure of just when and where he would start it.

It was then that I turned to Mr. Delano and said something like this: "The next time you see your distinguished nephew in the White House, I wish you would give him a message from me. Tell him that when it comes to war, if he is still in the White House, I hope he will do one particular thing. If the time should come when it seems necessary to take Republicans into his Cabinet, tell him, for the love of Mike, not to take in 'tame-cat' Republicans. Tell him not to take the kind of Republicans who are really halfway Democrats because they are friendly to him or he is friendly to them. Tell him not to take in Republicans such as Harold Ickes or Henry Wallace, who had lost their amateur standing in the G.O.P. even before they went into his Cabinet. Tell him to take the particular Republicans who have been chosen as leaders by the Republican party itself. They would be, of course, the most recent candidates for President and vice-president nominated by the Republican National Convention. If the war comes soon, as I believe it will, that would mean Landon and Knox."

My suggestion naturally brought on more talk, and both Mr. Delano and Dr. Merriam seemed to agree with me, and Mr. Delano said he would take the first opportunity of passing the notion along to President Roosevelt.

Then in the spring of 1939 came the march on Prague. At that time I was seeing the President very frequently in connection with the reorganization plans to be sent to the Congress under the provisions of the Reorganization Act of 1939.

One day at luncheon I said, "Mr. President, as you know, I have never ventured to talk politics to you, and, so far as I can recall, I have never said a word about any political question to you since you have been President." The President appeared to ponder for a moment and then said that he believed I was right; that we had always been so busy with our particular pidgin of administration that we had never had time to talk politics.

Then I said to him that he might put on his poker face, and, if he would just listen to what I had to say, I would not expect him to make any response whatsoever. I told him that I had endeavored to send a message to him through his Uncle Fred at the time of Munich but that I had discovered that Mr. Delano either had no opportunity to pass on the word or had forgotten to do it.

Thereupon I launched into my exposition of why I thought, if war came and he had to bring Republicans into the Cabinet, that under our system a direct coalition cabinet would not work at all, since there could be no responsibility to the party groupings in the Congress and since the President must always be solely responsible for the executive branch. Therefore, the demand for a so-called coalition could be met only by the selection of Republican leaders by the President.

He listened with an appropriate poker-face mask. I went on to say that if he took in Republicans, however able, however patriotic, and however devoted, their Republicanism might be questioned merely because he had named them. Therefore, I concluded, "If the time comes, you ought to bring in the two men chosen by the Republicans themselves—Alf Landon and Frank Knox."

When I had finished, he dropped the poker face. He spread his two hands out, palms down on the desk—a characteristic Roosevelt gesture at the moment of decision. He said, "You are right. If the time comes, that is what I intend to do, if there is any practicable way to do it. Thanks for the lecture on politics. It is a subject about which I know little and of which I hear less."

The next time I heard anything of that matter was early in September, 1939. Then there was war. Hitler had hurled his men and machines across the Polish border. What I had so confidently believed would happen from the hour the Germans were permitted to occupy the Rhineland had happened.

I saw the President several times during the week after the war began to discuss the executive orders and other documents relating to the establishment of the Executive Office of the President—the office that was to prove itself a mighty administrative engine for the accomplishment of our national purposes during the crowded and dangerous years to follow.

On one of these days the President told me that he had been thinking of my one political recommendation and that he had decided to give it a try. He told me that of course neither he nor anybody else could know what course the war would take. It was obviously a duty to prepare the thinking of the country for a globe-girdling, worldwide conflagration, and he said, in effect: "Sometime in the next two or three weeks I am going to invite a group of leading citizens of the country to come and talk the situation over with me. That will give me an excuse to ask Alf Landon and Frank Knox to come in here. I can look them over, and [this particular part of what he said I remember, I think, precisely] they can look me over from a little different angle than they used to in 1936."

A little later, on September 20, some fourteen eminent citizens came to the White House to talk with the President and Secretary of State Cordell Hull about the war policy that should be pursued by the people of the United States. More specifically, the talk centered on what to do about the repeal of the Embargo Act proposed so as to permit arms to be supplied to the countries fighting Hitler. The President already had called a special session of Congress to meet the very next day.

Among those who came to the White House conference were Alfred M. Landon and Frank Knox. Both had been advocating the repeal of the Neutrality Act, Governor Landon in speeches and statements made in Kansas and Colonel Knox in his newspaper, the *Chicago Daily News*.

Governor Landon, to use a phrase that was to be later associated with our naval operations, "broke silence" about the invitation to the White House. He issued a statement in Topeka before he entrained for Washington, another in Chicago on his way, and still another on the White House steps immediately after the conference. The others, or most of them at any rate, were discreetly silent, not only because of the importance of the occasion but also because in the very nature of the circumstances it was impossible at that time to reach any conclusions. Not only did Governor Landon make these public statements, but in the conference in the President's office itself he was markedly unco-operative. The President told me not long afterward that during the meeting Landon "acted like a bad little boy." At a still later time, Colonel Knox, in talking to me about the meeting, characterized Landon's behavior on that occasion in much saltier and more forceful words.

What Mr. Landon specifically said in Topeka on September 18, after receiving the invitation to the White House meeting over the telephone, was that he was glad to confer with the President; he had no hesitancy in accepting the invitation; and "It is not just a sophomoric expression with me to say that politics ends at the water's edge." On the next day, in Chicago, Governor Landon gave an interview in which he stressed the necessity of thinking about the domestic situation, saying, "War or no war, we cannot neglect our own affairs. In a few months, the nominating conventions will be upon us, and we cannot allow a foreign war to divert our attention from this job, much as the administration in power might be willing to have it diverted." In the White House meeting itself, Mr. Landon demanded that the Congress be kept in session for the duration of the "limited" emergency proclaimed by the President. He also, according to his statement given after the conference to the *New York Times,* announced that he had changed his mind and withdrawn his earlier indorsement of the repeal of the Arms Embargo Act, saying that the matter should be fully debated in the Congress.

Two days later, in New York, Mr. Landon gave an interview in which he demanded that the President then announce that he would not be a candidate for a third term. He was quoted in the *New York Times* as saying, "It is a matter of common knowledge that there are two groups in the Roosevelt Administration at Washington. One consists of those who are exulting in the advantage they think the European War has given Mr. Roosevelt. . . . The other group consists of equally good Administration men who are disturbed and frightened that violation of the third term tradition would be one more break in the dike of our popular government." Then he went on to say that if the President would announce that he would not accept a renomination, the opposition to the repeal of the Embargo Act might not be so serious.

The war in Europe went on, but after the destruction of Poland it settled down into the "Sitzkrieg," the "phony" war, and, simmering, seemed to be but little more violent than was the dispute in this country between the "interventionists" and the "isolationists," as each group was called by the other, about what would be its effects on the American people and what we should do about it, if anything.

Sometime during the next winter, I think it was January 2, President Roosevelt, through an intermediary, invited Colonel Knox to come into the Cabinet as secretary of the Navy. Perhaps it was not a direct invitation, but, at any rate, the President sounded out the colonel on the subject.

Knox was mightily interested, but he declined, saying that he felt he should not do so unless the President brought at least one other Republican into the Cabinet at the same time, so that it would be manifest to the country that the President was bringing Republicans to the national council table in their capacity as members of the Republican opposition and was not merely appointing an individual Republican personally acceptable to the President. Of this negotiation I knew but little at the time, and that only by rumor, a rumor that perhaps I would not have credited had I not had the earlier conversations with "F. D. R." But the next spring, the "Sitzkrieg" suddenly exploded into the "Blitzkrieg"; the danger to the United States was realized by millions who theretofore had wishfully thought that it was all only a European affair.

On April 9 the Germans invaded Denmark and Norway. On May 10 Germany invaded Holland, Belgium, and Luxembourg. The next day, May 11, Winston Churchill became prime minister of the United Kingdom.

Then, with rapidity that seemed at the time unbelievable, the Germans broke through the French lines at Sedan on May 16, and France lay prostrate before them as she had at the same place in 1870.

I saw the President several times in May, particularly to talk over the activation of the National Council of Defense and its Advisory Commission, which was accomplished late in that month. The President captured the imagination of the country and shocked its industrial leaders to the marrow of their bones by calling for fifty thousand warplanes a year. The Congress began to appropriate huge funds for defense. The alarm was communicating itself to the whole people.

The President invited Governor Landon to come to Washington to have lunch with him. Governor Landon again began to talk to the newspapers. The invitation to lunch was rescinded, to be reinstated a little later. The former governor of Kansas came, but I don't think the President said anything to him about coming into the Cabinet. Mr. Landon's public pronouncements again had made it too difficult. The following day, on May 23, Mr. Landon gave an interview in which he asked President Roosevelt to declare that he would not be a candidate for a third term, if the President expected Republicans to come into a "coalition cabinet." Mr. Roosevelt told his press conference that he was grateful for Governor Landon's suggestion.

The war was gathering fury. The Belgian king surrendered his army.

The British began their heroic retreat from Dunkirk. "The hand that held the dagger has struck it into the back of its neighbor," said President Roosevelt over the radio as Italy declared war on France and Great Britain. Paris fell on June 13. France surrendered.

At the same time, with the inevitability of the rising and the setting of the sun, the calendar was bringing around the quadrennial presidential election. There were many candidates, active, passive, or merely hopeful, on the Republican side. Willkie was creeping up in the Gallup Poll in a fashion alarming to the supporters of Dewey, Taft, and Vandenberg.

On the Democratic side there were also many candidates, but the answer to the great question of whether or not Mr. Roosevelt would break with tradition and run for a third term was unknown. "F. D. R." kept his own counsel.

Quite aside from the speculation on whether Roosevelt would or Roosevelt would not, quite aside from the speculation about the two great national conventions and the result of the November election itself, there was running that spring an undercurrent of serious discussion about how, in the presence of war in Europe and in the presence of the presidential election in this country, the foreign relations of the United States should be conducted. The problem was not solved by simply deciding to adopt a bipartisan foreign policy, for both parties had their quota of isolationists as well as of interventionists, while at the same time a majority of each party, at least in the Congress, was motivated by an intense desire to keep the United States out of the war, almost at any cost.

Among many serious-minded people, one of the things that seemed to be most dangerous was the President's custom of answering questions about foreign relations at his press conferences. It was argued that in such delicate circumstances no pronouncement by the chief of state should be made except in formal language, in writing, after careful consideration, and following exhaustive consultations with all persons in a position to know the facts. For just any newspaper reporter to ask just any question, and for the President to reply to it orally, and for one hundred and fifty different newspapers to interpret the result of that conversational exchange in one hundred and fifty different ways seemed to be as reckless as smoking a pipe in a powder magazine. The problem deeply disturbed the President. He knew quite well that, if he were suddenly to stop answering such questions, he would subject himself to attack as a supercensor by a large portion of the press and at the same time he would let loose an avalanche of persistent and insistent inquiries upon other agencies of the government, especially the Department of State.

To help him make up his mind what to do, he sought advice. I have no notion how many persons he consulted or who they were, but among them he did ask me. On May 29 he asked me to ponder the problem and see if I thought there was any way in which he could set up in the Department of State a unit which would command the confidence of the press, which would be able to maintain continuous contacts with the other governmental departments, with which he could keep in close touch, and to which all inquiries on foreign relations and on the effect of the war on the United States might be referred. He suggested that perhaps I ought to talk it over with Adolph Berle, then assistant secretary of state. Because he mentioned no one in the Department of State except Mr. Berle, I did not discuss it with any other person in that department, although I did explore the problem with a good many other men in and out of the government. This exploration I made, of course, apparently on my own motion and not as the agent or representative of the President. Just how many people I talked with, I do not now recall, but this I remember full well: with one exception, every person with whom I discussed it, in the government or out, was agreed that such a unit in the Department of State would not fill the bill.

Persons in other departments said that the State Department would not know and would refuse to learn enough of what was going on in the other departments of the government. Some of them were unkind enough to say that such a unit would not even know what was going on in other parts of the Department of State. The newspapermen with whom I talked simply said that, when the spokesman in the State Department gave a solemn answer to a sharp question, the drive to get the President's opinion on it would be tremendously enhanced and intensified.

The one exception was Mr. Berle, who argued with great cogency and extreme plausibility that the interpretation of the foreign policy of the United States was necessarily a part of the business of the Department of State and should be restored thereto, where it had been during most of the history of our country. He pointed out that in the past and, indeed, until the invention of the press conference, the President had never made offhand statements about our foreign policy; that, except when the matter was of the highest importance, such statements always had been left to the secretary of state or someone in his department. At the end of the conversation, very late in the afternoon, he drew toward him a small memo pad and on one page wrote an outline of what he thought should be the organization of an information unit in the Department of State to which the President should refer every inquiry the reply to which might affect our foreign policy.

A few days later, on June 5, I had lunch with the President in his office. I gave him a report of my several conversations and then handed him Mr. Berle's outline. He read it and then listened politely but, it seemed to me, with considerable indifference to my recital of Mr. Berle's arguments. He pulled down the corners of his mouth, shook his head, came forward with his hands outspread, palms downward on the desk, and said, "It won't do." He went on to say that the reason it would not do was a phrase that Berle had put in his little memorandum, a phrase about "any inquiry the reply to which might affect the foreign policy of the United States."

"To do that," the President said, in effect, "would be to close down the press conference entirely. There is no inquiry about anything in the United States the reply to which might not affect our foreign policy. We will have to search further. I think that Berle has shown me exactly what was really bothering me. If we can do anything about this problem, it will have to be something not so sweeping, and something that will set up some sort of standard which I can use to separate the questions that I can answer right here in this room from those that I ought to refer elsewhere. Think about it some more and come in, say, day after tomorrow. Talk to Steve Early about it."

I may have registered some slight astonishment when he told me to talk to Early, because, during the whole period that I had been discussing problems of reorganization and administration with him, I was under his strict injunction not to discuss my conversations with anybody in the departments or in the White House—an injunction that I faithfully observed, frequently to my embarrassment so far as my relations with the White House secretariat were concerned. The President caught my look of surprise and said, "Don't worry. I'll tell Steve you're coming to see him."

I did get in to see Mr. Early the next morning. He gave me what was for him a long lecture, for Mr. Early was never long-winded, on the relationship of public men with the press. I wish that that lecture could have been taken down and preserved for the benefit of posterity in general and students of public administration in particular. It was the considered opinion of a master who had then for seven years served as the press relations secretary for perhaps the most successful of all public men in public relations. He was to continue to serve in that capacity with Mr. Roosevelt through most of the war years. He was trusted by his chief, and he was both trusted and admired by the great majority of the journalists with whom he had to deal. Yet he was never loquacious. His taciturnity induced him to use short, clipped sentences. He sometimes matched a face empurpled with indignation with purple passages of scorn and wrath. He sometimes exploded into unprintable diatribes that would have done credit to the reputation of his distinguished kinsman, General Jubal A. Early of the Confederate Army. He could be conciliatory, assuaging, and apparently confidential, but one thing he never forgot, and that was his loyalty to his chief and his obligation to his job. And one thing he seldom did. That was to lecture.

Steve began his lecture with a question. Sitting on the top of his desk leaning over toward me as I sat in a chair, he fixed me with his eye and shot at me, "Do you know what public man in Washington handled his press relations better than any other?"

"Well," I replied without the slightest hesitation, "I suppose everybody knows that the Boss 'F. D. R.,' is the best there ever was."

"And that just shows how little you know about it," said Steve. "Of course I'm for the Boss all right, and he is pretty good, but there was one other who was so much better that it was nobody's business. We had one man here who really was good, and he was a Republican at that."

I registered astonishment and incredulity. Steve fixed me again with his eye and said, "I'll tell you who was the best. It was Henry L. Stimson."

And then he went on with his lecture about why Stimson, when he was secretary of state, did the best job that ever had been done with the newspapermen. Stimson not only told them frankly and candidly what was the news but took them into his confidence so far that when things arose that were not to be printed, the secretary of state did not have to beg them to keep silence and was not always compelled even to say the words equivalent in the late twenties to the current "That's off the record."

All this was leading up to just one thing, and that was that the President, in the presence of the burgeoning and spreading war in Europe and during the presidential campaign, ought not to answer questions about our foreign policy in a press conference but ought to get somebody with the skill, the knowledge, the experience, the patience, and the universally admitted patriotism of Henry L. Stimson to take over, for the entire government, press relations involving foreign policy.

I was impressed but was forced to ask the inevitable question: "But where is there such a man outside of Stimson himself?"

"Well," said Steve, spreading his hands, "there you are."

Thereupon I went in to see the President again. He asked if I had grown any new ideas on the problem of how to deal with foreign-policy questions in the press conference. I told him I had not but that Steve had, and that I was inclined to think that Steve might be right. The solution was Stimson.

The President said that it was not a bad idea; in fact, that it was a good idea. Of course, it was obvious that he had talked it over with Early and perhaps with others, but he was still disturbed. He did not know whether or not it would work. The upshot was that he asked me to undertake a poll for him.

"I want you to sound out some of the leaders of the press," he said in effect, "to see what the chances might be. Do you know Eugene Meyer of the *Washington Post?*"

I replied that I did.

"Well, I want you to go to Gene Meyer," resumed Mr. Roosevelt, in effect, "and ask him to arrange a meeting with Mrs. Reid of the *Herald Tribune* and Harry Luce of *Time,* at which you can put this whole thing up to them for me. They know the problem, of course. The thing to do is to ask them what they would think and what they think the other newspapers and magazines, especially those that will support the Republican candidate for President in the coming campaign, will think about setting up Harry Stimson as the mouthpiece for the government on news about the relation of the United States to the other countries of the world and especially to the war. They know Stimson, of course. I'm sure that they admire and trust him. I think they know that Stimson is on cordial terms with Cordell Hull. They know that he knows the Department of State, and you can tell them for me that I would give Stimson my complete trust and support. Come back and tell me what they say as soon as you can."

I telephoned at once to Mr. Meyer and went right down to the *Washington Post*. I opened up by telling him that I had come to see him at the request of President Roosevelt. That set off an admirable display of fireworks, which I rather enjoyed as I waited for the calm that nearly always follows one of Mr. Meyer's outbursts, the calm that has made him one of the great American public servants of the last three decades.

I explained my mission. He said he would telephone to Mrs. Reid and Mr. Luce, which he did. It turned out that, on account of previous engagements, the earliest possible meeting would have to be the following Tuesday. The arrangement was made to meet in Mrs. Reid's apartment in the Waldorf-Astoria on Tuesday, June 11.

I reported this to the White House and was told that the President then would like to see me the following Wednesday, June 12.

That night I took the train to Chicago, hoping to catch up over the week end with some of my accumulated work there before leaving the next Monday afternoon for New York.

On the way out, it occurred to me that it might be a good idea for me to talk to Frank Knox. I did not have any specific authority from the President to do so, but I was quite sure that I could rely on the colonel's discretion and that the President would be glad to get his views.

I did not know Colonel Knox very well. I had met him several times in large company, and I had had lunch with him and two or three other publishers once at the invitation of Dean Ackerman of the Columbia School of Journalism. I am sure he did not know me at all. But I did know his secretary, John O'Keefe, a young man who a few years before had taken a test in a competition that I had arranged for the selection of my own private secretary. O'Keefe had come out second in that competition, and I took the top man. However, I had been most favorably impressed in my interview with him at that time and had kept in touch with him occasionally by telephone. (It was a very good

thing for O'Keefe that I did not give him the job, for, if I had, he probably would not have reached the eminent position that he did in the
publishing world.) So, when I got to Chicago, I telephoned O'Keefe,
and he made an engagement for me to see Colonel Knox.

When I came in, the colonel was just looking at the noon edition of
the *Chicago Daily News* of Monday, June 10, fresh from press. It contained a front-page editorial concerning our national policy in the
Caribbean as affected by the war. He told me that it was a trial balloon
to test public opinion and that he was running it at the request of the
President, relayed to him through Secretary Ickes.

That circumstance, of course, permitted me quickly to get to my
business. I told him how disturbed the President was about handling
the foreign-policy news with both a war and a campaign raging and
what he had commissioned me to do. I said that on the next day I was
to meet Mr. Meyer, Mrs. Reid, and Mr. Luce in New York and also, of
course, that it was my duty to obtain from them their opinion about the
naming of Henry L. Stimson as the authorized spokesman for the
government in this field.

"It won't work," exclaimed Colonel Knox. "The idea is based on an
implicit agreement that neither side can possibly keep. The President
can't keep it because there will be questions that he will have to discuss
that inevitably will involve foreign affairs, if not that day, then the day
after or the next week. The newspapers and magazines couldn't keep
the agreement either. In the first place, there is nobody who could bind
them even in a preliminary agreement. And then there would be no
one to execute the agreement, even if the publishers entered into it in
absolute good faith. Any one of them any day might find something in
his own publication printed without his knowledge that might be considered a violation. I'm sure in my own mind that the scheme will not
work. You can tell the President what I think, but maybe you had
better not tell the three publishers, since I was not included as a member of that group which the President selected."

Colonel Knox, who had been leaning forward on his desk and talking with great earnestness, now leaned back in his chair and said, "Are
you going to see the President soon?"

"I have a date to see him next Wednesday to tell him what happened in New York with the publishers."

"Will you take a message to him from me?"

"Certainly," I said.

"Tell him that I deeply appreciate the honor he paid me when he asked me to come into the Cabinet. You know, I'm sure," he said, "that at that time I said I could not come unless some other Republican went in at the same time. Tell him that now I've changed my mind. The situation is so serious that I am willing to serve in any capacity that he wants me to serve and without any conditions whatsoever.

"Perhaps that's not quite the case," Colonel Knox went on. "There is one condition and one only, and that is that he doesn't call on me until after the Republican convention in Philadelphia. If that convention adopts an isolationist plank such as Bertie McCormick jammed through the Illinois Republican convention in Springfield the other day, I want to be there to lead the bolt out of the Republican convention."

"Very well," I said, rising to go, "I shall give both your messages to the President on Wednesday."

In some ways it was an odd assemblage in Mrs. Reid's apartment in the Waldorf-Astoria on Tuesday morning. There was Mrs. Reid, the extremely capable and most gracious woman who presided over the affairs of the *New York Herald Tribune* and directed its editorial policy; Mr. Meyer, a wealthy and successful businessman, who since World War I had devoted the major part of his time and his great talents to the public service in one capacity or another and who was then engaged in resuscitating the *Washington Post,* which he was to make into one of the greatest newspapers of the country. There was Henry R. Luce, of *Time* and *Fortune,* the survivor of that brace of youthful entrepreneurs who at Yale had put their heads together to create one of the most powerful publishing concerns in the world.

Each of them disapproved of President Roosevelt and, in varying degrees, violently objected to his plans and policies, his methods, and his manners. All three were passionately opposed to Roosevelt's presumptive candidacy for a third term. They did not know for sure whether or not he would run, but they did know for sure that, if he did, they would be against him and would exert their full influence, both through their publications and personally, to defeat him. (Later, Mr. Meyer, in view of the raging war, changed his mind and heartily supported Roosevelt for the third term.) They may have had their personal preferences among the aspirants for the Republican nomination for the President; indeed, Mr. Luce had almost a proprietary interest in one candidate who later was to be the nominee of the Philadelphia convention. Yet, all three were profoundly disturbed by the war, alarmed by the sweeping successes of Hitler's army, and fearful that England, now that France was almost surely gone, could not alone maintain the defense of the democracies. And, furthermore, whatever their personal opinions of Mr. Roosevelt, they had respect for the institution of the presidency of the United States and quite manifestly were ready and willing to give serious consideration to any suggestion made to them by the occupant of the White House and quite willing at his request to give him their advice.

Here was I, quite unknown, I believe, to either Mrs. Reid or Mr. Luce—since my former meetings with each of them had been casual and under circumstances which I might well remember but which they might well forget—possessing some slight acquaintance with Mr. Meyer, but an utter alien to that world in which newspaper and magazine publishers meet and move and have their being. I was known to them, I imagine, only as a person who had had some experience as a student of public administration and who had been chosen by President Roosevelt to be the chairman of the President's Committee on Administrative Management. Why the President had chosen me as his emissary to them, I am sure they could not imagine, nor could I.

I presented the problem to them as clearly, and as nearly in the President's own words, as I could: How should the President in his press conference deal with inquiries from the representatives of the press affecting the foreign policy and the foreign relations of the United States in a time of rapidly expanding war and in the year of a presidential political campaign?

The President, I told them, particularly wanted their advice about whether or not he should establish Mr. Henry L. Stimson, a Republican and a former secretary of state, as the spokesman for the government on all matters of foreign policy and foreign relations, with the understanding that the President would refer to Mr. Stimson every question asked in a press conference which he deemed to fall in this field. Furthermore, under this plan the President would arrange that Mr. Stimson himself hold frequent press conferences in which the inquiries might be addressed to him directly. As a part of this proposed scheme, the President undertook on his behalf and on behalf of Secretary of

State Cordell Hull to see that Mr. Stimson was kept fully and currently informed.

So far as the publishers were concerned, I told them that the President exacted no agreement from them, but, if they did approve the idea, he would like them to give their approval publicly, in order that he might have the support of their prestige in the publishing world in the establishment of the project.

As far as I was able, I refrained from discussing the proposal with the three publishers, except as they from time to time asked me for further exposition of what I thought the President had in mind.

Now, while Mr. Roosevelt had chosen three Republican publishers, and three most pronouncedly anti-Roosevelt publishers, before whom to put his proposal, he had with circumspect care not included any isolationist publisher.

Of course, the third term question could no more be kept out of that conversation than Mr. Dick could keep King Charles's head out of his history of England. And, of course, I could give them no enlightenment on that matter. I did not know whether or not Mr. Roosevelt intended to run for a third term. I did most ardently hope that he would. I even believed that he would. But, on that day, June 18, 1940, I doubt if anybody in the United States actually knew whether or not he would do so. And my doubt included Franklin D. Roosevelt as one person in the United States.

As the discussion went forward, two things took shape. First, it was thought that if such an arrangement were to be made, the President had selected in Mr. Stimson the best possible, or perhaps even the only possible, person to undertake the task. Second, there was an increasing doubt about the feasibility of the whole thing. It was pointed out that, even if Mr. Roosevelt were not himself a candidate, he undoubtedly would support the candidate of the Democratic party and that, as a candidate or as the supporter of a candidate, he could not "duck" all questions on foreign affairs by hiding behind the skirts of so eminent and respected a Republican as Mr. Stimson. All three made it clear that they harbored no such cynical suspicion of Mr. Roosevelt's intent, but they were equally sure that some sections of the press would put that interpretation on the plan.

In other words, as the discussion proceeded, they more and more came around to the position which Colonel Frank Knox in Chicago had stated instantly and without hesitation.

But no conclusion was reached, and I was asked to come back again later in the afternoon. Mr. Luce was late. He had to go over to the airport to meet Mrs. Luce, who was coming in from Europe. When he did come in, Mr. Luce was in no mood for further discussion. He had made up his mind that the plan would not work. After some more talk, Mrs. Reid and Mr. Meyer agreed with him. I did not dissent.

Then the question turned on what to do. It was a fact, as Mr. Roosevelt pointed out, that many newspapers were being adversely critical of the President's answering questions on foreign relations ad lib in his press conferences. So we got up a half-page memo in which the three publishers expressed the opinion that the most that could be done was for the President, when he made replies on matters of great importance, to reduce them to writing in order to avoid, as far as possible, either misunderstanding or distortion. That was that!

The next morning I went to the White House to see the President. I had two things to tell him. One was the result of the talk with the three publishers, and I handed him the half-page memo. The other was the message that Colonel Knox had intrusted to me for him. I told him that Colonel Knox had said he would withdraw all conditions and serve in any capacity in which the President desired him to serve, but that he did want to delay coming into the government until after the Republican convention in Philadelphia. And, of course, I told him why Knox wanted to wait. The President listened in silence, with his most immobile and expressionless poker face, until I was through with both messages. Then, after a pause, he threw up both hands, brought his palms down on the desk and said, "Good, now I am free to bring Harry Stimson in to be secretary of war and Frank Knox to be the secretary of the Navy!"

"But," I hastened to interrupt, "Colonel Knox said he did not want to come until after he had led the bolt out of the Philadelphia convention if that body adopts the McCormick isolationist platform."

"Oh!" said the President with a chuckle, "that just shows what a bum politician Frank is. If I bring him in now, he comes in as a Republican in good standing. If I wait until after he bolts Philadelphia and then put him in my Cabinet, that will be plain straight bribery. The

A Passion for Anonymity

Republicans must come in before their convention or not at all until after the election. That seems elementary to me, my dear Doctor!"

"Then," suddenly turning on me, "you think Knox will come now, don't you?"

"Of course," I replied, "he will come today if you want him."

"Today is the day for both of them. You sit right there in that chair while I call them up."

Then, greatly daring, I hazarded an interruption. "Mr. President," I said, "I believe that if Mr. Stimson comes in he will wish to be free to name his own assistant secretary."

The President's hand on the telephone hesitated. His Adam's apple went up and down rapidly several times. I had said to him a most painful thing. The secretary of war, Mr. Woodring, had not been in sympathy with the American policy regarding the European war. He had even, many persons thought, used delaying and obstructive tactics. On the other hand, the assistant secretary, Louis A. Johnson, had heartily supported the President's plans and program. It was a hard thing to ask him to do, to sacrifice Louis Johnson, who had so loyally fought his fights for him. But, at the same time, the President could not fail to recognize that I was right in my estimate of what Mr. Stimson would expect as a prerequisite of his acceptance of that appointment. He might perhaps not make the demand; indeed, he probably would not do so; but unless it were made clear to him that he would be free to select his own assistant, he simply would decline.

"You're right," finally said the President. "Sit right there."

He picked up the telephone. Mr. Stimson, it turned out, could not be reached until that evening. He put in the call for Colonel Knox. The colonel was out to lunch.

I left the White House. I still regret that Mr. Stimson and Colonel Knox were not in at the moment, because I should have liked to have heard a Democratic President offering two great Cabinet posts to two outstanding Republicans.

As quickly as I could get across Lafayette Park, I went to my room at the Hay-Adams and put in a call to Johnny O'Keefe at the *Chicago Daily News*.

"Where is the colonel?" I asked.

"At the Chicago Club for lunch."

[450]

"Get hold of him as quickly as you can," I said. "The President is trying to reach him from Washington."

"Someone just told me that," said Johnny O'Keefe, "but I thought he was kidding."

"It was no kidding," I said. "I was sitting there by the President's desk when he put in the call."

Colonel Knox did not wait to get back to the office of the *Chicago Daily News*. He called the President from the Chicago Club.

This was the end of my connection with the episode. I am quite sure that the President talked with others, perhaps with many others, not only about the particular appointments but about the two immediate, pressing problems: How he could manage the handling of questions relating to foreign affairs in the press conferences, and how he could bring Republicans whose loyalty as Republicans could not be questioned into the Cabinet in order to assure, as far as humanly possible, the non-partisan administration of the defense measures to which the United States was being compelled by the collapse of western Europe.

There is no doubt in my mind that his first intention, to which he clung for a long time, was to name Landon and Knox, on the theory that he would bring in the very men who had been chosen as leaders by the Republican party itself. As events seemed to make it more and more difficult for him to bring in Governor Landon, he turned to a consideration of Mr. Stimson, whose career both in the public service and in the Republican party was in itself a guaranty of his main purpose; but, at the same time, as long as he was pondering a solution of the problem of press conference questions on foreign affairs and especially as long as he was considering the setting up of an independent spokesman for the government, he could not consider Mr. Stimson for any other post. That is why, in my opinion, when I reported to the President that the publishers had concluded that the spokesman device would not work, he raised his hands and said, "That releases me. I can now bring in Harry Stimson as secretary of war."

Mr. Harold L. Ickes has ventured the opinion publicly that the suggestion to make Mr. Stimson secretary of war came from Justice Felix Frankfurter. I have no doubt that that is true or that, in any event, if the President suggested the matter to Justice Frankfurter, the latter gave it his wholehearted approval. Frankfurter began his career in the law as an assistant to Stimson when Stimson was United States district attorney for the southern district of New York, and the two had maintained their friendship. Mr. Stimson had heard from Grenville Clark some weeks before that his name had been suggested to the President, but Mr. Stimson had no notion that the President actually was considering him for the post.

As far as I know, Mr. Stimson never knew that the President was mulling over the notion of asking him to become the official spokesman of the United States government on foreign affairs. In Mr. Stimson's book *On Active Service* (1948) he told the story thus:

> In my New York office on June 19, 1940, I received a telephone call from the White House. I was called up by the President who offered me the position of Secretary of War. He told me that Knox had already agreed to accept the position of Secretary of the Navy. The President said he was very anxious to have me accept because everybody was running around at loose ends in Washington and he thought I would be a stabilizing factor in which both the Army and the public would have confidence.

To say that Mr. Stimson was surprised would be putting it mildly. He had known that Mr. Roosevelt was considering the appointment of one or more Republicans and that Frank Knox was among those being considered. Like everyone else, he knew that Secretary of War Woodring was at odds with both the President and large parts of the Army. He did not suspect, however, that these troubles might affect him. Some weeks before, he had heard from Grenville Clark that his name had been suggested for the job. Clark had coupled it with that of Judge Robert P. Patterson as assistant secretary. He knew too that this suggestion had reached the President. But that the President should have listened to it and acted upon it astonished him. His first reaction was to point out that he was approaching his seventy-third birthday. The President said he already knew that and added that Stimson would be free to appoint his own assistant secretary. Patterson's name was mentioned and approved by both men. Stimson then asked for a few hours in which to consult his wife and his professional associates.

> I then discussed it with Bronson Winthrop, George Roberts [two of his partners] and Mabel. They all advised me to accept. About 7 p.m. I telephoned the President and asked him three questions: (1) whether he had seen my radio speech and whether it would be embarrassing to him. He replied that he had already read it and was in full accord with it. (2) I asked him whether he knew that I was in favor of general compulsory military service,

and he said he did and gave me to understand that he was in sympathy with me. (3) I asked him whether Knox had accepted and he said he had. I then accepted [Stimson's Diary, June 25, 1940].

Stimson was later inclined to think this diary entry a trifle laconic; conversation with Franklin Roosevelt was seldom so stern and simple. It nevertheless contained the meat of what was said on both sides. Neither man mentioned any political aspect of the appointment. The only bargain struck on either side was an agreement that Stimson would be free to appoint Patterson as his own principal assistant. It was understood on both sides, then and later, that politics were not relevant; it was equally understood that Stimson was to be the undisputed head of his own department. These understandings remained unbroken to the end.

The two appointments were announced June 20. The Republican convention was to convene June 24. The announcement set off a series of explosions. There was hearty approval and violent denunciation. The chairman of the National Republican Committee read Stimson and Knox out of the party. The President was denounced for attempting to disrupt the Republican party on the eve of its convention, and he was praised for having taken the steps to insure that the administration of defense would be non-partisan and non-political. The event, however, clearly demonstrated, in my opinion, the wisdom of the President's action. There is in our constitutional system no room for a formal coalition government. The executive power is vested in the President of the United States and is indivisible. The legislative power is vested in the Congress of the United States, which consists of two chambers, each based on a different basis of representation. A formal scheme of coalition such as is not uncommon in a parliamentary form of government simply cannot be conceived of when one reckons with the separation of powers between the executive and the legislative branches and when one considers the differences between the Senate and the House of Representatives. The only possible way to approach a coalition under the Constitution and under our two-party system is to induce the co-operation of the two branches and of the two parties through informal *ad hoc* arrangements.

One example is the way in which President Roosevelt met the crisis of providing for national defense in a time of crisis and peril in June, 1940. He brought in Messrs. Stimson and Knox to be the heads of the

War and Navy departments in order to assure the country that, even in a year of a presidential election, the armed forces of the government, then about to be greatly expanded in both personnel and equipment, would be under the direction of men prominent in the affairs of the opposing party. Later, of course, in the defense period as well as after Pearl Harbor, the men who were brought into the Advisory Commission on National Defense and other war agencies were sometimes Democrats, sometimes Republicans, but the non-partisan character of the war agencies was so early established that even the newspapers rarely mentioned the party affiliation of the men brought in to head the new agencies.

In this case, there was no understanding with the other party. It would have been difficult, if not impossible, for Mr. Roosevelt at that particular time to have reached an understanding with the opposition. He simply assumed the co-operation of the other party and named two men to bring it about. He was accused, of course, of attempting to disrupt the Republican convention. I do not think for a moment that that was any part of his purpose, and, if it was, it certainly had no effect whatsoever. I also know, because it was implicit in what he said to me about Colonel Knox, that he was sure that he had to act before the Republican convention and not after. If he had waited, then it would have been necessary for him to have consulted the Republican nominee for the presidency, and it would have been almost impossible for that nominee—whoever he might have been—to enter into an understanding except upon conditions which would have been tantamount to the abdication of the presidential responsibility.

Another example, which has been the result of an understanding, is the bipartisan arrangement for this government's conduct of foreign affairs. Approaches to such an arrangement have been attempted several times in the past. The problem always has been difficult and remains so, since it is based on nothing more substantial than a general agreement, which sets up a not too clearly defined standard of conduct for the guidance of many persons in the executive and legislative branches and in the councils of the political parties.

Another, and perhaps the greatest, example in our history of such an informal coalition was that in which the energies and resources of the country were united by President Lincoln at the time of the Civil War. There were not then two parties, but four. The southern states had chosen to secede and it was the purpose of the United States to compel them by force, if necessary, to desist from their effort to destroy the Union. The President had taken into his Cabinet members of the new Republican party, of the northern Whigs, the southern Whigs, and the Union Democrats. He was forced by events to make some changes in the personnel of his Cabinet, but, until the end, it was a Cabinet of all parties. At the political crisis of the war itself, Mr. Lincoln had managed to keep the Republican party from even holding a convention, and in 1864, for example, in Baltimore, what was known as the Union Convention to nominate candidates for President and vice-president for the election of 1864 did not take place. The Democrats from the northern states met in Chicago and made their regular partisan nominations; the Republicans, the remaining Whigs, and the Democrats who wanted to adjourn partisan politics to maintain the virtual coalition nominated Abraham Lincoln of Illinois, a Republican, for President, and Andrew Johnson of Tennessee, a Democrat, for vice-president. The result of the election was not a foregone conclusion and indeed, as is well known, at one time Mr. Lincoln believed that he would be defeated by General McClellan, the Democratic nominee. Members of Lincoln's own party objected. Members of the opposition parties demurred. The South was waging war. Yet, through it all, the coalition survived, and by reason of that survival, the Union was saved and the nation survived. Yet it is important to remember that it was not a formal coalition and that there was no division of the executive power by agreement or otherwise, as was demonstrated in the famous incident in which the President took a vote with the Cabinet, every one of whom opposed him, and announced the vote, "Seven noes, one aye. The ayes have it."

CHAPTER XXXVI

WORLD WAR II AND AFTER

From the day of the invasion of the Low Countries, nobody any longer had any delusions about the confinement of the Nazi intent or about Hitler's purpose to attain world supremacy, unless it were, for a time, the Russians, who seemed to rely on the Molotov-Ribbentrop agreement, which had been reached only a few days before the invasion of Poland. In the United States, however, there were great hopes that this country would be able to stay out of the war, although we openly and avowedly sympathized with the western European powers and determined in every way short of war to assist them. In President Roosevelt's phrase, the great North American Republic proceeded to constitute itself "the arsenal of democracy."

There was the trade, widely denounced as of dubious legality, of old destroyers for island bases, which was followed by a long train of similar actions. The Nazi attack on Russia, the adhesion of Italy to the Nazi cause, the stirring of accelerated aggression on the part of Japan, the President's persistence, with the consent of the majority of the Congress, in adding more and more to the aid of Great Britain, as Great Britain came more and more to stand alone—all these things mounted into greater and greater national determination to aid in resisting the Nazi assaults. During that period of almost two years, until Pearl Harbor, I was busy doing chores of various kinds around Washington. Until the end of 1940 I was frequently at the White House. I was frequently in consultation with some of the departments and agencies of the government in Washington, but as the organizations for preparedness set up by the President within the Office of Emergency Management became more and more efficient and expanded more and more along definite lines, my consultations became more and more concerned with smaller and smaller events.

I had originally conceived of the Office of Emergency Management in the Executive Office of the President as a holding company—an agency which was to do little or nothing on its own but which was to establish continuous lines of instantaneous communication between the President and any of the defense organizations to be set up and which was also to serve as a catalyzer so that the President on his own motion at any time, without having to seek legislation from the Congress, could create, modify, consolidate, or dissolve any particular agency set up for the emergency. In that respect, despite many difficulties, I believe the agency justified itself, and materially advantaged the operations during the years of preparedness. It made possible the greatest effort ever made by any nation through its governmental machinery to equip an army and navy—the army and navy that won World War II.

At the same time, of course, I was still responsible for the Public Administration Clearing House. When, with the attack on Pearl Harbor, the war finally came, Mr. Emmerich was called back to Washington where he served as secretary of the War Production Board, and then, when the matter of war production became stalled in the bottleneck of housing for workers in munition establishments, he became commissioner of the public housing division of the newly created National Housing Agency, of which my nephew-in-law, John B. Blandford, Jr., was the administrator. That meant that I had to pick up my old lines in Chicago. Most of the heads of the several organizations established at 1313 East Sixtieth Street were called into the war effort in one way or another. That meant, so far as I was concerned, a great deal of consultation about the acquisition of personnel for the temporary conduct of many of those agencies.

Then also I was in daily, almost hourly, contact with agencies in the federal government in order to discover the right man for the right place in the ever recurring emergencies of personnel. I was busy. In fact, during the war, while I was able to escape a great load of responsibility, I was as busy as could be, day and night. However, even during that time, because I continued to refuse to accept any position of high responsibility, I never permitted myself to work as hard as I had before my heart attack in May, 1937.

To recall the incidents of that period would be simply to describe in detail another of the multiple facets of how Americans in the field of government worked for the common cause during World War II.

After the war effort got well along and the organizations set up to serve its effort were running fairly well, I persuaded Herbert Emmerich to come back to Chicago to become my assistant, with the idea that he would succeed me. And, in 1945, I retired as director of the Public Administration Clearing House. Mr. Emmerich succeeded me.

I never was quite able to take my retirement seriously. I did many things. I attempted at once to write an autobiography, but there were so many other things to do that it was years and years before I got through with it. During all that time I stood aside, rigorously determined not to interfere in any way with the operation of any of the institutions with which I had been connected. What happened was that I became by title a trustee of the Clearing House and became by edict a consultant for that institution; on the side, I offered a shoulder for weeping, a hand for holding, and an ear for hearing many persons in the field of public administration who sought me out.

Once in a while something would come along which would intrigue me into taking up something new. One of the most interesting and, to me, intellectually profitable adventures was the chance circumstance of my beginning a decade of close connection with the affairs of Puerto Rico.

One day in 1945, Dr. Rafael Cordero, the comptroller of Puerto Rico by appointment of the President of the United States, came into my office in Washington. He said that the governor, Rexford Guy Tugwell, and he were eager to get some expert and competent advice on the accounting and other fiscal-record procedures of the insular government and that Governor Tugwell had suggested that he talk with me about the problem.

I suggested that he arrange to have Public Administration Service make a survey of the fiscal records and accounting systems in Puerto Rico and then, if it seemed desirable, to devise and instal adequate new systems.

Later in 1945 the School of Public Administration of the University of Puerto Rico held a conference on the problems of public administration. The chancellor of the university, Dr. Jaime Benitez, whom I had known slightly when he was a graduate student at the University of Chicago, invited me to attend the conference and to make a speech. Mrs. Brownlow and I had a delightful three-weeks' visit in San Juan. It was evident to me that Governor Tugwell had succeeded in assembling one of the most capable corps of public administrators that I have ever seen around any government department in Washington, any state capitol, or any city hall.

Tugwell is a man of impressive personality, but I sometimes find myself unable to agree with his own estimates of himself. He seems to think that he is a great politician. I have had my doubts. He seems to think that he is a failure as an administrator. I think he is one of the best I have ever known. Perhaps in these few sentences I already have indicated that, during many years of close personal friendship, I never have been able to agree with him more than a few seconds about any particular thing to be done or not to be done. But we have been in general agreement on broad political policies nearly all the time.

After 1945 I made many visits to Puerto Rico. I have watched that beautiful island with its overcrowded population during a revolutionary decade make tremendous forward strides in many fields of governmental and human endeavor. And in Puerto Rico I found not only many good friends but, much more than that, the inspiration for a renewed faith in the processes of democracy. I found renewed faith in the possibility of the amalgamation of two different cultures and their differential adjustment to that scheme of government and of law which makes for political democracy and economic progress and which throws light on the forward path of peoples working with peoples for their mutual benefit.

When Tugwell became governor, he was greatly interested in extending the democratic privileges and responsibilities even further to the people than they had been in the past.

The leading Puerto Rican was the president of the Senate, Luis Muñoz Marin. In that position he became the leader of the new party that in a relatively short time attracted the support and the franchises of almost three-fourths of the Puerto Rican voters. Governor Tugwell began to urge President Roosevelt and, at the same time, leaders of both houses of Congress to take steps to advance the democratic movement in the island. As a result the Congress granted the authority to the President to name a Puerto Rican as governor. And when Tugwell's term expired, President Truman appointed Mr. Pinero, who had theretofore been the non-voting delegate with the title of resident commissioner of Puerto Rico in the United States House of Representatives.

Then came another step. The Congress and the President joined in the enactment of a law which provided that the governor be elected by the citizens of Puerto Rico. In the election of November, 1948, Luis Muñoz Marin became the first elected governor since the day the island was discovered and its first government established by Christopher Columbus. Governor Muñoz Marin was inaugurated at the beginning of January, 1949. A few weeks later some of the members of his Cabinet came to Washington to talk about a possible scheme for administrative reorganization of the insular government. I was known as the chairman of the President's Committee on Administrative Management, which had made the report on the reorganization of the United States government in 1937. In the meantime President Truman had appointed another commission on reorganization under the chairmanship of former President Herbert Hoover. To that commission Speaker Rayburn had nominated James H. Rowe, who had been an administrative assistant to both President Roosevelt and President Truman. Mr. Rowe and I were asked to serve on a reorganization commission for Puerto Rico. We accepted and chose as the chief of staff Arnold Miles, a graduate of Syracuse University, who had worked for several of the organizations in the Chicago cluster and who at that time was in the division of administrative management in the United States Bureau of the Budget.

Thus, in the first year of the first elected governor in the history of Puerto Rico, the governor turned to the problems of management. Mr. Rowe was made chairman of the commission. Work was begun early in the summer, and the report was submitted to the governor in October. That meant that I was more frequently in Puerto Rico than I had been before, stayed there longer, and had an excellent opportunity to look into all the problems of the government and its people.

Puerto Rico is a poor country. It has few natural resources, so far as mines or forests are concerned. It has rich and fertile land, but it also has a great deal of mountainous and untillable land and, in some areas, the handicap of aridity, which is not entirely balanced by other portions where the rainfall is excessive. Its greatest resource is people, and it has too many. The startling success of the sanitation and other health laws and regulations introduced by the Americans at the end of the Spanish-American War has made Puerto Rico the most thickly populated place in the entire Western Hemisphere. It seeks relief in emigration, and, as Puerto Ricans are citizens of the United States, they can go and come freely to the mainland, which Puerto Ricans usually call "the continent." But it has no lack of spirit.

Muñoz Marin as a political leader believed in planning, and, indeed, the insular government had paid more attention to planning, very largely under Tugwell's leadership, than had almost any other part of the United States. That planning was directed toward the establishment of an efficient, democratically responsible government which in turn would help to improve the economic conditions of all the people by every possible means: by improvement of agriculture, by improvement in the scheme of ownership and control of agricultural lands, by the introduction of industries, and by all those things that Governor Muñoz Marin later denominated "Operations Bootstrap," which has brought great economic improvement to the people of the island during the eight years of his administration.

The work of the organization commission was relatively easy; there were many differences of opinion, but compromises and agreements were reached with relative ease, and later the great majority of the recommendations of the commission were enacted into law by the legislature.

The commission followed in general the scheme that had been recommended by the Brownlow committee for the United States in 1937. It set up an Executive Office of the Governor to which was attached the governor's own staff, the planning agencies, the fiscal agencies, and the personnel agencies in such manner as to insure the co-ordination of over-all management.

But what was most exciting to me were the men assembled in the government. Many of them had been recommended or appointed in the first place by Tugwell. They were devoted to the interests of the people of the island, and above all they were of dedicated intelligence. The governor, who spent many years of his youth in New York and Washington as a journalist, who at times was best known for his poetry, who inherited his political acumen from his father, and who at last turned his whole being into an effort to improve the status of his people, was our frequent host at his official residence, the sixteenth-century La Forteleza. He was much impressed, through his long residence in the United States and his nativity and long life in Puerto Rico, with the fact that Puerto Rico might well be the bridge connecting the Anglo-European-American culture with the Spanish-Latin-American culture to the benefit of both. Thus arose his concept of the status of Puerto Rico, a change which was blessed by the Congress and the President. As a result of that change, Puerto Rico is no longer a territory of the United States. It is a commonwealth.

The great success of the program of industrialization of Puerto Rico, the introduction of hundreds of new industries, and the general economic improvement has testified to the success of the new plan. From the very beginning when the Foraker Act was passed, the Congress of the United States always has had the power to disapprove any law passed by the Puerto Rican legislature. But in the more than fifty years since that act, it never did so. Now, under the new scheme, the United States Congress still possesses the power to invalidate any act of the Puerto Rican legislature. On the other hand, under the new arrangement, the legislature of Puerto Rico can refuse to permit the application of an act of the Congress without its consent. Neither veto has ever been applied.

Puerto Rico now flies its own flag, the flag which for decades was assumed to be the symbol of revolution and rebellion and independence from the United States. It flies also the flag of the United States, and the two flags float together in harmony just as they do from the capitols of the forty-eight states and the commonwealths—the United States flag and the flag of the state or the commonwealth, together, testifying to the dual citizenship which is sometimes difficult to put into words but which is basic to the great political success of the United States of America.

During this time I had a finger in two other organizations. One was the National Institute of Public Affairs, set up in Washington with me as chairman of its board of trustees. It carried on, with the aid of a grant from the Rockefeller Foundation, a fourteen-year program attempting to bring into government service the most capable young men and young women being graduated from the colleges and universities of the country. The president of the corporation was Frederick M. Davenport, who about the same time had been appointed by President Roosevelt to be the head of the National Personnel Council. Every year Mr. Davenport selected, and this he did very largely in person, the ablest young graduates from the colleges and universities of the country in the field of government. Each of these, in groups varying from a minimum of thirty to a maximum of fifty, was brought to Washington to serve for a year as an interne in some department or agency of the government or in the office of some member of the Congress. These successive NIPA classes so clearly demonstrated the utility of such a system of selective personnel management that at the end of the experiment the task was assumed by the federal government operating through the United States Civil Service Commission—using not precisely the same methods of recruitment or training but, nevertheless, adapting from our experiment permanent modifications in the methodology of personnel management in the government. These NIPA internes in their turn began to consider themselves the members of an elite group. A few went into business management; some of them went into state and local government; but most of them remained in the federal government establishment or went into the work of the United Nations. In a way the NIPA was an extension of the apprenticeship system that the Public Administration Clearing House had conducted in its early days. In my own later life, this experiment has been tremendously profitable to me. It has kept, as it still keeps, me in touch with younger persons, many of them now occupying most important places in the administrative field. These contacts have flowered into friendship of a type that is particularly precious to a man in his late seventies. It gives me that rich experience which ordinarily comes to college teachers, for instance, who frequently find themselves drinking from Ponce de León's fountain of eternal youth because their work keeps them in touch year after year with a new crop of young persons who are willing, or at least nearly always willing, and sometimes even eager to talk to the old man.

Also during this interim I had another rich experience. Late in 1940 I joined Dr. William E. Mosher, dean of the Maxwell School of Citizenship and Public Affairs at Syracuse University, and some other friends and coconspirators in the establishment of the American Society for Public Administration.

In the enterprise we were aided by Donald C. Stone, who was himself a graduate of Dr. Mosher's school and who had worked intimately with me, first as the head of the staff of the Research Committee of the International City Managers' Association, which was blended into Public Administration Service, and then later as the head of the division of administrative management of the Bureau of the Budget.

The society was started off at a meeting called in the Wardman Park

Hotel in Washington. About two hundred and fifty persons were present, and all of them joined up. The abracadabra of drafting the constitution and setting up a group of officers and an executive committee was gone through. But there was no money. I was asked to support the infant organization with funds from the Clearing House. I declined. I said that I would consider it only after every like alternative source had been explored. I was determined that this new society, which we were setting up in an effort to bring together in one organization persons interested in administration in federal, state, and local government, should not be weighted down by a handicap that might be imposed upon it if it were to get the reputation of a PACH organization or a Brownlow organization or an effort to supplant any other organization in the field. There were two other possible sponsors. One was the Brookings Institution, headed then by Dr. Harold G. Moulton, and the other was the Institute of Public Administration, headed by Luther Gulick. I told the members of the committee who approached me that I would not even consider doing anything to help the new organization until after I had seen in writing the decision of both the Brookings Institution and the Institute of Public Administration to decline the task. After a month, the letters were brought to me. Brookings stepped aside. The Institute of Public Administration stepped aside. I then thought it would be safe for PACH to step in.

The society was launched. It was conceived as a national organization which would hold annual conferences, publish a monthly review, and encourage the creation in all parts of the country of local chapters for the discussion of administrative problems, techniques, and methods. The *Public Administration Review's* first issue came out early in 1941 following the first meeting of the society, which was held in conjunction with the meeting of the American Political Science Association in Chicago in the Christmas season of 1940. The device I used for its support was to have the society make the Public Administration Clearing House its secretariat. The society was to pay its own out-of-pocket expenses for the publication of the *Review* from its earnings, while PACH paid all the expenses for personnel. That went on for some years until the society had accumulated a surplus of something more than $10,000, a surplus, of course, which was an indirect subsidy from PACH. Then the Clearing House, as the secretariat, paid only parts of the salaries until, after a few years, the surplus was exhausted. The earnings from payment of dues and from subscriptions of the journal increased. But in 1956 it appeared that with special effort the society might attract members and increase its earnings so that it would become self-supporting. The Ford Foundation then gave it a developmental grant for five years, and the American Society for Public Administration was on its own.

That event coincided with the death of Public Administration Clearing House. The Spelman Fund, which had been the sponsor of, and had given the original support to, the Clearing House, was finally liquidated in 1950. At that time it turned over the balance of its available funds to the Clearing House. Later the Ford Foundation made two unsolicited grants to the Clearing House for continuing its work in the national and international fields, the total amounting to something more than a million dollars. This sum, together with the balance from the Spelman Fund and with the addition of occasional grants for special work from other foundations and a few private business concerns, was sufficient to carry the Clearing House through the year 1956.

However, as early as 1952, the director, Herbert Emmerich, and I, the former director, as members of the board of trustees, advised the board that unless further foundation grants could be obtained for the general work of the Clearing House, it was our opinion that the corporation should be liquidated.

It had been always my opinion, an opinion which was fully shared by Herbert Emmerich, that the Clearing House could not and should not attempt any activity which would bring in any independent income. To do so would have been to enter into direct competition with the various organizations which the Clearing House had in the beginning either assisted or housed or, in some instances, created and organized. "It is not right," we said, "for Grandfather to go into competition with the grandchildren."

The members of the board of trustees were persuaded that we were right, but they still thought that every effort ought to be made to find funds for the general, unspecialized, non-competitive, exploratory, and experimental work of the type the Clearing House had done in the past. Two or three years went by. None of the big foundations could see its way clear for further grants. So, at the end of 1956, after a full quarter of a century of activity in public administration in local, state, and federal government in the United States, in the other countries of the Western Hemisphere, in Europe, and in Asia, the Clearing House came to the end. Many of its functions were turned over to other agencies. The administration of the building at 1313 East Sixtieth Street in Chicago was turned over to Public Administration Service with the consent of the Board of Trustees of the University of Chicago. Many of the activities in personnel and publicity were assumed by the American Society for Public Administration. The task of keeping in liaison the organs of administration in the United Nations and the non-governmental organizations of administrators in Europe and the rest of the world, which had been carried on by the New York office of the Clearing House, was turned over to the Institute of Public Administration with a grant from the Ford Foundation to support it. In fact, all the activities, or practically all, were devolved upon other organizations, with the sole exception of what was really the most important part of the work of the Clearing House: exploration, imaginative experimentation, and all those numerous, complex, intricate lines of endeavor and communication that the Clearing House had so completely masked for twenty-five years under the web that was woven by its determined resolve to be what it first set out to be. And that was to model its work on that of a telephone exchange, to facilitate communication but not to indulge in conversation itself. Its guiding principle, sometimes suffering of course from temporary deviations, as do all guiding principles, was that of anonymity.

For that reason, I have said little or nothing in these memoirs about some other organizations of public administrators which the Clearing House helped to establish, always with the financial aid of the Spelman Fund in their beginning phases. All of them are now self-supporting and are integral and important parts of the American governmental (albeit not official) structure.

Among them are the American Society of Planning Officials, leading founders of which were Harold S. Buttenheim and Charles S. Ascher. I am glad to say that it was I who succeeded in persuading Walter H. Blucher to take the helm of that society, which he led with such great ability and success.

Perhaps the greatest credit for setting up the National Association of Housing Officials (now the National Association of Housing and Redevelopment Officials) is due to Ernest J. Bohn of Cleveland, with whom I worked in its initial phases, Coleman Woodbury, its first permanent director, and, of course, the inevitable Ascher.

Among others now quartered in the building known as "1313" is the Federation of Tax Administrators, the founders of which on their own motion sought out the Clearing House to ask assistance in its establishment.

Great as has been my interest in the work of these organizations, much as the Clearing House may have done to bring them into being, much as the Spelman Fund did to finance them, they and all the others in the cluster are autonomous, independent, and self-reliant.

I was always careful to try not to interfere in their operations, even when I was consulted. Once or twice I may actually have interfered in an emergency. But I always tried not to do so. My advice when sought was frank and candid, even forceful, but the decisions the organizations took were their own.

CHAPTER XXXVII

EPILOGUE

The title of this book is a contradiction in terms. In a long life a man may espouse many and various causes and, indeed, may have many passions for many things. If anonymity had been my ruling passion, it follows that there never would have been an autobiography. But it was only one of my passions, albeit an important one.

The first volume of these memoirs had another title, *A Passion for Politics*. That also was not a completely ruling passion. Sometimes I have ventured to say in the midst of controversies, usually oral, that in my considered view, government, politics, history, and administration are just one thing. My interest in politics, active since childhood, never obscured my interest in history. My later preoccupation with administration meant for me that I would no longer be absorbed in or venture to practice any of the methods by which political operations are conducted, nor was I ever to venture upon the techniques of the historian. I did undertake to be an administrator, and by that act I committed myself to pursue as far as possible a course of conduct in which acts would be more important than precepts and the accomplishment of programs infinitely more important than the projection of personality. Thus, there came about in my thinking, and, in so far as possible, in the conduct of the affairs of my daily life, a concentration of both thought and action that justifies to me, at least, the title of this volume.

The essential unity of government, politics, and administration, sometimes so vigorously denied by persons interested in one or the other, can be compared with the unity of any solid body. A cube, for example, has six sides. It is possible in studying a cube to consider the side one is looking at at the moment as though it were the whole cube. Nobody yet knows just what the man in the moon, with whose

Epilogue

face we are so familiar, has concealed on the other half of that globe. We have not seen the dark side.

Other solids have many more than six sides. A well-cut diamond has many facets, and one of its chief tasks, resulting not from its hardness and utilitarian use as a cutting instrument, is to exercise its charm by reflecting light; and this is accomplished by its many facets, each in its separate and distinct plane, contributing to the total effect. Its hardness is the function of its unity. Its brilliance is the function of its diversity. Yet, it is impossible to consider a human being's relation to a many-sided unit exclusively in unitary terms.

When one decides to take up the consideration of that phase of government known as administration, many aspects of person and personality retreat into the background. The process and the method increase in importance, and the tools to be used subordinate themselves to the purpose, plan, program, procedure, and accomplishment.

The prime requisite of successful administration of any large governmental unit is the devotion and dedication of anonymous persons. That is the reason that Tom Jones, out of his rich experience with the British Cabinet and with the British government, told me, when I asked him what President Roosevelt ought to do about administration, that the President should select assistants of high competency, great physical vigor, and a passion for anonymity.

Political leadership and sometimes military leadership as well do not easily tolerate a prominent lieutenant. If the second in command, or any down the rank, attracts too much attention to his person and his personality, he becomes a potential threat to the political prosperity of the politician at the top.

I know a good deal about this. I learned it during the course of my work as an administrator.

As a matter of fact, my reliance upon anonymity had begun much earlier. Most of the writing that I did when a journalist, especially that in which I combined the reporting of observed fact with the statement of opinion, was cheerfully written under the name of another man. When I first entered administration as a commissioner of the District of Columbia during World War I, I suddenly found that what I had considered the right thing to do when I was a reporter in the city hall was wrong. As a reporter, I thought that the business of the city hall and its officials was to make news for me to write. As a municipal administrator, I soon discovered that if everything that was planned or proposed was immediately put in the newspaper, nothing whatever could be done. It was the same job; but instead of being outside looking into the city hall, I found myself in the city hall looking out. I saw other facets of a solid—other facets that I had not consciously considered before and certainly had not thought important.

Still later the lesson was borne in upon me when I became the first city manager of Petersburg and then of Knoxville. It was with the greatest difficulty that I attempted—frequently unsuccessfully—to avoid publicity. I tried consciously but often without avail to give the mayor and the council the public credit for the decisions and leadership which actually were theirs. It was true, of course, that I made recommendations. It was true, of course, that I formulated policy, but I did not determine it. That was done by the council, and the leader of the council was the mayor. In Petersburg the mayor was a lawyer and a banker, a man of very great ability, an excellent speaker, and he fulfilled his role. I was successful in giving the mayor his rightful post as the chief political leader of the city government. In Knoxville I was unsuccessful because the mayor, a successful man, a man of very great ability in the administration of his own businesses, had discovered that secret of anonymity and found himself not only unwilling but unable to assume the political role. That thrust me into the vacuum and, as a very natural consequence, all but destroyed me.

Later, when it came to making a choice among a variety of attractive jobs that were available at the time, without any hesitation I fell into accord with a scheme to set up the Public Administration Clearing House to which I devoted the most active and, I flatter myself, the most fruitful years of my working life.

While there was a board of directors, and a beneficent foundation furnishing the money, it was I who determined the course of work of the new institution. Its purpose was to improve the communications among persons interested in government and in administration, and particularly among organizations of public administrators. It was supposed to be an effort to bridge the gap in administration between theory and practice, but the bridge was cantilevered from its firm base in practice toward theory, which alone could lend guidance and balance.

It imposed upon me and in turn I imposed upon the institution a general rule, which was not always successfully carried out but which was the main engine. It was the dedication to a ruling passion, the passion for anonymity.

The work of the Clearing House was to facilitate, to help financially, or in any other practicable way, the work of organizations of administration then existing, to induce the establishment of organizations in other fields where none existed, and then to devote its chief energies to persuading these organizations to exchange their information and intelligence—with the full consent, accord, and hearty support, of course, of my principal co-operators, Charles E. Merriam and Beardsley Ruml. This we thought could be done better, quicker, and more effectively by bringing the organizations together in one place. This was in order to prove our theory that informal communication is not only more rapid but more efficacious than the formal variety. We were persuaded to set up an apparatus in which that most intimate of all means of intercommunication among human beings could operate; the key was—propinquity.

In that purpose the Clearing House was effective. At the same time it was more and more necessary, because of the very success of the effort, to subordinate the role of the Public Administration Clearing House itself. Its job was not to lead but to serve. It existed not only for those organizations that happened to be brought into the camp by propinquity. It also existed to bring into that center all the intelligence it could assemble from similar organizations and persons interested in the processes of administration, not only in all parts of the United States but anywhere in the world. The plans along this line also met with some measure of success. In practice the reason that the Clearing House was able to pursue these activities was that it was supported by grants from philanthropic foundations. It was under no necessity to earn money. It was under no necessity to appeal for memberships. Indeed, if it had done either, it would have found itself immediately in competition with the very organizations and establishments it was founded to serve. At no time did it yield to the temptation to try to become self-supporting. All the other "1313" organizations at the beginning also were forced to rely upon help from foundations. But, in time, each became self-supporting. At the end of twenty-five years, it was obvious that the success of the Clearing House had destroyed many of the more obvious reasons why a foundation might give it money. After a useful life, it died an honorable death.

Of course, I did not always attain this anonymity, which I had decreed for the Clearing House, successfully for myself. Once in a while I would take on work to be done in this, that, or the other phase of administration which, by its very nature, attracted attention to me. That also was true of a good many of my assistants. It was true of my successor. But, in general and institutionally, the effort was crowned with success. The most prominent, the most marked, failure came when Franklin D. Roosevelt appointed me chairman of a three-man committee entitled the President's Committee on Administrative Management. My two colleagues were Luther Gulick, who had officiated as midwife at the birth of the Clearing House, and Charles E. Merriam, who was its father. PACH was Merriam's idea in the beginning. He had brought Beardsley Ruml, Guy Moffett, and the Spelman Fund into association with the notion. The three of them had selected me to attempt to carry it out.

At the beginning not much attention was paid to the President's committee. During the course of its work little was ever printed about it, simply because the committee itself and its staff—some staff members perhaps under duress—never once issued a statement. The report contained the "purple patch," the fatal phrase "a passion for anonymity." This phrase was received by the newspaper correspondents at President Roosevelt's press conference with guffaws of amusement and hoots of derision. They were the ones who wanted news, and wanted news for the most part which involved the names of some person, in order to enrich the story with that dramatic quality which inheres only in human personality.

And yet two years later the administrative assistants went into the White House, six of them then; now I don't know how many there are—maybe sixteen, maybe thirty-six, maybe more—but most of them are unknown in print; most of them never reach the headlines.

The simple rule that characterizes most administration of the affairs of government or business is that the hewers of wood and the drawers of water are the faceless ones, the nameless ones, but without their work nothing could be done.

In a sense the newspapermen were right in scoffing at the phrase. Their laughter proved the point. To be anonymous is to be unknown to newspapermen, as much as, if not more than, to anyone else. The newspapermen could well deny the existence of the anonymous man and, by denying it, demonstrate the success of the passion—and its existence.

In all this work of the Clearing House, I came more and more closely in contact with the social scientists, with the professors of the universities and the colleges, according them more and more admiration; I became more and more myself identified with them in thought if not in deed, considering myself toward the end to be much more, in my own fashion, an educator than an administrator, but never forgetting my proper role, never laying down rules to guide others, avoiding except on rare occasions that doom of the anonym which is the lifeblood of the professor—publication.

I might go on and on, but in these two volumes for the most part I have told my story. Here let it rest.

INDEX

INDEX

Index

consultant on government, Radburn (N.J.), 210–26
heart attack, 400–403
illness and recuperation, 197–98, 204, 401 ff.
on nature of political coalition in U.S. government, 453–55
political advice to Roosevelt, 433–35
Public Administration Clearing House, 227 ff.
public administration organizations, 141–49
Social Science Research Council, 292–301
Brownlow, Mrs. Louis
points out Chicago motto "I Will," 257–58
speaks of arrogance of office, 15
welfare activities of, 35, 132–33, 143–44
woman suffrage, 76
Brownlow, Ruth, marries Blandford, 137
Brownlow, Walter P., Republican boss of Tennessee, 163
Brownlow, William Gannaway, "Fighting Parson," 151
Brownlow Committee; see President's Committee on Administrative Management
Bryan, William Jennings, secretary of state, 28
Buchanan, Captain, Confederate veteran, 61–63
Buchanan, James P.
chairman, House Appropriations Committee, 350
opposition to President's Committee on Administrative Management, 350 ff.
Buck, Eugene, study of comptroller-general, 338
Budd, Ralph
Commission of Inquiry on Public Service Personnel, 292–93
PACH, chairman of board of trustees, 431
president, Association of American Railroads, 430
transportation adviser, 430
Budd, Robert D., engineer, Petersburg (Va.), 109, 111–12, 115, 130–32, 135
Budget; see Executive budget; U.S. Bureau of the Budget
Budget and Accounting Act, introduction of national executive budget, 303
Bunbury, Sir Henry N.
comptroller general of British General Post Office, 232
post office and telephone modernization, 232, 404

survey of government planning machinery, 404–8
Burchfield, Laverne, editor of report of President's Committee on Administrative Management, 383
Bureau of Municipal Research (New York City), 252–53, 302
Bureau of Public Personnel Administration; see Civil Service Assembly
Burlew, E. K., Department of Interior career official, 372
Buttenheim, Harold S.
editor, *American City,* 212
government public relations, 278–79
president of Snag Club, 220
Byrd, Harry F.
governor of Virginia, 253
Senator
chairman, Committee on Reorganization, 336 ff.
Brownlow advises Brookings as staff, 337
trustee of PACH, 253
Byrns, Joseph W., Speaker of House, 1935–36, 350 ff.

Cannon, Joseph G., "Uncle Joe," 66–68
Capital Traction Company, 91
Catt, Carrie Chapman, 74–76, 82
Charity; see Public welfare
Château d'Ardennes, PACH-sponsored conference on governmental planning held at, 404–8
Chatters, Carl, director of MFOA, 275
Chesapeake and Potomac Telephone Company, D.C. utility valuation, 91
Chevy Chase Club, Wilson refuses membership, 11
Chicago, "I will" motto adopted by Brownlow, 258
Childs, Richard S.
inventor of council-manager plan, 237, 253
organizer of "Short-Ballot" Association, 253
president, National Municipal League, 212
trustee of PACH, 253, 255
Churchill, Winston
on separation of powers in government, 392–93
and woman suffrage, 79
The City and the Citizen, Brownlow writes for Lawrence syndicate, 205–6

Index

Dawes, Charles G., Bureau of the Budget, 338, 419
Day, Ezra E., Rockefeller Foundation, 298
Deed restrictions
Ginter Park, 219
Radburn, 218–19
River Oaks, 219
Roland Park, 219
Defense Council; *see* National Defense Council
Delano, Frederic A.
chairman, NRPB, 285
discussion with Roosevelt on survey of executive, 300
"plan for a plan," 314, 324, 329 ff.
Dern, George H., secretary of war, 280–81
Des Moines, Iowa, commission form of government, 19
"Dictator bill"; *see* President's Committee on Administrative Management; Reorganization Act of 1939
Didisheim, René, PACH governmental planning conference, 406–7
Directory of International Organizations in the Field of Public Administration, 309
District of Columbia
Board of Trade, work of, on zoning ordinance, 97
Democratic National Committee, 13, 24
housing, 23
limited dividend, 210–11
intolerant of graft, 201
police
Capitol, 45
Department of Agriculture, 45
White House detail, 45
wartime growth, 65
District of Columbia government
alley-dwelling legislation, 23
auditor's office, 37–38
Brownlow as commissioner
advice from Wilson, 16–17, and Kutz, 22–23
learns to delegate, 64
papers ask dismissal, 87
president of commission, given title of governor, 56–57, 58
procedural reform, 21–23
resigns, 108
runs one-man show, 56
Selective Service Administration, 58–64
uses federal departments, 278

woman suffrage, 74–82
disagreement with Wilson, 76–79
youngest, 14
city council, the U.S. Congress, 100
commissioners, 3–102
collective responsibility, 19–22, 92–93
entertain city managers, 148–49
Gardiner succeeds Newman, 56–57
Knight succeeds Kutz, 56
Kutz, engineer, 3 ff.
legislative powers, 19 ff.
Police Union, 83–89
corporation counsel
assigned to public utilities commission, 91
Syme, 31–33
employees, public service, 38, 68–69
health department, 20, 33–36
home rule, 18, 100
hospitals, 35–37, 101
interdepartmental relations, 37–38
lobbies, control by, 10, 13
Organic Act of 1878, 20
police department, 14, 20, 24–30, 37–43
army MP's trained, 85–86
Brownlow wire-taps pro-German center, D.C., 47
Congress
forbids union, 89
increases pay, 89
corruption and discipline, 140–41
education of public, 41
employee standards, 38–39
favors to individuals, 40
Pullman appointed superintendent, 23–26
Police Union, 83–89
reforms, 38–43
Sylvester, superintendent of police, 24
traffic police arrest White House cars, 28–29
war effects, 44–55
woman suffrage, 76–82
arrests, 76–78
Women's Bureau, 42–43
prison reform, 36–42
public utilities commission, 4, 11, 14
valuation proceedings, 90–95
recreation and playgrounds, 20, 100–101
refuse disposal, 37, 65–68
cost survey, 65 ff.
Vare secures appropriation, 68
Shepherd, Governor, 201
Spanish flu, 69–73

[481]

A Passion for Anonymity

District of Columbia government—*Continued*
supreme court
  Siddons, Justice, 5, 11–12
utilities valuation, 94
welfare agencies, 20, 37
  Board of Charities, 34–35
woman suffrage movement, 74–82
World War I, effects of, 44–101
zoning ordinance, 96–98
  unchanged until 1954, 98
Dodd, William E.
ambassador to Germany
  Brownlow sees in Berlin, 309–10
University of Chicago, History department, 290
Dodds, Harold W.
executive secretary, National Municipal League, 211–12
at Princeton University, teaches classes in municipal government, 220
Donovan, Daniel J.
adjutant-general for Brownlow, 37 ff.
D.C. assistant auditor, 37–38
secretary D.C. commissioners, 60–61
"Doughnut Cabinet," Willard Hotel grill, 4, 8, 32, 98
Douglas, Lewis, director of the Budget, against loans and grants, 315, 317
Draft; *see* World War I, selective service
Dykstra, Clarence A., 345–46, 350–51
Public administration committee of the SSRC, study of the executive, 332

Eagleton, Dr. Clyde, Radburn citizens groups, 219
Early, Stephen
opposes President's Committee on Administrative Management, 348
on press relations, 441–43
Easby-Smith, James, D.C. lawyer, 58–60
Edson, John Joy, D.C. Board of Charities, 35–36
Egerton, M. W., Knoxville, temporary law director, 154–55, 164, 169
Egger, Rowland
Brownlow meets at Oxford, 231
Inter-American Municipal Organization, 409
international directory published, 358
IULA-IIAS, secretary, Joint Committee on Planning and Cooperation, 308–9
establishes common headquarters, 309
University of Virginia, Bureau of Public Administration, 230–31

850 East Fifty-eighth Street, Chicago, headquarters for public administration groups, 256–57
new agencies join, 288, 290
organizational autonomy, 290–91
Elections
presidential, 1932
  Brownlow concern, 270–71
    wants Baker as Democratic candidate, 270
  Roosevelt speeches, 271–72
presidential, 1936, unique results, 385
Eliot, Charles W., 2d
national planning, 314
secretary, NRPB, 314
Elliott, Harriet, consumer adviser, 430
Emmerich, Herbert
commissioner, National Housing Agency, 457
on costs of Radburn, 223–24
executive vice-president, City Housing Corporation, 212–13
Farm Credit Administration, 374
President's Committee on Administrative Management, 374
  Roosevelt's presentation of report, 391–92
Public Administration Clearing House, associate director, 402
succeeds Brownlow as director, 458
secretary, War Production Board, 457
Espionage, in World War I, 44–55
Europe, Brownlow travel fellowship, 227–33
Executive (the)
authority and responsibility, 326 ff.
Roosevelt
  sees needs, 315, 318, 325
  states needs to congressional leaders, 394–95
  Roosevelt and Brownlow agree, 338
  Brownlow sees as center of democracy, 335–36
IIAS, Warsaw meeting, 363–64
  President's Committee on Administrative Management, lessons learned from, 369–70
  U.S. delegation resolution, 365–67
Executive budget
milestone in federal administration, 303
proved in Illinois and New York state, 303
Executive Office of the President
Brownlow drafts Executive Order, 428–29

[482]

Index

emergency office provided, 428–29
President's Committee on Administrative Management, 313
Reorganization Act of 1939, 413 ff.
Reorganization Plan I, 1939, 416 ff.
strengthening, 371 ff.
use of the term given preference over "White House Secretariat," 376–77

Fair Lawn (N.J.)
Brownlow's house, 213–14
government, 213–17, 20
Radburn (N.J.), site of, 210
Federal-municipal relations, 278–79
in Europe and England, 263–65
Federation of Tax Administrators, 467
"Five-ring circus"; *see* U.S. government, administration under Roosevelt
Fleming, Colonel Philip, Public Works Administration, 285
Ford, Cornelius, public printer, 58–60
Forster, Rudolph, Roosevelt cites as truly anonymous, 397
Fort, Edwin J., nominated for president of City Managers' Association, 145
Fosdick, Raymond W., counsel, Rockefeller Foundation, 221, 235
Fowler, Dr., and D.C. Spanish flu epidemic, 69–70
Frazier, Spaulding, New Jersey municipal lawyer, 212, 215
Fulton, William M., Knoxville vice-mayor, 153–54

Gallinger, Jacob H., senator from New Hampshire and physician, Brownlow names D.C. hospital for him, 101
Galveston, Texas, commission form of government, 19
Garden cities; *see* City planning; Housing
Gardener, Helen, woman suffrage, 76, 82
Gardiner, W. Gwynne, succeeds Newman as D.C. commissioner, 56–57, 92
Gaus, John, research in public administration, 250
Generalist; *see* "Specialist vs. generalist"
Georgetown Gas Light Company, D.C. utilities valuation, 91
Germany
begins World War I, 10
"Blood purge," 309–10
Brownlow calls on Jeserich, 310
the Brownlows visit, 193–94, 309–10

espionage, 44–55
IULA meetings, Berlin and Munich, 358 ff.
Gibbon, Sir Gwyllym, British ministry of health, 232
Gill, German B., auditor at Petersburg, 117
Gold standard, U.S. abandonment of, 281
Goodwyn, Edwin P.
Petersburg, clerk of committees, 110–11
executive secretary, 119, 130–32
Government corporations, 391
Governmental centralization, Brownlow does not fear, 276
Governmental Planning Machinery (Bunbury report), 407
Governmental research; *see* Public administration
Governmental Research Association, 238
Governor's Conference, 249
Graft; *see* Morality in government
Graham, Edwin C., D.C. Board of Trade Zoning Committee, 97
Grayson, Admiral Cary T., woman suffrage, 77
Great Depression, 256–57, 261, 275
effect of
on cities, 275
on elections, 271
on Radburn, 224–25
Reconstruction Finance Corporation, 225
worsening, 272–73
Gregory, Thomas Watt, U.S. attorney-general, 12, 78
Gulick, Luther H., 136
Commission of Inquiry on Public Service Personnel
secretary and director of research, 293 ff.
incorporation of PACH, 254–55
Institute of Public Administration (N.Y.), 250, 252–54
host to ICMA, 222
President's Committee on Administrative Management, 339 ff.
Public Administration Committee, SSRC chairman, 298
study of executive, 332
and Senator Byrd, 349–50
top-management plan, 314
Gutiérrez, Gustavo, Cuban minister of justice, 409

Hall, Arnold Bennett, top-management plan, 314

[483]

Index

Hull, Cordell, Secretary of State, 317

Hutchins, Robert Maynard, president, University of Chicago, 271, 289

Ickes, Harold L., secretary of interior
administrator of public works under NRA, 282–86
asks PACH for tax study of Alaska, 281
for public works—not grants, 317
Pan-American Congress of Municipalities, 410
transfer of Office of Education, 419–20
views on management, 373

Ihlder, John, U.S. Chamber of Commerce, civic development, 210

Independent regulatory commissions, 391

Institute of Low Cost Housing of the Department of the Seine, 306

Institute of Public Administration
London
European–U.S. differences in research, 303–4
importance of meetings, 231
Oxford session, 231
publishes *Public Administration* (journal), 231
New York, 250–52
Bureau of Municipal Research, 252–53
houses International City Managers' Association, 222–23, 238
training school, 135–36

Inter-American Municipal Organization, 408–12
conferences
Chile, 412
Havana, 409–12
Panama, 412
Pan-American Congress of Municipalities, 410
permanent secretariat, 411–12
Spelman Fund grant, 411–12

Intergovernmental relations
bridge at Petersburg, 140
Spanish flu emergency in D.C., 70–73

International City Managers' Association, 238, 249–50
asked about needed public works, 284
Brownlow
election as president, 145–46, 150
establishes secretariat, 145–46, 222
interests Ruml in financing, 221–23
housed in Institute of Public Administration, 222

meetings
Asheville, 221–22
Chicago, 144
Cincinnati, 142
Kansas City, 145–46
Washington, D.C., 148–49
reception by Coolidge, 149
moves to Chicago, 222
and politics, 237
Spelman Fund grant, 227–28
Stutz, first permanent executive secretary, 146–48
resigns, 222

International Clearing House, 308

International Conference of American States; *see* Organization of American States

International Institute of Administrative Sciences
Joint Committee on Planning and Cooperation with IULA, 306–9
Lesoir, secretary, 232
Warsaw meeting, 358, 362–70
Brownlow diary of events, 363–67
Brownlow and Merriam joined by White and Rogers, 362
Magyary report and resolution, 363–68
resolution debated and revised, 363–68
Rogers criticizes, 363
Section III, chief executive and staff, 363–70

International Union of Cities; *see* International Union of Local Authorities

International Union of Local Authorities
conferences
Berlin-Munich meeting, 358–61
Brownlow assured of no Nazi incidents, 359
Brownlow finds himself in Hitler's seat, 359
Brownlow and Stutz, American delegation, 360–61
closing sessions in Munich, 361
Hitler receives delegation, 360
Jeserich proposes himself as vice-president, 361
London, 262
Lyons
on refuse disposal, 304–8
Stone, U.S. technical representative, 304
discussion of law and fact of municipal government, 261–65

[485]

Index

Index

Knoxville adopts, 152–53
Knoxville mayor's statement, 158–59
newspaper interest, 150–51
Petersburg (Va.), 105–40
Virginia law, 106
and politics, 237
public interest, 150–51
training, 135–37
effects of World War I, 57
in Europe and England, 263–64
financial administration, 117, 119–21
depression effects, 275–76
Knoxville, 154–56, 164–67, 170–77
Petersburg budget, 138–39
goals and functions, 239–48
IULA
conference at Lyons, 304–5
questions law and facts of administration, 261–62
national interest in 1922, 150–52
new towns, Radburn, 210–26
Petersburg (Va.) informed, 113–14
reform, 162
Knoxville, 198, 200–202
reports to Pan-American Congress of Municipalities, 410
research; *see* Public administration
Wilson's faith in citizens, 89
Munk, Frank, Masaryk Institute of Czechoslovakia, 406–8
Muñoz-Marin, Luis, governor of Puerto Rico, 460 ff.

Nashville Banner, 13
National American Woman's Suffrage Association, 74–76, 81–82
Congressional Union, 74–75
Woman's party, 75–82
National Association of Housing Officials, 466
National Association of Local Government Officials, 230, 265
National Conference on Improving Government, 250
National Conference of Social Work, Brownlow activities, 226, 228
National Defense Advisory Commission, 429 ff.
first meeting, 431
Knudsen asks, "Who is boss?" 431
National Defense Council, 425, 429–30
see also National Defense Advisory Commission, 429 ff.
National Emergency Council, 320 ff.
eliminated, 354–55

President's Committee on Administrative Management, 354–55
National Guard, 57–58
National Housing Association, Brownlow on advisory committee, 220
National Institute of Public Administration; *see* Institute of Public Administration, New York
National Institute of Public Affairs, Brownlow chairman of board of trustees, 462–63
National Municipal League
Brownlow
attends council meeting, 209, 211–12
Talks on Radburn, 220–21
Childs, President, 212
Cincinnati meeting, 220–23
council-manager government, 98, 136, 237
Dodds, executive secretary, 211–12
National Planning Board; *see* National Resources Planning Board
National Planning Committee; *see* National Resources Planning Board
National Resources Board; *see* National Resources Planning Board
National Resources Committee; *see* National Resources Planning Board
National Resources Planning Board, 418–19
Brownlow and SSRC point toward top-management study, 299–300
concern with government management, 326 ff.
Our Cities, 410
PWA asks for "plan for a plan," 314–15
Nesbitt, Charles F., D.C. superintendent of insurance, 8, 26
New Jersey, municipal law, 215
New Jersey League of Municipalities, Brownlow chairman of executive committee, 228
New York City Housing Corporation; *see* City Housing Corporation (N.Y.)
Newman, Oliver Peck
congressional appropriations, 37
D.C. commission president, 3–5, 8–9, 11, 13–14, 20–23, 37
goes into army, 57
recommends Brownlow for D.C. commissioner, 9
Washington Times, 8, 9–10
Wilson campaign, 8–9
Newspaper work
Brownlow, 8, 14, 96, 468
governmental relations, 7, 45, 468

[489]

Index

Index

Index

Temporary Executive Council, 318–20

memory, 384

outlines report of President's Committee on Administrative Management to Cabinet from memory, 385

press conference on report of President's Committee on Administrative Management, 396–97

press relations before World War II, 439 ff.

recommends increase of members of Supreme Court, 400

rejects Rockefeller Foundation for study of executive office, 333

restoring the economy, 281

summary of management authority asked of Congress, 386

and manner of presentation to congressional leaders, 386 ff.

tells Hopkins to create work program, 287

violates all rules of public administration, 432

wants Congress co-operation on administrative study, 338–39

wants survey made of administrative agencies, 329–30

Roosevelt, Theodore, President, 8, 11, 14

establishes FBI, 45

Treasury Department survey of administrative programs, 303

Roper, Daniel C., secretary of commerce

asks PACH to finance studies of currency and scientific research, 281

Brownlow asked to be assistant secretary, 277, 279–80

NIRA administrator, 282–84

Roosevelt campaign, 270–71

Rosenstock, Louis A., suggests Brownlow for Petersburg manager, 99

Rowe, James H., Puerto Rico administrative reorganization, 460

Rowell, Chester H.

editor of San Francisco Chronicle, 253

trustee of PACH, 253

Royal commissions of inquiry; see Social Science Research Council

Royal Institute of Public Administration; see Institute of Public Administration, London

Rule, William, editor Knoxville Journal and Tribune, 151–52

Ruml, Beardsley

administrative management, 314, 331

and Brownlow, first meeting, 221–23, 236

director, Spelman Fund, 220–21, 225, 236

financing of commissions of inquiry, 292

meeting at Geneva, 229–30, 233

member of NRPB, 332

Public Administration Clearing House born, 233

Roosevelt speech on agriculture, 271

Spelman Fund appropriation to PACH, 254 ff.

University of Chicago

dean of Social Science Division, 288–89

financing of University of Chicago Social Science Building, 289

Sabotage, in New York ports, 45–46

Sawyer, Colonel Donald H., PWA, 285

Schmitt, Bernadotte, University of Chicago History Department, 290

"Sectional" thinking versus regional planning, 268–69

Separation of powers, in American and English governments, 393–94

Shaw, Dr. Anna Howard, and woman suffrage, 74, 76, 82

Shepherd, Alexander R., governor of D.C., 201

Siddons, Frederick L., Brownlow predecessor on D.C. commission, 4, 9, 11–14

D.C. supreme court justice, 5, 8–12, 26–28

Wilson's close friend, 11 ff.

Sims, Elizabeth Virginia, marries Brownlow, 8

Sims, Paris, Brownlow's and wife's common ancestor, 187–88

Sims, Thetus W., 188

Brownlow's father-in-law, 8, 12–13

House committee on interstate and foreign commerce, 12–13

member of House D.C. committee, 8, 15

woman suffrage vote in House, 81

Sinnott, Arthur J., Newark Evening News, 30

Slum clearance; see District of Columbia government, alley dwelling legislation

Smith, Harold D.

Brownlow helps spell out functions of Executive Office of the President, 428–29

named budget director, 414 ff.

[495]

Smith, Thomas Vernor, University of Chicago Philosophy Department, 290
Snag Club (N.Y.), municipal government discussion, 220
Social Science Research Council
commission of inquiry on public service personnel, 292–98
Brownlow a member, 293
financed by Spelman Fund, 292
hearings in England, 293
Hoover's views, 394
plea for career service, 297
publications, 293, 298
purpose, 293
report, 296–98
commissions of inquiry as opinion surveys, 292, 298
composition, 292
Crane, president, 298
Merriam's initiative, 292
Public Administration Committee, 298–99
administrative management vs. reorganization, 348–49
applies for research grants, 298–99
Ascher chosen secretary, 299
Brownlow, chairman, 298–300
close relations with National Resources Committee, 300
discussion on survey of the executive, 300–301
meeting on "General Staff for the White House," 331 ff.
studies pointing to problems of top management, 299–300
Brownlow memo on research clearing house, 250–53
concern with government management, 326, 332 ff.
Gaus survey of research, 250
Gulick chairman, 250, 298
Harris chosen director of research, 299
meeting in Atlanta, 331–32
Rockefeller Foundation, 298
special studies, 299
study of over-all management in federal government seems sure, 332
White, chairman, 250, 298
Roosevelt wants survey made of administrative agencies, 329–30
Social service; see Public welfare
Spalding, Colonel George R., public works planning, 281–82
Spanish flu
D.C. hard hit, 69–73

government emergency measures, 70–73
War Industries Board, 70–73
Special privilege, Wilson ended era, 13
"Specialist vs. generalist," Brownlow, 280
Spelman Fund
aid to public administration organizations, 237–38
Brownlow travel fellowship, 225
center for associations of officials, 228–30
finances commission on public service personnel, 292–93
grant for public welfare officials, 225–26
grants to associations of public officials, 227–28
helps Inter-American Municipal Organization, 408, 411–12
IIAS-IULA joint committee ask aid, 308
Public Administration Clearing House
financing of *ad hoc* conferences, 273
funds appropriated by Spelman Fund, 254
plans approved by trustees, 249
Ruml, director, 220–23, 225, 236
supports *United States Daily*, 208–9
Spingarn, Mrs. Marian C., first policewoman, 42
Spoils system; see Patronage; Public service personnel
State government reorganization, 313
Illinois, 252, 300
Virginia, 349–50
State-municipal relations, 230, 262
European and U.S., 262–66
Staunton (Va.), first manager city, 141
Stein, Clarence S.
housing costs, 224
Radburn planner, 211–12
regional planning conference, 269
Sternberg, General George N., surgeon general of Army, 210–11
Stettinius, Edward R., Jr., head of War Resources Board, 426–28, 430
Stidham, Harrison, D.C. refuse contractor, 66–68
Stimson, Henry L., secretary of war, 433 ff.
Stone, Donald C., 463
Administrative Management Division, Bureau of the Budget, 428
director, Public Administration Service, 288
Public Administration Service, U.S. representative at Lyons conference of IULA, 304

[496]

Index

Index